# 75 YEARS
# OF
# IFMA
# 1917-1992

## THE NONDENOMINATIONAL MISSIONS MOVEMENT

Edwin L. Frizen, Jr.

William Carey Library
Pasadena, California

Published by
William Carey Library
P.O. Box 40129
Pasadena, California 91114
Phone (818) 798-0819

**Library of Congress Cataloging in Publication Date**

Frizen, E. L.
75 years of IFMA, 1917-1992 : the nondenominational missions movement / Edwin L. Frizen, Jr.
p. cm.
Includes bibliographical references (p. 461) and index.
ISBN 0-87808-235-2 (pbk.)
1. Interdenominational Foreign Mission Association—History.
I. Title. II. Title: Seventy-five years of IFMA, 1917-1992.
BV2360.F87 1992
266'.006'07—dc20 92-72008
CIP

Additional Cataloging note:
This publication contains a current history of the Interdenominational Foreign Mission Association of North America. It also provides significant historical information on North American Protestant missions in general and evangelical nondenominational missions, commonly referred to as faith missions, in particular.

Printed in the United States of America

# CONTENTS

**PART TWO**

**THE BEGINNING AND DEVELOPMENT OF IFMA**

**PART THREE**

**EXPANDING THE EFFECTIVENESS OF MINISTRY 1950-1992**

## PART FOUR

## LOOKING AHEAD

# FOREWORD

Jack and Grace Frizen—steady, stalwart, selfless, behind-the-scenes pioneers—did not merely join an organization, head it up for 28 years, and live to tell about it.

This book is a faithful, devoted account of that unique organization (the like of which there really is no other in the world).

But, this book is much more than the story of that amazing organization. It is the story of a highly crucial movement within the larger cause of global missions. Indeed, this particular organization and the book which sets it in historical context focuses attention on a very special, curious, vital phenomenon—that is widely misunderstood!

That is, quite a few people have confused "the church, the people of God," with particular congregational and denominational structures. For example, Episcopalians and Lutherans mean "denominations" when they speak of "the churches." Presbyterians consider the ultimate reality to be the regional "Presbytery." Baptists and Congregationalists—and the many unaffiliated congregations—are convinced that "the church" in its final reality is "the local church." In addition, many people within all three of these spheres are not sure what a mission agency is, where it is in the Bible, etc.

These are not marginal questions when all over the country (and all over the world) we see brand new independent congregations reinventing the wheel, so to speak, concluding superficially that there is no need for mission agencies at all: each local congregation should send out its own missionaries. If global, specialized mission structures are not legitimate or even necessary, then the whole story of the IFMA has got to be a pious fraud.

But it isn't. This book will show the God-given, God-guided, spiritual passion for the whole world in its classical role of a warm-hearted minority vision and cause, bursting out in fully legitimate structures before there ever were even "denominational missions." It then portrays that holy energy within the IFMA continuing to serve selflessly and impartially, in wholesome mutual inspiration and accountability, across many decades, emerging in our time as the sturdiest backbone of the entire mission movement.

So, delight yourself in the rich and rewarding details. Don't miss the larger and urgent significance of the very concept of the self-governed mission agency—just like the self-governed congregation—held in mutual accountability with other like organizations, fully legitimate as one expression of the people of God, the church of Jesus Christ.

This book is the best thing yet if someday the truth will be more widely known: all early missionary efforts, both in Europe and the colonies, were essentially nondenomination initiatives of an impassioned minority of individuals who could not have done what they did working through the bulky machinery of denominations.

As early as 1825 people like Bishop Hobart (an Episcopalian) thundered that nondenominational boards were "the work of man" while denominational boards were "the work of God."

Then, in the 1890s, the "whiz kids" from college, the SVM (the Student Volunteer Movement young people), came into the picture and put massive wind into the sails of specifically denominational structures, so much so that by 1925, 75 percent of all American missionaries were out under denominational boards (which, by the way, still were not suffering under "unified budget" restrictions). Somehow those students, unable or unwilling to read the record of the past, were caught up with the thought that if denominational enterprises were legitimate then nondenominational efforts were not. Presently, the student leaders, growing older, applied their doctrinaire insights to reducing the nondenominational missions to non-voting participants in the Foreign Mission Conference of North America. By 1917 (the year the IFMA was founded) it had become clear that this new blast of wind was hostile, in principle, to the nondenominational missions.

As this book delicately shows, the denominational missions came second, not first. They were the johnny-come-lately movement, not the other way around, and though denominational missions dominated the scene in 1925, by 1975—fifty years later—the majority of American missionaries were once again faithfully sent out by impassioned minorities within denominations and independent congregations, working through the good old nondenominational structures!

The IFMA is the largest and the strongest association in the world which steadfastly through withering and constant criticism from many denominational spokesmen upholds this nondenominational pattern, which is the most basic pattern in history. I cherish the thought that this will become plainer as time goes on.

This book is the first truly formidable step in that direction. Yet it is irenic in spirit, not at all combative. It does not so much argue the issue (as I have taken liberty to do here), but quietly describes what happened, relating what God has done. It is hard to argue with the facts. And Dr. Frizen and his wife, Grace, are selfless servants who now deserve a great deal of credit for the growth and development of the IFMA and of the marvelous record which this book portrays invitingly to readers in our time, when the record is now very plain!

Ralph D. Winter
U.S. Center for World Mission

# PREFACE

God has chosen to use people in accomplishing His purpose of man's redemption. Missions is the most serious work in which a person can be involved. It is with a sense of God's sovereignty and grace that the author is completing more than forty-two years in the cause of world evangelization, over twenty-eight years (September 1, 1963 - September 30, 1991) as executive director of IFMA, the Interdenominational Foreign Mission Association of North America.

The men and women who founded IFMA were mission pioneers. This book is about the movement that they started seventy-five years ago, in 1917.

The author is grateful to the IFMA Board for providing the time during the last year before their retiring for the Frizens to complete this history of the association.

Much appreciation goes to Dr. Ralph Winter who has been a mentor and encourager through the years. He graciously reviewed much of the manuscript and gave helpful counsel on the project. As an able historian, he has been persistent in stressing the necessity for an IFMA history and in keeping us focused on its completion.

Many thanks to a distinguished historian, author, theologian, teacher of the author's Sunday school class, and a good friend—Dr. Earle E. Cairns. Now retired from chairing the History and Political Science Department at Wheaton College, he willingly reviewed and commented on parts of the manuscript.

The generous and gracious assistance from the directors and staff of the Wheaton College Billy Graham Center Library and Archives was invaluable. They were superb in their warmth, their willingness to help, and in the provision of good facilities conducive to research.

To Mrs. Frizen, Grace—my partner in this project, who held us to a tight schedule, carried a heavy load of word processing, researching, writing, and editing—my absolute devotion and appreciation for forty-two years of partnering with me in world evangelization.

In his article, "Archival Alert—Rome 1980," in the October 1980 issue of Missiology, Dr. Arthur Glasser wrote:

> If a particular Christian community does not document its history, it is courting disaster. . . . It will not be able to defend itself against the inevitable challenges of its distinctives, much less clarify the misunderstandings that are also bound to arise. It will not even be able to judge itself soberly within the inescapable process of change that overtakes all institutions. Indeed, no community dares lose the inspiration of knowing in detail its origins.

It was the purpose of the author to record the origins of IFMA and to review its history for those that follow, that they may be able to evaluate the past for making decisions for the future. May they wait on God for His guidance and provisions as did those leaders who went before them.

# INTRODUCTION

One of the most significant developments in modern Christian missions has been the growth of nondenominational missions Nondenominational missions—or interdenominational, independent, faith missions—are agencies that are not connected with, nor directed by, any ecclesiastical organization. Although, they have close relationships with some denominational churches, being independent, faith missions have no denominational budgets to provide regular income.

Several features and strengths have contributed to the growth of nondenominational missions and to the impact they have had on missions strategy and world evangelization. While this book was largely written for the extended IFMA family, it is recognized that other readers may not be as well oriented to these missions. For that reason, in order to give a better understanding of the nondenominational missions movement, some of the distinctive features and strengths of faith missions are delineated here.

Although some features mentioned are not characteristic of nondenominational missions exclusively, they have figured prominently in these agencies in particular.

## DISTINCTIVES

### Finance

Nondenominational, interdenominational, or independent missions have been called *faith* missions because their financial structures are based on trust in God to supply financial needs through prayer. Through the years different interpretations of the faith principle have produced variations in financial practice.

Most missions have adopted as their interpretation of the faith principle *full information without solicitation.* Within IFMA, some missions do solicit funds. IFMA requires of its members that "each mission exercises faith in God for the provision of needs *without strong solicitation* for funds."

Funds received by nondenominational missions have generally been administered by one of three plans: (1) pooled support, (2) modified pooled support (pooling only personal allowance income), and (3) personalized support. Although there are published allowance rates, missionaries are not guaranteed a salary. Allowances are dependent upon funds received and cannot exceed the established rate.

**To Unreached People**

Since the major denominational missions stationed their missionaries primarily in the cities and coastal areas, the nondenominational missions purposed to reach the people and tribes of the interior. Reaching unreached people wherever they are remains the major focus.

**Interdenominational**

Independent missions are made up of men and women who are agreed on the basic essentials of the conservative evangelical Christian faith. Although they are *nondenominational* agencies, they are *interdenominational* in that the missionaries, directors, and staff come from different denominations and churches. These missions are directed by self-perpetuating boards of directors

**Field-Directed Work**

In most faith missions, the direction of the work in the field is done from the field, not by home directorates or executive staff.

**Mission Membership**

Mission members not only have a voice, but also a vote in the organization and conduct of mission affairs. In some, the missionary members elect the general director and other officers. In others, the board of directors elects them. In some, such as Overseas Missionary Fellowship, the general director has the authority to name his successor and other chief officers, after extensive consultation.

**Personnel**

Nondenominational missions have drawn their personnel from Bible institutes, Bible colleges, and Christian liberal arts colleges more than from seminaries and universities. This has changed considerably. However, usually, at least thirty semester hours of Bible study is required even for specialists with secular training.

**Prominence of Women**

Throughout their history, nondenominational missions have considered both husbands and wives as full missionaries, in contrast with denominational boards that have often appointed only the husbands. These missions pioneered in extensive use of single women, including interior evangelistic and church-planting ministries. Nondenominational missions have more single women as missionaries than single men. Although there are many qualified women, very few are appointed to prominent leadership roles on the fields or at home.

**Simplicity of Life Style**

Most missionaries serving with these missions have been characterized by a life style generally more simple than those with denominational agencies.

**Cooperation**

Nondenominational missions have traditionally been open to cooperation with other like-minded evangelical missions. In a number of instances, cooperation has led to mergers.

**Innovation**

Nondenominational missions have been innovative in their efforts to evangelize the unreached, hidden people of the world, pioneering and specializing in such ministries as education, missionary medicine, missionary radio and TV, gospel recording, Bible translation, and missionary aviation.

## STRENGTHS

**Dependence on Prayer**

Because faith is the basic principle of these missions, prayer has been the dynamic of their maintenance, growth, and ministry. Personal and corporate prayer has continually been an integral part of the nondenominational missions movement, involving both the missions' members and constituencies.

**Recruitment**

The continual emphasis on the responsibility of all Christians to consider missionary service has been a strength. The good relationship between nondenominational missions and interdenominational, independent Bible institutes and Christian colleges has facilitated recruitment. Strong recruitment efforts have greatly contributed to the growth of these missions.

**Lay Involvement**

Numerous people have become involved in missions by prayer support and financial participation as a result of the faith principle and personalized missionary giving.

**Social Aspects**

From the beginning of nondenominational missions, there has been an integration of social concerns and ministry. Numerous medical and educational missionaries have always had a prominent place. Relief and community programs have not been neglected. However, the primary focus remains on evangelism and the development of the church.

**Theological Position**
Nondenominational missions hold to the basic historical fundamentals of conservative evangelical Christianity, usually stated in detailed doctrinal positions. In their firm adherence to the inerrancy of the Word of God, nondenominational missions have avoided the grave dangers of syncretism and neo-universalism prevalent today.

## CONCLUSION

Not all nondenominational missions meet the standards set by IFMA or other associations of missions. The generalizations on the distinctive features and strengths that have been made are based on the missions that do meet these requirements. They represent the majority of missionaries who serve with nondenominational missions.

# PART ONE

# THE RISE OF NONDENOMINATIONAL PROTESTANT MISSIONS IN AMERICA

# 1

# THE CONTEXT: RELIGIOUS

Before the formation of mission societies in the New World, missionary outreach was carried on in the colonies under the auspices of societies organized and based in Europe.

Religion in America was never unified under a single dominant church, as in the European countries from which many of our forefathers emigrated. While the majority of the early Americans had a Protestant heritage, they came from various countries, having different religious persuasions. Earle Cairns has indicated that between 1607 and 1732 almost all of the denominations, representing Protestant churches that resulted from the Reformation, were established in America.[1]

Christianity, while dominant, has not been the only religious expression in America. Religious pluralism has been a factor on this continent since the Europeans arrived. The settlers of the original colonies came for a variety of reasons, but religious freedom was important to most of them. Many came for commercial or other purposes, but they usually maintained some religious connections.

As the country expanded westward, churches were among the first institutions to be established. Evangelical orthodoxy gave strong impetus to this church-planting expansion in which laymen and clergy were involved.

The rise of modernism and liberalism was to be expected in a nation that, from its beginning, has prized freedom of thought and expression. God's grace is evidenced in the measure of orthodoxy that has continued throughout America's history.

## AMERICAN PROTESTANT DENOMINATIONS

The earliest form of American Protestantism was the Anglican Church—the Church of England. It dates from the beginning of Jamestown Colony in 1607. The established church in the new colonies of Virginia, South Carolina, North Carolina, and Georgia was Anglican. It later became the established church in Maryland and several counties in New York state. Before the American Revolution, religious freedom was often earned through suffering, particularly in Virginia. The enactment of 1786 by the Virginia legislature declared that the government must not interfere in church affairs or matters of conscience, and that no citizen should suffer for his religious opinions. It became the cornerstone for religious freedom for the nation. Most Protestants accepted the fact of diversity of belief among denominations.

Although the Anglican Church prospered in New England, it was not the predominant church. The major denominational position of the New England Puritans was Congregationalism. They followed the Reformed tradition of theology.

Religion was central to New England society. Although only the religious leaders were expected to be learned in theology, everyone was expected to participate in the religious life of the settlements.

At the close of the colonial period, the Congregationalists and the Presbyterians were the largest denominations, accounting for almost 40 percent of all churches in the colonies. The Anglicans, Baptists, and

Quakers were equal in strength, accounting for 45 percent. The Dutch, French, and German Reformed churches made up another 10 percent.

Pennsylvania and the middle colonies were more open to diverse denominations, which helped to attract numbers of Quakers, Mennonites, Moravians, Lutherans, and Presbyterians.

The Great Awakening in the eighteenth century (1726-1756) strengthened evangelicalism through the preaching of Dutch Reformed Theodore Frelinghuysen, Presbyterian Gilbert Tennent, Congregationalist Jonathan Edwards, Baptist Shubal Stearns, Anglican Devereux Jarratt, and the man who made these revivals a movement—George Whitefield.

The Anglican Church was the denomination that was weakened most during the Revolutionary War—the War for Independence, 1775-1883. Up to then, the Anglican clergy had been supported by the Society for the Propagation of the Gospel in London. Its charter limited support to clergy within British colonies. Following the war, most of the clergy returned to England. A few who remained were able to get a properly consecrated episcopate and to call a convention in 1779 to adopt a constitution for the Protestant Episcopal Church in the United States.

The Methodists had been a part of the Anglican Church. They reorganized after the war. The Methodist Church was established in America with Thomas Coke and Francis Asbury as the first superintendents.

After the war, the churches responded with varying degrees of success to the spiritual needs of the western frontier. By 1850 the Protestant membership ranking had changed considerably. First were the Methodists; second, Baptists; then Presbyterians, Congregationalists, Lutherans, Disciples, and Episcopalians—in that order. The success of the Methodists was due in part to their sending clergy circuit riders to the frontiers. Baptist ministers, many of them lay preachers, accompanied people on their westward journeys. The Presbyterians responded to the calls for pastors to the new areas.

Church growth was seriously hindered by the defection of many of the educated classes to the acceptance of deism and other liberal tendencies among New England Congregationalists. It is said that in the Yale graduating class of 1800, there was only one church member. Such infidelity and skepticism was found at other leading colleges, such as Harvard and Princeton.[2]

By the middle of the eighteenth century, deism and free thinking were becoming widespread in Virginia.

When Timothy Dwight, grandson of Jonathan Edwards, became president of Yale College in 1795, he lectured and preached in chapel with such force that deism was eliminated. About one-third of the students were converted in 1802. Revivals spread to Dartmouth and Princeton, and on to other schools in the North and the South. Timothy Dwight wrote the hymn, "I Love Thy Kingdom, Lord."

Theological liberalism, which had been growing in Europe, was taking root in America. The move away from orthodox theology, particularly at Harvard College, and the preaching of men like William Ellery Channing, produced Unitarianism. Boston was its center. Immediately following the Great Awakening, the oldest Anglican church in New England, King's Chapel, became the first church to openly become Unitarian, led to this position by Harvard graduate James Freeman. Channing's Federal Street Church in Boston and Harvard College were the centers of liberalism.

Opponents to liberal theology were among the founders of Andover Seminary in 1807, Princeton Seminary in 1812, and Hartford Seminary in 1834.

The Second Awakening in the United States came soon after the Revolution and lasted into the first decades of the nineteenth century. Dr. Earle Cairns gives its dates as 1776 to 1810.[3] Calvinism, which was so strong in the Great Awakening, became less prominent because of the Arminian emphasis of the Second Awakening.

One of the results of the Second Awakening was the beginning of new denominations as evangelization spread westward. The United Brethren in Christ was formed in 1800. The Cumberland Presbyterian Church in 1810, and The Disciples—or Christian Church—followed in 1832. Both of these groups separated from the Presbyterian Church. The Christian Reformed Church was begun in 1857, with roots going back to congregations that left the Dutch Reformed Church in 1834. Other groups, including Adventists, Mormons, and Shakers, began on the frontiers.

Charles G. Finney was a popular revivalist who believed that the convert begins a new life in which *working* for God is just as necessary as *believing*. Finney, a lawyer-turned-revival preacher and professor, moved from his Congregational and Presbyterian connections to finally become Wesleyan in theological conviction.

Park Street Church, founded in Boston in 1809, became a strong center for missions activity and renewal in that city. In 1831 and again in 1857, Charles Finney preached a series of sermons there.

Biblical criticism, the German idealistic philosophy of Kant and Hegel, and the theory of evolution undermined belief in the authority of the Scriptures, and strengthened the growth of liberalism in America. They further paved the way for the social gospel that was to largely dominate Protestantism, starting in the last part of the nineteenth century.

## NONDENOMINATIONALISM

The revivals of the Second Awakening were in some respects nondenominational, since the meetings attracted people from various denominations, as well as the unchurched. Camp meetings were an important part of the evangelization thrust on the frontiers. And, surprisingly, they were accepted back in the East for a time.

The strong denominationalism of the churches in the East began to break down on the frontiers. Protestant services were held in schools and log cabins whenever a minister or lay preacher was available. Because there was not much opportunity to choose a particular denominational meeting, people attended whatever services there were. They found that the denominations actually had much in common. Many of the camp meetings were forerunners of later nondenominational Bible and missions conferences.

Church-related people in the East began to form nondenominational societies to pray for and support missionary work on the frontiers. Some of those societies were cent societies, female missionary societies, and youth missionary societies. Their membership came from all denominations.

For the fiscal year 1826-1827, ten of the fourteen leading benevolent societies that were listed according to income were nondenominational. Included among these were the American Education Society, American Bible Society, American Sunday School Union, American Tract Society, and American Home Missionary Society. Such societies were at the center of religious life of the country early in the nineteenth century.[4] More than 150 such organizations were identified by Charles Foster.[5]

In the last half of the nineteenth century, one of the foremost evangelists who strengthened the nondenominational movement was Dwight L. Moody. Born February 5, 1837, he was converted in 1855 in Boston through the follow-up of his Sunday school teacher, Edward Kimball. In 1856 at age nineteen, Moody moved to Chicago and became a successful shoe salesman and Christian witness. Two years after arriving in Chicago, he started a Sunday school for slum-area children, and soon was devoting full-time to evangelistic and welfare work. He was president of the Chicago YMCA and founded the church that is now Moody Memorial Church.

Shortly after the great Chicago fire of 1871, Moody and musician Ira Sankey held productive evangelistic and revival services in Great Britain for two years. Mr. Moody continued as one of the prominent evangelists of the world until his death in 1899. Dwight Moody was never ordained. He remained a layman who was instrumental in the leadership of many nondenominational institutions and organizations.

Arthur T. Pierson was a contemporary of Mr. Moody's. He was seminary trained, ordained, and spent much of his ministry as a Presbyterian minister. While pastor of Philadelphia's Bethany Church, founded by John Wanamaker, his scholarly but warm-hearted expository preaching drew invitations to speak at nondenominational conferences in America and Great Britain. Because of his missionary passion, he became the editor of *The Missionary Review of the World.* A number of prominent missions leaders were influenced through Dr. Pierson's ministry, including Henry W. Frost, Robert E. Speer, Samuel M. Zwemer, and D. M. Stearns.

## CHRISTIAN COLLEGES AND SEMINARIES

Harvard was founded as a strong Christian college in 1636 by the Puritans. It was followed by the Anglican's establishing William and Mary in 1693. Conservative Congregationalists founded Yale in 1701.

Dr. Earle Cairns observed:

> Higher education was strengthened by the founding of over a dozen new colleges between 1780 and 1830 by the Presbyterians and Congregationalists in order to meet the need for more trained ministers. Andover Seminary was founded in 1808 to meet the threat of Unitarianism in Harvard. Others, such as Princeton Seminary (1812), Auburn and Bangor, were founded soon after.[6]

Only 22 additional colleges were established during the eighteenth century. All were in the East and nearly all were

Christian, supported by various denominations. The nineteenth century saw 150 additional colleges started by 1860. Many of these were in small towns west of the Allegheny Mountains.

Wheaton College was founded in Illinois in 1860. New England Congregationalist Jonathan Blanchard was called to be the founding president. He was succeeded by his son, Charles A. Blanchard, in 1882. The Blanchard era at Wheaton lasted 65 years, until the death of Charles in 1925.

Wheaton quickly became known as a strong conservative evangelical nondenominational college. Many evangelical leaders of church, missions, education, business, and the professions have received their training and challenge for Christian witness at Wheaton College, which has been recognized through the years for its academic excellence.

## BIBLE SCHOOLS

The impetus for what was to become a strong American Bible institute and Bible college movement began with an editorial by Albert B. Simpson in 1880. A Presbyterian pastor in New York City, he proposed the establishment of a "specific missionary training college" to prepare for missionary service those not able to pursue full scholastic courses in regular colleges and seminaries.

During 1881, Simpson experienced physical healing of a heart condition, received baptism by immersion, and resigned from his church. He became pastor of the Gospel Tabernacle, which was officially organized in 1883.

That same year, A. B. Simpson began the Missionary Training College for Home and Foreign Missionaries and Evangelists, which developed into Nyack College and Alliance Theological Seminary. He sent the first missionaries from his church to Congo, now Zaire, in 1884. The organizations that he had begun were combined in 1897 to form the Christian and Missionary Alliance. Cross-cultural missions outreach remains the central focus of C&MA churches worldwide.

Meanwhile, some of D. L. Moody's friends in Chicago worked during the period after the Chicago fire, helping to train city missionaries. An organized training school was considered, but due to his evangelistic ministries in Great Britain and America, Mr. Moody was not able to give the leadership that would be required.

He agreed in 1886 to give time and effort to see the school started. The Chicago Evangelization Society was formed, initial funding secured, and a number of "Bible institutes" were held. This training of men and women in biblical evangelism to "fill the gap between the churches and the masses" was considered successful. In the spring of 1889, some 200 people gathered in "Mr. Moody's church" on Chicago Avenue to study for Christian service.[7]

The day came when Moody saw that the time was right to begin a more formal Bible school. Lots and buildings adjacent to the church were purchased. Mr. Moody persuaded Reuben Archer Torrey to become superintendent of the new Chicago Bible Institute, which opened on September 26, 1889. It later became Moody Bible Institute.

Now into its second century, Moody Bible Institute is the leading Bible institute in the world. While it offers accredited undergraduate and graduate degrees, it remains a Bible and missionary training school. Moody Bible Institute is a large and well-run organization, having divisions of education, including extension and correspondence programs; literature; radio; and films. Since its founding, MBI has maintained its firm commitment to urban and world evangelization.

Other nondenominational Bible schools soon followed, such as Boston Missionary Training School, 1889; Toronto Bible Training School, 1894; Practical Bible Training School, 1900; Providence Bible Institute, 1900; and the Bible Institute of Los Angeles (BIOLA), 1908.

Philadelphia School of the Bible opened October 1, 1914. The founding officers, who served on its initial board of directors, were Cyrus I. Scofield, president, William L. Pettingill, dean, and Frank W. Lange, business manager. These men were all involved with the missions that would organize the Interdenominational Foreign Mission Association of North America.

## NOTES

[1] Earle E. Cairns, *Christianity Through the Centuries*, rev. ed. (Grand Rapids: Zondervan Publishing House, 1967), p. 391.

[2] Earle E. Cairns, *Christianity in the United States* (Chicago: Moody Press, 1964), pp. 74-75.

[3] Earle E. Cairns, *The Endless Line of Splendor: Revivals and Their Leaders from the Great Awakening to the Present* (Wheaton, IL: Tyndale House Publishers, Inc., 1986), pp. 86-87.

[4] Charles I. Foster, *An Errand of Mercy* (Chapel Hill: The University of North Carolina Press, 1960), pp. 121-23.

[5] Ibid., pp. 275-79.

[6] Cairns, *Christianity Through the Centuries*, p. 456.

[7] August W. Williams, *Life and Work of Dwight L. Moody* (Philadelphia: P. W. Ziegler & Co., 1900), pp. 291-92.

# 2

# THE CONTEXT: POLITICAL AND SOCIAL

The exploration of Christopher Columbus for the Spanish Court was only one of several European explorations that touched on the Americas. After the voyages of Columbus in the 1490s, the papacy divided up the Americas between Spain and Portugal. North America was given to Spain. This angered other European nations. The English ignored the claim, as did the French, Swedes, and Dutch.

It is believed that the original settlers, the Indians, migrated from northeastern Asia.

## COLONIZATION

The colony of Virginia was among the oldest settlements in America. Several English expeditions reached America before Sir Walter Raleigh arrived in 1584. Both Martin Frobisher and Sir Humphrey Gilbert led expeditions in the last quarter of the sixteenth century, but neither established a permanent colony. Raleigh's group settled at Roanoke, but within a few years it had completely disappeared, possibly wiped out by an epidemic or massacre by the Indians. A search party in 1590 could find no trace of the settlement.

The beginning of Virginia is dated from the beginning of the Virginia Company in 1606. The first permanent English settlement in America was Jamestown in 1607. The colony was named in honor of Queen Elizabeth, the Virgin Queen of England.

At the same time that the Virginia Company was founded, the Plymouth Company obtained a charter for settling the country to the north of Long Island Sound, to which the English laid claim. But it was not until 1620 that the northern region began to be settled, under new charters.

The settlers of the northern region that became Connecticut, New Hampshire, Rhode Island, and Massachusetts (New England) were Protestants who were discontented with the Anglican Church, and others who were opposed to the crown and the government of England.

The present state of Maine was purchased by Massachusetts, which was the dominant northern colony. Religious differences and ideas of toleration led to the separation of the Puritan colonies—Connecticut, New Hampshire, and Rhode Island—from Massachusetts.

Lord Baltimore established a colony in 1632, named Maryland, to be a home of religious freedom for Catholics. From the start, Protestants outnumbered Catholics, since so few Catholics were interested in emigrating from their homeland. In effect, Maryland was founded on the principle that all people could have freedom of Christian worship. The established church in Maryland later became Anglican.

Quaker William Penn founded the colony of Pennsylvania. Later, there was a considerable immigration of German farmers and others into Pennsylvania.

Carolina was originally established by French Protestants. It fell into British hands at several points. It was subsequently divided into North and South Carolina.

There were a number of small Swedish and Dutch settlements between Maryland and New England, the main one being New Amsterdam, later named New York. These Swedish settlements were captured by the Dutch. The British took all of the settlements from the Dutch in 1664, but lost them again in 1673. They were later restored to England in 1674 by a treaty with Holland.

Before the end of the seventeenth century, the population

of the colonies had reached 220,000, with 95,000 in the southern colonies, 80,000 in New England, and 45,000 in the middle colonies. Most had been born in the colonies or had come from Great Britain when they were young.

The town of Savannah was settled in 1733 by Oglethorpe from England, who rescued a number of people imprisoned in England for debt. They became the first settlers of a new colony, Georgia. Later, a number of Protestants took refuge there, coming from The Tyrol, a region in western Austria and northern Italy that was a former Austrian crown territory.

To the south, the Spanish were established with headquarters at St. Augustine in Florida, the oldest city in the United States. It was founded in 1565 by Menendez de Aviles on the site of an old Indian village near Ponce de Leon's landing place in 1513. Pensacola was a settlement from 1559 to 1561, and was recolonized by Spain in 1698.

The British were established along the east coast from Savannah to the St. Lawrence River by 1750. The Allegheny and Blue Ridge Mountains were a barrier to spreading inland. The British had acquired Newfoundland and considerable northern areas by treaty from the French.

By the middle of the eighteenth century, there were British settlements along the American Atlantic coastline: the New England Puritans and free Protestants—Maine (belonging to Massachusetts), Connecticut, New Hampshire, Rhode Island, and Massachusetts; the Swedish/Dutch settlements now divided into New York, New Jersey, and Delaware; Maryland; Virginia; Carolina; and Georgia.

The French had settlements in Quebec and Montreal to the north and New Orleans and Mobile in the south. In the Peace of Paris in 1763, France ceded Canada to England, and relinguished Louisiana to Spain.

The French recovered Louisiana in 1800. Finally, it was bought by the United States Government in 1803. That was the abandonment of America by the French.

In 1763 the English captured Mobile from the French. It was taken from them by the Spanish in 1780. The Americans took Mobile from the Spanish in 1813. Toward the end of 1814, the American forces took Pensacola and St. Marks, overthrowing Spanish authority. The United States paid Spain five million dollars for Florida in February 1819, ending three hundred years of Spanish rule there.

Wars with the Indians and intercolonial wars were a considerable drain on the colonies.

The establishment of the colonies and immigration of peoples from many nations brought to the North American continent different cultures and political systems. They came to escape religious persecution, heavy taxation or other oppression of government, because of overcrowding in their own countries, for new commercial possibilities, to propagate the gospel, and others came simply for adventure.

With the increasing domination of the British in the American colonies, their political, cultural, and Protestant religious forms prevailed.

Although there was no caste system in America, there were classes among the people. The large landowners and prosperous merchants controlled local economic and political affairs. The clergy were highly regarded, both morally and socially. Skilled craftsmen and small farmers came next. They were prominent in New England especially, where many voted and served as town officials. Then came the unskilled, free workingman; next were the indentured servants; and finally slaves. The last three classes had no political power.

Some who came from England came with political experience that enabled them to begin new societies in America. Colonial assemblies were conscious of their rights, which helped them to challenge British royal authority. The remoteness of the colonies from London permitted them to handle their own business largely in their own way. But as time went on, crown authority intensified, forcing the colonies more firmly into the expanding empire. The growing requirements for goods and services became increasingly burdensome to the colonies, whose own needs were made secondary to those of the vast British empire. By the middle of the eighteenth century, the drawing of the reins more tightly came at the very time when the colonies were least willing for it. The result was the Declaration of Independence on July 4, 1776 and the American Revolutionary War in which the Americans won their freedom from England.

The Revolution made many notable changes, among which were destroying the authority of the crown of England over America, broadening the right to vote, making representation in the legislatures more equitable, and specifying liberties of the people.

The Revolution, also, brought about the downfall of the Anglican Church as the established church in certain areas of the colonies. It greatly weakened the Congregational Church, as well.

## SLAVERY

H. G. Wells observed that slavery began very early in the European history of America. He said, "No European people who went to America can be held altogether innocent in the matter."[1]

Tobacco growing began south of the Mason-Dixon line, and the warmer climate encouraged the establishing of large plantations with gang labor. "Red Indian" captives were tried but found to be too homicidal. Irish prisoners of war, convicts, and kidnapped children were sent to Virginia, as well as indentured servants.

The need for labor on the plantations of the West Indies and the American south seemed imperative. H. G. Wells further noted that it was a "very good and humane man indeed, Las Casas, who urged that negroes should be brought to America to relieve his tormented Indian proteges."[2] Bartolome de Las Casas (1474-1566) was a Spanish Dominican missionary, historian, and supporter of the Indians of Latin America, who himself had for a time been a planter and slave owner in Cuba until his "conscience smote him."

A Dutch ship brought the first Negro slaves to Jamestown in Virginia in 1619. By 1700 they were scattered throughout the colonies, but Virginia, Maryland, and the Carolinas were their chief regions of employment. The South developed large plantations with white owners and white communities of overseers and professional men subsisting on slave labor, which was necessary for maintaining the social and economic system that had grown up in the South.

With the growth of agriculture and cotton becoming a major crop, along with the expansion of settlements throughout the southern states, the use of Negro slave labor spread. Slaves were usually divided into three groups—field hands, house servants, and craftsmen. Many were quick to learn and became carpenters, masons, blacksmiths and wheelwrights. Negro slaves were considered property, and had no legal or political rights. They had no claim to a jury trial, and could not be witnesses against white people. While some owners were cruel and negligent about the physical well being of their slaves, many treated them well, both because they were human beings and because they were valuable property.

Almost the first outspoken utterances against Negro slavery came from agriculture-related German settlers in Pennsylvania. Quakers were strong in their opposition, as well. Harriet Beecher Stowe's book, *Uncle Tom's Cabin*, further inflamed northerners against slavery.

There were no large plantations in the North. There were communities of not-very-rich and not-very-poor farming men. Most slaves in the North were household servants. So, whether it was in jealous resentment of the prosperity and lifestyles of the southern plantation owners or sincere conscientious objections, opposition to slavery was more apt to develop and grow in the northern atmosphere.

H. G. Wells said:

> The north felt its cause a righteous one, but for great numbers of people it was not a full-bodied

> and unchallenged righteousness.
>
> But for Lincoln there was no doubt. He was a clear-minded man in the midst of such confusion. He stood for the Union; he stood for the great peace of America. He was opposed to slavery, but slavery he held to be a secondary issue. His primary purpose was that the United States should not be torn into two contrasted and jarring fragments. So through the long four years of struggle he stood out an inflexible conviction, a steadfast will.[3]

The Civil War preserved the union and abolished slavery. Writing about the period at the close of the Civil War, Michael Kraus said:

> Lincoln had lifted Americans to great efforts which saved their nation, "the last, best hope of earth." From the dangers of a divided land he delivered them to face the coming years with renewed confidence. A people who had braved the perils of pioneering the wilderness in the seventeenth century, who had brought forth a new nation in the eighteenth, and who were able to produce a Lincoln in the nineteenth century were endowed with a rich heritage to face the future.[4]

## THE INDUSTRIAL REVOLUTION

When extensive mechanization of production systems brought about a shift from home manufacturing to large-scale factory production, the result was significant and lasting social and economic changes. The Industrial Revolution began in England about the middle of the eighteenth century and by the end of the nineteenth century had spread throughout the world.

When the small farmers and the peasants in England were squeezed off the land by large landowners, the concentration of property was in the hands of a powerful and greedy class. Along with the change in ownership was an improvement in agricultural methods. This brought about an increase in wealth for the bigger owners, while the numbers of poor grew. The big and powerful owners grabbed the people's land and common pastures, assumed possession of the mines under their lands, and crushed down the small independent farmers and peasants to the status of poor laborers.

Concurrently with this change from traditional patch agriculture and common pasture to large and more scientific agriculture, great changes were going on in manufacturing. Throughout the course of history, manufacturing, building, and industry had been done by craftsmen working in their own homes. They were organized into guilds and were their own bosses. But in the eighteenth century, they began to be brought together into factories in order to produce things in larger quantities through a systematic division of labor. The employer became a person of much importance.

Mechanical invention produced machines driven by water power or steam that simplified the manual work of production. Watt's steam engine was constructed in 1765. The cotton industry was one of the first involved in factory production, then the woolen industry. Coal and iron industries changed. By 1800 this changeover from a small-scale business with small employers had become a large-scale business with big employers.

The machine and the employer now superseded the skill of the independent home-industry worker. He either became an employer or remained a worker and sank rapidly to the level of a mere laborer.

The immediate negative effect of the Industrial Revolution in the countries to which it came was upon the uneducated, leaderless, and increasingly-more-propertyless common people. The small farmers and peasants joined the families of the impoverished and degraded craftsmen in factories. Towns of shabby houses came into existence. Factories grew up, built as inexpensively as possible.

Around them were the cheaply-constructed homes of workers—without adequate space, without privacy, and at the highest rent possible. At first, the factory towns had no schools or churches.

During the last half of the nineteenth century, every part of American life reflected the growth of industry. The city seemed almost irresistible to many restless young people. Abandoned farms and overgrown fields bore witness to the urban movement. In many areas, the countryside was almost desolate as young men and women left the rural areas for the thriving manufacturing cities.

The urban population was swelled by the throngs of immigrants pouring into the country at an ever-increasing rate. Many had to live in crowded slums. Inventions and technological advance contributed to the rise of the cities and, in turn, were further stimulated by the pressing needs created by the rapid urban growth.

Lavish spending of the very wealthy was a characteristic feature of urban social life. Entertainment of the era grew more elaborate. Foster Rhea Dulles noted: "The Metropolitan Opera House was built in New York in 1883 to satisfy this urge for conspicuous display even more than to present operas."[5]

The life of the very poor was a sharp contrast. About one-tenth of the population of the cities lived in slums at the close of the nineteenth century. Buildings were close together, with little light or ventilation. Plumbing was primitive, rooms small, halls and stairways dark, and fire a constant danger.

The death toll in the slums was high, especially among children. Tuberculosis was widespread, as was typhoid, scarlet fever, smallpox, and diptheria. The slums were breeding places for disease, immorality, drunkenness, and crime.

Although the Industrial Revolution caused and still causes social and economic problems, it has brought about many good and profitable industrial and technological discoveries and changes. The invention of the steam engine, telegraph, telephone, the gasoline engine, and the discovery of electricity, as well as many other discoveries and inventions, made a great impact on westward expansion and the development of our nation. The growth of industries and manufacturing, and the achievement of technologies has made possible a better standard of living for Americans, inspite of the pockets of poverty and unemployment.

## NOTES

[1] H. G. Wells, *The Outline of History*, vol. 2 (H. G. Wells, 1920; rev. reprint ed. Raymond Postgate, New York: Doubleday & Company, 1961), p. 705.

[2] Ibid.

[3] Ibid., p. 795.

[4] Michael Kraus, *The United States to 1865* (Ann Arbor: The University of Michigan Press, 1959), p. 515.

[5] Foster Rhea Dulles, *The United States Since 1865* (Ann Arbor: The University of Michigan Press, 1959), p. 92.

# 3

# PROTESTANT MISSIONS IN AMERICA

The conversion of the Indians was emphasized in the charters granted by the British crown for establishing settlements in America. For instance, the Plymouth Colony Charter called for "the conversion of such savages as yet remain wandering in desolation and distress to civil society and the Christian religion." And the Massachusetts Bay Charter called upon the colonists to win the Indians "to the knowledge and obedience of the only true God and Saviour of mankind." William Warren Sweet pointed out that in the Plymouth colony, even during the hard early years, the Indians in the neighborhood were not neglected by the ministers, and in 1636 laws were passed providing for the preaching of the gospel among them. On the seal of Massachusetts Colony was an Indian, shouting the Macedonian call, "Come over and help us."[1]

Although this book relates to Protestant missions, it should be noted that the colonization efforts of the Spanish, Portuguese, and French were almost always done under the auspices of the Catholic Church. Priests usually accompanied these colonizing expeditions. This may have influenced the English, as Protestants, to emphasize the conversion of the Indians in their charters.

# THE BEGINNING OF CROSS-CULTURAL MINISTRY

The first Protestant cross-cultural missionary efforts in America were toward the end of the sixteenth century, according to Oliver Wendell Elsbree. Each of the three attempts by the English during the last quarter of the sixteenth century to propagate the gospel among the Indians of North America failed. Elsbree records:

> "The first of these efforts to attach the American natives to the Anglican Church was that made by Chaplain Wolfall who accompanied Martin Frobisher on his third voyage overseas and whose task it was not only to serve his white constituency but also "to reform these infidels [the natives] to Christianitie."[2] Likewise, Sir Humphrey Gilbert, when he obtained his patent for discovery, was invested with authority to establish in his colonies "the true Christian faith or religion now professed in the Church of England."[3] Both Frobisher and Gilbert failed to establish permanent colonies, and no results attended the efforts of their clergy to convert the savages.
>
> The name "Virginia" has survived to remind us of Sir Walter Raleigh and his premature hopes. Among his Roanoke colonists was Thomas Hariot who preached Christianity to the natives. A native "Lord" whose name was Manteo was baptized in 1587—probably the first red man to be received into a Protestant church in America. . . . His colony, however, was completely wiped out in some unknown manner. The relief expedition which went out in search of it in 1590 found not a trace of it.[4]

Probably the most well-known of the early missionaries in Virginia was Alexander Whitaker. The son of Dr. William Whitaker, professor of divinity at Cambridge and "one of the best known of the Puritan clergy of his day," Alexander built his parsonage in a group of new settlements seventy miles up the James River from Jamestown. "Thus Whitaker became the first country parson and missionary in Virginia." The Indian princess, Pocahontas, was among the Indian children that he taught and tried to Christianize. She was the first convert he won to Christianity, and to whom he subsequently gave religious instruction. Alexander Whitaker worked faithfully among the Indians until his death in 1617, which came by drowning in the James.[5]

Attempts at evangelization and education in Virginia stopped when a massacre by the Indians occurred in 1622. Because of the reaction to the massacre, no serious efforts of evangelization of the Indians was undertaken again. However, there were efforts in education of Indian youth.

The evangelization of the Indians was sanctioned by the crown, encouraged by the Anglican Church, and largely financed by collections taken in England. In the early years of colonization, most of the settlers were less interested in the spiritual needs of the Indians than in driving them out of their areas or eliminating them altogether.

It was primarily in New England that ministers and some laymen took seriously the missionary purpose of the charters. John Eliot and Thomas Mayhew, Jr. were the first missionaries to the Indians in New England.

Protestant missionary work began in New England on the island of Martha's Vineyard in 1643, some 23 years after the Puritans landed at Plymouth. While in England, Thomas Mayhew, Sr. obtained a grant to Martha's Vineyard and the surrounding islands. He sent his twenty-one-year-old son, Thomas, Jr., a Congregational clergyman, with a group of settlers to take possession of the islands in 1642. He followed a few months later and became the patentee and the governor.

Shortly after their arrival, the settlers called Thomas Mayhew, Jr. to be pastor of the settlement. With his congregation being small, in 1643 he began work among the several thousand Indians of the islands.

> Acquainting himself with the Indians, then mastering their language, he established a successful mission. The first convert among the New England Indians was Hiacoomes, who placed himself under Mr. Meyhew's [Mayhew] instruction for one year, then becoming a teacher, and later a preacher to his own people. In 1650 a number of these natives had abandoned their heathen beliefs and accepted Christianity. In 1651 Mr. Meyhew reported 190 conversions. On January 11th, 1651, Mr. Meyhew established the first school in New England for the instruction of Indian children. In October 1652, the first native church was organized, with 282 members. Mr. Meyhew having prepared for this a covenant in their own language. In 1657 Mr. Meyhew, while on his way to England to secure aid for his work, was lost at sea.[6]

His father, Governor Thomas Mayhew, Sr., although seventy years of age, learned the Indian language, and took up the work as an evangelist, continuing to preach to them until he was almost ninety-three years of age. Not long before Governor Mayhew died, grandson John Mayhew became the pastor of the island and began working among the Indians. A few years after John's early death in 1688, his son, Experience Mayhew, continued the Indian work for thirty-two years.

John Eliot was called "the apostle to the Indians." He graduated from Cambridge University in 1622, and taught in a church school in England until he sailed for Boston in 1631. Before coming to North America, Eliot had been ordained as a minister by the Church of England. He briefly pastored a church in Boston before accepting a call from a church in Roxbury, Massachusetts, in 1632, where he stayed until his death in 1690.

> In 1639 he was appointed with Welde and Mather, by the civil and religious leaders of the colony, to prepare a new version of the Psalms. Issued in 1640, this Psalter, called "The Bay Psalm Book" and later "The New England Version of the Psalms," was the first book printed in America, and subsequently went through twenty-one editions.[7]

Eliot became deeply interested in the Indians. Since the legislature passed an act for the propagation of the gospel among them, Eliot resolved to learn their language so that he could preach to them. He was assisted in his study of the language by a Pequot Indian who lived with him. He soon knew enough of the vocabulary and construction to translate the ten commandments, the Lord's Prayer, some texts of Scripture, and a few prayers. Finally, in October 1646 he delivered his first message to the Indians, the first sermon ever preached in a native tongue in North America.

Because of interest in Eliot's ministry, the Massachusetts Assembly passed an act ordering ministers to elect every year two from among their number to work as missionaries among the Indians.

By 1651 Eliot's converts were gathered into a community, forming their own town of Natick, seventeen miles southwest of Boston. He had translated the entire Bible into the Indian language by 1663. It was the first Bible printed in America. Among Eliot's original works in the Indian language were *A Catechism*, *Indian Psalter*, *Primer*, and *Indian Grammar*. Eliot died in 1690 at 86 years of age.

Only ministers that were called by a congregation were ordained. Workers who went directly into Indian mission work were often not ordained until a later date.

Richard Bourn is thought to be the first to be ordained for Indian missions. He had been a teacher of a group of Indians at Maktapog near Sandwich, Plymouth Colony. They were recognized as a church by civil and church leaders, and Bourn was ordained as their pastor on July 17, 1670.[8]

Four other prominent New England missionaries to the Indians were John Sergeant (Congregational), Eleazer Wheelock (Congregational), David Brainerd (licensed to preach by Congregational and later ordained Presbyterian), and Jonathan Edwards (a Congregational pastor who became president of the College of New Jersey at Princeton, a Presbyterian college).

While John Sergeant was a tutor at Yale College, he began ministering to the Indians. As a Congregationalist, he was ordained as a missionary to the Housatonic Mohegans by Governor Belcher at a council of the tribes at Deerfield. After learning their language, he set up a school for them at Stockbridge, Massachusetts. Sergeant was succeeded in that ministry by Jonathan Edwards from 1749 to 1758, with the next pastor being Stephen West.

Eleazer Wheelock was ordained on June 4, 1735 by the New Haven Congregational Association and called to the North Parish of Lebanon, Connecticut. He was one of the most active preachers during the revivals of the Great Awakening (1726-1756). For several decades he conducted the most extensive school of the New England missions to the Indians. Through the financial help of Joshua Moor, Wheelock was able to open a charity school, which was named Moor's Charity School. It was open to both Indian and white students. Converted during the Great Awakening, Samson Occum, a Mohegan, was the school's first graduate. Some Mohawk youth attended, as well.

As the school grew, it developed into Dartmouth College, which opened in Hanover, New Hampshire, in 1770. Its primary purpose was to train young white men for missionary work among the Indians. Inscribed on the great seal of Dartmouth College are the words *Vox Clamantis in*

*Deserto*, "the voice of one crying in the wilderness."

David Brainerd is probably the best known of all the missionaries to Indians during the period following the Great Awakening. Converted in 1739, he entered Yale College to prepare for ministry. He was the leader of his class and won distinction as a scholar. Because he favored the revival, which the college opposed, he made a disparaging remark about a tutor. That, along with the accusation of his having attended a Separatist meeting, led to his being expelled from Yale.

In 1742 Brainerd was licensed to preach in the Congregational Church. That same year, on November 22, 1742, he was commissioned by the New York-New Jersey Board of Commissioners of the Society in Scotland for Propagating Christian Knowledge. He was sent to work among Indians a few miles southeast of Albany. After receiving ordination from the New Side Presbytery in New York in 1744, he began Indian work in New Jersey.

Brainerd had suffered from tuberculosis since his student days. The severe exposure and hardships of travel brought his disease to a point of crisis. His condition was such that early in 1747 he could no longer continue his work. On October 9, 1747, he died at the home of Jonathan Edwards at Northampton. Brainerd was engaged to be married to Jerusha Edwards, Jonathan's daughter. His Christ-like character and his unswerving commitment to his Indian ministry, in spite of physical weakness and pain, made a deep impression upon his generation.

Largely using Brainerd's journals of his experiences, Jonathan Edwards published in 1749 *An Account of the Life of the Late Reverend Mr. David Brainard.* Partially due to Edwards' reputation as a theologian and preacher, this book had wide circulation and enormous influence in promoting missions. Henry Martyn and William Carey both made their decisions for missionary service after reading it. William Warren Sweet observed, "Indeed, David Brainerd dead was a more potent influence for

Indian missions and the missionary cause in general than was David Brainerd alive."[9]

Jonathan Edwards, a Congregational minister, was born in East Windsor, Connecticut, where his father, Timothy Edwards, was a minister. Jonathan graduated from Yale in 1720 at seventeen years of age, He continued several years of further study, and did some preaching and teaching at Yale before becoming the pastor at Northampton in 1726. For sixty years his maternal grandfather, Solomon Stoddard, was pastor there. Soon after beginning his ministry in Northampton, Edwards married Sarah Pierpont, daughter of Rev. James Pierpont of New Haven. She was described as being the ideal New England minister's wife. Jonathan Edwards' powerful preaching helped to start the Great Awakening.

Edwards succeeded John Sergeant in his ministry to the Mohicans at Stockbridge from 1749 to 1758, when he left to become president of the Presbyterian's College of New Jersey at Princeton. Jonathan Edwards died after receiving a smallpox inoculation during his first semester there.

The first Moravians arrived in America early in the 1730s. Missions was their main purpose in coming—to work among the Germans and the Indians. Their Indian work was primarily in New York and Pennsylvania, and in North Carolina after the Revolution.

The Quakers were interested in the Indians. George Fox repeatedly urged the spiritual claims of the Indian. As he traveled from Rhode Island south through Maryland and the Carolinas, he preached to the Indians when possible. William Penn often expressed a deep interest in the Indians spiritual welfare. In efforts to evangelize the Indians, such men as John Richards, Thomas Story, Thomas Chalkley, and John Woolman ministered as far as the western part of Pennsylvania and into Ohio.

The Indian missions, which were largely in New England from the 1640s, were the stimulus in America for all mission work that followed, both at home and abroad. They provided the patterns, the principles, the framework.

R. Pierce Beaver observed: "Out of the Indian missions came both the global evangelistic enterprise of all Protestantism and American 'home missions.' Inspiration, theory, and models were important gifts to the global mission."[10]

Working under extremely difficult and hazardous conditions, the early missionaries to the Indians exemplified commitment to evangelizing the unreached, simplicity of lifestyle, their own thorough preparation for ministry, determination in learning the language of the receptor people, and the importance of education in training national leadership.

The Great Awakening and later revivals stimulated the missionary movement, which gained more strength and momentum after the Revolution.

## THE EMERGING OF MISSION SOCIETIES

Societies, founded in Great Britain, supported the Indian work of the early missionaries. Although some funds came from individuals and churches in the colonies, it would be hard to determine the percentage of support that came from American sources.

It was the work of John Eliot that laid the foundation for the first Protestant mission. Reports of the Indian work, which were circulated in London, raised so much interest that the needs of the Indians were brought before Parliament. On July 27, 1649 an act was passed, A Corporation for the Promoting and Propagating the Gospel of Jesus Christ in New England. It recognized the need for the evangelization and civilization of the Indians, and made provision of funds for such work.

After Charles II was restored to the throne in 1660, that corporation ceased to exist. However, in 1662 the king issued a charter for a new company, The Company for the Propagation of the Gospel in New England and the parts adjacent in America. It was commonly known as The New England Company, and made grants for the work of Eliot, Mayhew, and others. It continued in operation until the Americans won their independence. The members of its board in New England were largely the same as the Indian Commissioners of the Society in Scotland for Propagating Christian Knowledge, which also had a New York-New Jersey Board whose responsibilities were eventually turned over to the Trustees of the College of New Jersey at Princeton. Founded in 1701 for work in Scotland, the Society was chartered in 1709, and began supporting Indian work in 1730 when it received a bequest for that purpose.

Appointed as the ecclesiastical representative for Maryland by the Bishop of London in 1696, Thomas Bray was instrumental in getting several societies started in Great Britain for work in the colonies. The Society for Promoting Christian Knowledge (1698) was for providing books and Bibles for Anglican clergy. The Society for the Propagation of the Gospel in Foreign Parts (1701) was to secure Anglican clergy for the colonies, and The Associates of Dr. Bray was a fund set up for educating Negro slaves.

The history of evangelization of the Indians and slaves by the colonies may have been different if more financial responsibility had been given to the churches in the colonies and to the colonists from the beginning. As it was, with most of the financial support coming from overseas that was withdrawn during and following the Revolution, there was no missions constituency within the colonial churches to carry on. After the Revolution, there was virtually no support for the Indian missions. With support cut off from England, the support for missionary effort begun before American independence became the responsibility of the churches in America. If there had been local supporting constituencies in the colonies, there would have been less of a decline in missions interest and involvement.

Chaney noted:

> By the end of the Revolution, the American missionary enterprise was in a generally deplorable condition. The Christian Indians were scattered and highly suspect. Their villages had been overrun, and their missionaries, who were mostly supported from Great Britain, were unpaid and poverty stricken. War had dispersed and destroyed many of the English churches, and many frontier settlements were completely abandoned. Inflation was rampant. Continental currency was almost worthless, and "hard money" was scarce. The fledgling country, and the various states, faced the great task of building a nation. In addition, the War had a general adverse effect on the spiritual life of the nation. Deism had never had such influential advocates. The future was dark.[11]

However, there soon was an awakening of interest and a seeming sense of urgency in the evangelization of all of America—the Indians, Negroes, those on the frontiers, and the influx of new settlers—the immigrants. The Concert for Prayer movement helped to prepare the way for the missions expansion following the Revolution. This non-sectarian prayer fellowship began in Scotland in 1744 and was quickly endorsed by pastors in Boston. Jonathan Edwards was one of its strongest proponents. He published an account of the Concert of Prayer, *An humble attempt to promote explicit agreement and visible union of God's people in extraordinary prayer for the Revival of Religion, and the advancement of Christ's Kingdom on earth, pursuant to Scripture promises and prophecies concerning the last time.*[12]

It had wide circulation in America and overseas, and stimulated many Christians to regular and united prayer for revival and the spread of the gospel. After 1795 the Concert of Prayer became widespread and continued for the next twenty-five years or so.

Another contributing factor to the renewed concern for evangelizing the unreached was the Second Awakening that spread throughout America. Dr. Cairns sets its dates as 1776 to 1810.[13]

About the time that the newly-formed Baptist Missionary Society in London (1792) sent William Carey to India in 1793, a movement began in America that resulted in numerous mission societies being organized in New England and the middle states among the Congregational, Presbyterians, Dutch Reformed, Baptists, Methodists, and Episcopalians.

Instead of organizing societies that would send missionaries overseas, the focus was on the needs in the new nation. The first societies organized in America were local in purpose. In 1787 some men in Boston established the Society for the Propagation of the Gospel among the Indians and others in North America. Several local Congregational societies came into being—The Missionary Society of Connecticut in 1789; the Massachusetts Missionary Society in 1790; The New Hampshire Society and The Vermont Society were also organized.

The New York Missionary Society, organized September 21, 1796, was called by Elsbree "the first voluntary interdenominational organization of a missionary character in the United States." Formed by ministers and laymen of New York City, mostly Presbyterians, Associate Reformed, Reformed Dutch, and Baptists, its immediate purpose was to take the gospel to southern Indians, particularly the Chickasaws of Georgia and Tennessee.[14]

This pattern of missionary society, of which the New York Missionary Society was a prototype, provided an open nondenominational policy of missionary membership and a broader supporting constituency. It provided a place where people with similar interests could work together. Hudson described the voluntary society:

> A voluntary society was an extra-church agency, formed for a specific purpose by individuals and not related structurally to the churches.

> Essentially a technique devised by British churchmen, the voluntary society was seized upon by American Protestants as a perfect instrument by which they could pool their efforts to influence public opinion, effect reforms, meet humanitarian needs, establish colleges, provide religious instruction, organize publishing ventures, and carry on extensive and wide-ranging missionary activities.[15]

The Northern Missionary Society in the State of New York, organized in 1796, and the New York Missionary Society sent workers to the Tuscaroras and other Iroquois in New York.

The Presbyterian mission outreach to frontier communities, settled regions without churches, Indians, and Negroes was supported for a number of years by individuals, presbyteries, and synods. The General Assembly was incorporated in 1799 and granted a charter by the state of Pennsylvania. The General Assembly served as its own missionary society until 1802 when it appointed a standing committee of missions.

In the early 1800s women's mission auxiliaries were established. They raised financial and prayer support, and provided Bibles, books, and other Christian literature for missions. Two of these women's organizations were the Boston Female Society for Missionary Purposes organized in 1800 and the Boston Female Cent Society in 1802.

Up to this time, the missionary movement in America was basically limited to work in new settlements and among Indians and slaves. The overseas mission advance from the United States began with the founding of The American Board of Commissioners for Foreign Missions in June 1810. The first five missionaries were sent to India in 1812.

Although it was organized by a Congregational body, it became nondenominational in 1812 when it elected Presbyterians to the board. Dutch Reformed were added in 1816. Valentin Rabe pointed out that the charter for the ABCFM was granted by the Commonwealth of Massachusetts, rather than by an ecclesiastical body.[16] Rabe also referred to the ABCFM as a "nondenominational agency."[17]

In 1817, the Presbyterian Church U.S.A., the Associate Reformed Church, and the Dutch Reformed Church founded the United Foreign Missionary Society. It later took over the New York and the Northern New York Societies. In 1826, it merged with the American Board of Commissioners for Foreign Missions. After the Civil War, the American Board became only Congregational again.

The General Missionary Convention of the Baptist Denomination of the United States of America for Foreign Missions was organized in May 1814. It was the first Baptist foreign missionary society and the first general organization of Baptists in the United States.

The Methodist Church formed its missionary society in 1819 as both a home and foreign mission. The Episcopal Church organized its domestic and foreign missionary society in 1821.

The nondenominational American Home Missionary Society, organized in 1826, was the first home mission on a nationwide scale. At first it was largely made up of Presbyterians, but a number of the local Congregational societies became affiliated with it. The Baptists organized their national Home Missionary Society in 1832.

Most of the Bible societies, which had been formed for local or state needs, were consolidated in 1816 to form the American Bible Society. The New York Bible Society, organized in 1809, did not join this group. Its name was changed to International Bible Society. It remains a strong cooperating agency for evangelical missions. The IBS and Living Bibles International merged in 1992, forming a new corporation, but continuing under the name, International Bible Society.

The American Bible Society and the United Bible

Societies have translated the Scriptures into hundreds of languages throughout the world. Their distribution system and subsidized pricing continues to make a significant contribution to ministries worldwide, particularly to cross-cultural outreach.

The American Education Society was also formed in 1816, the Colonization Society followed in 1817, The American Tract Society in 1825, the American Temperance Society in 1826, and the American Antislavery Society in 1833. These societies accepted the provision of literature as their part of the missionary outreach in the West and then in the South.

The voluntary nondenominational organizations and movements, beginning after the Revolution and continuing into the 1830s, reflected a strong conservative evangelical advance.

Ralph D. Winter stated, "Denominational leaders inevitably reacted as they saw so many of their key laymen and so much of their members' money flowing into these novel channels."[18]

Bishop John Henry Hobart expressed deep concern about Episcopalians cooperating with the voluntary societies. He was consecrated bishop in 1811, and was a strong leader of the Episcopal high-church party. Hobart wrote of Protestant supporters of these nondenominational organizations:

> They seldom bring into view the divine institution of the Christian Church, and the divine origin of its powers. In their language, and in their practice, they reduce this sacred institution, which, founded by a divine hand, is animated and governed by him, to whom "all power is given in heaven and on earth," to a level with those associations which have no higher origin than human power, and no other object but human policy.[19]

## THE HOME MISSIONS MOVEMENT TO THE FRONTIERS

The migration to the West was largely made up of individuals and families seeking better opportunities. Coming from different ethnic and religious backgrounds, most did not move together in homogeneous religious groups with their own pastors. When a missionary preacher or circuit rider came, people gathered as much for social, as religious, reasons. This helped to produce on the frontiers what Mode called "the process of interdenominationalizing the sectarian mind of the community."[20]

The early camp meetings were popular partly because of the large number of people that gathered for several days of teaching and fellowship. Denominational distinctives were blurred as men of differing denominations shared the same platform.

One of the important missionary organizations of the frontier era was the American Sunday School Union. Sunday school advocate Francis Scott Key could hardly have known that his poem would be immortalized as the new nation's national anthem, or that the Sunday school organization over which he presided as vice president would shape and strengthen the moral fabric of the nation he loved. Yet, Americans still sing the "Star Spangled Banner" and the American Missionary Fellowship is still vibrantly alive.

The American Missionary Fellowship, which was known to Francis Scott Key as the American Sunday School Union, traces it roots back to the First Day Society, a Sunday School organization established in 1790. Bishop William White, minister at Philadelphia's Christ Church, in which George Washington and Benjamin Franklin worshipped, visited England where he observed the work of Sunday school pioneer Robert Raikes. Already concerned about the number of illiterate unchurched children in Philadelphia, Bishop White seized on Raikes' solution and excitedly brought the idea home to America. He assembled a group of prominent Philadelphia Christians—physicians, merchants, a minister, and a publisher—and challenged them with the prospect of organizing Sunday schools.

On December 26, 1790, the charter of the First Day Society was drawn up, and on the second Sunday of March 1791, the first two Sunday schools met in the Philadelphia area, one for boys and one for girls. The children were taught to read and write, using the Old and New Testaments as the primary texts. The main purpose of the schools was to lift the moral and religious character of the students. Since, for another generation, the churches did not see this work as a part of their responsibility, the society became a voluntary nondenominational organization.

The Sunday and Adult School Union was organized in 1817. It was designed to be a "Union" of all Sunday school societies. It began a lay, nondenominational movement, representing 11 associations. The Union grew quickly. By the end of the seventh year, some 720 groups from 17 states were members. It excelled in producing Sunday school books, including song books and other literature.

The Union had a missionary vision and purposed to see Sunday schools planted throughout the country. It cooperated with Bible societies in Bible and Christian literature distribution, and sponsored schools among Indians and Negroes.

By 1823 there was a large publishing work, auxiliary groups in 19 states and 3 full-time missionaries. The first full-time Sunday school missionary employed by the Union was Rev. William C. Blair. During his first year, he traveled by horseback some 2,500 miles, covering 6 states, "founding 61 Sunday schools, visiting 35 others, reviving 20, and establishing 6 tract societies and 4 adult schools."[21]

A new constitution of the American Sunday School Union was adopted in 1824 by the managers of the Sunday and Adult School Union, and actually amounted only to a change in name. The same managers were elected to the successor organization and all assets were transferred.

In fact, during the 1820s, the board of managers of the American Sunday School Union served as the managers of the First Day Society. In effect, the two organizations were already united in the 1820s.

Dr. E. Eugene Williams, general director of American Missionary Fellowship, said, "Although the First Day Society affiliated with more than ten other societies in the 1817 organization, it retained its autonomy and continues to exist under the auspices of American Missionary Fellowship. It is the oldest existing Sunday school society in the world."[22]

This ministry has operated under a number of names. The full name of the mission was First Day Society from 1790 to 1817. The New York Sunday School Union, organized in 1816, merged with it in 1817. It operated as the Sunday and Adult School Union from 1817 to 1824. The Female Sunday School Union, organized in 1816 merged with it about 1820. The mission operated as the American Sunday School Union from 1824 to 1974. The Maranatha Settlement Association merged with it in 1968. It has operated as American Missionary Fellowship since 1974.[23]

The ASSU worked to make its educational program complementary to the educational responsibility of the family, church, and state. However, as the settlers moved west and as the missionaries traced a parallel path, they found that there was an enormous need, particularly in many of the frontier villages and countryside where no religious instruction was being given.

In 1830 a plan was adopted to plant Sunday schools in the most needy areas of the "Valley of the Mississippi," an area of some fourteen states or territories. The plan caught the imagination of much of the settled part of the nation. Funds were raised in large meetings in Philadelphia, New York, Boston, Washington, and Charleston. Addresses endorsing the project were given by such men as Lyman Beecher, Daniel Webster, and Francis Scott Key.

This resulted in the planting of 4 to 5 thousand new Sunday schools, with many growing into churches. About 90 missionaries were employed and about 1,000,000 books were put into circulation. A similar ASSU program in the southern states produced significant and lasting results. To help meet the huge demand for Christian literature, the ASSU provided 1,000 libraries of 120 books each.

During the 1850s, the issue of slavery became more pressing and it became difficult for missionaries from the North to be accepted for work among slaves in the South. During the Civil War, the ASSU suffered financially, limiting its missionary activity. At the end of the war, missionaries were reinstated in the South and in the North. New schools for blacks were started.

The period from 1870 to 1915 saw a continually increasing effort in evangelistic outreach. At the beginning of the twentieth century visits to families in remote areas to provide Christian literature increased to 95,000 a year. The number of missionaries was doubled. One missionary, Martin B. Lewis, was able to start over 1,000 Sunday schools in Minnesota and Wisconsin. In 1915 it was estimated that almost 132,000 schools had been formed in which 700,000 teachers had worked with more than 5,000,000 students.[24]

The expansion of denominations was helped considerably by this nondenominational movement.

Today's frontiers have expanded to include the inner city, multicultural ministries, and rural America. Missionaries still start Sunday schools, but they have broadened their church-planting methods to include Bible studies, released-time classes, and Christian camping. Thousands of churches in the United States owe their origin to this mission.

Much space has been given to the ministry of the American Missionary Fellowship for several reasons: (1) it was one of the earliest nondenominational missions to be organized in America; (2) its ministry has been noticeably extensive and effective, including a significant cross-cultural outreach, and (3) it is a highly respected member of the IFMA and has been in existence longer than any other IFMA member mission. The IFMA is a fellowship of mission agencies, working cross-culturally in North America and throughout the world.

## BIBLE AND MISSIONARY CONFERENCES

The nondenominational Bible conference movement was one of the major methods used by conservative evangelicals toward the end of the nineteenth century to counter the liberalism of Protestant schools and prolific writings of liberal clergy. Bible conferences brought together believers across denominational lines for fellowship and confirmation of conservative evangelical belief.

The first conferences were meetings of a few concerned men for Bible study and prayer. Ernest Sandeen traced the origin of what became known as the Niagara Bible Conference to men affiliated with the premillenarian publication, *Waymarks in the Wilderness*. James Inglis, David Inglis, and Charles Campbell were the editors. Several other men got together with these editors for a small conference in New York City in 1868. They were George S. Bishop, a Reformed church pastor in Orange, New Jersey; L. C. Baker, a Presbyterian minister from Camden, New Jersey; George C. Needham, a Christian worker who had emigrated from Ireland; George O. Barnes and Benjamin Douglas. In the years following, these men sponsored Bible conferences in Philadelphia, St. Louis, and Galt, Ontario.[25]

After the deaths of a few of these leaders, there was a lapse in the meetings until younger men caught the vision for such Bible and prophetic conferences, with emphasis on the imminent second coming of Christ. A planning meeting was held in 1875 in Chicago with James H. Brooks, pastor of the Walnut Street Presbyterian Church, St. Louis, Fleming H. Revell, publisher, and Philip P. Bliss, a singer and evangelist.

The resulting conference was held in 1876 at Swampscott, Massachusetts, with Adoniram J. Gordon, Baptist pastor in Boston, and William J. Erdman, a Presbyterian minister, among the speakers. Both of these men, along with Arthur T. Pierson, were among the continuing popular Bible conference speakers. In addition to their premillenial position, they were strong foreign mission advocates.

From 1877 the conference met for the next five years in different resort grounds from Maine to Michigan. From 1883 to 1897 it settled at Niagara-on-the-Lake, Ontario. The "Niagara" conferences ended in 1900 at Asbury Park, New Jersey.

During the years of its existence, at least 120 prominent conservative evangelical speakers took part in the sessions, which normally lasted for 8 days. There were 5 messages throughout the day, except for Sunday, which featured one message in the morning, communion in the afternoon, and a missionary message in the evening. Among the missionary speakers were Presbyterian Jonathan Goforth and J. Hudson Taylor of the China Inland Mission.

One of the lasting results of the Niagara conferences is the list of essential doctrines attributed to a "Niagara Statement" of 1895. Those include the inerrancy of Scripture, deity of Christ, virgin birth, substitutionary atonement, resurrection, and Christ's bodily second coming.[26] Sandeen reproduced "The 1878 Niagara Creed," which included fourteen articles.[27]

A well-attended Bible and prophetic conference was held at New York City's Holy Trinity Episcopal Church in November 1878, instituted by the same leaders as the Niagara Conference. The premillenarian view of the second coming of Christ was emphasized. The second of this series was held in 1886 at Farwell Hall in Chicago, and the third in Allegheny, Pennsylvania, in 1895.

Another conference center with great significance, particularly for its influence on missions, was started by

Dwight L. Moody at Northfield, Massachusetts, his birthplace and home. The first conference in 1880 drew some 300 people for Bible study and a Concert of Prayer. Spiritual power was the main emphasis of this ten-day meeting.

The 1885 conference, the third to be held, stressed Christian life and service. Foreign missions was emphasized. One of the key speakers was J. E. K. Studd (brother of C.T. Studd) of London who spoke of the English student movement and the "Cambridge Seven." They were seven outstanding men from Cambridge University who went to China early in 1885 as missionaries with China Inland Mission—D. E. Hoste, Stanley Smith, C. T. Studd, Montagu Beauchamp, C.P. Polhill, A. T. Polhill, and W. W. Cassels. Adoniram J. Gordon spoke with power on the Christian life. The conference ended with a call for a world conference on missions, which later took place in 1888 at Exeter Hall, London. Arthur T. Pierson was chairman of the committee that drafted the "call"—"An Appeal to Disciples Everywhere."[28]

## STUDENT MISSION INVOLVEMENT

The student societies of the eighteenth century evidently did not result in any student foreign missionary movement, although students were involved in various forms of outreach among American Indian tribes. Early in the nineteenth century, student emphasis on missions was prominent.

Samuel J. Mills, Jr. was presumably the first American college student to propose to a praying group of fellow students at Williams College that they dedicate their lives for overseas missionary service. Mills was one of seven children of a respected pastor in Torringford, Connecticut, who was one of the leaders of a movement of revival in that area. But it was young Samuel's mother who had early committed him to the Lord for missionary service. She related the missionary passion of men like John Eliot and

David Brainerd. She kept the needs of the world before him. His personal commitment to missionary service became a reality to him while attending Morris Academy.

Upon entering Williams College in the spring of 1806, Mills joined a small group of believers to pray for revival among the students. The prayer time was held in fields away from the college since such activity was not appreciated by the majority of the students.

As the group began to pray one August afternoon, a thunderstorm passed over, causing them to move underneath a haystack to continue their meeting, which has since been called "the haystack prayer meeting." Mills presented the foreign missionary need so forcefully that three of the other four joined him in purposing for missions service, possibly in Asia. Others joined them in this resolve during the next two years. This group, organized in 1808, was known as the Society of the Brethren.

There were no American missions for sending missionaries overseas at that time. The existing mission agencies were concentrating on the needs of the expansion of the frontiers and work among Indians and Negroes.

After graduation from Williams, Mills and several of his companions entered the new Andover Seminary. There they maintained their interest in overseas service. Mills convinced his friends that American churches should send them rather than their applying to the London Missionary Society. And so it was that in 1810 a petition was submitted to the meeting of the General Association of the Congregational Churches of Massachusetts, requesting that a foreign mission be established and offering themselves as missionaries. It was signed by Adoniram Judson, Samuel Nott, Jr., Samuel Newell, and Samuel Mills, Jr.

## THE RISE OF FOREIGN MISSION BOARDS

As a result of the petition by Mills and his friends, the American Board of Commissioners for Foreign Missions was established in 1810. The first group of missionaries was ordained and sailed for Calcutta in 1812. They were Adoniram and Ann Judson, Samuel and Rosanna Nott, Samuel and Harriet Newell, Gordon Hall, and Luther Rice. The wives were appointed as assistant missionaries.

Through Bible study on the long voyage to India, although on different ships, the Judsons and Luther Rice became convinced of believers baptism by immersion. After their arrival in India, they were baptized by William Carey, and they resigned from the American Board. Luther Rice returned to America to offer his service and the Judsons as Baptist missionaries. This led to the formation of the General Baptist Convention of the Baptist Denomination of the United States of America for Foreign Missions in 1814. Rice was asked to remain in America as administrator of the new agency. The Judsons, who were in Burma, remained there to establish the first Baptist mission.

When the others left for Calcutta, Samuel Mills, Jr. was asked by the American Board to seek additional volunteers in the colleges and to help some home missions projects of the Board. At this time, there were only 25 colleges in America and only a few had as many as 100 students enrolled.

Mills died in 1818 on board ship when returning from an exploratory trip to Africa. While his missionary career was short, the foreign mission enterprise, which he helped to start, grew in America.

The Methodists organized their domestic and foreign society in 1819; the Episcopal Church missions society, organized in 1821, included both domestic and foreign. Most of the denominational groups formed foreign mission agencies in the first half of the nineteenth century.

The first Young Men's Christian Association (YMCA) was organized in London in 1844. In the United States, the first one was formed in Boston in 1851. More than 200 had been organized by 1861. The flow of people into the nation's cities came from farms and rural areas where usually churches had been a prominent part of their lives. The YMCAs sought to reach them as soon as they arrived in the cities. Evangelism was a priority in the early years of the YMCA movement.

The first Young Women's Christian Associations (YWCA) began to appear in the United States in the 1860s. They were for reaching the young women who were working in the cities. The first ones were started in the 1850s in Germany and Great Britain.

Both YMCAs and YWCAs were organized in colleges and universities in the United States and Canada, and by the 1880s these nondenominational organizations had largely become the stimulus of religious life among students in these two countries. National associations of both YMCA and YWCA were formed, and later international associations were established.

Interest in missions had been revived in a number of colleges by the close of the 1870s and beginning of the 1880s, particularly in the Interseminary Missionary Alliance organized in 1880 and the medical students missionary conferences.

The evangelistic ministry of Dwight L. Moody was effective in colleges and universities in Great Britain, then in America. This paved the way for the nondenominational YMCA college division's 26-day conference held at Moody's Mount Hermon boy's school in Massachusetts in 1886. Some 250 students from 90 schools attended. There was intensive Bible study, emphasizing the importance of God's Word and work. Powerful missionary meetings were held, featuring testimonies of 10 international students and sons of missionaries. Dr. Arthur T. Pierson challenged and motivated the students with the idea of "the evangelization of the world in this generation." Only 10 percent of the students were purposing for foreign work when they came. The number quadrupled by the end of the conference.[29]

Before the Mount Hermon conference ended, it was decided that a team of volunteers should travel to the colleges across America to present the missionary challenge. Robert Wilder and his Princeton classmate, John N. Forman, whose parents were missionaries, spent the next year traveling from college to college. By June 1887 some 1,600 men and 500 women had volunteered for missionary service.[30]

Along with Luther D. Wishard, the first national college secretary of the Intercollegiate YMCA, and his assistant—Charles K. Ober, other key student leaders who kept the foreign missions vision before the students were John Forman, John Mott. Robert Wilder, and his sister, Grace. Their efforts were greatly strengthened by the establishing in 1888 of the Student Volunteer Movement for Foreign Missions as the missionary arm of the Student Christian Movement. The SVMFM is commonly referred to as the Student Volunteer Movement. John R. Mott was made chairman of this new organization. By the time he stepped down from this position in 1920, more than eleven thousand student volunteers had gone from the colleges into world missions.[31]

## NONDENOMINATIONAL FOREIGN MISSIONS

In the last half of the nineteenth century, a number of nondenominational missions came into being, sometimes referred to as faith, independent, or interdenominational missions. Almost all of the organizers and early leaders were active as clergymen or lay men and women in evangelical churches in the various denominations. This was before the rise of the independent Bible-church movement.

While the increasing liberalism of the period was undoubtedly recognized as an unwelcome development, it was not the immediate cause for founding nondenominational missions. Rupert is correct in stating that the first motivation of the independent mission pioneers was "the desire to proclaim the gospel throughout the world."[32]

The first major factor was the recognition that all people

were not being reached with the gospel of God's saving grace through Jesus Christ. The denominational agencies were not sending missionaries into the interiors. They were not reaching women in *purdah* or the *harem*. The unreached people and places of the world provided strong motivation for the development of the nondenominational missions movement. Thus, missions such as the China *Inland* Mission, Regions *Beyond* Missionary Union, Sudan *Interior* Mission, and Africa *Inland* Mission were formed. Usually these nondenominational missions were founded by strong natural leaders who were burdened to reach a particular people or area of the world not being served by other missions. This concern for penetrating the frontiers has influenced many missions to seek more personnel in order to expand into new places and/or types of service.

Concerned women in 1860 reluctantly founded one of the first nondenominational foreign mission agencies in the United States. For years they had tried to convince the denominational "men's boards" to send single women missionaries to work among the women and children of Asia. The denominational boards of the day considered sending single women as missionaries too hazardous. When their answer remained negative, the Woman's Union Missionary Society was formed in 1860. This was five years before the founding of the China Inland Mission in England in 1865.

Almost forty years later Pandita Ramabai, a converted Indian widow from a strong Hindu background, spoke throughout North America, telling of the desperate plight of widows and orphaned girls and their need for shelter and salvation. As a result of this visit, the American Council of the Ramabai Mukti Mission was established to assist the ministry which she had started at Kedgaon, Poona District, India.

Second, the theological issue was a major factor in the emergence and growth of the nondenominational missions movement. As the leadership of the denominational boards was increasingly assumed by those holding a liberal theological or social-gospel position, more workers and support came to the nondenominational missions. This was based upon the convictions and decisions of individual Christians and individual churches that wanted the missionaries they sent out and supported to go with agencies that held firmly to the authority of the Scriptures and demonstrated evangelistic fervor. Nondenominational missions have through the years required that each missionary sign a conservative evangelical statement of faith and agree to notify the mission if there is a change in his/her doctrinal persuasion.

Third, the financial factor was a major issue. When the denominational boards did not have sufficient funds to send out additional workers for expanding into new areas, nondenominational agencies were formed to operate on the basis that the Lord would provide by faith the support needed for ministries that He directed His servants to enter. Thus, for well over a hundred years, nondenominational missions have been referred to as *faith missions.* While accepting this designation from others, and seeking to operate according to their interpretation of the faith principle, they recognized that faith and trust in God for His provisions are exercised by others, including boards which have an identifiable church or denominational constituency. The success of deputation by individual missionaries seeking the Lord's seal on their calling by provision of their support needs has substantially increased the number of missionaries serving with these agencies.

The fourth factor that contributed to the establishment of some nondenominational mission agencies was an experience of theologically conservative evangelical cooperation. This was usually combined with a mutual recognition of an unmet need. This factor was present in the establishment of most of the early nondenominational missions. Since the missionaries and missions leaders were drawn from various denominations, the agencies were known as interdenominational, or nondenominational. An example following World War II is SEND International, formerly the Far Eastern Gospel Crusade. It was formed by a number of men and women who worked together in Christian witness activities during the War. Those serving with American armed forces in the Philippines saw the need for establishing a nondenominational Bible training school to prepare Filipino Christian workers from various churches and denominations. In Japan they saw the need for an evangelistic church-planting ministry. Other post-World-War-II organizations had a similar beginning, such as Mission Aviation Fellowship, Far East Broadcasting Company, Pacific Broadcasting Company, Greater Europe Mission, and several schools for missionaries' children.

This concern for the use of available methods and resources led to the establishment of many missionary service agencies, such as the Bible House of Los Angeles and the Home of Onesiphorus. These were followed by the World Radio Missionary Fellowship, Gospel Recordings, Mission Aviation Fellowship, Wycliffe Bible Translators, and similar specialized mission agencies. In recent years, the majority of new nondenominational missions being formed are such specialized agencies.

A factor in growth and development of the nondenominational movement is that, from the start of the movement, these mission agencies were fed personnel by the nondenominational Bible conference and Bible institute/college movements, which developed almost simultaneously with the missions. Many missionary candidates received their calling to missionary service from mission leaders and missionaries who spoke at Bible and missions conferences in various parts of North America. Having a strong emphasis on the biblical basis of missions and the believer's responsibility, they strengthened the nondenominational missions movement. The majority of missionaries associated with these missions received some, if not all, of their Bible and theological training in Bible institutes or colleges, or in independent nondenominational Christian liberal arts colleges or seminaries.

These factors that helped to give rise to nondenominational missions were directly related to theological changes and influences that arose during the last part of the "Gilded Age" of American history and the "Great Century" of foreign missions. These factors are not mutually exclusive. It is evident that several of them, in various combinations, were influential in the founding of all these agencies.

Nondenominational missions that were founded before the end of the nineteenth century, which became members of the IFMA, include the following:

1790 - The First Day Society (now American Missionary Fellowship)
1852 - The Indian Female Normal School & Institution Society, organized in England (became Bible and Medical Missionary Fellowship; now InterServe International)
1860 - Woman's Union Missionary Society of America to Heathen Lands (merged with InterServe in 1976)
1865 - China Inland Mission (now Overseas Missionary Fellowship)
1878 - Livingstone Inland Mission (now RBMU International)
1881 - North Africa Mission (now Arab World Ministries)
1887 - Chicago Committee for Hebrew Christian Work (now American Messianic Fellowship)
1889 - Cape General Mission (now Africa Evangelical Fellowship)
1889 - Ramabai Mukti Mission
1890 - Central American Mission (now CAM International)
1890 - The Scandinavian Alliance Mission (now The Evangelical Alliance Mission)
1892 - World's Gospel Union (now Gospel Missionary Union)
1893 - Ceylon and India General Mission (became International Christian Fellowship; merged with SIM in 1989)

1893 - Poona and Indian Village Mission (became International Christian Fellowship; merged with SIM in 1989)
1893 - The Pocket Testament League, organized in England; in U.S. 1917
1893 - Soudan Interior Mission (became Sudan Interior Mission, now SIM)
1895 - Africa Inland Mission (now Africa Inland Mission International)
1897 - Egypt General Mission (merged into UFM International)

## MISSION CONFERENCES PRIOR TO 1892

The presence in the United States of the renowned British missionary churchman, Dr. Alexander Duff, was the stimulus needed to call the first nondenominational missionary conference at the Presbyterian church on Fifth Avenue in New York City on May 4-5, 1854. Nearly 300 evangelical clergymen were delegates. Eighteen mission officers and 11 missionaries participated.

The subjects discussed have continued to be of interest to mission leaders through the years: missionary deployment, field comity, and the need of candidates. There was unanimous agreement that pastors were the key to securing candidates.

In his address at the public meeting at the close of the conference, Dr. Duff mentioned that all missionaries of the Bengal area of India, representing all denominations, had met every month for the previous twenty years to consult together on mission issues.[33]

An intermission conference was convened in London on October 12-13, 1854. The discussions were limited to general principles since only a few mission secretaries were able to participate, along with other members of the principal agencies.

In March 1860 a Conference on Missions was held in Liverpool, with 120 officers and missionaries of 25 British societies. Two missionaries from North America also participated. Some public meetings—devotions and missions information—were held during the week. About 23 papers or addresses were given in the closed sessions, and resolutions were adopted on various subjects.

Eighteen years later, another conference was held from October 21-26, 1878 at the Conference Hall, Mildmay Park, London. These were public meetings, but there were 158 official representatives, coming from 26 British, 6 American, and 5 other European agencies. At least 47 papers and addresses were given, plus short addresses and responses on the many subjects covered.

Intermission conferences were held in mission lands. A one-day conference of six English and American missions met in Kobe, Japan, on May 13, 1881. Out of that meeting came a resolution to hold a general convention of all Protestant missionaries, which was held in Osaka on April 16-21, 1883.

The largest international, interdenominational missions conference up to that time was the Centenary Conference on Foreign Missions held June 9-19, 1888 in London, in which 1,576 people participated. Of this number, 183 were from the United States and 30 from Canada. Women made up 429 of the participants. In 1860 not one woman had attended. In 1878 only 5 women took part.

The Student Volunteer Movement for Foreign Missions held its first international convention February 26 - March 1, 1891 in Cleveland, Ohio. Participants included 558 students from 151 schools, 31 missionaries, and 32 representatives of mission boards. Rev. and Mrs. Frederick A. Steven of China Inland Mission and Dr. and Mrs. George D. Dowkontt, representing International Medical Mission, spoke at this convention. The Dowkontts were the parents of IFMA's George H. Dowkontt, also a physician.

At the second Student Volunteer Movement conference

held in 1894 in Detroit, speakers included Hudson Taylor, Geraldine Guinness, and Henry Frost of the China Inland Mission; Spencer Walton of South Africa General Mission; and William E. Blackstone, founder of Chicago Hebrew Mission now the American Messianic Fellowship.

In 1896 the International Students Missionary Conference was held in Liverpool. Among the missionary participants were representatives of China Inland Mission, North Africa Mission, South Africa General Mission, and the Zenana Bible and Medical Mission. At its 1900 meeting held in London, there were representatives from the Ceylon and India General Mission, China Inland Mission, North Africa Mission, Regions Beyond Missionary Union, South Africa General Mission, and the Zenana Bible and Medical Mission. Although some of the names of these missions have changed, they all are IFMA member agencies.

## FOREIGN MISSION CONFERENCE OF NORTH AMERICA

The Interdenominational Conference of Foreign Missionary Boards and Societies in the United States and Canada was held January 12, 1893 at the Presbyterian Mission House in New York City. In 1911 the name was shortened to Foreign Mission Conference of North America (FMCNA). Twenty-three mission boards and committees, including the American Bible Society, YMCA, China Inland Mission, and Southern Baptists, were represented. Dr. Frank F. Ellinwood of the Presbyterian Board had precipitated the meeting and served as host. Among the sixty-eight participants were laymen Robert E. Speer, John R. Mott, and Frederick A Steven, who represented the China Inland Mission.

At the conclusion of this first meeting of current mission secretaries, it was recognized that the interaction was profitable and a similar meeting was planned for the following year. The second conference in this series was held January 17, 1894. In the third conference in 1895, it was decided that the meetings should be continued on an annual basis. Presbyterian W. Henry Grant was made the continuing secretary. Committees were appointed for conference arrangements, editing the annual report, and a study committee on self-support for mission churches.

By 1896 there were nine working committees, including one to study the issue of Chinese indemnities, and another to work on an ecumenical missionary conference. This committee work resulted in the Ecumenical Missionary Conference in New York in 1900.

The conference was well established in 1897, but it was still only an annual conference. There was no defined membership, no constitution, no creedal statement, and no continuing body of officers. By 1898 the growth of the conference resulted in the adoption of a rule for membership. Foreign mission boards in the United States and Canada could send executive officers, plus two additional representatives. Missionaries on furlough and others could be elected by the conference corresponding members. Preparations for the 1900 New York conference were the main issue of the 1899 conference. No separate session was held in 1900.

The conferences of 1901-1903 discussed cooperation, such as in the German missionary council. The subject of a permanent committee was raised again in 1904. A paper was presented that included the constitution of the German council, *Ausschuss*, the standing committee of German Protestant missions that had been formed in 1885. The discussion resulted in the appointment of a committee on reference and arbitration to study the matter and poll the participating mission boards, but the conference was hesitant about moving toward such a committee. The study continued in 1905 and 1906. At the 1907 meeting, a new nine-man Committee on Reference and Counsel was appointed, having limited authority. There was to be no interference in the internal affairs of any society. This committee now served as the representative of the annual conference between sessions. Adoption of the constitution was deferred in 1909 until the next conference.

# ECUMENICAL MISSIONARY CONFERENCE NEW YORK 1900

The Ecumenical Missionary Conference New York 1900 was the most genuinely international and interdenominational of all missionary conferences up to that time. Beside the scores of boards from the United States and Canada, ninety-eight boards from fifteen other countries were represented by hundreds of missionaries, officials, and representatives. The meetings were held in Carnegie Hall, with afternoon sessions held in nine prominent churches in New York City. The conference began on Saturday afternoon, April 21, 1900 and continued through Tuesday, May 1.

The meeting was called by a group of leading citizens of Philadelphia and New York. Former President Benjamin Harrison presided at the opening session. As honorary chairman of the conference, he gave the welcome address. The president of the New York Chamber of Commerce chaired the evening session. President William McKinley and New York Governor Theodore Roosevelt each gave an address of welcome, with a response by Benjamin Harrison.

The first morning session considered the "Authority and Purpose of Foreign Missions." J. Hudson Taylor (China Inland Mission) spoke on "The Source of Power," and Robert E. Speer (Presbyterian USA) on "The Supreme and Determining Aim." The afternoon program consisted of 10 different sessions covering areas of the world. The tenth of these was at Carnegie Hall, considering "Hebrews in All Lands." Dr. Arthur T. Pierson chaired this meeting and spoke on "The Jewish Question." Some of these afternoon meetings had as many as 19 missionary speakers in one session. The registered delegates and missionaries totaled some 3,200.

No count was given of public meeting attendance, but some 60,000 people were reported to have visited the missions exhibit areas. Visitors from near and far secured over 50,000 tickets for the Carnegie Hall and alternate meetings. Thousands more attended the sectional and overflow meetings that needed no tickets. Among those who lined up to get any available seat were people representing all classes, but the majority were reported to be people of education and refinement.

The significance of the New York Conference was given in a powerful article written by Robert E. Speer,[34] who at that time was secretary of the Board of Foreign Missions of the Presbyterian Church, USA. The final remarks of the honorary president of the conference, former United States president and general, Benjamin Harrison, give an added perspective on the value of the conference.

The New York 1900 Conference was both public and promotional. It raised the consciousness of America and beyond of the value of missions. While there were many excellent papers and reports given, they were in large measure an apologetic for missions, as well as an overview of all that missions involved and was accomplishing worldwide. The intermingling of a large number of missionaries and mission leaders from around the world did much to foster understanding and a spirit of oneness among the professional mission workers gathered from many sending and receiving countries.

The 1900 conference paved the way for Edinburgh 1910, the most influential in the history of mission conferences.

## WORLD MISSIONARY CONFERENCE 1910

In contrast to the New York 1900 Conference, the purposes and planning for the World Missionary Conference held in Edinburgh in 1910 were quite different. It developed a conference model more closely resembling some of the intermission conferences that were being held in "mission field" countries. The Decenniel Missionary Conference at Madras in 1902 and the Centenary Missionary Conference at Shanghai in 1907 were helpful examples of conference programming, featuring discussions of problems and issues, rather than mission promotion.

The international planning committee, made up of five North Americans, ten British, and three continental Europeans, agreed that the 1910 conference should be a definite study conference. The committee met for four days in July 1908 at Oxford. They determined to limit the conference to an in-depth study and discussion of eight subjects:

1. Carrying the gospel to all the non-Christian world
2. The church in the mission field
3. Education in relation to the Christianization of national life
4. The missionary message in relation to non-Christian religions
5. The preparation of missionaries
6. The home base of missions
7. Relation of missions to government
8. Cooperation and the promotion of unity[35]

Eight commissions of 20 members each were appointed and given the responsibility to collect and organize information on these subjects. A list of some 160 names of the most qualified men and women to serve on these commissions was prepared. Only 11 were not able to accept a place on the commission, due to unavoidable circumstances.

Edinburgh 1910 was truly a world conference, but it was also basically a conference representing the world's missionary home bases. Only 17 of the 1,200 delegates represented the younger churches. However, the influence of these few was enormous. Another group of delegates that had great influence was the younger leaders, most of whom were Student Christian Movement men, such as John R. Mott, Joseph H. Oldham, Robert E. Speer, and William Temple.

While Edinburgh 1910 did not launch the Ecumenical Movement, it hastened that movement's beginning. Edinburgh was certainly a great conference, probably the most influential of missions conferences. Some said that Edinburgh 1910 was the greatest. But from a conservative evangelical point of view, it had a dark side to it, also. Three principles that were emphasized at Edinburgh 1910 became the framework for the formation of the Ecumenical Movement. They were:

1. The principle of bringing together officially appointed delegates, responsible to their boards. Previously, it was simply assemblies of individuals.
2. The principle of broad denominational inclusiveness, joining Catholic and Protestant elements.
3 Edinburgh launched international, cooperative Christian endeavor on essential tasks without demanding prior theological consensus and by agreeing to hold in abeyance theological differences.[36]

The appointment of the Edinburgh Continuation Committee, chaired by John R. Mott and employing J. H. Oldham as full-time paid secretary, was another "first" in missions conferences.

The World Missionary Conference 1910 at Edinburgh was a watershed event, both for the Ecumenical Movement and for conservative evangelicals who would begin the IFMA in the following decade.

## NOTES

1 William Warren Sweet, *The Story of Religion in America* (New York: Harper & Row; reprint, Grand Rapids: Baker Book House, 1973), p. 156.

2 William S. Perry, *The History of the American Episcopal Church*, 1587-1883, vol. 1 (Boston: 1885), p. 7, quoted in Oliver Wendell Elsbree, *The Rise of the Missionary Spirit in America 1790-1815* (Williamsport: The Williamsport Printing and Binding Co., 1928; reprinted, Philadelphia: Porcupine Press, Inc., 1980), p. 7.

3 Ibid., p. 9.

4 Ibid., pp, 18-19.

[5] Sweet, *The Story of Religion in America*, pp. 30-31.

[6] William Munsell Bliss, ed., *Encyclopaedia of Missions*, vol. 1 (New York: Funk & Wagnalls, 1891), p. 455.

[7] Ibid., p. 354.

[8] R. Pierce Beaver, "Foreword: The Significance of the Early Sermons," in *Pioneers in Mission: The Early Missionary Ordination Sermons, Charges, and Instructions*, ed. R. Pierce Beaver (Grand Rapids: William B. Eerdmans Publishing Company, 1966), p. 5.

[9] Sweet, *The Story of Religion in America*, p. 162.

[10] R. Pierce Beaver, "The Churches and the Indians: Consequences of 350 Years of Missions," in *American Missions in Bicentennial Perspective*, ed. R. Pierce Beaver (South Pasadena: William Carey Library, 1977), pp. 275-76.

[11] Charles L. Chaney, *The Birth of Missions in America* (South Pasadena: William Carey Library, 1976), p. 128.

[12] Oliver Wendell Elsbree, *The Rise of the Missionary Spirit in America 1790-1815* (Williamsport: The Williamsport Printing and Binding Co., 1928; reprinted, Philadelphia: Porcupine Press, Inc., 1980), pp 135-36.

[13] Earle E. Cairns, *An Endless Line of Splendor: Revivals and Their Leaders from the Great Awakening to the Present* (Wheaton, IL: Tyndale House Publishers, Inc., 1986), pp. 86-87.

[14] Elsbree, *The Rise of the Missionary Spirit in America*, p. 51.

[15] Winthrop S. Hudson, *American Protestantism* (Chicago: The University of Chicago Press, 1961), p. 82.

[16] Valentin H. Rabe, *The Home Base of American China Missions 1880-1920* (Cambridge, Massachusetts: Council on East Asian Studies at Harvard University, 1978), p. 17.

[17] Valentin H. Rabe, "Evangelical Logistics: Mission Support and Resources to 1920," in *The Missionary Enterprise in China and America*, ed. John K. Fairbanks (Cambridge, Massachusetts: Harvard University Press, 1974), p. 58.

[18] Ralph D. Winter, "Protestant Mission Societies: The American Experience," *Missiology: An International Review*, April 1979, p. 147.

[19] John Henry Hobart, *The Corruptions of the Church of Rome Contrasted with Certain Protestant Errors* (N.Y., 1818), 8-13, 22-7, quoted in H. Shelton Smith, Robert T. Handy, and Lefferts A. Loetscher, *American Christianity*, vol. 2 (New York: Charles Scribner's Sons, 1963), p. 77.

[20] Peter G. Mode, *The Frontier Spirit in American Christianity* (New York: The Macmillan Company, 1923), p. 107.

[21] Edwin W. Rice, *The Sunday School Movement and the American Sunday School Union* (Philadelphia: The Union Press, 1917), pp. 68-69.

[22] E. Eugene Williams, information to author, January 1992.

[23] Ibid.

[24] Barbara A. Sokolosky, ed., *American Sunday School Union Papers 1817-1915* (Sanford, NC: Microfilming Corporation of America, 1980), p. 10.

[25] Ernest R. Sandeen, *The Roots of Fundamentalism: British and American Millenarianism 1800-1930* (Chicago: The University of Chicago Press, 1970; reprint, Grand Rapids: Baker Book House, 1978), p. 134.

[26] Stewart G. Cole, *The History of Fundamentalism* (New York: Richard R. Smith, Inc., 1931; reprint, Westport, CT: Greenwood Press, Publishers, 1971), p. 34.

[27] Sandeen, *The Roots of Fundamentalism: British and American Millenarianism 1800-1930*, pp. 273-77.

[28] Arthur T. Pierson, *The Crisis of Missions* (New York: Baker & Taylor Co, 1886), pp. 365-70.

[29] Arthur T. Pierson, *Forward Movements of the Last Half Century* (New York: Funk & Wagnalls Company, 1900), p. 158.

[30] Clarence P. Shedd, *Two Centuries of Student Christian Movements* (New York: Associated Press, 1934), pp. 266-68.

[31] Ibid., p. 275.

[32] Marybeth Rupert, "The Emergence of the Independent Missionary Agency as an American Institution, 1860-1917" (Ph.D. diss., Yale University, 1974), p. 112.

[33] *Ecumenical Missionary Conference, New York, 1900, vol. 1* (New York: American Tract Society, 1900), p. 21.

[34] *Ecumenical Missionary Conference, New York, 1900, vol. 2* (New York: American Tract Society, 1900), pp. 58-64.

[35] W. H. T. Gairdner, *Echoes from Edinburgh 1910* (New York: Fleming H. Revell Company, 1910), pp. 17-19.

[36] William Richey Hogg, *Ecumenical Foundations* (New York: Harper & Brothers, Publishers, 1952), 139-40.

# 4

# THE CONTEXT: 1910-1917 WHY IFMA?

The previous chapters gave an overview of the rise and expansion of the Protestant missions movement in America from colonial times to the beginning of the twentieth century. A brief summary was given of some of the religious, social, and political context in which mission agencies were formed and ministered during that period. In this period of 1910-1917, liberalism and secularism largely characterized the immediate context in which the IFMA was organized.

## THE INFLUENCE OF EDINBURGH 1910

The World Missionary Conference in 1910 at Edinburgh, Scotland, produced a radical change in the cooperation among mission agencies. Latourette wrote, "Largely because of the influence which issues from Edinburgh 1910, the ecumenical movement became widely inclusive."[1] This was a decisive factor that contributed to evangelical agencies seeking their own cooperative structures.

A number of missions that later became members of IFMA participated in Edinburgh 1910. These included Africa Inland Mission, Ceylon and India General Mission (International Christian Fellowship), China Inland Mission (Overseas Missionary Fellowship), North Africa Mission (Arab World Ministries), Regions Beyond Missionary Union

(RBMU International), Scandinavian Alliance Mission of North America (The Evangelical Alliance Mission), South Africa General Mission (Africa Evangelical Fellowship), Woman's Union Missionary Society (merged into InterServe International), and Zenana Bible and Medical Mission (InterServe International).[2]

The International Missionary Council formed in 1921 at Lake Mohonk, New York, was connected with Edinburgh 1910 through the Edinburgh Continuation Committee of which John R. Mott was chairman and Joseph H. Oldham, executive secretary. They both continued in these same responsibilities in the IMC. Mott was a Methodist layman. Although not theologically trained, he played an important part in most phases of the ecumenical movement. Oldham became editor of the *International Review of Missions*, which began in 1912.

Before the outbreak of World War I, Mott held some twenty-one regional and national conferences in Asia to encourage further cooperation. However, the war delayed plans for the formation of the IMC.

At the Lake Mohonk organizational meeting, fourteen countries were represented by sixty-one delegates, of whom only seven came from the young countries of the Third World. As an aftermath of the war, the Germans did not participate in this gathering.

Under the strong leadership of Mott, Oldham, and their associates in London and New York—and a broad set of purposes—the International Missionary Council extended itself in many directions as a central planning and coordinating agency for the major Protestant missions. IMC-sponsored conferences were held in Jerusalem, 1928; Madras, 1938; Whitby, 1947; Willingen, 1952; Ghana, 1957; and New Delhi, 1961.[3]

By the Jerusalem conference, the IMC's position on the authority of Scripture had weakened. The missionary's obligation to share the gospel message of redemption through Jesus Christ was questioned. Many no longer believed that redemption through Christ is the only means of man's salvation.

## THE GROWTH OF LIBERALISM

During the latter part of the nineteenth century, called by Latourette the "Great Century," and characterized as "a time of unequalled expression of the vitality inherent in the Christian faith,"[4] powerful theological changes were at work. In part, this was an outgrowth of some of the sociological influences that challenged Christian theology, such as the dismal urban conditions and other problems resulting from industrialization.

The American churches did not seem to realize how nationalistic they were. Sidney Mead, a former president of the American Society of Church History, observed, "The situation was ironic. While Protestant leaders were very much aware of the evils resulting from a formal connection between church and state, they were, to say the least, less conscious of the equally grave perils in religious endorsement of a particular way of life."[5]

It is generally thought that Protestant churches in the United States were quite orthodox in their theology during the first half of the nineteenth century. Several factors contributed to the gradual rise of liberalism by the beginning of the twentieth century. Historians and theologians have identified a number of men and their challenges to supernatural or orthodox Christianity. Immanuel Kant and his idealistic philosophy substituted human reasoning for God's divine revelation. Friedrich E. D. Schleiermacher pointed to man's experience as the basis of faith. These philosophical ideas were among the strands of thought which combined to form a new liberal theological climate. Earle Cairns concluded, "These views of the philosophers congealed into concepts of the fatherhood of God and the brotherhood of man so characteristic of Liberalism."[6]

These philosophies were quickly brought to the United

States through books and professors who had gone to Europe, primarily to Germany, for graduate study. Such travel increased as steamships became more plentiful and the price of passage declined.

Other challenging strands included the developing thought in psychology, science, and higher criticism. At the end of the nineteenth century and the beginning of the twentieth, E. D. Starbuck and William James were very influential in undermining the supernatural in the evangelical experience of conversion. They reduced such experiences to human and natural effects. Looking at the implications of the work of these men, historian Gaius Atkins stated, "Religion had now to reckon with psychology."[7]

William James fervently promoted American pragmatism. That this philosophical formulation was detrimental to the evangelical position is seen in the assessment by Henry Commager. "It cleared away the jungle of theology and metaphysics and deterministic science and allowed the warm sun of commonsense to quicken the American spirit as the pioneer cleared the forests and the underbrush and allowed the sun to quicken the soil of the American West."[8] Some of the theological issues that were rejected by this philosophy included the assurance of salvation and the biblical moral code. James was followed by John Dewey who moved the emphasis of philosophy away from individual salvation to the reconstruction of society.

Just as psychology and philosophy were intertwined in the writings of James and others, so was scientific theory mixed with philosophy in men like Charles Darwin, Asa Gray, and John Fiske. The influence of the evolutionary theory, promoted by these men, hastened the decline of orthodox belief in favor of liberal theology. Darwin's philosophy of evolution was one of the destructive philosophies that contributed to the abandonment of orthodox theology.

Preachers and writers, such as the influential Lyman Abbott and Henry Drummond, worked to reconcile

Christian teaching and evolution. President McCosh of Princeton did the same. Scientists, such as John W. Draper and Andrew D. White, intensified the conflict between science and theology. One of the most influential elements in the development of liberalism was the importation of higher criticism from Europe, which gave a naturalistic historical interpretation to the cultural development seen in the Bible.

The critics of the Bible examined its various parts to determine their dates, authors, and value. Their interpretations were usually done in the light of evolutionary hypothesis. Evangelicals did not accept the claim that the major proponents of higher criticism practiced scientific objectivity. The leaders of this movement on the continent, particularly in Germany, were generally rationalists who rejected any idea of supernatural revelation.

The first chapter of a four-volume edition of *The Fundamentals* gives an historical account of higher criticism. Canon Dyson Hague presents three arguments to demonstrate that higher critics did not exhibit the spirit of scientific and Christian scholarship. First, the leaders who gave impetus to the movement based their theories "largely upon their own subjective conclusions." Second, many of the strongest proponents were Germans, "and it is notorious to what length the German fancy can go in the direction of the subjective and of the conjectural." Third, the men in leadership of this movement "were men with a strong bias against the supernatural."[9]

The social gospel posed another threat to biblical theology of the day. Problems of urbanization and industrialization in America gave liberal ministers cause to urge the Christian church to alleviate the ills of society. Respected people like Washington Gladden, Henry Ward Beecher, Phillips Brooks, and Josiah Strong were early leaders of the social gospel movement. It grew in strength during the years just before World War I, and "became the church party platform of all theological progressives, liberals or modernists."[10]

For seven years Walter Rauschenbusch served as pastor among the working people on New York City's West Side. Later, as professor of church history at Rochester Seminary, he remembered the pressures borne by these people and wrote *Christianity and the Social Crisis*. He concluded:

> The swiftness of evolution in our own country proves the immense latent perfectibility in human nature. . . .
>
> If at this juncture we can rally sufficient religious faith and moral strength to snap the bonds of evil and turn the present unparalleled economic and intellectual resources of humanity to the harmonious development of a true social life, the generations yet unborn will mark this as that great day of the Lord for which the ages waited, and count us blessed for sharing in the apostolate that proclaimed it.[11]

Ten years later, in the month that the United States entered World War I, Rauschenbusch gave a series of lectures at Yale School of Religion, calling for a "theology large enough to contain the social gospel, and alive and productive enough not to hamper it."[12] He believed that if Christian doctrine was not changed to include social salvation, it would be abandoned, especially by workingmen, college, and seminary students. Walter Rauschenbusch did not foresee that the change he recommended would cause an equal, if not greater, abandonment of biblical faith and theology.

The liberal teaching current at the time of the founding of the IFMA included many elements, which, together, became increasingly hostile toward the personal message of salvation. Liberalism emphasized man's freedom of choice and natural capacity for doing good. It did not regard human nature as depraved and in rebellion against God.

The erosion of orthodox theology began to produce grave changes in the denominational missionary program.

Until well past the Civil War, the missionary enterprise of the major Protestant denominations emphasized evangelism, winning individual converts to Christ. However, during the last of the nineteenth century and the beginning of the twentieth, this understanding of missions started to change, particularly among the top denominational leadership. Mead affirmed:

> Since the missionary enterprise was central in each denomination, it was recognized that those who would define its nature would control the denomination's life. Hence the movement generated the drive to shift the conception of the evangelistic work of the churches from individualistic revivalism to social reconstruction, and its success in this respect should not be underestimated.[13]

## FACTORS CONTRIBUTING TO THE FOUNDING OF IFMA

Missions involved in the founding of the Interdenominational Foreign Mission Association of North America in 1917 had participated in the Foreign Missions Conference of North America since 1893, and similar meetings in Great Britain. Why, then, was the IFMA formed?

First of all, there was a growing reaction on the part of key denominational mission leaders against the nondenominational "faith" mission agencies. On a practical level, this reaction was due to their belief that the nondenominational missions were funded by donations that otherwise would have gone to the denominational missions. This has remained a key point of tension throughout the history of nondenominational missions in North America.

The mainline denominations failed to recognize that their departure from orthodox theology caused many of their members to seek other ministries to support, which still held to the inerrant Word of God and to a conservative evangelical position. It should be noted that through the years, evangelical church membership has increased considerably, as well as the numbers of evangelical missionaries, while church membership of the mainline denominations has noticeably decreased, as well as the numbers of their missionaries. There appears to be a direct correlation between liberalism and the decrease in church membership and missions involvement.

As far back as 1897, denominational leaders, meeting in what became the Foreign Missions Conference of North America, indicated their problems with nondenominational missions. At the 1897 meeting, the Methodist Episcopal Mission corresponding secretary, Dr. A. B. Leonard, presented a paper on "independent Missions," listing his objections to such missions. He concluded his paper by stating, "Independent missions are unnecessary."[14]

The first response was from Dr. Arthur J. Brown, one of the mission secretaries of the Presbyterian Church in the U.S.A. He spoke on behalf of all denominational boards when he concluded, "The prevalence and popularity of these independent agencies doubtless have a great deal to do with the alarming financial condition of all these Boards." Dr. Samuel W. Duncan, foreign secretary of the American Baptist Missionary Union, agreed. In regard to the support being given to the nondenominational missions, he added, "I consider it to be one of the disintegrating tendencies of the present time."[15]

On a more theological level, some of the denominational leaders were against the conservative evangelical position of the nondenominational agencies regarding biblical inerrancy, the premillenial position of the second coming of Christ, and other scriptural truths held by nondenominational missions. These were viewed as limiting the desired cooperation on the broadest possible level, including Roman Catholic and Eastern Orthodox participation, especially after Edinburgh 1910.

Toward the end of the nineteenth century and early

twentieth, while there were cooperative intermission conferences, much of nondenominational work of earlier years was changing to denominational work.

At the meeting of 1898 and again in 1911, the Foreign Missions Conference of North America adopted a constitution that effectively limited the membership to denominational mission officers. The nondenominational mission representatives, who up to 1910 had served as members, speakers, and members of committees, were now reduced in 1911 to "corresponding members." Thus, the nondenominational mission agencies were given second-class status, and their influence and contribution were effectually silenced or ignored by the Foreign Mission Conference leadership. Participation in the FMCNA by the missions that later founded IFMA noticeably diminished after that action.

The year of the Edinburgh Conference, 1910, and the years immediately following, coincided with the rapidly-spreading social gospel movement. It was during the years 1910 to 1915 that the twelve-volume set, *The Fundamentals*, was published. Edited by Dr. A. C. Dixon, pastor of Moody Memorial Church; Rev. Louis Meyer, a Jewish Christian; and Dr. Reuben A. Torrey, dean of Moody Bible Institute, these books raised issues of importance and set forth Christian truths as held by conservative evangelicals.

Three hundred sets of *The Fundamentals* were published in the first printing, and sent to pastors, missionaries, and other Christian workers. The entire project was underwritten by two brothers, Lyman and Milton Stewart. This set of books has had wide circulation since that first printing. The Bible Institute of Los Angeles reprinted it in a four-volume set in 1917. In 1972, Baker Book House reprinted the four-volume set. The most recent publication of *The Fundamentals* was in 1988. Edited by George M. Marsden, the four-volume set is included in the forty-five volume facsimile series, *Fundamentalism in American Religion 1880-1950.* The series reproduces some extremely rare material, which documents the development of one of the major religious movements in our time.

In 1917, the year of the founding of the IFMA, Dr. William B. Riley, pastor of First Baptist Church of Minneapolis and superintendent of Northwestern Bible Training School, authored *The Menace of Modernism*. After tracing the effects of modernism in the pulpit, in the universities, and in denominational colleges, he applauded the rise of conservative evangelical Bible conferences and Bible schools, and their resistance to liberalism. In his closing chapter, Riley called for a "confederacy" of believers who would hold to the fundamentals of the faith and take the great commission seriously. He concluded, "It remains now, as it ever has, for the Church within the church to realize the responsibility of world evangelism."[16]

Liberalism, modernism, and the social gospel swept through the colleges, seminaries, and churches of the major Protestant denominations.

In a study of the period of 1880-1920, William R. Hutchison indicated that after the beginning of the twentieth century liberalism greatly increased among the missionaries and mission boards of the mainline Protestant denominations. He further stated that this spread of liberalism was enhanced through organizations such as the Student Volunteer Movement and the YMCA.[17]

Pioneer missionary outreach to the sub-Sahara "Soudan" was undertaken by missionary volunteers who were challenged through a Bible conference program of the Kansas state YMCA. Five of the first nine missionaries of the Kansas-Sudan Missionary Movement died of African fever in 1889-1890. This faith mission project was condemned by critics. Even Frank F. Ellinwood, secretary of the Presbyterian mission board, who was generally supportive of the faith missions of George Müller and J. Hudson Taylor, concluded that these early Sudan missionaries "to all appearances died from insufficient support, and from a persistent reliance on faith instead of medicine in extreme sickness." Ellinwood further said, "The principle of faith missions has undoubtedly been reinforced by the kindred doctrine of faith healing. . . . Public sentiment throughout Christendom condemns those misguided young missionaries."[18]

The international leadership of the YMCA, including John R. Mott, worked to see that this mission project was separated from any affiliation with the YMCA. George S. Fisher, Kansas state YMCA secretary who promoted the Sudan missionary project, was ridiculed by the increasingly liberal YMCA national leadership for promoting the faith principle for his staff support, and his belief in the verbal inspiration of the Scriptures, the infallibility of the Word of God, and the premillenial position.

Fisher, with the help of Reuben A. Torrey and other conservative evangelicals, reorganized the mission project, and in 1892 formed the World's Gospel Union, which in 1901 was changed to Gospel Missionary Union, a member of the IFMA since January 1946.

Dr. Arthur T. Pierson was criticized by the YMCA leadership for editorial encouragement of the Sudan project. He responded by saying that the death of these young missionaries "may be God's way of restraining all excess of zeal and deepening all real consecration." Pierson then asked if "the YMCA was drifting toward a certain exclusiveness and in danger of becoming a sort of religious club, with athletic culture and good fellowship, but a lack of the evangelistic and missionary spirit."[19]

Dana Lee Robert believes that the YMCA retained broad support in American Christianity by not accepting the faith mission theology and practice. She concluded that John R. Mott was influential in steering the YMCA toward an "inclusive liberalism."[20]

The twentieth conference of the Foreign Missions Conference of North America was held at Garden City, New York, January 15-17, 1913. The following is from the report of that conference:

The Committee of Reference and Counsel has been approached during the year by the representatives of several regular missionary Boards, and asked to give counsel and cooperation in the adjustment of certain difficulties which have arisen between these Boards and certain independent missionary movements and organizations which had entered the areas within which these Boards were working. . . . There are several elements in the problem which present serious difficulty. The independent movements or missions involved are frequently under the leadership of some individuals whose motives or policies in promoting missionary work are without check from any definite Board, missionary organization or even missionary constituency to which appeal could be made. It is largely, therefore, a question of dealing with certain individuals and personalities. In addition to this there is frequently a measure of irresponsibility and of inexperience, due to the fact that these missionary movements have been in existence for but a short time and their continuance is not altogether assured. The difficulty of arriving at an understanding with some of these independent movements is aggravated by the fact, that their promoters are often located in remote sections of the United States and of Canada so that personal interviews with the leaders are not always possible, while it is equally difficult to bring these leaders into fellowship with regular Boards and their leaders.

. . . Most important, however, is it to press upon the constituencies of the Christian Churches of America the wisdom of withholding endorsement from special missionary undertakings, unless a thoroughly responsible leadership has been first assured, and these special efforts

> have been properly correlated with the regular and established lines of missionary work undertaken in the name of the organized Church. The evils of independent and un-correlated missionary efforts are so great that we cannot permit ourselves to relax in any effort to educate the Christian public with reference to these dangers. The difficulties of over-lapping in the cultivation of the field at home are great, but the most serious and lamentable consequences are to be found in the friction and the working at cross purposes in the foreign field itself, wherever such independent and uncorrelated missionary efforts are to be found.[21]

The antipathy of denominational mission leadership against the nondenominational *faith* missions movement continued to grow during the first decades of the twentieth century and beyond. When the nondenominational missions were maneuvered out of full participation in the Foreign Missions Conference of North America, the stage was set for the founding of the Interdenominational Foreign Mission Association of North America, which is an association of nondenominational missions.

In considering the context in which the IFMA was organized, it seems that several facts are quite clear.

First, the denominations, or at least the leaders of the Foreign Missions Conference of North America, had departed from orthodox theology. They did not agree with the conservative theology of the nondenominational missions in their positions on basic biblical doctrines, such as the inspiration of Scripture, the deity of Christ, virgin birth, the lostness of man, the vicarious atonement of Christ, the second coming of Christ, the resurrection, and eternal punishment of the wicked. For theological reasons, the nondenominational missions did not agree with the Continuation Committee of Edinburgh 1910 on its principle of broad denominational inclusiveness, joining Catholic and Protestant elements.

Second, in 1911 the FMCNA limited its membership to leaders of denominational missions. The nondenominational leaders, who previously had been members, served on committees, and were conference speakers, were limited to being corresponding members. This, in effect, was the squeezing out of the nondenominational missions from the FMCNA.

Third, theologically conservative nondenominational missions could not possibly have permitted their missionary work to be "properly correlated with the regular and established lines of missionary work undertaken in the name of the organized Church," which was dominated by liberalism, modernism, and the social gospel.

The China Inland Mission withdrew from the Edinburgh 1910 Committee in 1916 because it objected to the committee's position which implied "tacit approval of the Roman Catholic theology and soteriology.[22] In 1917 Dr. Frost saw the organization of the IFMA as an alternative to the Foreign Missions Conference of North America and urged the nondenominational missions that had been involved in the FMCNA to organize.

## THE IMMEDIATE CONTEXT: POLITICAL AND SOCIAL

Changes came swiftly in the United States during the time when the nondenominational, or independent, *faith* missions were being organized. During and after the Civil War, industrialization of the country proceeded rapidly. The textile industry expanded greatly in the South, and the tobacco industry flourished. Deposits of coal and iron in Tennessee and Alabama produced the start of a southern iron industry. However, agriculture remained the primary business of the South.

American industry, particularly in the North, bounded forward on every side. Some of the main industries included iron and steel mills, oil refineries, and breweries. The population more than doubled from thirty-one to sixty-six million during the period from 1860 to 1900.[23]

Some fifteen million of this increase was due to the great waves of immigrants that provided manpower for expanding industries, particularly in the larger cities. While the conditions for poorer workers worsened, the owners of great industries, business, transportation lines, etc., developed into a millionaire class. Historians estimate that during this same period at the end of the nineteenth century, millionaires in the United States increased from only three to at least thirty-eight hundred.[24] The richest class was composed of the owners of factories, mines, railways, and urban property. By comparison, while the income of the ordinary wage earner improved slightly, his condition actually worsened due to rising costs. With the increase of social problems, trade unions were able to develop an increasingly strong base, and socialistic ideas began to cause unrest.

Material prosperity for the upper and middle classes was due in part to the great number of inventions that flooded America after the Civil War. Some of the important ones included the web-printing press, cable communication, commercial typewriter, telephone, linotype machine, automobile, motion pictures, and the airplane. All of these were to have direct application to missions.

American college graduates sought advanced studies and research programs in Europe. They were particularly welcomed in Germany, and many pursued doctoral work in science, economics, history, theology, and classical literature. Upon their return, they taught in American colleges the progressive philosophy and theology, socialistic economics and methods of critical inquiry that they had absorbed abroad. This added greatly to the ferment of sociological, philosophical, and theological thinking throughout American educational institutions.

For some thirty years after the Civil War, the American people were so concerned with expansion of the West and increase of industry that they had little interest in foreign affairs. The war with Spain was a turning point. The United States soon became a world power, with possessions or protectorates in the Atlantic and the Pacific. Increasingly, American governmental and commercial representatives were added to the American community overseas, along with foreign missionaries already resident in remote areas of the world.

On the world scene, American politics through the end of the nineteenth century lacked particular interest.[25] The Beards evidently agreed with this assessment of the period when they indicated that the "political power was being shifted from party to party and dissipated among an ever-changing army of captains and subordinates, most of them nameless in history."[26]

When Paul Graef suggested that a meeting be held to consider matters of mutual concern to nondenominational mission leaders, there was a ready response. The time was fortuitous. The year 1917 was a critical one for overseas missionary activity.

Just a week after the March 31st meeting of mission leaders in Philadelphia, the United States entered World War I. President Woodrow Wilson had campaigned for reelection the preceding year, displaying a deep desire for peace without American entry into the war. However, the position of neutrality, while apparently an expression of the will of the American people, was difficult to maintain. Relations with Great Britain and the Allies were becoming more and more strained due in part to President Wilson's attempt as a "neutral power" to negotiate directly with the Germans for peace. These efforts were not successful. The tide turned after German submarines sank three American merchant ships in mid-March. After a week, called "Wilson's Gethesemane,"[27] the President summoned Congress into special session on April 2 and presented his war resolution, which was adopted by the Senate and the House.

It was in this context that the IFMA was born. Modernism infiltrating churches and missions, and theological liberalism that increasingly departed further and further from biblical truth, forced theologically conservative nondenominational missions to organize.

## NOTES

[1] Kenneth Scott Latourette, "Ecumenical Bearings of the Missionary Movement and the International Missionary Council" in *A History of the Ecumenical Movement 1517-1948*, 2d ed., eds. Ruth Rouse and Stephen Charles Neill (Philadelphia: The Westminster Press, 1967), p. 357.

[2] World Missionary Conference, 1910, vol. 9 of *The History and Records of the Conference Together with Addresses Delivered at the Evening Meetings* (New York: Fleming H. Revell Company, n.d.), pp. 42-63.

[3] Arthur P. Johnston, *The Battle for World Evangelism* (Wheaton: Tyndale House Publishers, 1978), pp. 57-100.

[4] Kenneth Scott Latourette, *The Great Century: Europe and the United States of America A.D. 1800-A.D. 1914*, vol. 4 of *A History of the Expansion of Christianity* (Grand Rapids: Zondervan Publishing House, 1970), p. 457.

[5] Sidney E. Mead, *The Lively Experiment: The Shaping of Christianity in America* (New York: Harper and Row Publishers, 1962), p. 156.

[6] Earle E. Cairns, *Christianity in the United States* (Chicago: Moody Press, 1964), p. 148.

[7] Gaius Glenn Atkins, *Religion in Our Times* (New York: Round Table Press, 1932), p. 38.

[8] Henry Steele Commager, *The American Mind: An Interpretation of American Thought and Character Since the 1880s* (New Haven: Yale University Press, 1950), p. 97.

[9] Canon Dyson Hague, "The History of the Higher Criticism" in vol. 1 of *The Fundamentals*, ed. A. C. Dixon, Louis Meyer, and R. A. Torrey (Chicago: Testimony Publishing Company, 12 vols., 1910-1915; reprinted in 4 vols., Los Angeles: Bible Institute of Los Angeles, 1917; reprinted in 4 vols., Grand Rapids: Baker Book House, 1972), pp. 11-14.

[10] Mead, *The Lively Experiment*, p. 179.

[11] Walter Rauschenbush, *Christianity and the Social Crisis* (New York: The Macmillan Company, 1907), p. 422.

[12] Walter Rauschenbusch, *A Theology for the Social Gospel* (New York: The Macmillan Company, 1917), p. 9.

[13] Mead, *The Lively Experiment*, p. 179.

[14] *Fifth Conference Foreign Mission Boards United States and Canada 1897* (New York: Foreign Missions Library, 1897), p. 122.

[15] Ibid., p. 123.

[16] William B. Riley, *The Menace of Modernism* (New York: Christian Alliance Publishing Company, 1917), p. 180.

[17] William R. Hutchison, *The Modernist Impulse in American Protestantism* (Cambridge, Massachusetts: Harvard University Press, 1976), p. 155.

[18] Frank F. Ellinwood, *Questions and Phases of Modern Missions* (New York: Dodd, Mead and Company, 1899), pp. 134-36.

[19] Arthur T. Pierson, "Editorial Notes on Current Topics," *The Missionary Review of the World*, vol. 13, 1890, p. 951.

[20] Dana Lee Robert, "Arthur Tappan Pierson and Forward Movements of Late-Nineteenth-Century Evangelicalism" (Ph.D. diss., Yale University, 1984), p. 271.

[21] *Foreign Missions Conference of North America, Being the Report of the Twentieth Conference of Foreign Missions Boards in the United States and Canada* (New York: Foreign Missions Library, 1913), pp. 130-31.

[22] Arthur P. Johnston, *World Evangelism and the Word of God* (Minneapolis: Bethany Fellowship, 1974), p. 130.

[23] Winston S. Churchill, *The Great Democracies*, vol. 4 of *A History of the English-Speaking Peoples* (New York: Dodd, Mead & Company, 1958), p. 314.

[24] Charles A. and Mary R. Beard, *The Rise of American Civilization: The Industrial Era* (New York: The Macmillan Company, 1930), pp. 383-84.

[25] Churchill, *The Great Democracies*, p. 313.

[26] Beard, *The Rise of American Civilization: The Industrial Era*, p. 287.

[27] Arthur S. Link, *Woodrow Wilson and the Progressive Era: 1910-1917* (New York: Harper & Brothers Publishers, 1954), p. 275.

# PART TWO

# THE BEGINNING AND DEVELOPMENT OF IFMA

# 5

# THE IFMA ORGANIZED

The significance of the gathering brought together by Wall Street broker Paul H. Graef, a Presbyterian layman and member of the board of the South Africa General Mission on March 31, 1917, was not anticipated beforehand and certainly not fully understood at the time. None of those gathered that day had any idea that it was the initial step leading to the founding later that year of the Interdenominational Foreign Mission Association of North America, an association that would bring together dozens of nondenominational missions in a united effort to penetrate frontiers and take the gospel to all people. The IFMA, the first association of missions in North America, would provide a framework for cooperation among nondenominational missions. It would establish standards for membership, doctrine and purpose, organization, finance, operation, and personnel by which the Christian public would be assured that they could support member missions in full confidence.

## THE PRELIMINARY MEETING

Convened at the Philadelphia School of the Bible in Philadelphia, the eleven men participating in that historic meeting were Charles E. Hurlburt, Orson R. Palmer, and Howard B. Dinwiddie of the Africa Inland Mission; Luther Rees and Frank W. Lange of the Central American Mission; Henry W. Frost and Frederick A. Steven of the China Inland Mission; Arthur J. Bowen, John C. Medd, William H.

Hendrickson, and Paul H. Graef of the South Africa General Mission. Rowland V. Bingham of the Sudan Interior Mission sent a letter from Toronto, wishing God's blessing upon the meeting and expressing his regret at not being able to attend.

Mr. Hendrickson, secretary of South Africa General Mission, was named chairman of the meeting and Mr. Dinwiddie, associate general director of the Africa Inland Mission, secretary, with the understanding that it did not imply that they would continue in those offices or that there would necessarily be any further meetings.

Mr. Hendrickson called for suggestions of discussion topics. It appears from Mr. Dinwiddie's minutes that Mr. Hurlburt, Mr. Steven, and Mr. Graef were the major participants in the discussion.

Mr. Hurlburt was general director of the Africa Inland Mission and maintained his office in Africa. At the time of that meeting, he was on assignment in North America, giving oversight to the expansion of the mission, seeking additional workers, and emphasizing to American Christians the secret of the "victorious life."

Several items for discussion were presented by Mr. Hurlburt who felt that the most important matter for discussion was the consideration of the question of making the missionary message more effective to potential candidates and supporters of mission work. He expressed his conviction that there was a great need for the sense of missionary responsibility on the part of all Christians; that they should not only give and pray for missions, but they should feel it incumbent upon themselves to become involved individually in active work for missions. Mr. Graef said that he had received in a conversation the suggestion of the great need for arousing a missionary spirit among professing church members to a greater extent than exhibited at present.

The second item for discussion, suggested by Charles Hurlburt, was how far the mission boards represented at the meeting, and other similar missions, might work together. He stressed the value and importance of frequent meetings of officers and council members of the various nondenominational mission boards for conference and prayer. Mr. Hurlburt further expressed the earnest desire that there might grow out of such meetings a system of transcontinental Bible and missionary conferences in which the fundamentals of the faith and arguments for worldwide evangelization could be clearly presented, "together with such teachings of the victorious life and complete surrender as might be needful to secure desirable candidates for the mission field."

Mr. Hurlburt's third item for consideration was the importance of union meetings being held for the public, with representatives of the different boards participating.

Mr. Steven felt there was need for mutual agreement of all bodies participating in such union meetings, regarding appeals for funds. He also "called attention to the need of safeguarding any union meetings or any federation of mission boards from one-man movements, or from boards under unwise leadership that might seek admission." Frederick Steven pointed out that the boards represented that day differed from some other agencies, particularly in the uncompromising adherence of those present to five specific beliefs: the deity of Christ, the vicarious atonement of Christ, man's fallen condition, the plenary inspiration of the Scriptures, and the premillenial return of Christ.

It was suggested by Mr. Graef that a committee be appointed to guard against undesirable mission boards being admitted to a union that may be established among the boards present, or similar boards.

As the discussion progressed, Mr. Hurlburt said that it would be better not to have any organization to which a mission could belong, or from which a mission could be excluded; that it would be better to have merely a working understanding without organization. It was Mr. Steven's opinion that "organization must be avoided, and if it should come, should be of the slightest and flimsiest nature possible." CAM layman Luther Rees said, in his judgment, what was needed was not organization, nor federation, but cooperation.

Organization could have ended with that discussion. However, at that point Henry W. Frost, North American director of the China Inland Mission, came into the meeting. After he was briefed on the progress of the discussions, he expressed his belief that the various missions should get together. He wondered why they had not done so already. He expressed his personal opinion, and felt he was expressing the attitude of the officers of the China Inland Mission, that they would welcome meetings among the leaders of different missions once or twice a year, if only for the very important matter of prayer. He believed, however that boards would learn a great deal from one another in the discussions in such meetings.

Mr. Frost indicated he was willing to go beyond this. The minutes record:

> He thought there ought to be an organization that would give definite hold upon this work of cooperation; . . . . He referred to the great blessing that had resulted from the annual meeting and conference of the China Inland Mission, . . . and expressed his belief that similar conferences between boards of sympathetic belief would result in similar blessing.

He cautioned, however, that any show of opposition to any existing denominational boards should be avoided, that any organization that may emerge from the present discussions should be distinct from any other organization already formed, for the purpose of cooperation between mission bodies.

In his last comment, Mr. Frost was undoubtedly referring to the Foreign Missions Conference of North America. It is interesting to note the similarity between its name and the name he chose for the new association—Interdenominational Foreign Mission Association of North America.

There came to be general agreement with Mr. Frost's statements. Orson R. Palmer, North American home director of the Africa Inland Mission and pastor of Berachah Church in Philadelphia, commented that the matters presented had been very much upon his heart, and that he enthusiastically favored Mr. Frost's suggestions. After expressing his agreement with the suggestions, Arthur J. Bowen, deputation secretary for Canada and the United States for South Africa General Mission, "called attention to the fact that it was necessary for the individual boards to continue their own individual missionary meetings."

Another meeting was proposed for September 29 to be held at Princeton, New Jersey. Mr. Frost was appointed chairman of a committee to arrange for the fall conference.

## THE ORGANIZATIONAL MEETING - 1917

The minutes record that on Saturday, September 29, 1917 a conference of representatives of several nondenominational foreign mission societies was convened in the prayer-meeting room of the First Presbyterian Church of Princeton, New Jersey. Henry W. Frost, chairman of the meeting, William H. Hendrickson, and Orson R. Palmer were the only participants who had attended the March meeting. At the time of this September meeting, Charles E. Hurlburt of the Africa Inland Mission was on his way back to his headquarters in Kenya.

The eleven other participants were Rodger B. Whittlesey of the China Inland Mission; Benjamin S. Stern, J. Davis Adams, and J. R. Schaffer of Inland South America Missionary Union; E. R. Garnsey, Lewis Sperry Chafer, and Mrs. Chafer, representing the South Africa General Mission; Rowland V. Bingham and Mrs. Bingham, Sudan Interior

Mission; and Mrs. Frank Marston and Miss Clara E. Masters of the Woman's Union Missionary Society.

After reviewing the deliberations of the March meeting, Henry Frost said that while the September meeting grew out of the previous meeting in March, it was unrelated officially. The purpose of the meeting was briefly stated: to consider the advisability of establishing an informal organization of nondenominational foreign mission societies in order to call mission officials to a yearly conference for prayer, fellowship, and mutual help.

Chairman Henry Frost indicated that he had "a serious sense of the importance of the issue of the meeting for weal or woe." He warned that there was a possibility of reaching conclusions that would not be helpful; therefore, he urged caution. He added that no effort would be made to bind the missions to any action that might be decided upon there, or to compromise the doctrinal basis and policy of their individual organizations. He felt, however, "that there was a service that we could render to each other for mutual good and the advancement of the work of evangelization; if we could realize that service, we should never regret our actions today."

A loose form of organization was suggested, which would provide spiritual fellowship, the sharing of helpful mutual experiences, and a united testimony that would hasten the evangelization of the world.

Mr. Frost submitted for discussion a list of eight articles that were considered in detail, one by one. They were provisionally adopted by unanimous vote for future ratification by individual missions. The document recommended by Mr. Frost and provisionally accepted was as follows:

### Articles of Agreement

> First, that the representatives of the Interdenominational Foreign Mission Societies presently assembled decide, subject to the ratification of the Societies represented, that a confederation

of persons shall be formed which shall be known as the Interdenominational Foreign Mission Association of North America.

Second, that the purpose of the Association shall be three-fold: one, to secure spiritual fellowship and intercessory prayer; second, to open the way to mutual conferences concerning missionary principles and methods; and third, to make possible the bearing of a united testimony to the need of a complete and speedy evangelization of the world.

Third, that the Association membership shall consist of the officials of those Societies which shall be asked by the Executive to join the Association, which, through official channels, shall accept the invitation given, and which, in taking this course shall subscribe to this Agreement and the Doctrinal Basis of the Association.

Fourth, that the officers of the Association shall be a President and a Secretary-Treasurer, that the Executive shall consist of these two persons and five others, and that all these seven persons shall be appointed for a term of two years, by, at least, a two-thirds majority vote taken and recorded at each alternate annual meeting of the Association.

Fifth, that the meetings of the Association shall be held, at least, once a year, at the time and place appointed by the Executive of the Association.

Sixth, that the Doctrinal Basis of the Association shall be as follows: (1) The plenary inspiration and divine authority of the Scriptures; (2) The Trinity, including the Deity of Christ; (3) The fall of man, his moral depravity and his need of regeneration; (4) The atonement, through the substitutionary death of Christ; (5) Justification,

> apart from works and by faith in Christ; (6) The bodily resurrection of Christ, and also of the saved and unsaved; (7) The unending life of the saved and the unending conscious punishment of the lost; and (8) The personal premillennial coming of Christ.
>
> Seventh, that the relationships of the Societies and their officials to the Association shall be an entirely voluntary one, it being understood that it shall rest with each and all concerned whether connection with the Association shall be begun, and whether, if begun, it shall be continued.
>
> Eighth, that each Society of the Association shall be asked to subscribe to its general fund—in order to provide the necessary expense of printing, postage, etc.—the sum of from one to five dollars per annum.

The final item of business was the election of the first slate of officers and members of the executive (official board). Elected unanimously were Henry W. Frost (CIM), president; J. R. Schaffer (ISAMU), secretary-treasurer; and Rowland V. Bingham (SIM), Orson R. Palmer (AIM), Paul E. Graef (SAGM), Clara E. Masters (WUMS), and Frank W. Lange (CAM). Each of the organizing missions was represented on the board of the newly-formed association.

The Central American Mission was represented at the March meeting, but was not officially represented at the September meeting. Nevertheless, Frank Lange was elected a member of the first board, and Central American Mission is considered a founding mission, along with Africa Inland Mission, China Inland Mission, Inland South America Missionary Union, South Africa General Mission, Sudan Interior Mission, and Woman's Union Missionary Society.

## THE CONFIRMATION MEETING - 1918

The second meeting of the Interdenominational Foreign Mission Association of North America was held December 11-12, 1918 at Berachah Church in Philadelphia. The board had prepared a program for a two-day Bible and missions conference. The morning sessions were reserved for business. The afternoon sessions were for the presentation of the overseas work and workers of member missions. Inspirational addresses were given in the evening.

Fifteen delegates participated in the business sessions, representing six missions: Africa Inland Mission: Mr. DeGroff, Howard B. Dinwiddie, Robert C. McQuilkin, Orson R. Palmer, and George Rhoad; Central American Mission: Frank W. Lange; China Inland Mission: Henry W. Frost and Roger B. Whittlesey; Inland South America Missionary Union: J. Davis Adams, J. R. Schaffer, and Mr. Thomas; South Africa General Mission: A. W. Bailey and William H. Hendrickson; and Woman's Union Missionary Society: Mrs. Frank Marston and Miss Clara Masters. Dr. F. W. Troy of Brooklyn was speaker.

A telegram was received from Mr. Bingham of Sudan Interior Mission, giving several items for the agenda. William L. Pettingill—CAM Board member, a noted Bible expositor, educator, author, and one of the editors of the Scofield Bible—had expected to be present but C. I. Scofield's critical illness prevented his attending.

The minutes of the 1917 organizational meeting in Princeton and the Articles of Agreement were read. It was reported that these had been circulated to member missions and ratified. Before final adoption there was discussion of the basis of membership. Mr. Whittlesey, secretary-treasurer of China Inland Mission, moved to amend the third article to read: "Third, that the Association membership shall consist of the officials of those Societies which shall be asked by the Executive, *after full consideration of their spiritual standing and financial methods*, to join the Association."

After this action, the minutes of the September 1917 organizational meeting were adopted as amended. The amendment gave the board the responsibility to check into the spiritual reputation and financial operations of prospective member missions. From the beginning of the association, accountability and openness were established in the important areas of spiritual and financial standards.

It was recognized that both Canadian and United States organizations were to be a part of the association, representing North America.

Delegates recommended the names of a number of missions to be invited into membership. Those listed were Bolivian Indian Mission, Central American Mission, Ceylon and India General Mission, Evangelical Union of South America, Indian Christian Mission, Mission to Lepers, San Pedro Mission to the Indians, Sudan United Mission, and Zenana Bible and Medical Mission. The inclusion of the Central American Mission in this list may indicate that CAM had not yet ratified the Articles of Agreement, even though Frank Lange represented the mission on the association's board.

Consideration was given to the possibility of the cooperation of missions in Bible conferences. J. Harvey Borton, chairman of the board of the Victorious Life Conference, and Robert C. McQuilkin, secretary of the conference, spoke on the opportunity and renewed demand for Bible conferences throughout the United States and Canada. Mr. McQuilkin, who had left his position with *The Sunday School Times* to further prepare for missionary service in Africa, was a delegate of the Africa Inland Mission. Borton and McQuilkin emphasized the three dominant Bible conference emphases: the person and work of Christ, with emphasis on His second coming; the great missionary program of the church; and the victorious life of the believer.

The ship that the McQuilkins were to take to Africa on November 30, 1918, *The City of Lahore*, burned in New York harbor and sank, along with all of their belongings, except some suitcases. The Lord never opened the way for them to go as missionaries, although four of their five children served overseas, and now several grandchildren are missionaries. In 1923 Dr. McQuilkin became the founding president of Columbia Bible College in South Carolina, which has expanded to become a leader among conservative evangelicals in preparation for missions and church ministries. Its program includes a Bible college, seminary, graduate school, extension department, radio station, and a secondary school named Ben Lippen. Hundreds of alumni are in Christian ministries worldwide.

In the afternoon and evening public sessions, reports and messages were given by both mission executives and missionaries on furlough. Among the missionary speakers were Rev. and Mrs. George Rhoad of the Africa Inland Mission of British East Africa (Kenya), and A. W. Bailey of the South Africa General Mission from Angola, Portuguese West Africa.

## THE THIRD ANNUAL MEETING - 1919

The Third Annual Meeting of the association was called to order by IFMA President Henry W. Frost on October 22, 1919 at the Africa Inland Mission home in Brooklyn, New York.

The board had decided not to include any public sessions in the program of this annual meeting. This was to allow the missions leaders more opportunity to interact among themselves in fellowship and prayer. Also, it was planned to allow "intimate and confidential consideration of matters of special importance and of common interest to the missions belonging to the association."

There were fourteen delegates, representing eight missions. The Bolivian Indian Mission, the most recent mission to participate in this fellowship, was represented by W. H. Strong. The Evangelical Union of South America had evidently been accepted into membership, since their secretary, George Smith, was elected to the board at this meeting. The Bible House of Los Angeles may have been accepted, as well. A payment by the Bible House of dues of $5.00 was recorded as received November 10, 1919.

The Articles of Agreement were amended to allow for a vice-president and additional members to the board. The incumbent officers were reelected for another two-year term. Orson R. Palmer was elected vice president. New board members were E. A. Brownlee, Canadian secretary for the China Inland Mission; George Smith, secretary of Evangelical Union of South America; and William H. Hendrickson, secretary of South Africa General Mission.

A question from the previous annual meeting, relating to Canadian meetings of the association, was considered. Because of distance and expense, the chairman mentioned the possibility of holding two meetings. Rowland Bingham, who was the only Canadian resident present, was asked for his opinion. With foresight on the issue of unity and cooperation, Mr. Bingham favored one central meeting to strengthen the character and work of the association. This position prevailed and provided the pattern of an annual meeting of the association, with representatives from mission members from both Canada and the United States. One annual meeting including both countries has continued to be followed since the IFMA was organized. Recognizing the benefits of Canadian participation, the amendment to the Articles of Agreement stated that three of the nine members of the association's board shall be residents of Canada.

A practical cooperative effort was proposed that related to the exchange of candidate procedures among member missions.

Mr. Bingham recommended that the board contact U.S. Secretary of State Lansing on behalf of member missions "to see if it is possible to secure for American missionaries permission to land in the various countries under the jurisdiction of Great Britain, France, Belgium, and other countries, by reference directly to their ambassador at Washington without the long delay incident to the country of landing."

Dr. Henry W. Frost wrote an article in 1919 for the CIM's *China's Millions*, in which he stated his interpretation of the rise of nondenominational missions. At the time of the writing, he was president of the Interdenominational Foreign Mission Association. The following is taken from Dr. Frost's revision of his article for the Africa Inland Mission publication, *Inland Africa:*

> Devoted men, while remaining in their denominational connections, began to plan and produce new Christian activities, simple in form, sound in doctrine, and making much of prayer, faith, and dependence upon the Holy Spirit. It was out of this condition of things that interdenominational movements arose, including interdenominational missions.
>
> And it is important to note that these last did not come into existence simply because there were large unoccupied fields of labor. Waiting fields gave direction to the movements which took place; but the cause of them lay behind and was far more significant in character. The fact is that spiritually minded men and women were once more reaching out after apostolic conditions, both in faith and practice; and, at times, not being able to express these in and through their denominations they felt constrained to act independently of them. It was in this way that independent missions came to be organized, and in this manner that they were founded upon doctrinal and spiritual bases of a primitive and positive kind. It follows that most of these missions continue to lay firm and strong emphasis upon evangelical truth, and continue to seek to

> maintain both their personnel and service in full harmony with apostolic teaching and example.
>
> This brief resumé of church history has been given in order to set forth a few simple but important conclusions, these being as follows: First, there is good reason to believe that the existing interdenominational mission societies have come into existence as a direct result of the Holy Spirit. Second, the Spirit, in bringing into existence these societies, has had for His object, not only the occupying of unoccupied fields, but also and particularly the safeguarding of imperilled fundamental doctrine and revitalizing the spiritual life of the Church. Third, the various interdenominational missionary societies are not schismatic, either in character or spirit; they are, on the contrary, operating within the Church, and hence, while independent in government, are *undenominational in form and interdenominational in fellowship*, allowing to their members a full expression of denominational preferences and activities. Fourth, these interdenominational societies, having chosen to establish themselves upon apostolic truth, and having sought to restore to the Church her full spiritual privileges, have laid themselves under heavy obligation before God and men to maintain their testimony and life. And, finally, the above being true, it is manifestly the case that such organizations should be earnestly and continually prayed for, that they may be kept in purity of doctrine and fulness of life, and, thus, that they may fulfill the divine purpose of their creation and being.[1]

By the close of 1919, the IFMA was established and was well on its way to becoming a significant impetus in a united effort for world evangelization. It is with a sense of

God's exceeding grace and goodness that we mark the advance and development of the IFMA in the history of foreign missions, recognizing that a great portion of the missionary enterprise is borne by nondenominational conservative evangelical missions.

## NOTES

[1] Henry W. Frost, "The Rise of Interdenominational Missions," *Inland Africa*, February 1920, pp. 1, 4-5.

# 6

# SOME FOUNDING LEADERS

There were a number of men and women who were active in founding and establishing the IFMA. Some were more prominent in the work of IFMA than others. Eight men, who were well known through their public ministries and influential in churches and among their peers in missions leadership, were Rowland V. Bingham, Arthur J. Bowen, Joseph A. Davis, George H. Dowkontt, Henry W. Frost, Robert Hall Glover, Paul H. Graef, and Charles E. Hurlburt.

In the early years of the association, it appears that Mr. Graef and Dr. Frost were the most influential in determining the direction of the IFMA and setting standards that are still in effect. However, the IFMA bears the mark of all of these men.

## ROWLAND V. BINGHAM

Sudan Interior Mission
(SIM)

Rowland Victor Bingham, born in 1872, became a man of many achievements as a pioneer missionary, journalist, editor, minister, and leader of various Christian enterprises. The second of seven brothers and one sister, his homeland was Surrey, South England. It was in his town of birth, East Grinstead, that the China Inland Mission was formed in 1865. Bingham's father operated a brickyard and sawmill, along with other building operations. He died from vaccination poisoning during a smallpox scare. Rowland, at the age of thirteen, left home to help his mother by earning his own living as a pupil/teacher. Three years later when he was sixteen, he left England for Canada. He was converted the year before in a Salvation Army service, and shortly after arriving in Canada became a Salvation Army officer.

A few years later, after speaking at a meeting in Toronto, he was invited to lunch at the home of Mrs. Gowans, a quiet Scottish lady. She told of her eldest son's call to be an ambassador of Christ in the "Soudan." Bingham had studied mission fields of the world and became convinced that the Sudan, with an area larger than India and some sixty-to-ninety-million people without a gospel witness, was the place that needed him most. He called on Mrs. Gowans the next day to say that he expected to sail in two weeks to join her son, Walter, in Britain and to go on with him to Africa.

No mission agency in North America or Britain would send missionaries into this area. In response to the call of God, Walter Gowans and Rowland Bingham, decided to go out alone, trusting God and the prayerful backing of Mrs. Gowans. Bingham resigned from the Salvation Army about the time that two other friends did. One was Peter W. Philpott, founder of Philpott Tabernacle in Hamilton, Ontario, and later pastor of Moody Memorial Church in Chicago. The other was A. W. Roffe who for many years was Canadian superintendent of the Christian and Missionary Alliance.[1]

In New York, twenty-year-old Rowland Bingham met Thomas Kent, a college friend of Gowans. Kent determined to be the third member of this pioneering group, who called themselves the Soudan Interior Mission. By December 1894, just a year after their arrival in Nigeria, Gowans and Kent both died in their attempt to reach Kano. A few months later, weakened in health, Bingham returned to North America, recognizing the need of some form of organization and home base. After taking some medical training at a hospital in Cleveland, he enrolled in Albert B. Simpson's

Bible school in New York City. During his time there, he pastored a small church in Newburgh, New York.

Mr. Bingham organized the Africa Industrial Mission in 1896. He married Helen E. Blair on May 24, 1898. The Binghams left the church in Newburgh seven months later and returned to Toronto, trusting God to provide their needs.

The name of the mission was changed in 1905 to Africa Evangelistic Mission, and to Sudan Interior Mission in 1907.

Another attempt to open the Sudan in 1900 failed, and Mr. Bingham was sent home after a near-fatal bout with malaria. After his convalescence in England, he returned to Toronto and soon found four new candidates willing to take up the work. Finally, the first station was occupied in Nigeria in 1901, and from that time on, under the leadership of Mr. Bingham, the mission became a vital church-planting force in West Africa and later in Ethiopia.

For the next forty-one years, Rowland V. Bingham gave himself unstintingly to the direction of the Sudan Interior Mission and other evangelical ministries. Through many trials of every kind, his faith and determination did not waver. He always kept before himself the "other sheep" who needed to be reached in Africa, North America, and throughout the world. Not one of the founders of IFMA or early leaders were more dedicated to evangelical cooperation and the practice of practical, biblical Christian unity than Rowland V. Bingham.

One of the ministries that he was instrumental in founding was *The Evangelical Christian*, which replaced *The Faithful Witness* that had been turned over to him in 1904. Beginning as a missionary journal, it broadened to cover the general evangelical religious field without losing its primary focus on missions. *The Evangelical Christian* was never an SIM publication, although Mr. Bingham was editor for twenty-five years. Begun by faith, the periodical continued for some seventy years as a powerful voice of conservative evangelical Christianity, with a special emphasis on world evangelization.

Another vital evangelical enterprise that Bingham founded and led was a Christian publishing house. Evangelical Publishers was started in 1912 to produce books true to the fundamentals of the Christian faith, which were intended to offset the teachings of liberalism that appeared to dominate religious thinking.

Rowland V. Bingham cooperated fully in the establishment and growth of the IFMA. He sent a letter expressing his regret at not being able to attend the March 31, 1917 preliminary meeting and wishing God's blessing on the gathering. Both Mr. and Mrs. Bingham participated in the organizational meeting on September 29, 1917. He was elected to the first board of the new association, and gave it valuable support until his death in December 1942. At the 1919 meeting in Brooklyn, he was instrumental in confirming the North American character of the IFMA—the joining of both Canada and the United States in only one annual meeting of the association.

Dr. Bingham founded the independent Gowans Home for Missionaries' Children in 1923. Through the years, this facility provided a home in Collingwood, Ontario, for hundreds of children of evangelical missionaries, regardless of mission or denomination.

Bingham organized the Canadian Keswick Conference in 1924 with two primary aims: (1) deepening the spiritual life, and (2) strengthening the missionary cause. Besides promoting missions at Keswick, Bingham used the summer conference as a place of training and preparation of missionary candidates.

During his lifetime, he served on the boards of several missions, representing ministries worldwide, and on the board of Toronto Bible College, as well. At the beginning of World War II, Dr. Bingham became deeply interested in the Soldiers' and Airmen's Christian Association, which was set up to provide Christian centers for military personnel throughout Canada. He was untiring in his efforts to strengthen soul-winning and discipling ministries.

Dr. Rowland V. Bingham was a highly regarded Christian leader, unswerving in his conservative theological position, and committed to evangelical cooperation.

## ARTHUR J. BOWEN

South Africa General Mission
(Africa Evangelical Fellowship)

Arthur John Bowen was born in south Wales in 1871 and was reared in a Christian home. He had a solid basic education, supervised by his mother who was a public school principal. He worked as a teenager for the Great Western Railroad in Great Britain, but resigned at age twenty for missionary work with the Congo Balolo Mission.

Bowen received fifteen months of missionary training at Harley College in London before leaving for Africa in December 1892. During that time, Dwight L. Moody spoke at Spurgeon's Metropolitan Tabernacle on the subject, "Be Filled with the Spirit." The truth of that message made a deep and lasting impression on Mr. Bowen, which was reflected in his sixty years of missions service.

During his first furlough from Africa, he was married in March 1897 to his childhood schoolmate, Jessie Dove Gibbs. They sailed the next month for the Congo. While Mr. Bowen was translating the Acts of the Apostles, Mrs. Bowen studied the language and supervised the household. She soon came down with malaria. She suffered so greatly, and without relief, that within the year they had to return to England.

Back in England, Mr. Bowen taught at Harley College and was deputation secretary for the mission. After a year and a half, Mrs. Bowen regained her health. Since she could not return to the Congo, they decided that Mr. Bowen should return to continue the translation projects. He did that for two years, completing the translation of the Gospel of Matthew and the Acts of the Apostles into Lomongo. Upon his return to England, Bowen represented the work of the mission throughout the British Isles for two more years. He translated the Epistles to the Corinthians, compiled a Lomongo grammar, and continued teaching at Harley College.

The Bowens finished their association with the Congo Balolo Mission in 1903. The mission had been reorganized in 1900, becoming the Regions Beyond Missionary Union, now RBMU International.

They felt led of God to minister in Canada. Arthur Bowen was ordained at their farewell meeting. During the next decade, he was a pastor in three areas of Ontario.

Mr. Bowen was invited in 1913 to serve as the first deputation secretary in Canada for the South Africa General Mission (now Africa Evangelical Fellowship). After laying the foundation for the SAGM to be officially organized in Canada, his work was expanded in 1917 to include the United States, as well as Canada, from a base in Chicago. He was a dynamic missions speaker.

When William H. Hendrickson died in December 1920, Arthur Bowen was chosen to succeed him as general secretary of SAGM. Upon his retirement as general secretary at the end of 1947, Bowen was succeeded by Ezra Shank. After retirement, Mr. Bowen continued to carry on his effective ministry of promoting missions until he was well into his eighties.

In his biography of Mr. Bowen, Ezra Shank wrote of him following his trip to Africa in 1922:

> Newspapers carried headlines, such as these: *The Brooklyn Daily News:* "African Missionary's Trips Total 33,000 Miles in a Year;" *The Chicago Daily Journal:* "Savage Africa Called Tame;" and *The Grand Rapids Press:* "Field Secretary to Lecture Here After Long Sojourn in Heart of African Wilds."
>
> Thus, the vivacious Welshman became the flaming evangel of missions. . . . He became one

> of the most popular missionary speakers on the North American Continent, and one whose opinions were sought and his counsel appreciated.[2]

Both Mr. Hendrickson and Mr. Bowen attended the 1917 preliminary meeting that led to the founding of IFMA. After the family moved to Brooklyn, New York, in 1921, Arthur Bowen was faithful in his work with the IFMA, serving on the board and as president from 1939 to 1943.

## JOSEPH A. DAVIS

### Inland South America Missionary Union (South America Mission)

For Joseph A. Davis, the path to missionary service and leadership was not a smooth, direct route. He was born May 4, 1879 in Detroit, Michigan. His father managed the family's prosperous hardware business. Religious training for Joseph, his two brothers, and a sister was left to his mother, a devout Roman Catholic.

At the University of Detroit, Joseph earned his bachelor, master, and law degrees, while working as a part-time reporter for a city newspaper. During this time, he became an agnostic.

After practicing law for several years, he became involved in politics as a way to better serve humanity. A group soon backed Joseph for nomination for a judgeship. He became thoroughly disillusioned when he discovered that his backers really wanted a judge to cover for their less-than-honorable plans. He withdrew his name, left Detroit and the practice of law.

Davis worked his way west for several years, doing odd jobs while living for worldly pleasure. His health had deteriorated by the time he reached the San Francisco area.

In Oakland, he sought help at the Home of Peace, which, he thought, was a sanatorium. Mr. and Mrs. Montgomery, the Christian owners of this missionary rest home, orphanage, and school, opened their door and hearts to Davis. The prayers and witness of this Christian community resulted in his conversion. While working at the Home of Peace in 1909, he met and married Mabel A. Kleis who was teaching at the orphanage school. Mabel committed herself to missionary service early in life. Joseph Davis had received a call to missions at the time of his conversion. South America was the direction indicated, but they were uncertain about the steps to take.

Joseph now worked for Scribner's publishers, and began disciplined Bible study on his own and through correspondence courses. He participated in tent and street meetings and a prison ministry. After a few years, Mr. Davis was called to pastor a Baptist church in Denver. The pastoral work was satisfying and the congregation wanted them to stay, but they continued to sense a call to Latin America.

They wrote to mission societies, but could not discover one that was interested in the unreached Indians of South America. Finally, they put a fleece before the Lord. Besides travel expenses, they figured they would need one thousand dollars. Almost immediately a member of the church felt constrained to ask if they were still thinking of going to South America. When the response was positive, she brought them exactly the amount they had put before the Lord. In obedience, they resigned from the pastorate.

By September 1914, the Davis family, which now included a son and two daughters, arrived in New York with Mrs. Whitmore, a member of the Denver church. World War I had started the month before, but they were soon able to secure passage to England and from there to Argentina, although through dangerous seas. They arrived safely in Buenos Aires a month later, but a sister ship was sunk.

They settled in a small village to begin language study. Soon, their money was gone, but the Lord provided employment, teaching English to the sons of a wealthy family. After two years, Mrs. Davis became too ill to stay.

While Mrs. Davis was recuperating in Detroit, Joseph spoke in churches and helped in the family business. After some months, they moved to Chicago to study at Moody Bible Institute. In addition to their studies, they recruited four new missionaries to join them and Mrs. Whitmore in beginning a new work in Paraguay. Calling themselves the Paraguayan Mission, they began work among the Guaranis Indian tribe. They started with evangelism, colportage, women and children's work. A school for Guarani children, with night classes for adults, was soon begun.

In 1919, they once again had to return to the United States to care for Mrs. Davis' serious health problem. It was to be a permanent move, since they were not able to return.

The Paraguayan Mission merged into the Inland South America Missionary Union, which was led by experienced missionary John Hay from Scotland. Joseph Davis was asked to become U. S. deputation secretary for the ISAMU, which had been represented in the States for almost a decade. The ISAMU was one of the founding missions of the IFMA in 1917.

Joseph Davis soon became the administrative leader of the mission. Both he and Mrs. Davis thrived under the new responsibilities. By 1932, sixty-five additional missionaries had gone to the fields under their leadership.

In 1932, the ISAMU was separated into two missions: the ISAMU in the United States, and the British mission, under the leadership of the Hays, was named New Testament Missionary Union. Joseph Davis became the general director of the U. S. mission, and its name was changed to South America Indian Mission. By 1939 the mission headquarters was moved from New York City to West Palm Beach, Florida. After his death in 1958, Mr. Davis was succeeded as general director by G. Hunter Norwood, Jr.

During their years in New York, Mr. Davis became heavily involved in the IFMA. He served as an officer of the association for fifteen years, including a term as president.

## GEORGE H. DOWKONTT

South Africa General Mission
(Africa Evangelical Fellowship)

Rev. George H. Dowkontt, M.D., became a board member of the IFMA in 1921, and from 1926 to 1943 conscientiously served as secretary of the board and the association. Dr. Dowkontt had worked as a medical missionary in Africa. When he returned to the United States, he helped to establish the Samaritan Hospital in New York City. He also continued his leadership of the International Medical Missionary Society, which had been organized by his father, Dr. George D. Dowkontt.

George Harry Dowkontt had been reared in a Christian home that was dedicated to medical missionary service in the inner cities of England and America. His father was a medical steward in the British navy for some seventeen years. After leaving the navy, he worked at the Liverpool Medical Mission, ministering to the poorest of the poor through his medical knowledge and gospel witness. When young Harry Dowkontt was ten years old, the family moved to the United States to help to start a medical mission in inner-city Philadelphia.

After the father, George D. Dowkontt, had earned his medical degree, and while Harry was a student at Dwight L. Moody's Mount Hermon boys' school, the family moved to New York City in 1881. There, Dr. George D. founded the New York Medical Mission. The medical missions were operated on a nondenominational *faith* basis, trusting the Lord for the supply of all needs. The slum-area patients were unable to pay for medical treatment.

Harry worked his way through his educational training. He attended the first student conference at Mount Hermon in 1886. He was among the initial one hundred students to join the Student Volunteer Movement, which resulted from those weeks of meetings. Harry continued his preparation for Christian service at Pennington Seminary in New Jersey and at Princeton College. He earned his M. D. degree in 1896.

Dr. Harry Dowkontt represented medical missions as speaker and participant at conferences of the Student Volunteer Movement and Foreign Missions Conference of North America. He was one of the people on the Bible and missions conference team sponsored by the IFMA. Among other responsibilities, Dr. Dowkontt took care of travel arrangements and the missions book table.

He became pastor of the South Brooklyn Baptist Church. Among his many activities, Dr. Dowkontt was superintendent for over thirty years of the Fulton Street Noon Prayer Meeting, which was a respected and productive evangelical ministry that continued for almost ninety years. The meetings were held daily in rented rooms in an office building at 113-115 Fulton Street, New York City. Occasionally, these rooms were used for various IFMA meetings. Dr. Dowkontt served as a board member of a number of IFMA member missions: American European Fellowship, Bolivian Indian Mission, Ceylon and India General Mission, India Christian Mission, Orinoco River Mission, and South Africa General Mission.

## HENRY W. FROST

China Inland Mission
(Overseas Missionary Fellowship)

The family of Henry W. Frost were deeply committed Christians. His father was a successful financier who worked in various cities. Henry was born in Detroit, began school in Stanford, Connecticut, continued in Chicago and New York City, and then went to Princeton where he completed three years of college studies. For health reasons, he left for outside work with his father and brother. He soon was put in charge of the construction of the gas and water works in Attica, New York. He continued in Attica, building up a prosperous flour mill. During this time, alone with the Lord, he had a definite experience of conversion, and was changed from a churchman to a committed Christian.

In 1883 Henry Frost married Abbie Ellinwood, a graduate of Houghton Seminary and teacher of Latin and music. That summer, just before the wedding, the first Bible Conference was held at Niagara-on-the-Lake. Conference Chairman Dr. William J. Erdman consented to spend a week in private Bible study with Henry. Soon after, Frost was approached by an elderly man from the village of Attica Center, inviting him to speak to a group who wanted to start Sunday services in an unused church. He was about to refuse when he remembered his prayer of the night before, asking the Lord to lead him in his Christian witness.

This first experience led to many others until he and Mrs. Frost felt God's leading to go full-time into home missionary work in New Brunswick, New Jersey, among the poor working class. Henry's father took over the management of the mill and pledged to support his son and daughter-in-law. After an effective ministry in urban mission work, Henry attended a session of the Niagara Bible Conference in 1885. There, at the age of twenty-seven, he heard his first missionary messages, which were given by William E. Blackstone of Chicago and Jonathan Goforth of Knox College, Toronto. He immediately saw that his life must be given, not just to those in New Brunswick who needed him, "but to those who needed him most."[3] Through a book purchased at the conference, *A Missionary Band*, he was introduced to the faith mission concept of J. Hudson Taylor and the China Inland Mission. The following year at the Niagara Conference, through a message by Dr. Arthur T. Pierson, Henry was challenged again for missions.

Another year passed during which he continued service in needy areas in New York City and throughout the state of New York. He experienced a growing missionary conviction. However, Mrs. Frost, who was occupied with their growing family and the care of her invalid father, did not see how they could enter overseas missionary service.

Henry Frost continued to be burdened for China and the China Inland Mission. With his wife's approval, he wrote to the mission, but was not encouraged by the leadership because of his being twenty-nine years old and the responsibilities he had.

He was soon speaking in a two-week evangelistic crusade that was sponsored by three churches in northern New York. During his prayer and study times, he became convinced that he should go to London to talk personally with Hudson Taylor and Benjamin Broomhall about opening a branch of China Inland Mission in North America.

He made the voyage in 1887, but was disappointed when these two mission leaders did not agree that the CIM should internationalize by setting up a branch in North America. Before returning to New York, Frost asked Mr. Taylor if he would be open to an invitation to speak at the Niagara Conference on his way back to China. The positive response was Frost's first encouragement during his trip to London.

On his way to China in 1888, J. Hudson Taylor stopped in America to speak at the Niagara and Northfield conferences. As a result of his meetings, spontaneous offerings were given for the support of new workers in China. Dr. Taylor was not eager to add North American missionaries to the CIM, but he did spend much time in prayer to discern the Lord's will.

God quickly answered. By September, fourteen Canadian young people had volunteered to form the first North American team to go to China with Dr. Taylor. The first meeting of the North American council was held September 24, 1888 in Toronto. Mr. Frost was named secretary-treasurer for the United States, and the next year was asked to move to Toronto to serve both countries. Soon, he was made director for North America, and Mr. Frederick A. Steven became secretary-treasurer.

During the 1890s, Mr. Frost made three extended trips to China, while Mrs. Frost and the council carried on the work in the Toronto mission home. On one China trip, he became quite ill, which required time for recuperation away from the mission. On another trip, just after the Boxer Rebellion, Dr. Frost experienced shipwreck.

The Philadelphia-area property for the mission headquarters and home was provided in 1901. Mr. and Mrs. Frost reluctantly left the strong supportive group of mission friends in Canada to start over in the United States, with very few contacts. Again, by faith, God worked, and as in Canada, the Lord raised up praying friends who became missionaries and mission supporters, all without appeals for money. The "faith principle" of not soliciting funds for the work was strongly endorsed by Dr. Frost for the following reasons:

> First, I did not wish to do anything to divert money from the regular denominational channels of missionary giving; second, I preferred to receive gifts which were voluntary and would be accompanied by love and prayer; third, I desired to set such an example of dealing with God in respect to prayer for daily needs as would encourage the faith of faint-hearted Christians; and fourth, I was anxious to try out the promises of God, such as seeking first His kingdom and His righteousness, and thus discover for myself and the work if the earthly things would be added to us.[4]

Mr. Frost was instrumental in starting the mission's Prayer Union in Canada, which grew to over two thousand members, besides similar groups that followed in England, Australia, and New Zealand. He saw the vital connection between prayer and blessing in the work of the mission. *Men Who Prayed* and *Effective Praying* were two of his books.

Henry Frost was well respected wherever he traveled. The mission became better known in the United States through his ministry. His testimony was deeply appreciated by church leaders in the Philadelphia area who recommended him for ordination. He was ordained by the

Philadelphia Presbytery in July 1904. After hearing his earnest message, "Prevailing Prayer," at Moody Memorial Church in Chicago, Thomas E. Stevens was led to found the Great Commission Prayer League in 1910. Mrs. William Borden and her son, William, committed themselves to the Lord's work in China as a result of his message, "The Spiritual Condition of the Heathen." The biography of William Borden's short life is recorded in the book, *Borden of Yale '09.*

Westminster College, New Wilmington, Pennsylvania, conferred on Mr. Frost the Doctor of Divinity degree in 1922 in recognition of his contribution to Christian life and literature.

Dr. Frost and the China Inland Mission were accepted by the denominational missions leadership. There is no question but that this was largely because of Henry Frost's character, gifts of leadership, and effective ministry of preaching and writing. It is interesting to note that Mrs. Frost—Abbie Ellinwood Frost, who had considerable gifts and abilities, as well—was a niece of Dr. Frank Ellinwood, secretary of the Presbyterian USA Board of Missions, and was a cousin of Dr. Edmund K. Alden, secretary of the American Board of Foreign Missions.[5]

At the time of the founding of the IFMA, Henry Frost had become one of the most respected mission leaders in North America. He gave strong leadership to the association for the first ten years of its history, serving as president from 1917 to 1927.

## ROBERT HALL GLOVER

China Inland Mission
(Overseas Missionary Fellowship)

Robert Hall Glover, M.D., F.R.G.S., was greatly used of God as a physician, missionary, mission executive for two agencies, missions professor, and author. Born and educated in Canada, he was a missionary in China for nineteen years and founded two Bible schools while there. In 1913 he was elected foreign missions secretary of his mission agency, the Christian and Missionary Alliance. He held this post until 1921. At a special meeting in 1921, the IFMA Board approved setting up a separate office for the IFMA, with an invitation extended to Dr. Glover to become full-time secretary. After thought and prayer, Dr. Glover decided not to accept this proposal.

That same year Dr. Glover sought out Dr. Henry W. Frost in Princeton to discuss an invitation from Dr. James M. Gray of Moody Bible Institute to direct and enlarge the missions department of the school. Dr. Frost encouraged him to accept it, although he thought how good it would be to have this friend as a colleague in the work of the China Inland Mission. Dr. Glover did accept Dr. Gray's invitation.

As a result of five years of teaching at Moody, he developed his lecture materials into the widely-used text, *The Progress of World-Wide Missions*. Dr. Glover was well prepared to teach and write on the subject, since in his service as a missionary and administrator, he had traveled over one hundred thousand miles in foreign lands, visiting missions in Japan, Korea, China, the Philippines, Indonesia, India, Africa, the Near East, and Latin America.[6] During his years of teaching and counseling at Moody Bible Institute, some two hundred MBI students entered foreign missionary service.

Dr. Frost was able in 1926 to secure Dr. Glover as assistant home director for the China Inland Mission. That was an unsettled time in China as missionaries faced the "evacuation of 1927." Because of these complications, D. E. Hoste, the CIM general director, asked Dr. Glover to visit China to become better acquainted with CIM personnel and to share in deliberations of the mission leaders, concerning problems and opportunities. Spending 1928 there, the Glovers returned to speak throughout North America and to help secure new workers. Dr. Glover was in great demand as a missionary speaker. For almost twenty years, he warned of the communist advance in China.

Starting in January 1930, Dr. Glover began a fifteen-year ministry as home director for the China Inland Mission in North America. After he turned over that responsibility to Herbert Griffin in 1946, the Bible House of Los Angeles published Dr. Glover's book, *The Bible Basis of Missions.*

He made a significant contribution to the IFMA, serving fourteen years on the board, nine as president and five as vice-president. Robert Hall Glover died in 1947.

## PAUL H. GRAEF

The man who had the original vision for organizing IFMA was Paul H. Graef, a Wall Street broker. A lay Bible teacher at Bedford Presbyterian Church in Brooklyn, he served on the boards of several missions, including the South Africa General Mission (Africa Evangelical Fellowship), Inland South America Missionary Union (South America Mission), and the American Board of Missions to the Jews (Chosen People Ministries). Mrs. Graef was active in the ministry and on the board of managers of the Woman's Union Missionary Society.[7]

A South Africa General Mission editorial stated:

> Mr. Graef, Chairman of the Executive Committee . . . finds time for God in the midst of an active business life, giving himself much to the work of the Gospel at Home, and being keenly interested in its prosperity through the Mission in South and South-Central Africa. He brings a happy quota of initiative and hopeful zeal.[8]

Paul Graef was a member of the IFMA Board from 1917 to 1943, serving as vice president from 1922 to 1943. He was a willing worker, and a member of many IFMA special committees. In 1937 he made several hundred copies of his book, *Eye to Aye*, available to member missions.

The last mention of Mr. Graef is found in an IFMA resolution by the board on October 22, 1943:

Resolved: that this Association acknowledge with deep gratitude to God the long years of service and fellowship our Brother Paul H. Graef contributed, the vision of his which was instrumental in bringing the Association into being, and his unflagging interest in its welfare ever since.

We extend our sympathy in connection with his decreasing strength of body, and pray not only that "the inward man may be renewed day by day," but also that the fruitfulness of his Christian testimony may increase to the glory of God.

## CHARLES E. HURLBURT

Africa Inland Mission

Charles E. Hurlburt established the Africa Inland Mission as a major missionary force in Africa. After the early death of Peter Cameron Scott, Mr. Hurlburt, chairman of the North American Council of the new mission, was appointed general director in 1897.

Born in Dubuque, Iowa, in 1860, Hurlburt grew up in Oberlin, Ohio, where he attended school and joined the First Congregational Church. Charles was the oldest of four children and still a youth when his father died. He was forced to provide support for his mother, brothers, and sister at an early age. He worked on farms, in factories, and eventually started a plumbing business.

Family circumstances prevented his becoming a missionary as he desired. He worked for the YMCA in his spare time. Sometime after his marriage, he turned over his successful plumbing business to his brother and accepted full-time employment at the YMCA at a much-reduced salary. He was made state secretary of the YMCA in Pennsylvania in 1889. Although he had many opportunities for service in this position, he was not sure he was doing the work God had for him.

Hurlburt and several others met with Peter Cameron

Scott in Philadelphia on May 6, 1895 to consider ways and means of strengthening the work of missions in Africa. From this meeting, the Africa Inland Mission was born. A few months later, Scott was on his way to Kenya with the first team of eight workers. Nineteen months after the Philadelphia meeting, Peter Cameron Scott died of black-water fever in Kenya. A year after his death, because of illness and other circumstances, only one missionary remained in AIM work in Africa.

The AIM's Philadelphia Council met to consider the possibility of closing the mission. Instead, upon the advice of Dr. Arthur T. Pierson, Mr. Hurlburt was asked to go to Africa to survey the field. That trip assured him of God's direction for his life, and he resigned from the YMCA. He was appointed AIM general director in 1897, and in 1901 took his wife and five children—along with some new workers—to rebuild the work in Kenya.

Kenneth Richardson, who served his first missionary term while Charles Hurlburt was general director, wrote of him:

> Bwana Hurlburt, while different from the founder of the Mission, was well fitted for work on the foreign field. His resourcefulness was amazing. He could apply mind and hand to almost any emergency, and accomplish most tasks with complete mastery. In those days, when qualified men were scarce in that part of the world, his abilities were put to full use. As a dentist, he was ready to help the missionaries and a host of appreciative officials and settlers also.[9]

Hurlburt was a rugged, dynamic, affectionate leader, and a spiritual father to new missionaries. He put great stress on prayer, was a deep thinker, and read widely. While on furlough in 1908, he was summoned to the White House to brief President Theodore Roosevelt on East African affairs, including big-game hunting. He was a delegate to the World Missionary Conference at Edinburgh in 1910, and was a highly-respected leader within the nondenominational missions movement.

Hurlburt was the only IFMA mission leader to speak at the 1925 Foreign Missions Convention in Washington, DC. Speaking on the topic, "The Gospel among Primitive People," he referred, also, to President Theodore Roosevelt's visit to the Africa Inland Mission headquarters in East Africa. After inquiring about AIM's work, meeting some African Christians, and going into their homes, Roosevelt commented to Mr. Hurlburt, "I like your finished product. It is the right sort of thing to do."[10]

It was appropriate that much of the discussion at the preliminary meeting that led to the founding of the IFMA followed an outline of issues given by Charles E. Hurlburt. For some thirty years, he gave effective leadership and stability to the Africa Inland Mission. When on furlough or assignment in North America, he participated meaningfully in meetings of the IFMA.

The IFMA was largely shaped by Charles Hurlburt and the other men mentioned in this chapter. Their practice of cooperation and unity determined to a large extent the position of the IFMA. They set forth the strong doctrinal basis on which the IFMA continues, and the standards required of its members. As it is important to study the founding leaders, it is helpful to know the missions, as well. The next chapter will give a brief overview of the IFMA's seven founding organizations. Each one continues to be represented in the association's membership in 1992.

## NOTES

[1] J. H. Hunter, *A Flame of Fire: The Life and Work of R. V. Bingham, D.D.* (Toronto: Sudan Interior Mission, 1961), p. 48.

[2] Ezra A. Shank, *Fervent in Spirit: The Biography of Arthur J. Bowen* (Chicago: Moody Press, 1954), p. 170.

[3] Dr. and Mrs. Howard Taylor, "By Faith . . . " *Henry W. Frost and the China Inland Mission* (Philadelphia: China Inland Mission, 1938), p. 50.

[4] Henry W. Frost, "Shut up to God," in *The Fire Burns On*, comp. Frank Houghton (London: Overseas Missionary Fellowship, 1965), p. 94.

[5] Taylor, "By Faith . . . " *Henry W. Frost and the China Inland Mission*, p. 30.

[6] Delavan L. Pierson, "By Way of Introduction," in *The Progress of World-Wide Missions*, 4th ed., rev., ed. Robert Hall Glover (New York: Harper & Brothers Publishers, 1924), p. viii.

[7] August B. Holm, telephone interview with author, 15 January 1981.

[8] *South African Pioneer*, August-September 1913, p. 3.

[9] Kenneth Richardson, *Garden of Miracles: A History of the Africa Inland Mission* (London: Victory Press, 1968), p. 46.

[10] Charles E. Hurlburt, "The Gospel Among Primitive Peoples," in T*he Foreign Missions Convention at Washington 1925* (New York: Foreign Missions Conference of North America, 1925), p. 95.

# 7

# THE FOUNDING MISSIONS

Present at the first meeting in March 1917 were representatives of the Africa Inland Mission, Central American Mission, China Inland Mission, and South Africa General Mission. Three other missions—Inland South America Missionary Union, Sudan Interior Mission, and Woman's Union Missionary Society—were represented at the organizational meeting in September that year. These seven organizations are the founding missions of the IFMA.

## AFRICA INLAND MISSION

Peter Cameron Scott, founder of the Africa Inland Mission, was born in Glasgow, March 7, 1867. With his godly parents, he left Scotland in 1895 and settled in Philadelphia. After a crisis experience, he surrendered his life to the Lord, trusting Him for both spiritual and physical health. Scott entered the New York Missionary Training College. He not only worked to support himself during his training, but spent time in personal evangelism among men in the slums.

Ordained by Dr. A. B. Simpson, he sailed for Africa in November 1890 under the International Missionary Alliance. In less than two years in the Congo, Scott had buried his brother and had to leave Africa himself because of constant fever. After recovering, he shared his vision for a line of mission centers through East and Central Africa with Dr. Arthur T. Pierson who was impressed with the possibilities.[1]

The denominational mission boards were sending few new workers out, particularly to the interior of Africa, primarily for two reasons: lack of funds and health conditions. It is doubtful that Peter Cameron Scott would have been accepted for service by any denominational board because of educational and health reasons.

A sponsoring committee was soon formed under the leadership of Dr. Pierson, with Charles E. Hurlburt, James H. McConkey, Orson R. Palmer, William C. Pettingill, John Steele, and Reuben A. Torrey as members.[2] It was organized as the Philadelphia Missionary Council and served several small mission projects. The North America mission office was located at the Pennsylvania Bible Institute in Philadelphia of which Charles Hurlburt was president.

The new mission would focus on the unreached tribes in the interior of Kenya. The first workers under the Africa Inland Mission were Peter and his sister, Margaret, along with six others, who sailed in August 1895.

Another party arrived shortly after that, which included Peter Scott's parents and his younger sister, Ina. Four stations were opened and a school started in the first year. Peter Cameron Scott sent only one annual report to the home council. During his fourteenth month back in Africa, he died of blackwater fever on December 4, 1896.

After the death of Scott, the mission passed through deep waters. One after another, valuable workers died; others had to leave for health reasons. Some left to serve Africa in other ways.

When the home council learned of Peter's death and that all but one of the missionaries had left the work, they questioned the continuation of the mission. Dr. A. T. Pierson convinced them that it was a time for advance, not retreat. Charles Hurlburt was appointed general director and went to Africa for a two-month survey trip. Mr. Hurlburt's burden for the people of Africa increased. He felt that he should move to the field. Thus, he and his family left for Kenya in October 1901. In 1903 he established the headquarters and main center for the work at Kijabe, about thirty-five miles northwest of Nairobi.

From this renewed start, Charles E. Hurlburt was used of the Lord to direct the expanding work of the AIM and to fulfill the mission of Peter Cameron Scott. The work in Tanzania was started in 1909. The first station was received from the Church Missionary Society of England. The first survey trip was made into the Congo in 1910, and in 1912 the work opened there. The outreach of the mission continued during World War I.

A review of the statistics indicates that in 1910 the Africa Inland Mission had 59 missionaries.[3] Records for 1915-1916 show the number of missionaries had more than doubled, to 133.[4]

The annual report for the year ending February 28, 1919 lists 157 missionaries on the field, 8 enroute, and 21 at home, not including home staff workers.[5] In spite of war conditions—the hazards of ocean travel and the mobilization of men for the military—more workers were going out.

Charles Hurlburt became general director emeritus in 1925, and leadership in America was passed on to Henry D. Campbell. Ralph T. Davis served as U. S. home director during the years of 1941 to 1955, when he was chosen international general secretary at AIM's Jubilee Conference in Kijabe, Kenya. By then the missionary staff had grown to 500, serving in 6 African countries.

Peter Stam III served as Canadian director from 1964 to 1977. Douglas Harris followed from 1977 to 1980. In the United States, Sidney Langford was home director from 1956 to 1977.

As international general secretary of the mission from 1955 to 1963, Dr. Ralph Davis coordinated all sending and receiving countries. Following Dr. Davis' death in 1963, these responsibilities were divided for the next ten years among the field and home directors and the honorary chairman of the international conference.

Based in Kenya, Norman Thomas was international

general secretary from 1973 to 1978. He was succeeded by Richard Anderson, M.D., who filled this office until 1990.

The work of the AIM, now approaching its centennial in 1995, has continued to develop and expand. The Africa Inland Church is self-supporting, having its own leadership, training schools, and mission board. National pastors have not been supported by mission funds since 1930.[6] An interdependent relationship exists between the mission and the church. The mission cooperates with the AIC churches in outreach to unevangelized areas, and in educational and other support ministries.

Dr. Anderson, international secretary, reported that for AIM's 85th year (1980) the mission set eighteen goals, ten of which were related to unreached people groups. Working closely with the AIC churches, The AIM helped: (1) to identify and prepare to evangelize unreached people throughout its areas of Africa, (2) to clarify in each country the needs for Bible teaching of believers and to decide how to satisfy them, (3) to accelerate Africanization of present AIM ministries, (4) to encourage cross-cultural African missions, (5) and to continue to provide scholarships for advanced theological training.[7]

Upon the retirement of Dr. Anderson in 1990, Dr. Fred Beam was elected to succeed him, with his office in Bristol, England.

On the North American scene, Peter Stam changed from Canadian director to U.S. director, serving from 1977 until his retirement in 1987. The current U.S. director is a third-generation AIM-er, Dr. Ted Barnett. An educator by profession, Dr. Barnett was nine years with BIOLA University and four years at Campus Crusade's International School of Theology before accepting this position with AIM.

In Canada, Rev. Frank Frew, former AIM Kenya leader, succeeded Peter Stam as Canadian director. He was followed by the current director, Dr. Gordon Dorey.

At the AIM bienniel international council meeting held in England in 1991, mission-wide ministry plans were once again updated. The council affirmed a commitment to place church-planting teams in 20 additional unreached people groups by 1995, AIM's 100th year. A goal of placing missionaries in 20 of Africa's needy urban areas was adopted, as well. It is recognized that, when met, these goals will only partially fill the existing needs in the 14 African countries in which AIM works. Surveys indicate 108 distinct ethnolinguistic groups in these fields not yet reached with the gospel by any evangelical church or mission.[8]

At the end of 1990, 656 of AIM's staff came from the United States and Canada: 456 career missionaries, 41 short-term, 82 summer and under one year, 60 home staff with missionary status, and 17 home staff without missionary status. Accepted candidates from the U. S. and Canada numbered 83—56 career and 27 short-term. Coming from other countries were 191 career and 9 short-term missionaries, bringing the total cross-cultural career missionaries to 647 and short-term to 50. They serve in Central African Republic, Chad, Comoro Islands, Kenya, Lesotho, Madagascar, Mozambique, Namibia, Reunion, Seychelle Islands, Sudan, Tanzania, Uganda, United States (Newark), and Zaire

Leaders of the Africa Inland Mission have participated in the work and meetings of the IFMA since its beginning. From 1917 to 1992, twelve North American AIM officials served on the IFMA board, six were officers and three—Henry Campbell, Ralph Davis, and Peter Stam—were president of the association. Dr. Ted Barnett was elected to the IFMA board in 1990.

## CENTRAL AMERICAN MISSION

(CAM International)

The Central American Mission was founded in 1890 by Cyrus Ingerson Scofield, the editor of the Scofield Reference Bible. Albert T. Platt, president of CAM International, noted, "Interesting that it was a biblicist with strong theological convictions who became concerned for the salvation of those in his Samaria. Dr. Scofield would be pleased to note that this has not changed in 90 years at CAM."[9] This strong emphasis on conservative evangelical theology, along with training and outreach throughout Central America and Spanish Europe, continues in CAM's second century.

Prayer had a prominent place in the beginning of the Central American Mission. Mrs. Robert Ross and Mrs. Robert Lang, wives of coffee plantation owners and discerning Christians, committed themselves to pray that God would send missionaries to their adopted land of Costa Rica. Although there was an English church in San Jose, which had been started by Scottish Presbyterians, Indian and Spanish-speaking areas were virtually unreached with the gospel.

During the 1880s, Dr. Scofield was pastor of the First Congregational Church of Dallas, Texas. For several summers, he attended the Niagara Bible Conference. The ministry of J. Hudson Taylor caused Dr. Scofield to study the importance of missions as seen throughout the Bible. In 1888 he became aware of the deep spiritual need of Costa Rica and shared his findings with a small group of dedicated men in his church, calling them into a prayer fellowship. Luther Rees made further study of the spiritual need in other Central American countries and found there was only a small Presbyterian work in Guatemala and a Moravian work in Nicaragua. Dr. Scofield became convinced that God would hold North Americans responsible for these in America's "Samaria" who were not being reached with the gospel.

Upon further inquiry, it was found that none of the existing mission boards were prepared to begin new work in Central America. Therefore, on November 14, 1890, in Dr. Scofield's home, the Central American Mission was organized. Mr. Rees was made chairman; Dr. Scofield, secretary; and two other laymen rounded out the initial council.[10]

From the beginning, CAM was characterized as evangelical, evangelistic, and nondenominational. The inspiration of Hudson Taylor is seen in the adoption of the faith basis for financial support.

Within four months of the initial published call for prayer for missionaries, the first ones—Mr. and Mrs. W. W. McConnell—were accepted and sailed for Costa Rica. They were welcomed joyfully in February 1891 by Mrs. Ross and Mrs. Lang as answers to prayer. By the end of the first decade, twenty-five CAM missionaries were at work in parts of four of the republics.

CAM has endeavored to give nationals prominent roles in the ministry. Mildred Spain wrote:

> It was Mr. Boyle's purpose to put into active service as many believers as possible, and even in these early days he made remarkable progress in the matter. A portion of a letter of June 1, 1896, from San Jose, gives the idea:
>
> "The work grows. The largest audience ever assembled here, 92 persons, was gathered Sunday night. One of our deacons preached a good sermon.
>
> "During Sunday, several of the brethren were out in the neighboring towns evangelizing.
>
> "The church is now entirely self-sustained. The members take turns at preaching and all expenses are paid and accounts are kept by them, through the deacons. I shall preach to the English-speaking people at 11 a.m. Sunday, and at 5 p.m. to the Jamaicans. Two weeks later, Mr. Boyle reported:
>
> "The meeting last Sunday gathered 100 souls. Senor Gongora, the national pastor, preached. He is suffering much persecution."[11]

After some thirty years, the results of evangelism and church-planting efforts brought about the beginning of educational and other supporting institutional ministries to assist the believers of the growing number of churches.

CAM missionaries have undertaken responsibility for Bible translation in several tribal languages. While still a CAM missionary, Cameron Townsend, founder of Wycliffe Bible Translators, began translating the New Testament into Cakchiquel. He started the Nimaya school for the Cakchiquels in 1919 and Robinson Bible Institute in 1923.

The churches took over the responsibility for the Christian elementary and secondary schools. The mission gave emphasis to the development of schools of theological education—in cooperation with the churches—in both Spanish and Indian languages. Besides Bible institutes, seminaries have been formed in Guatemala and Mexico.

Dr. Emelio Antonio Nunez of Central American Theological Seminary in Guatemala is one of the leading theologians in Latin America and is in demand as a speaker at international meetings. He is respected for his solid biblical exposition and clear conservative evangelical position.

Radio stations in Guatemala, Nicaragua, and El Salvador extend the evangelistic and discipling ministries of the mission and churches. Besides clinics operated by missionary nurses, CAM helped to establish a hospital and a school of nursing in Honduras.

A large printing and literature center was established in Puebla, Mexico, to provide materials for the churches. Bookstores and correspondence courses are used in various countries. The mission and churches have shown Christian love and compassion through participation in relief and rehabilitation projects following natural disasters.

Work in Panama was begun in 1944. Mexico was surveyed in 1955, and the first worker entered in 1956. In 1971 the mission expanded to Spain. The missionary team there was strengthened by a church leader from El Salvador who joined Central American Mission. After entering Spain, the mission name was changed to CAM International.

At the end of the 1970s, mission staff totaled 251 missionaries, serving in evangelism, church planting and development, educational, and support ministries.

National churches with which the mission is in partnership continue to multiply. The number of churches and congregations in the 6 Central American countries was 1,276.

The CAM board in 1981 approved opening the southwestern part of the United States as a field of ministry. Experienced field leaders, Jim and Cathy Paul, were asked to direct this work. New Orleans was recognized as part of CAM's North American field. Two couples were assigned to church planting among the city's 175,000 Spanish-speaking people. By 1989 the board had voted to expand to any place in the U. S. where a concentration of at least 100,000 Hispanics are located. Missionaries are provided upon the invitation of a sponsoring church.

The Central American Theological Seminary (CATS) has been training pastors and other Christian workers for more than sixty years. It held its first conference on worldwide missions in 1981. As outgrowth of that conference, CAM-related churches formed the Evangelical Missionary Agency. One of the non-Indian CATS graduates and his family are working as cross-cultural missionaries, doing Bible translation in the Chuj dialect. The complete Chuj Bible is expected to be completed by 1995.

The Evangelical Missionary Agency and the Africa Inland Mission agreed to a partnership arrangement to facilitate sending Central Americans to assist in evangelism and church development in Africa.

At the third CATS world missions conference in April 1991, Dr. Jonathan Chao, president of Christ's College in Taipei, Taiwan, presented the challenge of China. The conference was followed by a consultation on missionary training in the Third World. Toward the close of 1991, the transfer of CATS to a Guatemalan Christian association was completed after more than a decade of planning and work with churches and the Guatemala government.

In recognition of CAM's one hundred years of missionary service in Costa Rica in 1991, CAM-related churches sponsored two weeks of special services and events. One week was devoted to a world missions conference. Dr. Theodore Williams, a national missions leader from India and president of the World Evangelical Fellowship, was the featured international speaker.

CAM-related churches, known as *Iglesias Centroamericanas*, are affiliated internationally through biennial congresses, which bring together church and CAM leaders, along with large numbers of church members. The sessions, both inspirational and instructional, provide a forum for positive interchange of ideas geared to advancing and strengthening the ministry of the churches on the local, regional, national, and international levels.

At the end of 1990, CAM's staff totaled 258. They represented 189 career, 7 short-term, and 7 summer-and-under-one-year missionaries, 35 home staff with missionary status, and 20 without missionary status. There were 29 career and 3 short-term candidates that had been appointed to CAM's fields.

## CHINA INLAND MISSION

(Overseas Missionary Fellowship)

The work of Dr. Karl F. A. Gutzlaff in China interested many Europeans in the needs of inland China. His visit to England led to the formation in 1850 of an organization that became known as the Chinese Evangelization Society. Its purpose was to further the promulgation of the gospel in China by native evangelists. The goal was to send European missionaries to work in inland China, and, if possible, to serve alongside national workers.

At twenty-one years of age, James Hudson Taylor sailed for China on September 19, 1853. As CES' first English missionary, he worked for several years under its auspices. After a friendly separation from the mission, Taylor worked independently until health problems caused him to return to England at the end of 1860.

For two years prior to his return to England in 1860,

Hudson Taylor traveled with Rev. W. C. Burns in evangelistic work in several provinces. The experience convinced him that a special order of Chinese evangelists would be needed to reach the millions of China with the gospel.

Taylor reported that there were only ninety-seven Protestant missionaries in all of China in 1865, and these were all located in ten or eleven port cities. He became burdened for the souls of two hundred million Chinese in the inland provinces for whom nothing was being done. He urged his own mission, Chinese Evangelization Society, and other missions to move inland, but they all declined. They had neither men nor money for expansion.

Back in England, Hudson Taylor had an experience that changed his life, and led to his being known as the father of faith missions. J. Herbert Kane recorded Dr. Taylor's account, as follows:

> I had the growing conviction that God would have me seek from Him the needed workers, and go forth with them. But for a long time unbelief hindered my taking the first step. Yet what was I to do? The feeling of blood-guiltiness became more and more intense. Perishing China so filled my heart and mind that there was no rest by day and little sleep by night, till health broke down. On Sunday, June 25, 1865, unable to bear the sight of a congregation of a thousand or more Christian people (in Brighton, England) rejoicing in their own security while millions were perishing for lack of knowledge, I wandered out on the sands alone, in great spiritual agony; and there the Lord conquered my unbelief, and I surrendered myself for this service.[12]

Two days later, on June 27, 1865, Taylor received a check for ten pounds, and deposited it in a bank in the name of *China Inland Mission.* He then began to pray for twenty-four workers to go with him to China. On May 26, 1866,

Hudson Taylor, his wife, four children, and sixteen workers sailed for China on the *Lammermuir.* By the end of that year, twenty-four workers were settled in four central stations in China.

During the first 10 years of the mission, the number of missionaries reached 44, including wives. Stations were opened in 4 of the 13 provinces in which Hudson Taylor wanted to see work begun. In 10 more years, 7 other provinces had resident CIM missionaries. In 1885 alone, 40 new missionaries arrived. The following year the CIM had 152 missionaries, not including wives.

A well-rounded study program was prescribed for new missionaries. For six months, European and Chinese teachers gave careful instruction in the Chinese language. Other subjects studied included geography, government, etiquette of the country, phases of religious thought, and the best method of communicating the gospel to the people. After this, new missionaries were assigned to an inland station to continue their studies under the supervision of experienced missionaries, and to assist in gospel outreach as they were able. They followed a course of study divided into six sections, each one completed by an examination. At the end of two years, if satisfactory progress was made, they were assigned to assist an experienced district missionary. After five years, and passing all examinations, the missionary was given responsibility for a station or district.

Superintendents over a number of districts were chosen from missionaries with ten-to-thirty years experience. The superintendents formed the general council of the mission. Church planting in unreached areas remained the primary focus, involving a team ministry of foreign and Chinese workers. Some eighty-nine churches had been established by 1890.

Some 60 or 70 of the 380 missionaries in 1890 were either supported by their own private means, or received their support from special friends. They did not receive funds from the *pro rata* sharing from the general funds as the other missionaries.

Hudson Taylor and the general council were quite conscious of church polity differences and tried to cluster together missionaries who held similar views on church government.

The distinctive features of the CIM were stated as:

> First. Its interdenominational charter.
>
> Second. That the workers have no guaranteed salary, but trust in the God whom they serve to supply their needs, and are not disappointed in their trust.
>
> Third. That the direction of the work in the field is carried on, not by home committees, but by senior and experienced missionaries, who help and guide as they are able, those who have less experience in the Lord's work in China.
>
> Fourth. That no personal solicitation or collection of funds is made, voluntary contributions alone being received; to which we may add, that the names of donors are never published, but each one receives a dated and numbered receipt, by which he can trace his own contribution into the list of donations and hence into the annually published accounts of the mission.[13]

One hundred new workers sailed in 1887. In 1900 during the Boxer Rebellion, 58 missionaries and 21 children were killed. After this, another large influx of workers were received. The membership had grown to 1300 by 1929.[14] This was remarkable since there was a mass evacuation of inland China in 1927. Dr. Herbert Kane stated, "Missionary work in China, more than any other field, has been hindered by political unrest. Shortly after their arrival in China, the first contingent was almost wiped out."[15]

Unrest continued with one riot, uprising, revolution, or war after another until the Communist takeover in 1949. Mission orders were then given for the complete evacuation of all China Inland Mission personnel as local conditions permitted. The last of CIM's missionaries was finally evacuated in July 1953.

Missionaries were redeployed to other unreached areas of Asia. Permanent headquarters was set up in Singapore. By the end of 1955, mission membership totaled 552. Overseas Missionary Fellowship became its new name, and its publication, *China's Millions*, was changed to *East Asia Millions*. The emphasis on reaching out to unevangelized tribes and people continues.

The OMF opened its membership in 1965 to men and women of all nationalities and races. At the end of 1979, the mission reported an international staff of 777 missionaries, serving in Bangladesh, France, Hong Kong, Japan, Indonesia, Korea, Malaysia, Nepal, Philippines, Saipan, Singapore, Taiwan, and Thailand. In addition, there were 111 staff members with missionary status in the sending countries.

Dr. James Hudson Taylor III, a great grandson of CIM's founder, left his position as president of China Evangelical Seminary in Taiwan, to join OMF as general director in August 1980, the seventh in its history.

The priorities of OMF have been evangelism and church planting. It is still involved in educational ministries, medicine, Christian literature production and distribution, and other support ministries, including prayer conferences. A strong focus has been maintained on ministering to unreached people—refugees, professionals, industrial and other workers in the growing cities, slum dwellers, tribal people, students, and the Chinese.

A few months before entering the mission's 125th year, OMF's Central Council, meeting in September 1989, reviewed the current status of evangelization in Asia and called for churches in the West to make the evangelization of Asia their highest priority for the coming decade. The central council recommitted itself by covenanting to increase its efforts in the following ways:

1. To reach Asians wherever they are found, thinking ethnically rather than geographically
2. To recruit more Christian professionals for both creative-access and open-access nations
3. To place more missionaries in pioneer urban ministries
4. To cooperate with growing Asian churches in mobilization and training for local and a worldwide evangelization
5. To care for the uncared for

> In the face of this immense task and the second coming of Christ, our first call is to holiness, our general director has reminded us, a holiness that proclaims the uniqueness of Christ, submits to His Lordship, lives for His glory, and abandons all to fulfill His commission.[16]

Since OMF limits the term of its chief executive officer to age 60, James Taylor selected for his successor the OMF director of overseas ministry, David Pickard, who became the new general director on May 10, 1991. Dr. and Mrs. Taylor moved from Singapore to Hong Kong, and, as consulting directors for Chinese ministries, are supervising the OMF China program, the Pray-for-China Fellowship, radio and literature programs, and other church ministries to extend the mission's vision of the church in Hong Kong.

During the 1980s, the OMF strengthened its missionary force with Asian missionaries. By the end of the decade, 8.5 percent of its 1000 missionaries were Asians, serving in cross-cultural ministries in countries other than their own homelands.

In addition to its staff from other countries, at the close of 1990, the Overseas Missionary Fellowship had 408 people from Canada and the United States. They represented 309 career, 13 short-term, and 34 summer-and-under-one-year missionaries, and 52 home staff with missionary status.

From the beginning of IFMA in 1917, the China Inland

Mission/Overseas Missionary Fellowship has contributed considerable leadership to the association. Henry W. Frost was president for the first ten years of its existence. He was followed by Robert Hall Glover who was president for the next nine years and vice president for five, serving fourteen years altogether. Other CIM/OMF leaders who served as president of the association were Herbert M. Griffin, and J. Morris Rockness. George A. Southerland, Daniel W. Bacon, and David J. Michell each served as vice president. Ernest E. Heimbach was treasurer. Four others were on the board: E. A. Brownlee, Roger B. Whittlesey, H. E. V. Andrews, and William W. Tyler.

## INLAND SOUTH AMERICA MISSIONARY UNION

(South America Mission)

The British branch of the mission was founded by Scotsman John Hay in 1902 as the Paraguayan Evangelistic and Medical Mission. The first station was opened at Concepcion in the north of Paraguay.

As the work began to spread into Argentina and Brazil in 1904, the name was changed to Inland South America Missionary Union.[17] The work was difficult because of illiteracy and fanaticism of the Indians. Work began in the south in 1908 and response was greater, due in part to a greater density of population. An English soldier, who served in the area shortly before that time, stated:

> Of course, we know that they are uncivilized and savage and have never been taught a word about God and religion as we have; therefore, we ought to pity and, if possible, help them. Why don't some of the missionaries come out here? . . . I am sure that three or four missionaries a year would do more than ten regiments.[18]

According to 1910 statistics, the Inland South America Missionary Union had eight missionaries on the field.[19]

Statistics prepared for the 1916 Panama Congress showed that by 1915 four more missionaries had been added.[20]

Available records indicate that a meeting of the United States Council of the Inland South America Missionary Union was held in New York City on October 18, 1910. John Hay was recognized as founder and director of the mission. Three men from this group were a part of the IFMA organizational meeting in September 1917—Benjamin S. Stern, J. Davis Adams, and J. R. Schaffer who was elected secretary-treasurer.[21]

After giving up his law practice in Detroit, Joseph A. Davis traveled west. Professing to be an agnostic, he met some practicing Christian believers in California and was converted. A few years later, after his marriage, he pastored a church in Denver. Concerned for the Indians in South America, the Davis family went to Paraguay in 1914 to work among these unevangelized people. They called their work the Paraguayan Mission.

Joseph Davis and John Hay met in 1916 and realized they had a common evangelical emphasis and objectives. Their friendship led to the merging of the Paraguayan Mission into the Inland South America Missionary Union in 1919. Davis returned to the United States that year for family health reasons and became the American director of ISAMU. The board of directors voted to incorporate in the state of New York in 1921. The official date of the completed incorporation was November 10, 1922.

Bolivia was added as a field in 1922 and Peru in 1923. From the beginning, the work has been pioneer in nature. An objective is to present a clear gospel witness to the unreached Indian tribes and mixed-blood people, and to establish indigenous national churches.

When the first missionaries arrived, the Indians were still in their aboriginal state. A graphic first-hand account of the physical and spiritual difficulties faced in attempting to present the gospel to an unreached Indian tribe in Brazil was recorded by Mrs. Arthur F. Tylee in her book, *The*

*Challenge of Amazon's Indians.* This is the story of the first attempt to evangelize the Nhambiquara Indians during the years 1924 to 1930. The preliminary party was composed of Alexander Rattray Hay and Arthur F. Tylee of the Inland South America Missionary Union, and Leonard L. Legters of the Pioneer Mission Agency.

The tragic conclusion of the initial work among this tribe came in November 1930 when a group of the Indians visiting a remote mission station suddenly attacked the missionaries and their Brazilian helpers. Mr. Tylee, their young daughter and only child, nurse Mildred Kratz, and three Brazilian helpers were killed. Only Mrs. Tylee survived the attack.[22]

Work continued and has developed among the Indians throughout the past sixty years, in spite of the murders all the privations, isolation, and loneliness.

John and Alexander Hay, along with the Canadian and British missionaries, withdrew from the mission in 1932 to form the New Testament Missionary Union.

In 1934 the Inland South America Missionary Union began work among Indian tribes in Colombia. The mission name was changed to South America Indian Mission, and by 1939 the American headquarters had moved from New York to Florida.

In addition to the pioneering evangelistic and church-planting work, gospel day schools, Bible institutes, medical, and literature work are emphasized.

General Director Joseph A. Davis participated actively in the affairs of the IFMA. He was elected to the board of directors, and served as president of the association. After his death in 1958, G. Hunter Norwood, Jr., was named general director. In 1970 the word *Indian* was dropped from the name of the mission, and it became South America Mission to better reflect the increased scope of ministry.

Robert D. Anderson, who served in Peru in Indian work and as director of a Bible institute, was placed on loan to serve as general secretary of the *Concilio Nacional Evangelico del Peru* 1968-1970. Anderson succeeded Hunter Norwood as general director of the mission in 1984. He has served on the IFMA board almost continuously since 1972.

To assist in the outreach to Indian tribes, SAM developed its own aviation division—SAMAIR. Indian churches related to SAM have grown in their missionary vision for unreached tribes. SAM assists by providing transportation for national missionaries and supplies to more remote tribal areas. The mission provides training programs for prospective national missionaries to supplement the Bible institute curriculum.

Church-planting schools, such as the two-year program at SAM's Urban Training Center in Bolivia, are producing new indigenous congregations in urban areas. Partnership with the existing evangelical churches is a significant focus of SAM ministry.

At the end of 1990, South America Mission had a staff from Canada and the United States of 148, which included 106 career and 18 summer-and-under-one-year missionaries, 18 home staff with missionary status, and 6 home staff without missionary status. In addition to these, 18 career and 6 short-term candidates had been appointed by the board and were in their final preparation before leaving for their fields of service.

## SOUTH AFRICA GENERAL MISSION

(Africa Evangelical Fellowship)

The founding of the South Africa General Mission came from God's working in the hearts of several people. As with the majority of nondenominational faith missions, it was born through prayer. A young soldier, who was passing through Cape Town, South Africa, was so stirred by the appalling conditions existing near the military camps that he wrote a strong letter to the editor of a periodical. The challenge of his letter was met by two responses from different areas of the world.

One response came from George B. Howe, whose health had been impaired by the fevers and privations of military campaigns in Zululand. He went to Cape Town and opened a home in 1880 to which he could invite soldiers. Being familiar with the temptations peculiar to military life, Mr. Howe sought to help them withstand "by introducing them to a new Captain under Whom they were invited to serve."[23]

The other response came from England, where Mrs. Martha S. Osborn, widow of a major general that had served in India, read the soldier's letter. For about two years while she was still in India, Mrs. Osborn read the Bible. She attributed her conversion to that experience. After leave in England, her health did not permit her to return to India with her husband who had about a year left before his retirement.

Mrs. Osborn was a counselor during the London Moody-Sankey meetings in 1875. After that experience, she had a deep desire to serve the Lord, and was looking to Him for direction regarding a life ministry.

Following General Osborn's completion of his tour of duty, he returned to England with an incurable disease. After his death, Mrs. Osborn started a rescue mission in a rented stable, which became known as "The Drunkard's Church." While involved in this ministry, she read the soldier's letter that graphically portrayed the conditions in South Africa, the land of her birth. It seemed to confirm a missionary call to her to return to that country. She wrote to her father who still lived there, and he confirmed the evil conditions that existed.

Arriving in Cape Town, Mrs. Osborn learned of the work of Mr. Howe and joined forces with him. The work developed with several homes opened for soldiers and sailors, a work for business girls, and other ministries as personnel became available. For spiritual fellowship and advice, Mr. Howe and Mrs. Osborn turned to Dr. Andrew Murray.

A well-respected minister of the Dutch Reformed Church of South Africa, Dr. Murray had found a group of intercessors in an early pastorate through whom he had been impressed with a sense of urgency for the evangelization of the Africans. Thus, he gave his support to worthy missionary projects. In addition to writing devotional books for which he is well known, Dr. Murray was a prominent conference speaker. At the Keswick Convention in England, he met William Spencer Walton, who was a prominent evangelist and hymn writer. One of his hymns is "In Tenderness He Sought Me."

On his return to Cape Town, Dr. Murray recommended that Mr. Howe and Mrs. Osborn invite Mr. Walton to join them for a special evangelistic campaign. After some time of daily prayer, it was decided that Mrs. Osborn should go to England to extend a personal invitation to Mr. Walton. She also made some contacts for the future of the work in South Africa while she was there. In order to interest friends and to solicit prayer for the special campaigns, she started a quarterly magazine in October 1886, which became the SAGM's *South African Pioneer.*

Spencer Walton arrived in Cape Town in 1888 to a welcome by Dr. Murray, Mr. Howe, Mrs. Osborn, local ministers, and Christian leaders. In Cape Town the meetings had to be moved twice to larger buildings. The meetings moved from Cape Town to other towns. Some 500 converts were recorded throughout South Africa. After 4 months, Walton returned to England, but it was agreed that his ministry should continue in South Africa. With the encouragement of Dr. Murray, Mr. Howe and Mrs. Osborn asked Walton to return to direct the work they had begun.

Mr. Walton decided to form a mission if Dr. Murray would serve as president. On his way back to England, much time was spent in prayer over a large map of Africa. Swaziland, in particular, claimed his attention. In England, Walton consulted with J. Hudson Taylor, F. B. Meyer, and others. He enlisted the support of Christian leaders willing to serve as council members. The mission was legally organized on March 12, 1889 as the Cape General Mission.

Mr. Walton returned to South Africa in September with five young men for the work. Toward the end of the month, Mrs. Osborn signed over to Walton the ministries and assets of the work she had started in Cape Town.

The first station in Swaziland was opened in June 1891. Two years later, three more stations were opened. By this time, Mr. Howe and Mrs. Osborn had been married in London in 1890, and had left the Cape General Mission to begin a work in Zululand, which was called the Southeast Africa Evangelistic Mission. In January 1894, the two missions joined to form the South Africa General Mission.

The work continued to grow with stations added in Angola, Mozambique, Nyasaland, and Northern and Southern Rhodesia, in addition to Swaziland and the Union of South Africa. Councils were formed in England, the United States, Canada, and Cape Town. Dr. Murray remained president until his death in 1917. As executive director, Mr. Walton traveled extensively on behalf of the mission, not only in Africa and the British Isles, but in North America, as well. His leadership was cut short in 1906 by his death, following an appendectomy.

From the beginning, the SAGM was international, nondenominational, and evangelistic in character. The work was definitely influenced by Dr. Andrew Murray who was theologically conservative. He was moderator of the South African Dutch Reformed Church six times and led the opposition to liberalism in that church. Dr. Murray was the motivator for the missionary awakening of his denomination.[24]

In the early days, the work was primarily itinerant preaching, Scripture translation, Christian training and educating young people, Bible training for Christian workers, Bible conferences, and medical clinics. These ministries produced many churches throughout southern Africa.

The SAGM was incorporated in the United States in 1910. William H. Hendrickson served as secretary from its beginning in North America until his death in December 1920. He was succeeded by Arthur J. Bowen.

Both Hendrickson and Bowen attended the preliminary meeting on March 31, 1917 that led to the founding of IFMA. Until his death, Mr. Hendrickson was active in IFMA meetings and a member of the board.

At the end of 1947, Mr. Bowen retired and in January 1948 Ezra A. Shank was elected home director for the United States. The title was later changed to executive director.

Mr. Bowen and Mr. Shank were active members of the IFMA Board and served terms as president of the association. Robert Fine was a member of the board at the time of his death in 1981.

Since Mr. Shank's retirement in 1967, others who have served as executive director are Dr. Robert L. Foster, 1967-1969; Dr. Terry Hulbert, 1970-1971; Mr. Allan A. Habbick, 1972; Dr. David Stone, associate executive director 1973-1974; Rev. Robert Fine, associate executive director 1973-1974, executive director 1974-1981; Rev. Philip Gammon, September 1982 - July 1985; Mr. Bjarne Nyborg (interim), September 1985 - September 1986; Dr. Geoffrey Griffith since October 1986.

Because the mission had expanded its work into countries other than the Republic of South Africa, the name of the mission was changed to Africa Evangelical Fellowship in 1964. In addition to its evangelism, church planting and development, the mission has established Bible institutes, teacher-training institutes, high schools, hospitals, leper colonies, work among the blind, and other ministries.

The AEF continues to advance into new areas in southern Africa, as the Lord provides workers. At the 1987 international council meeting, the mission approved entry into southern Tanzania to work among the Makonde people in cooperation with the Africa Inland Church and the Africa Inland Mission. At the invitation of existing evangelical churches and groups, reentry into Madagascar was worked out. Outreach to Muslims and the Makua people were included in AEF's focus on unreached people groups.

Centennial celebrations and special meetings were held

in South Africa and sending countries during 1989, praising God for the churches that have been raised up throughout AEF's 100 years of ministry. There has been a recommitment to the mission's outreach and discipling purpose and objectives, working toward the fulfillment of the great commission.

At December 31, 1990, AEF had staff from Canada and the United States totaling 260 people. These represented 182 career, 4 short-term, and 45 summer-and-under-one-year missionaries; 20 home staff with missionary status; and 9 home staff without missionary status. The board had appointed 1 short-term and 48 career missionary candidates who were in their final preparation for leaving for their fields.

Africa Evangelical Fellowship was working in 13 countries or islands at the close of 1991, and had called for at least 350 additional workers.

## SUDAN INTERIOR MISSION
(SIM)

Walter Gowans, Roland Bingham, and Thomas Kent—concerned with the spiritual needs of the people of the "Soudan"—went to Africa in 1893 as independent missionaries because they could not interest any mission society in the Sudan. It was then one of the world's largest totally unevangelized areas, without a resident missionary among its estimated 60-to-90-million people.[25]

Calling themselves the Soudan Interior Mission, Gowans, Bingham, and Kent expected to set up a base on the shores of Lake Chad. However, in Lagos, Nigeria, they were refused inland passage by the Royal Niger Company. Gowans and Kent started out on an overland trip to Kano, enroute to Lake Chad. Bingham was to supervise their supply line, since he was too ill for such travel in the interior toward their goal, the "Soudan." By the end of 1894, both Gowans and Kent had died, and within six more months Bingham had to return to Canada because of illness and lack of co-workers. There was no board or council behind them at that time.

Bingham organized the Africa Industrial Mission in 1896. The plan was to propagate the gospel by means of self-supporting missionary colonies, which would start African-operated agricultural and handicraft projects. The first North American council was formed by Mr. Bingham in May 1898 in Toronto.

With two companions, Bingham again sailed for Nigeria in 1900, but, because of illness, this attempt also was unsuccessful. The next attempt by four pioneer missionaries sent out by Bingham and the mission council resulted in establishing the first station at Patigi, Nigeria, in April 1902. A new station was opened in each of the next two years.

In order to emphasize its purpose, the name of the mission was changed in 1905 to Africa Evangelistic Mission. In 1907, the name became Sudan Interior Mission.

By 1923 the SIM had 72 missionaries in Nigeria, making it the second largest mission in the country. The Church Missionary Society of Britain had 87 missionaries at that time.[26] The SIM reported that 35 self-supporting churches and 12 additional regular preaching points had been established. They were ministering to a Christian community of some 6,000 people.[27]

SIM entered Niger in 1924, and in 1927 work was begun in Ethiopia. Mr. Bingham ministered in Australia and New Zealand in the mid-1920s, and councils were established in those countries. Because of the time and expense required for missionaries from "down under" to travel to West Africa, Bingham was considering the possibility of a field in East Africa. Upon learning of the organization of the new Abyssinian Frontiers Mission by experienced missionaries—Tom Lambie, M.D.; George Rhoad; and Alfred Buxton—he contacted them, and a merger was effected in 1927 that was beneficial to both missions. By the end of the year, SIM's first nine missionaries in Ethiopia had arrived with all financial needs met for the new undertaking.[28]

One of the first tribes to be contacted in southern Ethiopia was the Wallamo (Wolayta). In 1928 there was not a single known believer. Nine years later, when the missionaries were all expelled by the invading Italian army, there was one organized church of 48 believers. The church leadership was only minimally grounded in the Scriptures. Illiteracy abounded and the full Bible was not available to them. After 5 years, when the first SIM personnel were able to re-enter Ethiopia, the church was found to be amazingly alive and reproductive. One church had multiplied to 100 churches. Forty-eight believers had multiplied to 10,000.[29] Missionaries were warmly welcomed by the church that had grown during severe persecution.

The SIM opened work in Upper Volta in 1930 and in the Republic of Sudan in 1936.

While the work of the mission has continued to extend its outreach and ministries, the real strength of the SIM ministry is seen in the strong national churches that have developed and grown at a rate greater than that of the mission. The Evangelical Churches of West Africa (ECWA) was organized in 1954 and was officially recognized by the Nigerian government in 1957. SIM missionaries in Nigeria work under the direction of the national church. The working relationship between ECWA and SIM is a good model of partnership. Such a dynamic relationship requires continuous interdependent interaction between the leaders of both groups.

Throughout its history, SIM has been nondenominational, evangelical, and international. Financial support has been secured on a faith basis by freewill contributions. Ministry includes evangelism, literature, radio, and education. Extensive medical work, relief, and development projects have been carried on, as well. Books could be written on each of these ministries, such as the Kano (Nigeria) Eye Hospital, the leprosy and other medical ministries, *African Challenge* magazine, radio station ELWA in Monrovia, Liberia, the SIMAIR aviation ministry, publishing, bookstores, and correspondence ministries.

In spite of the withdrawal or curtailment of the missionary force from SIM's two largest fields of Nigeria and Ethiopia, at the end of 1980 the mission recorded 1,187 members. General Director Ian M. Hay noted, "SIM has about the same number of missionaries now as it had 15 years ago, but the church has nearly tripled. In terms of achieving our goal, the gifts and prayers and involvement of God's people are bringing greater returns than ever."[30]

Not only have the churches grown, particularly in Nigeria and Ethiopia, but the outreach of ECWA churches continues to expand under its own mission board, the Evangelical Missionary Society. Harold Fuller wrote:

> The number of EMS missionaries has steadily increased, until in 1979 there were 130 couples, or 260 missionaries, counting husband and wife. Since 1950, more than 300 missionaries have been sent out, serving in 50 distinct language groups. The ECWA church base for this operation numbers 1,400 local congregations, but many of them are small subsistence-level groups.[31]

ECWA takes its responsibilities for cross-cultural and local evangelism seriously. Dr. Fuller further stated:

> When her leaders accepted the challenge of the Nigerian Congress on Evangelization to reach everyone in Nigeria with the gospel in a two-year period, they calculated they would need 150 evangelists for their part. They mobilized 50 vernacular Bible school seniors to start with. For the remainder they called on 100 churches to release their pastors for a one-year "sabbatical" to evangelize unreached people.[32]

When asked who would support them, ECWA leaders said let the churches continue their salaries, and let the elders and deacons pastor the churches while they are away. Toward the end of the 1980s, the EMS had some

800 Nigerians in missionary service.

The decade of the 1980s was a time of profound change for SIM. Two successful international mission mergers were accomplished. The Andes Evangelical Mission, with 66 missionaries, became SIM's South America field on January 1, 1982. The merger with International Christian Fellowship on January 1, 1989 added 153 missionaries and Asia as a field. The ministries and number of missionary staff in South America and Asia have grown significantly since the mergers.

After the merger with Andes Evangelical Mission in 1982, the mission's name was changed from Sudan Interior Mission to SIM International. When it merged with International Christian Fellowship and became a worldwide society, in terms of both sending and receiving countries, its name was changed again. In 1991 the *official* name became SIM. However, in cases where further definition is necessary, the board approved the use of Society for International Ministries.

The Evangel Fellowship is the association of churches related to SIM around the world. The fellowship represents more than 7,000 congregations and 3,000,000 people in 13 national church fellowships in Africa, Asia, and Latin America. Mission outreach was the major emphasis of the Evangel Fellowship meeting in Ethiopia in 1989.

SIM is seeking to increase its staff by 7 percent a year to help to meet the needs it has in its fields. Wars, political unrest, and natural disasters of famine and floods have caused grave problems for both missionaries and national believers. In spite of these, the church continues to grow.

The internationalizing of SIM grew in this decade, not just through mergers, but also through churches and missions in Asia channeling their missionaries to SIM. The mission has entered a number of unreached people groups in cooperation with national churches.

SIM became a partner, along with Far East Broadcasting Company, Trans World Radio, and World Radio Missionary

Fellowship (HCJB), in the missionary radio cooperative, The World by 2000. Begun in September 1985, their joint statement of intent declared:

> We are committed to provide every man, woman, and child on earth the opportunity to turn on their radio and hear the gospel of Jesus Christ in a language they can understand so they can become followers of Christ and responsible members of His Church. We plan to complete this task by the year 2000.

Since the beginning of the IFMA, the Sudan Interior Mission has been prominent in its leadership. General Directors Rowland V. Bingham, Guy Playfair, Raymond Davis, and Ian Hay, as well as U. S. and Canadian Directors M. A. Darroch, W. J. Trevor Ardill, Jack Phillips, and Larry Fehl have served on the IFMA Board. Davis and Hay served, also, as president of the association. Referring to the office of president of IFMA, Ezra Shank wrote, "This is an honor bestowed upon few men and bespeaks the trustworthiness and statesmanship of the person chosen to this highest position in the missionary enterprise."[33]

SIM reported that at the end of December 1990 its staff from Canada and the United States numbered 969, representing 613 career missionaries, 141 summer-and-under-one-year missionaries, 168 home staff with missionary status, and 47 home staff without missionary status. Additional staff coming from other countries were 367 career and 22 short-term missionaries. The number of accepted candidates reported were 120 career and 3 short-term from North America; and 26 career and 4 short-term from other countries. These candidates were in their final stages of preparation before leaving for their fields.

As of December 31, 1991, the worldwide SIM missionary family was 1,950, made up of 1,785 career missionaries, 165 short-term and associate missionaries, and 529 retired.

## WOMAN'S UNION MISSIONARY SOCIETY

(Merged into InterServe)

One of the factors leading to the significant involvement of single women in the missions movement was the concern of women to reach other women for Christ. It was the social systems of the East—primarily the *purdah*, the *zenana*, and the harem, which isolated women—that aroused Christian women of the West to carry the gospel where, without women, it could not be taken. Many women of Asia were inaccessible to a Christian witness by male missionaries. Missionary wives did what they could, but because of heavy responsibilities for their own families during the nineteenth century in foreign lands, most had little or no time for ministry. The denominational boards would not send single women because of travel conditions and other hazards.

While on his way home to America from Asia in 1834, missionary David Abeel of the American Board, challenged the people of England concerning the condition of women in China and India. He brought the same appeal to America, urging that single ladies volunteer for service, and that women of the church organize to support them. It was a revolutionary concept.

There was an immediate response in Great Britain, with women of various denominations forming in 1834 the Committee for the Promotion of Female Education in the East. In 1852 the Indian Female Normal School and Instruction Society was organized. The 1891 *Encyclopaedia of Missions* states that the society originated within the Church of England and was supported both by its members and a "nonconformist constituency." On the field, it cooperated with all orthodox missionary societies.[34]

There was a division in this mission in 1880. One group became the Church of England Zenana Missionary Society, and the other became the Zenana Bible and Medical Mission. The church in India and Pakistan asked the Zenana

Bible and Medical Mission in 1952 to send out men as well as women. Because of the inclusion of men as missionaries, the name was changed in 1957 to Bible and Medical Missionary Fellowship. In 1979 it became BMMF International; and in 1986 it was changed to International Service Fellowship, commonly known as InterServe.

Mrs. Thomas C. Doremus heard David Abeel in 1834 call for single women to minister to women and girls in the Orient. Although she was a prominent Christian and influential in New York, she could not persuade the denominational boards to send out single women. For twenty-five years, Mrs. Doremus led the crusade on behalf of the women of the Orient. Dr. Herbert Kane recorded that after years of failure and frustration, this tenacious little woman approached those gentlemen for the last time. Meeting with the same response, she rose with determination, flounced her large hoop skirt, and with great dignity announced, "If you men won't do it, we will!"[35]

In 1860, while on furlough, Baptist missionary Ellen Bullard Mason (Mrs. Francis Mason) spoke in Boston, New York, and Philadelphia, calling for the formation of a women's society to commission and support single ladies who could give their full time to the evangelization and education of women and children.

Responding to this challenge, on November 16, 1860, nine women in Boston, most of whom were from Baptist churches, organized The Society for the Promotion of Female Education in the East. A year later this group merged with a similar society in New York, which had been organized on January 15, 1861 by a group led by Mrs. Doremus and Mrs. Mason. The new organization was named the Woman's Union Missionary Society of America for Heathen Lands. Mrs. Doremus was its first president, serving until her death in 1877.

Sarah Haines Doremus was born August 2, 1802 in New York City, the second of seven children. She was married in 1821 to Thomas C. Doremus, a wealthy dry-goods merchant.

Formerly a Presbyterian, Sarah Doremus joined her husband's church, the South Dutch Reformed Church in New York City.

The Doremus home was always open to missionaries of different denominations. Although frail of health, Mrs. Doremus was well organized and was involved in many missionary and charitable organizations, often as president. These included a support committee for Greek women oppressed by the Turks; a society in support of a women's mission at Grand Ligne, Canada; New York Female Bible Society; the Charitable Women's House and School of Industry; the first Woman's Hospital; the Presbyterian Home for Aged Women; and the Gould Memorial for Italo-American Schools. She taught Sunday school and Bible classes in her church, ministered to soldiers during the Civil War, and was a good wife and mother to nine children.

Sarah Doremus never forgot the appeal of David Abeel in 1834 on behalf of the women of the East. At a meeting on January 9, 1961, the report by Mrs. Mason of the continuing need galvanized Mrs. Doremus and the women meeting under her leadership to organize a "woman's mission to women" one week later. By unanimous consent, Mrs. Doremus was elected president; Miss Sarah D. Doremus, secretary, and Mrs. Richard L. Wyckoff, treasurer. Board members and collectors were elected, as well.

The mission was to be "an independent undenominational society of women with a management of unsalaried officers (in this country) to send out single women, untrammeled by family cares, to Christianize heathen women who can not be reached by men missionaries."[36]

On January 15, 1861 at the new mission's second meeting, a constitution and bylaws was adopted. The next month—on February18—the first missionary candidate, a Miss Kay, was accepted as a worker for Burma. At the March 18 meeting, the first children's mission band and their gift of $20.00 was reported by Mrs. S. E. Warner, a member of the Clinton Avenue Congregational Church of Brooklyn.

The purpose of the new society as stated in the constitution was to provide an organization through "which women of all evangelical denominations may work together efficiently, by distinct voluntary effort for the salvation of their perishing sisters."[37]

From its beginning, the basis of WUMS was nondenominational. The organizing members came from six denominations—Baptist, Congregational, Dutch Reformed, Episcopal, Methodist, and Presbyterian. It proposed to send out single ladies only. Converts through their ministry would unite with existing churches. The society endeavored to be a helper to many churches, rather than to establish churches.

Financially, the original plan which WUMS followed had 100 women serving as collectors to receive contributions from the groups of interested women, or auxiliaries. By 1890 the support groups had grown to 26 auxiliaries and 178 bands in 15 states and the Canadian province of New Brunswick. During that year over $60,000.00 was collected, and the missionary force had reached 63. In addition to its missionaries from North America, WUMS had a large full-time national staff of Christian doctors, nurses, teachers, and evangelists.

The Woman's Union Missionary Society had an impressive list of "firsts." The *first* single missionary to Burma, Miss Sarah H. Marston from South Baptist Church in Boston, sailed on November 24, 1861 and opened the *first* school for Burmese girls.

Miss Harriet G. Brittan, an Episcopalian, had gone to Africa as a missionary in 1854, but had to leave due to recurring fever. After returning to America, she became associated with the Woman's Union Missionary Society and left for Calcutta on July 1, 1863, the *first* single American missionary to the *zenanas* (women's quarters) in India. She began a program of teaching secluded women to read, along with a simple presentation of the gospel, and directed a dozen or more Indian and Anglo-Indian Christian teachers who visited and taught in the *zenanas*.

An orphanage was opened where many girls came to Christ and were educated. WUMS also opened the *first* day school for girls in Calcutta, which earned the highest reputation for scholarship and Christian culture. Many graduates became doctors and teachers. For almost 75 years, the Calcutta work prospered from the educational and evangelistic foundation laid down by the organizing genius of Miss Brittan.[38] The work was turned over to another society in 1938, since it was isolated from WUMS stations up country and in another language area.

*Zenana* teaching among Muslims and Hindus in India began in Allahabad in 1868. Central Girls School was the *first* Christian school for high caste girls in the city. Later other cities were entered—Cawnpur (Kanpur) Jhansi, and Fatehpur. Ministries included day and boarding schools, hospitals, a nurses' training school, a nursery for babies, a rescue home for girls, and a Bible school.

The work opened in China in 1869 in Peking when WUMS began the *first* day and boarding school for girls. Missionary nurse Elizabeth McKechnie was the *first* nurse to enter China. The Margaret Williamson Hospital, built in Shanghai in 1883, was the *first* hospital for women. Dr. Kane, who served with CIM in China, wrote:

> For seventy years this efficient hospital, staffed entirely by women doctors and nurses, has never closed its doors. Through the dreadful ordeals of the Boxer Year, the revolutions of 1911 and 1927, the Sino-Japanese War, and now the Red Revolution, these valiant women have stayed by their posts in the face of personal danger to succor their more needy sisters—the womenfolk of China.[39]

WUMS cooperated with two other women's boards to organize in 1920 a school of nursing and a medical school for women.

Missionaries had to withdraw from China in 1950,

leaving their Chinese doctor and nurse colleagues to carry on alone.

WUMS missionaries entered Japan in 1871 and opened the Doremus School for Girls, the *first* girls' boarding school for women in Japan. A Bible school was begun in 1883 from which hundreds of young women went with the Christian message to all parts of Japan, Formosa (Taiwan), Korea, Manchuria, and China.

The last field WUMS entered was Nepal. Two WUMS nurses began working there in 1967 in affiliation with the United Mission to Nepal.

Up to the time of the merger in 1976, WUMS continued its work in Japan, India, and Pakistan. Although turned over to Japanese, WUMS was involved in teaching at the 1200-girl school in Yokohama that it had founded. WUMS continued to operate the Bible training school for women, also in Yokohama. The work in India was primarily in the United Provinces. The mission had a Bible training school for women at Allahabad; two hospitals—at Jhansi and Fatephur; orphanages, schools, and day schools in Fatephur and Kanpur. Work in India also included dispensaries, and zenana work among Hindus. WUMS work in Pakistan was in Multan where it operated a women's and children's hospital, and carried on some *zenana* work among Muslims.

WUMS' name was changed in 1911, deleting "for Heathen Lands." At its 110th Anniversary Meeting on January 29, 1971, another name change was announced, from Woman's Union Missionary Society of America to United Fellowship for Christian Service, in order to attract male missionaries. Another departure was the addition of men to the board. Five years later—on January 1, 1976—UFCS was merged into the Bible and Medical Missionary Fellowship (BMMF), now InterServe, combining the ministries of two of the oldest missions in the IFMA. The impetus for organizing both of these agencies had come from the appeal by David Abeel in 1834.

From the beginning of the IFMA, representatives of

WUMS were active in the affairs of the association. WUMS had two representatives at the September 1917 organizational meeting. Miss Clara E. Masters, who was at that meeting, represented WUMS from 1917 to 1933, serving for a number of years on the IFMA Board. WUMS President Elizabeth Jaderquist Paddon (Mrs. Wallace Paddon) represented the mission from 1950 until her death in 1968. She, too, served on the IFMA board. Her sister, Mrs. Helen Jaderquist Tenney, was a WUMS delegate to the IFMA Annual meetings, as well as to the IFMA/EFMA-sponsored 1966 Congress on the Church's Worldwide Mission.

InterServe, into which WUMS merged, reported at the end of 1990 a staff of 104 coming from Canada and the United States. They represent 72 career, 4 short-term, 8 summer-and-under-one-year missionaries, 4 home staff with missionary status, and 14 home staff without missionary status. The mission draws additional missionaries from Europe, Australia, and New Zealand, as well.

## NOTES

[1] Catherine S. Miller, *Peter Cameron Scott* (London: Perry Jackson Limited, 1955), p. 25.

[2] Ralph T. Davis, "Africa Inland Mission," in *The Encyclopedia of Modern Christian Missions*, gen. ed. Burton L. Goddard (Camden, NJ: Thomas Nelson & Sons, 1967), p. 5.

[3] James S. Dennis, Harlan P. Beach, and Charles F. Fahs, eds., *World Atlas of Christian Missions* (New York: Student Volunteer Movement for Foreign Missions, 1911), p. 96.

[4] Foreign Missions Conference, "Statistics of Protestant Foreign Missionary Societies of the United States and Canada, 1915-1916," *The Missionary Review of the World* January-December 1917, pp. 88-89.

[5] Charles E. Hurlburt, "Annual Report," *Inland Africa*, October 1919, p. 3.

[6] Davis, "Africa Inland Mission," in *The Encyclopedia of Modern Christian Missions*, p. 6.

[7] R. J. D. Anderson, "Eighteen Goals in Eighteen Months," *Inland Africa*, January-March 1980, p. 3.

[8] "AIM's International Council Focuses Vision for Future," *AIM International*, Summer 1991 (Pearl River, NY: Africa Inland Mission), p. 8.

[9] Albert T. Platt, "Still at It," *CAM Bulletin*, Fall 1980, p. 3.

[10] Mildred W. Spain, *And In Samaria*, rev. and ext. (Dallas: The Central American Mission, 1954), p. 9.

[11] Ibid., p. 26.

[12] J. Herbert Kane, *Faith Mighty Faith* (New York: Interdenominational Foreign Mission Association, 1956), p. 45.

[13] Edwin Munsell Bliss, ed., *The Encyclopaedia of Missions*, vol. 1 (New York: Funk & Wagnalls, 1891), p. 275.

[14] Arthur F. Glasser, "Overseas Missionary Fellowship," in *The Encyclopedia of Modern Christian Missions*, gen. ed. Burton L. Goddard (Camden, NJ: Thomas Nelson & Sons, 1967), p. 521.

[15] Kane, *Faith Mighty Faith*, p. 26.

[16] "OMF Covenants to Increase Its Efforts," *East Asia's Millions*, January/February 1990, p. 307.

[17] Alexander Rattray Hay, "New Testament Missionary Union," in *The Encyclopedia of Modern Christian Missions*, gen. ed. Burton L. Goddard (Camden, NJ: Thomas Nelson & Sons, 1967), p. 478.

[18] Homer C. Stuntz, *South American Neighbors* (New York: Missionary Education Movement of the United States and Canada, 1916), pp. 89-90.

[19] Dennis, Beach, and Fahs, eds., *World Atlas of Christian Missions*, p. 97.

[20] Stuntz, *South American Neighbors*, pp. 202-04.

[21] General Director of South America Mission G. Hunter Norwood, Jr., telephone interview by author, 5 March 1981.

[22] Mrs. Arthur F. Tylee, *The Challenge of Amazon's Indians* (Chicago: Moody Press, 1931), pp. 86-91.

[23] Ezra A. Shank, *Fervent in Spirit: The Biography of Arthur J. Bowen* (Chicago: Moody Press, 1954), p. 138.

[24] D. G. L. Cragg, "Murray, Andrew 1827-1917," in *The New International Dictionary of the Christian Church*, gen. ed. J. D. Douglas (Grand Rapids: Zondervan Publishing House, 1974), p. 685.

[25] Kerry Lovering, "Sudan Interior Mission," in *The Encyclopedia of Modern Christian Missions*, gen. ed. Burton L. Goddard (Camden, NJ: Thomas Nelson & Sons, 1967), p. 616.

[26] Harlan P. Beach and Charles H. Fahs, eds., *World Missionary Atlas* (New York: Institute of Social and Religious Research, 1925), p. 88.

[27] Ibid., p. 109.

[28] Rowland V. Bingham, *Seven Sevens of Years and A Jubilee: The Story of the Sudan Interior Mission* (Toronto: Evangelical Publishers, 1943), p. 81.

[29] Raymond J. Davis, *Fire on the Mountains*,(Grand Rapids: Zondervan Publishing House, 1966), p. 109.

[30] Ian M. Hay, "How to Measure a Mission," *Africa Now*, November-December 1980, p. 11.

[31] W. Harold Fuller, *Mission-Church Dynamics* (Pasadena: William Carey Library, 1980), p. 236.

[32] Ibid., pp. 240-41.

[33] Shank, *Fervent in Spirit*, pp. 171-72.

[34] Edwin Munsell Bliss, ed., *The Encyclopaedia of Missions*, vol 2, p. 491.

[35] Kane, *Faith Mighty Faith*, p. 157.

[36] Helen Jaderquist Tenney, "No Higher Honor," Folder 1, Box 2, Collection 44, Billy Graham Center Archives, Wheaton, Illinois, p. 18.

[37] Ibid., p. 20.

[38] Helen J. Tenney, "Woman's Union Missionary Society of America," in *The Encyclopedia of Modern Christian Missions*, gen. ed. Burton L. Goddard (Camden, NJ: Thomas Nelson & Sons, 1967), p. 693.

[39] Kane, *Faith Mighty Faith*, p. 160.

# 8

# IFMA DEVELOPMENT 1920-1949

Within the original purposes of the Interdenominational Foreign Mission Association were fellowship and learning from each other. The association would provide a place for mutual help and a united testimony. It was soon evident, however, that in matters of common interest and concern to the ten member missions, it was best if they could be considered and dealt with collectively. One of the first instances recorded was in 1919 when the association approached the Secretary of State's office to secure permission for American missionaries to land in various countries by making arrangements directly through consular offices in Washington.

## 1920-1929

The decade of the twenties was significant in the development of the association. In many ways, the IFMA was molded in its outreach and ministry during these years. The need for closer cooperation of nondenominational missions was recognized. This was reflected in three questions discussed at a special IFMA meeting in New York on June 24, 1921. They were:

1. What are the present-day needs that call for close cooperation of the faith missions with each other?

2. Can the organization and work of the Interdenominational Foreign Mission Association be enlarged to meet the present-day needs for cooperation? If so, how?
3. Shall the IFMA employ a secretary and rent a central office? If so, how shall the financial needs be met?

Throughout this period the minutes contain a variety of suggestions for projects and programs that could be accomplished together. Some were:

1. Joint councils in various cities to represent all faith missions
2. Attractive, helpful and instructive joint literature, presenting the work of all members of the association
3. Joint conferences and meetings of various kinds
4. United efforts in securing passports and permits
5. United efforts in purchasing office supplies and outfits
6. A full and frank interchange of information about candidates and missionaries upon request
7. Literature, meetings, and other ways to emphasize the theological position of faith missions and to call attention to the unoccupied fields of the world

Many suggestions remained in the proposal stage because of lack of staff to give time to intermission cooperative work. Member missions themselves had few workers spending full-time in administration with the mission. Men like Orson R. Palmer, home secretary, and Oliver M. Fletcher, general secretary of the Africa Inland Mission, were busy pastors, as well. Others, like Dr. Henry Frost, were advanced in years and fully occupied with speaking, writing, and general oversight responsibilities for the largest of the nondenominational missions.

A recurring recognition throughout the decade was the need for an office and a full-time executive secretary. At the IFMA Special Meeting in 1921, a motion was carried, which stated:

> That it is the sense of this meeting that there should be in existence a secretary and an office, which shall be a center of information and service for all the interests which are recognized as being for the mutual advantage of those interdenominational missions, and as may become associated with them.[1]

During this decade, the Articles of Agreement was amended and the name changed to "Articles of Association," and a series of bylaws were adopted The executive committee was changed to "general committee." It would consist of one representative from each mission society. The officers of the association would be elected from among that group. The purpose statement was strengthened. In addition to "holding mutual conferences concerning mission principles, methods, and actions," it was agreed to add "and to cooperation in the same." The article of the doctrinal statement on the Trinity was expanded to mention "the personality of the Holy Spirit," in addition to stressing the deity of Christ. The article on the second coming of Christ was changed to substitute "bodily and visible return of Christ" for the phrase "premillenial coming of Christ."[2]

A significant feature of the new bylaws provided that the representation of member missions be according to the number of missionaries supported by North American funds. This proportionate basis was followed, also, for the dues structure of the association. Another important item was the principle of unanimity, which included approving missions for membership and effecting changes in the bylaws.

During the 1920s, the association sponsored a series of summer Bible and missionary conferences, first at Montrose, Pennsylvania, and later at Stony Brook, Long Island. Winter conferences were held in New York City for missions representatives and council members. In addition to Bible messages, a number of mission topics were profitably considered, including the preparation of missionaries, candidate contacts, deputation, furloughs, methods of evangelization, as well as home administration problems.

IFMA Annual Meetings provided opportunity for mutual cooperation and interchange. There were discussions on the mission periodical, the candidate, administration, missionary support, home councils and field administration, and the authority of district councils.

Missions agreed that the publication of missionary support figures should include personal allowance, plus related mission expense at home and on the field.[3] Health information forms for furlough missionaries were published by IFMA for use by member missions. "A Call to Prayer for China" was published and thirty thousand copies distributed.

Six additional missions were accepted into membership in the twenties:

1922 - India Christian Mission
1923 - Ceylon and India General Mission (became International Christian Fellowship, which merged with SIM)
1924 - Heart of Africa Mission
North East India General Mission
1929 - American-European Fellowship
Latin American Evangelization Crusade (became Latin America Mission)

The Heart of Africa Mission was active in meetings from 1924 to 1926, but there is no mention of it after the 1926 Annual Meeting.

At the 1929 Annual Meeting, the secretary was instructed to prepare a booklet about IFMA's fifteen member missions, presenting facts as to the organization, location of each mission, the number of missionaries, annual income, and property.

Financing the association office appeared to be an insurmountable problem. It is somewhat difficult to understand why these men who had great faith when it came to the supply of workers and funds for their missions were not led to exercise faith for the supply of qualified personnel and needed support for the association.

## 1930-1939

By the first IFMA meeting of the decade of the thirties the booklet, *Faith Missions*, was published. The association was committed to do everything possible to develop interest in the common task of member missions — world evangelization.

Dr. John. E. Jaderquist (1866-1946) was appointed western field representative of IFMA in 1932. As a young man, Jaderquist was a missionary in Africa. After returning in 1892, he became affiliated with the Christian and Missionary Alliance and served as district superintendent in New York State, publications secretary, and member of the C&MA Board of Managers. Following his years with the Alliance, he was associated with the Bible House of Los Angeles. Dr. Jaderquist was active in the IFMA from 1919 until his death in 1946, serving as a vice president for a number of years. He was the initiator of the IFMA cooperative missions conferences held on the Pacific Coast each year, which stimulated much interest in missions. His two children, Helen Jaderquist Tenney (Mrs. Merrill) and Elizabeth Jaderquist Paddon (Mrs. Wallace) were both deeply involved in missions through the Woman's Union Missionary Society and the IFMA.

At the 1932 Annual Meeting, the need for mission accreditation was stressed by Mr. Philip Howard, Jr., of *The Sunday School Times*. The Committee of Reference was named to provide information concerning any societies of the association at any time it was required.

Rev. Will H. Houghton, pastor of Calvary Baptist Church in New York City and later president of Moody Bible Institute, suggested a possible missions youth auxiliary movement to attract more young people to involvement in world evangelization. To follow up this discussion, the executive committee made arrangements for a missionary rally at Calvary Baptist Church. The Church made available a missionary radio broadcast, featuring leaders of member missions, each one speaking weekly for a month.

Robert Glover, Philip Howard, and George Rhoad were assigned to prepare a leaflet on behalf of the association in answer to the unscriptural positions taken by the Commission of Appraisal of the Laymen's Foreign Mission Inquiry. The contrast between statements of the commission and passages of Scripture were noted.

Also in 1932, discussions were held in relation to the ministry of the association, including cooperative deputation work, conferences, and common literature. This interaction resulted in positive cooperation in these areas. Paul Graef suggested that the IFMA publish its own quarterly periodical. However, the IFMA prayer and praise news bulletin, which became the *IFMA News*, did not become a reality for another eighteen years. In the meantime, clippings of member missions' activities were sent to various Christian publications.

Annual cooperative missions conferences were sponsored by IFMA in a number of cities in New Jersey, New York, Maryland, and Pennsylvania. The variety of speakers from member agencies represented a global dimension of missions. Bible teachers, such as John Linton, Peter W. Philpott, and Harry Ironside, participated. In addition to sharing the need for expanding missionary outreach through new workers and supporters, there was a need to communicate the Bible basis of missions and to demonstrate evangelical cooperation.

There is no question about the devastating effect the *Laymen's Inquiry* had upon Protestant missions programs and support. However, mission executives and missiologists can find much helpful information in its documents. One example is the article, "Recruiting and Selecting New

Missionaries," by Charles H. Fahs that was published in 1933.[4] Of the many helpful insights given by Fahs, one is a clear presentation of the qualities to be looked for in missionaries in light of changing relationships between churches overseas and founding missions.[5]

A three-paragraph statement of organization and purpose, adopted previously, was reaffirmed at the 1935 Annual Meeting.

> The Interdenominational Foreign Mission Association of North America was formed in 1917 by a group of existing foreign missionary societies, not denominationally related, holding identical doctrinal convictions, and adhering to similar missionary principles and practices.
>
> The Association is not designed to superimpose any administrative authority over the distinctive work of its member missions. Its purposes are as follows: first, to promote spiritual fellowship and intercessory prayer; second, to provide for mutual conferences concerning missionary policies, methods, and procedure; and third, to present a united appeal for hastening the completion of the task of world evangelization.
>
> Member missions of the Association unite in testifying to the faithfulness of God in supplying the means for the carrying on of their Christ-appointed task. They do not go into debt, nor authorize personal solicitation of funds, nor pursue popular methods of raising money, but look to the Lord in faith and prayer, and minister to their workers and carry forward their work in the measure in which God provides through the voluntary contributions of His people.

A question raised at the 1935 Annual Meeting related to the use of the term "faith missions:"

> Do you favor the use by ourselves (e.g., in our printed pamphlet) of the name "Faith Missions," a term which the Missions within the I.F.M.A. did not themselves originate or assume, but which was first applied to them by others by way of designating their distinctive financial policy and practice, or do you think it might be better for us to refrain from using that term in speaking of ourselves? On vote it was decided that hereafter the name "Faith Missions" should be excluded as a heading to any publication, but that following our full title there might be an explanation to the effect that this is a fellowship of units popularly called "Faith Missions."

The question of limiting membership in IFMA to nondenominational missions was asked of the delegates at that meeting.

> Do you favor the Association's continuing to limit its membership to approved missions which adhere strictly to the faith policy and practice as regarding financial support, or do you think it is preferable for the Association to widen its fellowship to include missions which are one with us in sound doctrine and also in the aim, character, and methods of their missionary work, irrespective of their financial policy or of their being nondenominational?

After discussion, the annual meeting voted to continue limiting membership in the association to nondenominational agencies.

The IFMA position in relation to the Foreign Missions Conference of North America was clearly stated in 1937. Because of its theological inclusivism, it was agreed that the IFMA had no sympathy for the FMCNA's position and could not have spiritual fellowship with it.[6]

The use of *interdenominational* in the IFMA's name was considered in 1937. It was agreed that the word should be retained since some missionaries of member missions received support from denominational churches, and there was fellowship with evangelical churches of various denominations on the fields.

During this decade, which covered the time span from the depression to the start of World War II, IFMA meetings considered issues such as missionary support, funding the general fund, the purpose and length of furloughs, ordination of national workers, and the spread of communism.

Of eleven missions that applied for membership during the 1930s, only the Orinoco River Mission was accepted. The others were tabled or rejected because they did not measure up to the faith basis of support, were considered denominationally related, did not meet financial and/or administrative standards, did not have a responsible functioning council in North America, had too few missionaries, were not sending agencies, or were not involved in cross-cultural mission work. Membership was withdrawn from one mission in 1939 because of persistent questions over a period of several years, during which unsatisfactory answers were given concerning the administration of the mission and the conduct of its work.

## 1940-1949

IFMA Bible and missions conferences moved west in 1941—to Detroit, Grand Rapids, Indianapolis, St. Louis, and Wheaton. Dr. Harry Ironside, pastor of Moody Memorial Church, was the principal speaker; Arthur J. Bowen of South Africa General Mission (Africa Evangelical Fellowship) presented the work of the association; Ralph T. Davis, using a large map, presented the various fields of the world; and George H. Dowkontt, a physician and council member of several missions, manned the literature table and was in charge of finances, paying hotel and railroad expenses, and accounting for offerings. Conferences continued in various cities throughout the decade.

The decade of the 1940s was a turning point in the IFMA, and 1943 was a key year. Participating missions more than doubled from the previous year's annual meeting, and there were three times as many individual delegates. Ralph T. Davis of the Africa Inland Mission was elected president of IFMA, along with a slate of officers who brought new vision and vitality to the association. Davis gave strong leadership to IFMA, and was a firm believer in evangelical cooperation. He was instrumental in helping to bring evangelicals together for the initial meeting in Chicago from which the National Association of Evangelicals developed.

Luncheons were held the fourth Thursday of each month in New York City. Council members and missionaries on furlough met for fellowship and prayer, as well as "to hear some outstanding speakers." An annual IFMA dinner was begun in New York, also.

Up until 1944, the affairs of the association were directed by the executive committee and the general committee. The bylaws were amended at the annual meeting in September 1944 to provide for the "official board." IFMA Bylaws Article V, as recorded in the minutes reads:

> There shall be elected as officers of the Association a President, two Vice Presidents, a Secretary-Treasurer, and not less than three nor more than five additional Board members, which group shall be known as the Official Board of the Association.

The executive committee would "be elected by the Official Board from among their number and shall consist of not less than three and not more than five members, to include the President and Secretary-Treasurer."

## COMMITTEES

It was in this decade that committees began to function as a prominent part of the IFMA. In addition to the Program

Committee for the annual meeting, the Conference Committee, and the Policy Committee, others were appointed.

The Literature Committee was to supervise the production of general missions literature. The annual meeting voted in 1943 that publications would carry the imprint of the IFMA only, and a logo was designed to enable missions to identify themselves as a member of the association. Until then, literature had carried a list of all member missions. This would no longer be done, but missions could order literature with their own imprint. The 1944 Annual Meeting minutes recorded "the exceptionally fine reception the I.F.M.A. literature has had." The minutes noted that during the previous year there was a drop in literature distribution—only 195,000 pieces were distributed.

During the 1940s, seventeen mission pamphlets were produced for distribution by member missions and churches. Titles were: (1) *Preparation Now for Post-War Missionary Advance*, (2) *India Calls You*, (3) *Africa: The Land of Possibilities*, (4) *Post War Missions: A Fresh Challenge*, (5) *How to Put on a Missionary Program in the Local Church*, (6) *The Divine Logic of Foreign Missions*, (7) *Introducing IFMA*, (8) *Men Wanted*, (9) *The World at a Glance*, (10) *Why Missions in South America*, (11) *Central Asia*, (12) *Prayer and Missions*, (13) *Missionary Qualifications*, (14) *India*, (15) *The Missionary Call*, (16) *How to Promote Missions in the Local Church, and* (17) *Europe.*

Three new committees were established in 1943. Dr. Howard Ferrin, president of Providence Bible Institute, spoke at the 1943 IFMA Annual Meeting on future radio and educational possibilities. As a result, committees were set up for radio and education. The Radio Committee was to investigate the advisability and possibilities of radio ministry on the mission field. The Educational Committee was to coordinate action between member mission societies and various training schools, with a view to improvement in missionary preparation of students. Dr.

Harold Cook of Moody Bible Institute was a prominent speaker at IFMA meetings on missionary qualifications and preparation.

The Articles of Agreement was revised in 1945. Some moderation of the strong faith financial stand of the association was taken by deleting "and do not resort to financial appeals" from the membership standards.

Two committees were appointed in 1949. The temporary Committee on Latin America was made the first standing area committee. Its purpose was to represent missions of the IFMA working in Latin America in matters of united effort and study. At the recommendation of the Policy Committee, the Public Relations Committee was appointed and made responsible for "publicity of the IFMA, accrediting of societies, and the defense and promotion of the Faith Mission Movement."

## PRESENTATIONS AND DISCUSSIONS

Annual meetings provided a forum for presentations and discussions on pertinent topics. Some of these during the forties were: (1) Qualifications of a Missionary, (2) Qualities of a Missionary, (3) Deputational Work, (4) Our Social Contacts, (5) What Can IFMA Do for the Pastor?, (6) The IFMA Aiding the Local Church and Christian Organizations, (7) The IFMA: A Channel for the Student and Volunteer, (8) What Can the IFMA Do to Render Service to Member Missions?, (9) Problems Relative to the Better Training of Students for the Mission Fields, and (10) Messages on Mutual Helpfulness: from the Pastor's Standpoint and from the Field Standpoint.

Practical assistance to missions included information on income tax, IFMA Missionary Certificate recognition by the Passport Division of the U. S. State Department, and help in securing surplus materials from World War II.

## MEMBERSHIP

This was a decade of membership expansion. Ten missions were accepted into membership:

1941 - Soldiers and Sailors Gospel Mission (Gospel Mission of South America)
1943 - Sudan United Mission (North American branches merged into TEAM)
Unevangelized Fields Mission (UFM International)
1945 - Scandinavian Alliance Mission (The Evangelical Alliance Mission)
Russian Gospel Association (Slavic Gospel Association)
India Mission (International Missions)
West Indies Mission (Worldteam)
Gospel Missionary Union
1948 - Mexican Indian Mission (merged into UFM International)
1949 - Wycliffe Bible Translators

Ten missions that applied for membership were not accepted.

In 1941 Paul Graef raised the question of limiting membership to sending agencies with a minimum of ten missionaries. Retroactive action was taken, resulting in the elimination of the Bible House of Los Angeles from IFMA membership. However, in 1942 an exception was made, and it was reinstated into membership, which this literature agency had held since 1919.

Initial discussion was held on the possibility of a classification of associate membership, which would make it possible for certain other missions to belong to the IFMA.

A question dealt with in 1935 was brought up again in 1946. Why did not the IFMA accept denominational missions that were faith missions in principles and practice? No answers were recorded in the minutes, but the nondenominational limitation remained in force.

As this was a decade of growth, it was also a decade of loss. Through death, the IFMA lost three of its most prominent and long-time leaders: Dr. John. E. Jaderquist, Dr. Robert Hall Glover, and Mr. Paul H. Graef.

## OTHER ASSOCIATIONS

During the 1940s both the National Association of Evangelicals (NAE) and the Evangelical Foreign Missions Association (EFMA) were organized to provide additional platforms and services for evangelical churches and agencies in the United States. The EFMA's name was changed in 1990 to Evangelical Fellowship of Mission Agencies.

### National Association of Evangelicals

A group of American evangelical leaders met in Chicago at the Moody Bible Institute during the first week of October 1941 for prayer and discussion regarding cooperative efforts. J. Elwin Wright was the moving force behind this meeting. He was the leader of the New England Fellowship, which, since 1929, had raised an evangelical response to the liberal Protestantism, Roman Catholicism, and Unitarianism of that area. The NEF Conferences of 1939-1941 called for evangelical cooperation on the national level.

Ralph T. Davis, general director of the Africa Inland Mission, wrote to four Bible institute presidents in December 1940, and later sent a general letter to a large number of evangelical leaders on behalf of united evangelical cooperation.[7] This was followed by a tour by Dr. Wright to consult with evangelical leaders across the United States.

The group that gathered in Chicago in 1941 unanimously called for a national conference of evangelicals to represent denominational and nondenominational churches, missions, schools, periodicals, and other interested organizations. This national conference, which led to the founding of the National Association of Evangelicals, was called to order on April 7, 1942 at the Hotel Coronado in St. Louis. Some of the speakers included J. Elwin Wright,

Harold John Ockenga, William Ward Ayer, Stephen W. Paine, and Robert G. Lee. The St. Louis conference produced a tentative constitution, including a statement of faith. It approved the plan for a constitutional convention to be held the following year. Ralph T. Davis was elected secretary of the new association, an office which he filled for a short period, but was not able to continue due to his heavy responsibilities with the Africa Inland Mission.

More than a thousand evangelicals met May 3, 1943 at the LaSalle Hotel in Chicago. The participants came from some fifty denominations, as well as independent religious organizations and local churches. Being committed to a conservative theological position, they gathered together with enthusiasm. James Deforest Murch, one of the early NAE participants and historian, noted, "In an atmosphere akin to Pentecost the 'National Association of Evangelicals' was born."[8]

Clyde W. Taylor who gave effective leadership to the NAE for more than thirty years summarized the founding and purpose of the National Association of Evangelicals in two sentences:

> Starting as a prayer meeting about two years previously and planned at a conference in St. Louis in 1942, NAE became a constitutional entity in April, 1943. The purpose back of NAE was to bring together in fellowship and cooperation for united witness and voice, as well as for necessary action, a large number of smaller denominations in the United States.[9]

The NAE is not a council of churches. Its membership is a voluntary association of evangelical denominations, local churches, organizations, and individuals. It serves, but does not control, its members.

The National Association of Evangelicals held its fiftieth-anniversary convention March 3-5, 1992 at Chicago's Hyatt Regency O'Hare Hotel, with the theme "Forward in Faith—

50 Years of Evangelical Cooperation." The author serves on the NAE's Board of Administration.

## Evangelical Foreign Missions Association (Evangelical Fellowship of Mission Agencies)

Mission agencies, affiliated with NAE churches and organizations, were represented in the initial Missions Commission of the NAE. Clyde W. Taylor opened the NAE Office of Public Affairs in Washington, DC, in 1944 in order to better represent and serve evangelical churches and missions.

Since IFMA would not accept denominational agencies into its membership, a group of mission executives met during the 1945 NAE convention, and a committee was appointed to prepare a constitution and bylaws for a new evangelical missions association. On September 19, 1945 the constitution of the Evangelical Foreign Missions Association was approved, and the incorporation was completed by the end of December. The first EFMA annual convention was held in Minneapolis, Minnesota, in April 1946. Fifteen mission agencies were received as charter members.

Dr. Clyde W. Taylor became the first executive secretary of the EFMA and continued in that office until his retirement in 1975. At one time, he served concurrently as general director of NAE, director of NAE Office of Public Affairs, executive director of the EFMA, and international secretary of World Evangelical Fellowship.

As executive director of the IFMA from September 1, 1963 to September 30, 1991, for over twenty-five years the author had close association with Dr. Taylor, a statesman in evangelicalism and world missions. He often said, "Evangelicals cooperate very carefully." Clyde Taylor was consistent in cooperation. During the last half century, there were few national and international efforts of evangelical cooperation which were not influenced by this man. He was a catalyst, a motivator, and an encourager. He held a high view of the church, and believed that the church is the chief vehicle through which God is working out His redemptive purposes.

Membership in the EFMA is open to all qualified evangelical agencies, both denominational and nondenominational. Pentecostal and holiness groups are welcome.

The 1946 IFMA Annual Meeting voted unanimously not to become related to the EFMA. The EFMA was still a young association compared to the thirty years history of the IFMA. Also, while the IFMA was committed to evangelical cooperation, it was not ready for any official relationship with evangelical denominational groups. Since its beginning in 1917, the IFMA was known for its independent nondenominational stance. It continued to be known for its solid stand against liberalism, and its role as an accrediting association of nondenominational mission agencies grew.

## NOTES

[1] Interdenominational Foreign Mission Association, Minutes of Special Meeting, 4 April 1921.

[2] Interdenominational Foreign Mission Association, Minutes of Annual Meeting, 19-20 October 1922.

[3] Interdenominational Foreign Mission Association, Minutes of Annual Meeting, 9 November 1926.

[4] Charles H. Fahs, "Recruiting and Selecting New Missionaries," in *Home Base and Missionary Personnel, vol. 7: Laymen's Foreign Missions Inquiry Fact-Finders' Reports*, ed. Orville A. Petty (New York: Harper & Brothers Publishers, 1933), pp. 1-43.

[5] Ibid., p. 9.

[6] Interdenominational Foreign Mission Association, Minutes of Annual Meeting, 28 January 1937, p. 2.

[7] Ralph T. Davis, letter to four Bible institute presidents, 11 December 1940, Records of American Home Council of the Africa Inland Mission, Folder 27, Box 14, Collection 81, Billy Graham Center Archives, Wheaton, Illinois.

[8] James Deforest Murch, *The Protestant Revolt* (Arlington, VA: Crestwood Books, 1977), p. 251.

[9] Clyde W. Taylor, "Implementing Our Evangelical Unity," in *Dynamics of Christian Unity*, ed. W. Stanley Mooneyham (Grand Rapids: Zondervan Publishing House, 1963), pp. 89-90.

# PART THREE

# EXPANDING THE EFFECTIVENESS OF IFMA MINISTRY 1950-1992

# 9

# PROGRESSION 1950-1992

At the beginning of 1950, the IFMA office was located in space provided by the Africa Inland Mission at its headquarters in Brooklyn, New York. August B. Holm was IFMA Secretary-Treasurer and carried on the work of the association, along with other ministry at AIM. At the June 1950 meeting of the board, Ralph T. Davis reported that the space would be needed for new AIM personnel. It was also reported that J. O. Percy, SIM secretary, offered to assist Mr. Holm with the IFMA office responsibilities. They were authorized to secure other office space and to seek secretarial assistance.

The IFMA established its own executive office at Room 715, 1860 Broadway, New York City, on July 25, 1950. After thirty years of occupying office facilities provided by the missions of the elected officers, the association began to put emphasis on its own identity. The IFMA had been incorporated in the state of New York in 1948 when a gift of oil, gas, and mineral rights for land in Latimer County, Oklahoma, was deeded to the association on July 15, 1947 by Carlton Weaver. Incorporation was necessary in order to own the rights. The gift came through the recommendation of Philip Howard, Jr., editor of *The Sunday School Times*. He was also on the board of Belgian Gospel Mission. Mr. and Mrs. Howard had been missionaries with Belgian Gospel Mission, which merged with Greater Europe Mission in 1971.

The 1949 and 1950 Annual Meetings were held at the Inter-City Tabernacle in Lansing, Michigan. Through contact during the meetings, Cora E. Goble was led to leave the Tabernacle staff to serve as IFMA office secretary. The coming of Miss Goble on January 8, 1951 provided more efficient service. She continued with the IFMA until December 1973 when the office was moved to Wheaton, Illinois.

John O. Percy of the Sudan Interior Mission was elected secretary of the IFMA Board at the 1950 Annual Meeting. He was reelected to that position until 1954 when he was made administrative vice president.

The IFMA Board took action in 1956 to invite Mr. Percy to become general secretary, the first full-time executive officer of the association. On March 1, 1957, the association purchased a building at 308 West 105th Street, New York City, to serve as its headquarters. It was IFMA's fortieth anniversary year.

Because of increasing property problems and requirements, the IFMA Board in March 1960 authorized the sale of the New York building and the relocation of the office to New Jersey. Suitable property was found at 54 Bergen Avenue, Ridgefield Park, New Jersey, and the office was moved August 30, 1960.

Mr. Percy submitted his resignation from the IFMA on November 28, 1961, to be effective March 31, 1962. During the following months, a number of men were considered for the job. In February 1963, IFMA President Vernon Mortenson (TEAM) contacted the author who was on furlough from Far Eastern Gospel Crusade's Philippine Field. He became executive secretary of IFMA on September 1, 1963. One of the founders of Far Eastern Gospel Crusade (SEND), the author served four years on the FEGC Board of Directors and three years on the executive staff as home secretary/treasurer before leaving for the Philippines in 1954. While there, he was on the field council and was treasurer/business manager. He represented the mission on several intermission boards and committees.

Mr. Holm began the *IFMA Prayer Bulletin* in February 1950. It was intended to be "used of God to promote a greater bond of prayer fellowship between every Society of the IFMA."[1] It ended with the November-December 1954 issue and was replaced by the more widely-circulated *IFMA News* in January 1955. It was discontinued after the Fourth Issue (October-December) 1991.

An annual listing of minimum personnel needs of member missions is published, entitled *IFMA Opportunities*. One important service of the IFMA office was the bulletin, *IFMA Update: Government and Business*, which kept member missions informed on the latest tax and government matters relating to mission agencies, as well as business items and financial management. The office receives many inquiries about missions matters. Requests for assistance, personal interviews, and consultation increased dramatically at the Wheaton location.

Dr. John Frame, a medical missionary who had returned to the United States, was appointed medical consultant to the IFMA in 1953. Dr. Frame worked with the IFMA in designing four forms: "Medical Examination," "Medical History of the Missionary Candidate," "Medical History of the Returned Missionary," and "Children's Medical Examination." These forms are still available from IFMA, and are used by some member missions, as well as by other agencies. Through the years, many missionaries went to Dr. Frame's New York City office for physical examinations.

A library of missions books was set up in the IFMA office in 1953. It was envisioned as a reference and, possibly a lending, library. Beginning with 150 books, it now contains over 3,500 volumes on missions and missions-related subjects, plus numerous periodicals and other items. It is used as a reference library by IFMA staff and missions, as well as by students, primarily on the master's and doctoral levels. Since moving to Wheaton, the IFMA library has been cataloged.

A monthly book-purchasing service was begun in 1958 for missionaries of member missions. A subscriber agreed to IFMA's choosing one book each month. This service continued until 1979, when it was discontinued due to lack of staff to handle it.

Throughout the '50s and early '60s, the monthly luncheons were held in New York City, as well as an IFMA Annual Dinner. The West Coast IFMA group continued twice-yearly meetings.

At the IFMA Mission Executive's Retreat in 1960, Philip Howard, Jr. (*The Sunday School Times*), moved and it was carried that the IFMA seriously consider the appointment of commissions to make studies of the Congo, Cuba, and other areas of interest the board considered necessary. Information from the studies would be available to member missions.[2]

Arthur Glasser (OMF), Ralph T. Davis (AIM), and Kenneth Strachan (LAM) were appointed to an IFMA Commissions Committee to study subjects for commissions. The committee recommended that five study commissions be named to detail an evangelical strategy to consider the following:

1. The Ecumenical Movement of the World Council of Churches
2. The changing posture and program of Romanism
3. The nature and influence of nationalism
4. The problems of recruiting noncaucasians as missionaries
5. The widespread acceptance of universalism by Barthian theologians[3]

At the 1962 Annual Meeting, the matter of study commissions and desk men was tabled until asked for by the IFMA Board. Some of the suggested areas of study were dealt with in IFMA meetings and articles in periodicals, including the IFMA/EFMA-sponsored *Evangelical Missions Quarterly*, since 1964.

The IFMA Board felt in 1973 that a move from the property in Ridgefield Park was necessary. After considering other possible locations in metropolitan New York, Philadelphia, and Chicago, the decision was made to locate in Wheaton, Illinois The primary reason for choosing Wheaton area was the central geographic location. The proximity to O'Hare Airport and to other Christian organizations was an important consideration, as well.

After renting for about two-and-a-half years, a suitable lot at 370 South Schmale Road in Carol Stream, on the north side of Wheaton, was purchased, and the IFMA had its own headquarters building constructed in 1976. Through proceeds from the sale of the Ridgefield Park building, contributions by member missions, and a matching grant, the building was completely paid for in 1978.

Forty-five missions were accepted into IFMA membership from 1950 to 1980. Many others that inquired or applied did not qualify. Thirty-five more missions were approved from 1981 to 1991.

The author informed the IFMA Board in 1986 that it needed to consider a schedule for leadership transition, a successor as executive director. Since no action had been taken by the March 1989 IFMA Board Meeting, the author presented his projections regarding his retirement as executive director. A policy was adopted for normal retirement of the executive director at age sixty-five with a possible year-by-year extension, as approved by the board.

The author provided a notebook of documents and suggestions for the board president and search committee. Subsequently, an invitation was extended to Dr. John H. Orme to join the IFMA staff on September 16, 1990 as executive director designate, to become executive director on October 1, 1991. After stepping down as executive director on September 30, 1991, the author remained on staff through September 1992 as consulting director.

Dr. Orme is a graduate of Philadelphia College of Bible and Dallas Theological Seminary where he earned a doctorate in theology. He came to IFMA from a background of teaching overseas and in the United States, as well as experience in the pastorate. As missionaries, Dr. and Mrs. Orme served for fourteen years with CAM International where he taught at the Central American Theological Seminary in Guatemala. After returning to the United States, he was professor and director of missions at William Tyndale College. Immediately before coming to IFMA, he was associate pastor at Highland Park Baptist Church in Southfield, Michigan.

## IFMA COMMITTEES

The association concluded its 1949 Annual Meeting by approving the three-fold recommendation of the Policy Committee:

1. That definite steps be taken leading to the occupation of unoccupied areas and the evangelization of poorly evangelized areas
2. That the IFMA be expanded by inviting into our fellowship worthy societies not now able to meet all the requirements of this organization, by granting associate membership in ways to be defined
3. That we study and wrestle with the major problems which face the missionary enterprise today

The association endeavored to implement this through the appointment of special committees to supplement the efforts of the officers and board. Throughout its existence, much of the IFMA ministry has been accomplished by committees composed of mission executives.

Starting in the late 1950s, IFMA began to participate in cooperative committee work with the Evangelical Foreign Missions Association (Evangelical Fellowship of Mission Agencies). After the first joint study conference of the two associations in 1963, the cooperative committees increased.

Previous committees that were joint with EFMA for a period of time were: (1) Summer Institute of Missions Committee, (2) Committee to Assist Ministry Education Overseas (CAMEO), and (3) Committee on Bible Society Concerns.

Current IFMA committees that were also joint committees with EFMA from the late 1950s until 1991 were: (1) Africa, (2) Asia, (3) China, (4) Islamics, (5) Latin America, (6) Evangelical Missions Information Service (EMIS), and (7) Personnel Committee.

Only two IFMA committees are currently joint committees with EFMA. They are Evangelical Missions Information Service (EMIS) and Personnel Committee. Most of the committees that were joint now function with a board-appointed coordinator who may appoint others from IFMA missions to assist on a task-force basis as the need arises.

Current IFMA committees that were never joint with EFMA are: (1) Business Administration Committee, (2) Cooperation and Amalgamation Committee, (3) Europe Committee, (4) Frontier Peoples Committee, (5) Jewish Ministries Committee, (6) Missions Evaluation Committee, (7) North America Committee, and (8) Theological Commission.

After beginning cooperation with EFMA in joint committees, IFMA kept its own committees to deal with IFMA missions' needs. However, after committee cooperation began with EFMA, service to IFMA missions dwindled during the 1970s, particularly among the IFMA "area" committees that were joint with EFMA—Africa, Asia, China, Islamics, and Latin America.

In 1981 the author urged the IFMA committees, especially on Africa, Asia, Islamics, and Latin America, to become more active in serving the particular needs and interests of IFMA missions, in addition to their activities in the joint committees with EFMA. Area committee work in relation to IFMA missions' needs had increasingly diminished since the beginning of joint committees with EFMA. Nondenominational missions have their own distinctive needs that are often different from denominational missions. Also, nondenominational missions can get geared up for action faster than denominational missions. A missions department within a denomination often has to wait for approval from the leadership of its denomination before acting.

New IFMA committees that were instituted in the 1980s were a Theological Commission and three new area committees: Frontier Peoples, North America, and Jewish Ministries. The Europe Committee, which had functioned from 1962 to 1969, was reactivated in 1984. None of these were joint with EFMA.

Strategy group sessions for each area committee were included in the program of annual meetings. Papers or presentations were made on assigned topics, followed by discussion and recommendations for action or for implementation. IFMA sends a form each year to each member mission, requesting the name of the person to whom information should be sent for each committee or function, such as each specific area committee, business, finance, data processing, etc. That person is responsible to see that each person within his/her mission that should get the information does receive it. If it should go to the mission's overseas offices, he/she is responsible to send it. These people are called "mission contacts" for business, finance, candidates, Africa, etc.

Throughout the past decade, IFMA committee chairpersons have met with the IFMA Board at its spring meeting to give reports and to interact with the board. They share progress, planning, and prayer concerns relating to their areas. During this meeting, the board and the area committee chairpersons pray together for the personnel and work of the missions served by the committees.

Area committees met at the IFMA Annual Meeting, as well as in their strategy sessions. Most of them had several conference calls each year.

Dr. G. Dal Congdon, from TEAM's South Africa Field, was loaned to IFMA from August 1984 to August 1990. During these six years, he gave valuable assistance, primarily through the coordination of seven IFMA area committees: Africa, Asia, Europe, Frontier Peoples, Islamics, Latin America, and North America. Dr. Congdon worked directly with the chairpersons of the committees, and in consultation with the author, in assessing needs of the missions within specific areas, determining needs for new and/or increased outreach, and developing strategies.

The author continued to coordinate the joint IFMA-EFMA committees, as well as all other IFMA committees

As a result of the board/area committee chairpersons discussions in March 1985, a position statement was prepared, entitled "IFMA Committees: Purpose and Objectives" A copy of this was given each year to all committee chairpersons, and a copy was included in the conference book as general information for all delegates to the IFMA Annual Meeting.

## IFMA Committees: Purposes and Objectives

### Purpose

To care for the overall concerns of a region or major ministry on behalf of the IFMA, as specified under the following objectives:

### Objectives of IFMA Area Committees

1. Identify key issues affecting the work of the gospel in the region, relating specifically to IFMA-wide concerns expressed by the committee or board
2. Research to provide information that will assist member missions to function effectively
3. Mobilize action on assignments, on a task-force basis
4. Communicate information of regional interest, as follows:

   a. Reports to the IFMA Executive Director for editing and circulation
   b. A position paper for the IFMA Annual Meeting, which will include presenting issues, needs, concerns, and proposing action
   c. Information to member missions in the region on methods, resources, and tools found effective
5. Interact appropriately with other evangelical committees having similar concerns

Objectives of Other IFMA Committees

1. Identify key issues within the emphasis of the committee's concern, which affect the work of IFMA member missions
2. Research to provide information that will assist member missions to function effectively
3. Mobilize action on assignments, on a task-force basis
4. Communicate information on the committee's area of concentration, as follows:
   a. Reports to the IFMA Executive Director for editing and circulation
   b. A position paper for the IFMA Annual Meeting, which will include presenting issues, needs, concerns, and proposing action
   c. Information to member missions on methods, resources, and tools found effective
5. Interact appropriately with other evangelical committees having similar concerns

Discussions began between the board and committee chairpersons in 1990 about the possible restructuring of IFMA committees. Rather than continuing to appoint standing committees, a chairperson or coordinator could be appointed and, as needed, a task force could be named. This system has been working well for some of the joint IFMA-EFMA committees since 1987.

Because of the IFMA leadership transition to Dr. John

Orme as executive director, the change in committee structure was not implemented until the IFMA Board appointments at the 1991 Annual Meeting. Coordinators were appointed at that time to replace most standing committees.

The IFMA Executive Director serves as a participating member of all committees appointed by the IFMA Board. He attends all meetings and participates in all telephone conference calls. He is responsible to see that copies of all committee minutes are provided to members of the IFMA Official Board and that reports of each committee are presented at the Annual Meeting

With the appointment of coordinators instead of standing committees, the coordinator will continue to carry on his/her responsibilities in consultation with the executive director. The appointment of others on a task-force basis will also be done in consultation with him.

Committee members are not paid for their service on IFMA committees. The committee members' missions contribute the time and expertise of their staff members, but all member missions share in the travel and committee-related expenses through dues paid to the association.

Throughout the history of the IFMA, dues of member missions have been kept to a minimum. Because of the minimal staffing of the IFMA office, the association committees have had to be working committees. The accomplishment of any IFMA committee depends largely on the ability and willingness of its chairman, and his/her mission's appreciation of the benefits of this intermission cooperation by permitting him/her to devote time to see that the committee's goals are met.

Discussions for several years have sought for ways to make the committees more effective. Questions were raised about the need for standing committees. There was agreement that the key to profitable committee work is a chairman or leader who is able to give time to the work. Restructuring to a task-force basis or, more simply, the appointment of a coordinator with authority to call upon others for help as needed, was considered.

The approaching change in executive leadership of IFMA was taken into consideration. After a little over twenty-eight years in the position, the author stepped down as IFMA Executive Director on September 30, 1991, a few weeks after the 74th IFMA Annual Meeting. Dr. John H. Orme became executive director on October 1, 1991.

At the 74th Annual Meeting, the board made the decision to continue the Business Administration Committee as an IFMA standing committee. Joint IFMA and EFMA standing committees that will continue are only Evangelical Missions Information Service (EMIS) and the Personnel Committee. Coordinators were appointed for other areas of interest.

This action is expected to help to provide added flexibility and ease of administration for the decade of the 1990s, and for the new executive director as he becomes more oriented to the operations and needs of the association.

## LITERATURE AND PUBLICITY COMMITTEE

For many years, the production of literature demanded the most committee work. In addition to producing a large variety of pamphlets, the committee prepared advertisements for a number of Christian periodicals. Some were to call Christians to pray for missions; others were promotional and informational on the IFMA. For a number of years, J. O. Percy prepared the missions page in each issue of *The Voice*, the periodical of the Independent Fundamental Churches of America (IFCA). *The Missions Annual* was published by IFMA from 1958 to 1962. It contained statistics, articles, and general information on IFMA missions, world needs, and outreach.

At the 1953 IFMA Annual Meeting, Mr. Percy reported his contact with J. Herbert Kane, out of which grew the suggestion that Dr. Kane write or edit a book on the history of the nondenominational missions of IFMA. *Faith Mighty Faith* was published in 1956.[4]

A letter was received by the committee in 1955 from Arthur Glasser, at the request of Miss Marjorie Glover, asking for suggestions of someone to bring up to date Robert Hall Glover's book, *The Progress of World-Wide Missions*.[5] The Literature and Publicity Committee suggested that Dr. Kane do the revision.[6] The revised and enlarged edition came out in 1960.

The five morning messages given by IFMA missions executives and missionaries at the annual missionary conference of Calvary Independent Church, Lancaster, Pennsylvania, March 8-15, 1959 were so timely that the IFMA published them under the title, *Witnessing*.[7] The book, *Facing the Unfinished Task*, came out of the IFMA-sponsored Congress on World Missions in 1960.[8] The IFMA worked with Back to the Bible Broadcast in 1961 in publishing *The Final Destiny of the Heathen* by Richard Wolff.[9]

At the IFMA Annual Meeting in 1959, Dr. Paul E. Adolph presented "The Physical and Emotional Stress of Missionary Work," and it was printed in *The Sunday School Times*. It was revised with an additional chapter, "The Missionary on Furlough," and published in 1965. The booklet, *The Physical and Emotional Stress of Missionary Work*, is available from the IFMA office and continues to be used by some missions in their candidate orientation programs.

The booklet, *Next Steps*, was originally printed and copyrighted in 1949 by the Moody Bible Institute. Permission was given for the IFMA to print it in 1960. It was revised and printed again in 1966. Written by Harold R. Cook, it continues to be good counsel to volunteers for missionary service.[10]

The IFMA continued to publish and distribute brochures on missions during the 1960s and 1970s. The IFMA publishes and distributes the brochure, *IFMA Standards* (Appendix A). It is used widely by member missions, with their own imprints, to demonstrate to their supporting constituencies the extensive standards that missions must meet and maintain to qualify for membership in IFMA.

In 1984, two IFMA missions executives in Canada, Charles Tipp of InterServe Canada and Harold Fuller of SIM Canada, designed a poster, *Reaching the World for Christ*, that had a wide circulation. It was, also, printed in Spanish by the IFMA/EFMA Latin America Office in Quito.

Available as a brochure that opens to eight-and-one-half inches by seventeen inches, it has maps in six colors of the continents of the world, with population by areas, and statistical information on various religions and unreached people. Since 1986, it has been updated and reprinted four times as a brochure. Several hundred thousand copies have been distributed with the IFMA imprint and imprints of various missions, both IFMA and non-IFMA.

Most other missions literature is now published in cooperation with the Evangelical Missions Information Service (EMIS), a joint corporation of the IFMA and the EFMA.

## LATIN AMERICA COMMITTEE

At the 1949 IFMA Annual Meeting, Karl D. Hummel of the Central American Mission read the following report:

The Temporary Committee on Latin America submits the following report in the form of a recommendation:

> We recommend that a committee on Latin America, under the auspices of the IFMA and subject to the Official Board of the same, be appointed for the purpose of representing the missions of the IFMA working in Latin America, in matters of united effort and study.

The committee would provide official representation, if necessary, and would be a clearing house for investigation, information, and mutual consultation on the part of IFMA member missions.

Under the leadership of Kenneth Strachan (LAM), chairman, and J. Hubert Cook (EUSA), secretary, in January 1950 the committee initiated a study of the following problems or situations:

1. Survey as to the present occupation of Latin America on the part of all existing missionary societies, including also a survey of Indian work
2. The problem of relationships on the field, including national intermission councils, church bodies, and international bodies
3. A study of the mutual problem of candidate training and orientation for the Latin American field[11]

In addition to the fourteen IFMA missions working in Latin America, a letter and questionnaire was sent to EFMA missions in Latin America, the Christian and Missionary Alliance, the Association of Baptists for World Evangelism, Baptist Mid-Missions, and the Independent Board of Presbyterian Foreign Missions.[12]

At its meeting on March 20, 1950, a report on the survey was given. Plans were made for a cooperative candidate orientation program for Latin America. A one-day conference on Latin America was planned for October 20, in connection with the IFMA Annual Meeting. The minutes record the following:

> The problem of relationships in Latin America, especially in view of the evident determination of the I.C.C.C. to force the issue, as demonstrated in a letter received . . . was discussed. It was agreed that leadership in the fight against modernism and opposition to the W.C.C., and to unite evangelical forces, should be in the I.F.M.A.[13]

In 1952 the committee decided to sponsor a Pan American conference of IFMA-related missions and church leaders to be held in Costa Rica. However, at the 1952 Annual Meeting, the committee decided it would be best to have a preliminary conference in this country. At the 1953 Annual Meeting, the following was reported:

> First, it is of interest to note the important position of IFMA Missions serving in Latin America. It may not be generally known that there are 15 Member Missions with at least 1,500 missionaries on the field. According to the Missionary Research Library report, this represents 39.2% of all Protestant missionaries in Latin America, the largest body of evangelical workers in that area.
>
> Six or seven of these missions are definitely planning advance into new areas in Mexico, Argentina, Brazil, Uruguay, Panama, and, we understand, also Paraguay, leaving only Puerto Rico without an IFMA mission in the country.
>
> In spite of areas of opposition and persecution, such as is being experienced in Colombia, Latin America today presents a greater opportunity than ever before in the history of evangelical missions in those lands. In the light of the aforementioned facts, we feel that IFMA Missions are in a strategic position and at an opportune time in Latin America, and our meeting together for mutual help and discussion is, therefore, a tremendous necessity.
>
> Second, to help bring this about, the Committee has been active during this past year. At a meeting of delegates from the member missions working in Latin America, held in Chattanooga during November of last year, plans were initiated for a Conference of mission representatives. The committee worked towards bringing this about, and a meeting was held in Lancaster, Pennsylvania, during the Missionary Conference of the Calvary Independent Church.
>
> . . . Careful plans have been made for the series of sessions being held concurrently with

> this Annual Meeting, in which we are considering the extent and nature of present missionary occupation as a basis for specific planning for advance, occupation and correlation of missionary activities on the part of the IFMA Societies working in Latin America.
>
> Third, our present projects include a number of undertakings, the most important and greatest of which is a survey of missionary distribution in Latin America. This survey is not to be a general report listing the number of missionaries in each section, but rather it is a detailed study, province by province, showing such things as the location of missionaries in each country, the areas within each country either unoccupied or inadequately occupied, the areas of concentrated population and the extent of missionary effort in these areas, etc. Further, it is to include a study of the minority racial groups found in Latin America, such as the reported 1,000,000 Japanese in Brazil, the 200,000 Hindus in Trinidad, the reported 50,000 Cantonese in Cuba, the Jewish population, the English-speaking Negro population on the mainland, etc.
>
> As far as we can ascertain, there is no such report now available, not even covering one country.
>
> Projected also are plans for definite coordination of missionary advance efforts, which should result in the avoidance of overlapping and the mutual approval and good will of neighbor missions.

At the November 1953 meeting of the committee, data was presented from the General Survey of Evangelical Work in Latin America. The detailed survey was not yet completed. Also, at that meeting the following questions were discussed:

1. Do we think it advisable that there be organization ties among our missionaries on the field?
2. Should we try to get them together in fellowships for national planning and presentation of their problems to the government?
3. Is there any feeling that we should have representatives from different fields meet together?
4. Should we as IFMA missions seek to organize national churches into conferences?
5. What should be done about the education of national Christians to assist in organizing these?
6. What should be the IFMA attitude toward assisting fellowships and organizations?
7. Is the best approach to this matter of cooperation the chosen instrument method of mission cooperation?

The committee arranged a Bible-teaching tour for L. E. Maxwell of Prairie Bible Institute who visited a number of IFMA missionaries and fields in 1955.

After the resignation of Kenneth Strachan as chairman in 1954, the Latin America Committee was largely inactive during 1956 and 1957. In 1958 the Executive Committee of the IFMA met and considered the possibility of a joint committee on Latin America to be composed of IFMA and EFMA members. The 1959 Annual Meeting passed the following motion:

> That the I.F.M.A. authorize participation in a joint IFMA-EFMA Evangelical Committee on Latin America for consultation on missionary work in Latin America. As amended, it is understood that the I.F.M.A. representatives of this joint committee shall constitute a Standing Committee on Latin America of the I.F.M.A. to function as in the past.

Since 1959, most of the work of the Latin America Committee has been done in cooperation with the joint committee with the EFMA. This will be discussed further in Chapter 11, Cooperative Committees.

The IFMA Latin America Committee seldom met alone without its EFMA counterpart, except for a meeting during the annual meeting to report on the work of the joint committee, and to discuss issues of interest to member missions. Throughout the 1980s and through 1991, area committee strategy group sessions were scheduled into the annual meeting program. The sessions at annual meeting became the Latin America strategy group, with one or two presentations on assigned topics, followed by discussion. The written committee reports continue to be put into the conference book, to be read before the business sessions, with only questions or clarifications during the meeting.

The committee began a project in 1987 to collect case studies from each IFMA mission in Latin America, regarding leadership training programs for Latin church leaders. Information was gathered from both the member mission headquarters in North America and from field personnel. Summaries of material received was shared in 1988 and 1989 with member missions having ministries in Latin America.

The project of the IFMA Latin America Committee for the past two years has been one of interest and help to member missions working in Latin America, as well as to the Missions Commission of the World Evangelical Fellowship. First, the project was to find what is being done in preparing Latins to serve in cross-cultural ministries. Second, the project was to research books and teaching materials, and to compile a bibliography of mission publications in Spanish and Portuguese.

At the request of Dr. William Taylor, executive director of WEF's Missions Commission, the IFMA Latin America Committee is continuing to work on a more complete bibliography that will be distributed to IFMA missions having work in Latin America. It will be put in a standardized data base so that the COMIBAM office in Guatemala can continue to revise and update the information.

This committee gave a grant of $2,000.00 in November 1990 to the Missions Commission of WEF to be used for writing and producing a basic textbook on biblical missiology. It is being prepared by Dr. Emilio Antonio Nunez, related to CAM International.

The IFMA committee is currently working on researching what IFMA member missions are doing in Latin America regarding mission-related ministry of nationals, how and what to pay them, and the method of channeling funds to Third World leaders, which includes (1) pastors involved in church planting, (2) supporting a para-church ministry, and (3) supporting Latin missionaries going to other cultures and countries.

John Miesel of UFM International has chaired this committee for several years. It continued to contribute much to the effectiveness of member missions in Latin America. At the 1991 Annual Meeting, Mr. Miesel was appointed coordinator for Latin America and can name others to assist on a task-force basis, as needed.

## AFRICA COMMITTEE

At the 1950 Annual Meeting, the reports of the Latin America Committee precipitated a motion to establish an Africa Committee. Ralph T. Davis was appointed chairman and convened the first meetings on December 21, 1950 and January 24, 1951. The main issue discussed in these sessions related to evangelical relationships in Africa in light of projected visits by J. Elwin Wright, representing the World Evangelical Fellowship, and Carl McIntyre, representing the International Council of Christian Churches. The IFMA leaders were concerned about divisions that would probably be introduced into the African continent by these two organizations. It was agreed that background information should be sent to IFMA mission field leaders to inform them of these developments.[14]

Outside of discussions during the IFMA Board and Annual Meetings, there is no record of special meetings of the Africa Committee from the early 1950s until 1959.

A special meeting of representatives of IFMA missions working in Africa was held in New York on December 9, 1959. The meeting was called by IFMA President Ralph Davis, after receiving a letter from Peter Letchford of South Africa General Mission. A proposal had come from believers in the Durban area of South Africa for some kind of evangelical union—the various national groups of Christians, which came into being through the ministry of various mission boards, would come together in an organized association or fellowship. Mr. Letchford wrote:

> The above proposition, originating from native believers in Durban, brings to my mind once again the suggestion I made to you . . . namely, that those members of I.F.M.A., who have worked on the African continent, might give consideration to the formation on a continent-wide basis of a Fellowship which would give an opportunity for a closer association and fellowship to those whom the Lord has won for Himself through our joint testimony. The last thing we would want to start is a "super-church." But even as we here in North America became aware of the desirability of closer association together, and thus I.F.M.A. came into being, so now the time may be opportune for us to encourage the formation of an "African Evangelical Fellowship," which would provide similar benefits for our African brethren.[15]

It was noted at this meeting that the WCC had appropriated men and money to organize churches. They were by-passing the nondenominational missions, going directly to the national pastors and churches and establishing relationships with them.

The Africa Committee report to the 1961 Annual Meeting included the following summary of activities:

> The Committee has met twice during the year. After our first meeting, materials dealing with communism and lessons learned by CIM in China were distributed to our societies. Questionnaires also were sent to member societies to gain information as to places where evacuated missionaries might be re-allocated and where temporary housing might be had in case of evacuation.

Other matters were discussed, including warnings about the inroads of the World Council of Churches and its influence in Africa. The Committee recommended the formation of evangelical fellowships to give churches a united evangelical voice.

Since 1962, the IFMA Africa Committee has largely functioned as a part of the joint IFMA-EFMA Africa Committee.

Separate IFMA Africa Committee meetings were held to discuss the IFMA responsibilities related to the joint committee program. Such meetings or conference calls also helped to guide the chairman as he prepared the program for the Africa strategy group sessions for the IFMA Annual Meetings.

After several years of consideration of committee structure and function, it was decided by the IFMA Board to appoint an Africa coordinator to carry on the work formerly handled by the chairman. A standing committee was not appointed at the 1991 Annual Meeting. The board named Rev. Gary Corwin (SIM) as coordinator for Africa. If he needs help, he may call on others from any of the IFMA member missions working in Africa on a task-force basis.

## BUSINESS ADMINISTRATION COMMITTEE

One of the strongest IFMA committees through the years has been the Business Administration Committee. Before forming a committee, officers, such as Ralph T. Davis and J. O. Percy, made a number of contacts with various government officials and shared with the member missions the information they received.

In April 1957, administrators representing missions related to IFMA, EFMA, and The Associated Missions of the International Council of Christian Churches met together to discuss issues of mission administration.[16] The administrators met under the chairmanship of the IFMA General Secretary.[17] As a result, a *Mission Administration Manual* was published by IFMA in 1958 with an initial run of 350 copies. There was such a demand for the manual that a revised edition was published in December of that year.

A special memo was issued in October 1959, concerning the proper receipting procedures of contributions. In 1961 the IFMA issued a *Supplement to Manual on Business Administration*, dealing with various aspects of Internal Revenue Service regulations pertinent to mission organizations. This supplement resulted from a May 1961 meeting of twenty mission administrators.[18]

At the 1961 Annual Meeting, Philip Armstrong (FEGC), Vernon Mortenson (TEAM), and J. O. Percy (IFMA) were named as the IFMA Business Administration Committee and commissioned to arrange an informational seminar for IFMA mission administrators before the end of the year. For the past thirty years, the Business Administration Committee has continued as one of the IFMA's most active committees. It functions on behalf of evangelical missions as follows:

1. Interpreting and instructing missions in relation to government matters, including tax and retirement regulations
2. Providing guidance and assistance relating to accounting and financial reporting for missionary organizations
3. Planning the IFMA Mission Administration Seminar biennially to update administrative information on these and other matters, such as office systems, equipment, and management

IFMA was incorporated in Canada in 1975. The incorporation there provides a Canadian association that is recognized by the Canadian government, enabling IFMA to be more effective in assisting its missions in Canada. IFMA missions and other Canadian agencies have benefited greatly through the efforts of Mr. Jack Phillips (SIM), IFMA Business Administration Committee member, and Mr. Ron Knechtel, IFMA's Canadian consultant.

The effectiveness of the IFMA Business Administration Committee is also shown under the section on Mission Administration Seminars in Chapter 12, Conferences.

The Business Administration Committee remains an IFMA standing committee.

## EUROPE COMMITTEE

Following the 1960 Congress on World Missions, representatives of member missions working in Europe met together during the IFMA Annual Meeting. By 1962 a committee was formed with Rev. Walter Frank of Greater Europe Mission as chairman. Their first project was to collect information on mission work throughout the continent. *Survey of Missions Working in Europe* was published in 1964.[19]

The committee continued to meet each year through 1969, sharing information on radio opportunities, group travel flights, schools for missionaries' children, cooperation in ministry, saturation evangelism, opportunities in Eastern Europe, and analysis of the unfinished ministry in Europe.

For the next fifteen years, coordination of information of interest to missions in Europe was handled by the IFMA Executive Director. Consultation between missions was handled individually, as needed.

Because of developments on the continent and to avoid duplication of efforts, an IFMA Europe Committee was reappointed in 1984. Missions were facing issues similar to the ones raised during the 1960s. A new generation of mission leaders was participating in the meetings.

Papers were assigned for a two-day Europe briefing held in June 1986, considering: (1) coordination of ministries in Eastern Europe, (2) relationship or role of IFMA missions in Europe, (3) missionary support levels, and (4) schooling of American children. A report of conclusions and recommendations arising from the briefing was shared with member missions at the 1986 Annual Meeting.

Because ministry involvement in Eastern Europe was significantly different from work in Western Europe, the annual meeting strategy group sessions were handled separately. The committee requested a survey of Eastern Europe ministries and opportunities from Slavic Gospel Association's research department. Missions starting new ministries in Eastern Europe were urged to consult with experienced missions for orientation and guidance.

Concern was expressed about the apparent lack of adequate training and experience in evangelism for new missionaries who desired to work in fields where the dominant tradition is Roman Catholic, Eastern Orthodox, or liberal Protestant. This concern was shared with the American Association of Bible Colleges, Association of Evangelical Professors of Missions, and the Association of Church Missions Committees.

Member missions with evangelism training programs in areas of large ethnic concentration, such as American Missionary Fellowship, International Missions, Open Air Campaigners, The Pocket Testament League, and Worldteam, were requested to accept candidates from other missions into their training programs.

A meeting of the committee and a briefing on Europe were held March 26-27, 1987 in Glen Ellyn, Illinois. Presentations on Eastern Europe were made by Mrs. Anita Deyneka of Slavic Gospel Association and Dr. Mark Elliott, director of the Institute of East/West Studies at Wheaton College. Copies of these addresses were later sent to all IFMA missions having an interest in Eastern Europe.

The other half of the time together was spent considering the ministry relationship between IFMA missions and churches in Europe. A position statement, "A Call to Biblical Evangelism and Church Planting," was approved as follows:

## A Call to Biblical Evangelism and Church Planting

BECAUSE of increasing encouragement from various Christian sources to carry out the mandate of Christ within existing heretical and nominally Christian churches in Europe; and
BECAUSE to do so inevitably compromises certain and specific biblical doctrines which relate to faith (Acts 4:12) and obedience (Gal. 1:6,7; Phil. 1:27b; Acts 5:29; 8:4; 13:15-41; 18:4-11; 19:8); and
BECAUSE to do so is either to ignore, bypass, or cut off the existing national Bible-believing fellowships of evangelical churches in Europe,

The IFMA Europe Committee calls upon IFMA member missions working in Europe to:

AFFIRM long recognition of the existence of evangelical Bible-believing churches in the countries of Western Europe;
AFFIRM the necessity of church-planting missions and Christian workers to identify culturally and spiritually in fellowship with Bible-believing evangelicals;
AFFIRM the conviction that the message of redemption must be disseminated through scriptural methods, consistent with biblical teaching and ethics;
AFFIRM that the unity of the body (Eph. 1:20-23; 4:4-5) must be based upon scriptural truth and must not be distorted in order to accomplish the work of evangelism;
AFFIRM that the Bible-believing evangelical church is the means both taught and demonstrated in the New Testament to accomplish the divine purposes of God;

AFFIRM that implicit in biblical evangelism is a reproducing church that teaches the whole counsel of God, which does not encourage converts to remain in heretical churches (Acts 19:10, 18-20);

AFFIRM the necessity to proclaim the distinctives of evangelical Christianity, particularly the redemptive message of the gospel with its demands upon all men, and that these must be proclaimed in total dependence upon God to accomplish salvation;

THEREFORE, in grateful recognition of the success of our European evangelical brethren in planting biblical churches long before the arrival in Europe of North American-based missions, we renew our commitment to work harmoniously alongside them, demonstrating our oneness in Christ, as together we strive to plant more churches and to strengthen the existing evangelical church for the honor and glory of God.

The IFMA Europe Committee presented an extensive outline of discussion items for the Europe strategy sessions at the 1987 IFMA-EFMA Study Conference in Orlando, Florida.

The committee met twice in 1988. Europe Committee Chairman George Murray (Bible Christian Union) and committee secretary Andrew Semenchuk (Slavic Gospel Association) prepared a five-page report on how missionaries in Western Europe can help with ministries in Eastern Europe for the September 1988 IFMA Annual Meeting strategy sessions. There was discussion also on the support structures of IFMA missions in Europe.

The committee continued to plan helpful, stimulating strategy sessions for the annual meetings of 1989 to 1991. Much of the interest focused on the expanding opportunities in Eastern Europe.

IFMA sponsored a special Eastern Europe Consultation on May 10, 1990 in Rosemont, Illinois, near O'Hare Airport. Sixteen representatives from twelve missions participated, sharing information on mission activities and relationships.

Because of escalating changes in Eastern Europe, IFMA consultations were held in Lancaster, Pennsylvania, both in March and September 1991, with invitations extended to EFMA missions, as well.

At the 1991 Annual Meeting, the board named Rev. George Murray as coordinator for Europe, with authority to ask others from any IFMA mission working in Europe to assist on a task-force basis, as needed.

## PERSONNEL AND STUDENT AFFAIRS COMMITTEE

The IFMA Board met in an extended session at Williams Bay, Wisconsin, September 24-26, 1964. This retreat was planned to give time for an in-depth study of various issues affecting the ministry of member missions. Two of the agenda items were redeployment of missionaries and student recruitment. From the consideration of these personnel issues, the Committee on Student Affairs was envisioned. It was established the following week during the IFMA Annual Meeting, with Virgil Newbrander (FEGC/SEND) and Delbert Kuehl (TEAM) as members.

The committee functioned on behalf of the association by considering matters of personnel recruitment and student relations. It met with representatives of student groups, including a consortium of students from Christian schools. The committee worked with Inter-Varsity Christian Fellowship (IVCF), Intercristo, and other organizations to coordinate relationships and activities on behalf of member missions. Two members of the committee were selected to serve on the IVCF Advisory Committee.[20]

From 1967 to 1971, the committee held a seminar for personnel workers at Missionary Internship in Detroit. On December 9, 1971, the joint IFMA-EFMA Personnel and Student Affairs Committee was formed. Since then annual workshops have continued under the sponsorship of the joint committee. The Personnel Committee is one of the two joint IFMA-EFMA standing committees that is continuing. The other is Evangelical Missions Information Service.

With the assistance of the author, representatives of the personnel departments of member missions in the Northeast formed a steering committee for sponsoring an annual Collegiate Mission Seminar for interested students from schools throughout the area for four years, 1973-1976. Students, faculty members, and IVCF workers participated in planning and conducting these seminars. Because of decreasing student involvement and reassignment of mission personnel, the seminars were discontinued.

## THE AMALGAMATION COMMITTEE

The Amalgamation Committee was formed in March 1965 to investigate possibilities, interests, and problems relating to mergers, amalgamations, and similar situations, particularly within IFMA missions, but not necessarily limited to them.

The first meetings were designed to get the subject of mission mergers out into the open for discussion. At the 1966 IFMA Annual Meeting, it was reported that almost every IFMA mission had a representative at one of the regional sessions. In Toronto approximately twenty-two people attended, representing sixteen IFMA missions. In Philadelphia twenty-seven people represented eighteen missions. In Chicago sixteen attended, representing nine missions, and in New York sixteen people represented twelve missions.

At a meeting of the IFMA Board in July 1967, the name of the Amalgamation Committee was changed to Cooperation and Comity Committee, which was more representative of the broad area of intermission relations that the committee hoped to serve. While still ready to be of assistance and encouragement in bringing about actual mergers between societies, the board and the committee felt there was a great deal to be done in fostering cooperation and united action short of merger. It recommended further study and action in the following areas of potential intermission cooperation:

> 1. Possible integration of various aspects of home and field operations without actual merger
> 2. Writing and publishing articles and reports
> 3. Cooperation in reaching the unreached
>
> Recognizing our responsibility for total world evangelization, we urge all member missions to be constantly alert for unevangelized areas or special needs not being met. If the society is not able to meet these needs, IFMA would be happy to recommend additional members which might be able to assist. The area committees of IFMA/EFMA should make the analysis of the unfinished task a major portion of their responsibility and recommend open areas to member missions for action.
>
> Before a mission enters a new area as an independent organization, it should consider whether it will be able to go into the area in sufficient strength to make a significant and sustained impact. It should be sure that it is able to provide adequate supervision for new workers. Although there may be room for additional missions, it should consider whether churches resulting from its ministry could become a part of an existing evangelical church fellowship.[22]

From 1965 to 1972, the committee was very active, sponsoring a preliminary survey of member missions, giving special presentations at IFMA Annual Meetings, conducting workshops, producing cooperation and merger materials, and serving as consultants to member missions. During this period, a number of mission mergers were accomplished and cooperative programs initiated and stimulated.

Mergers from 1966 to 1971 included: Oriental Boat Mission with International Missions; United Faith Mission and Pioneer Bible Mission, Ceylon and India General Mission and Poona Inland Village Mission into International Christian Fellowship; Practical Missionary Training into Central American Mission; Central Alaskan Mission into Far Eastern Gospel Crusade; Mexican Indian Mission into Unevangelized Fields Mission; Belgian Gospel Mission into Greater Europe Mission; and Missionary Services into MAP International. Most of these were absorptions by larger missions. One merger of two larger missions was between the Evangelical Union of South America and the Gospel Missionary Union. Of course, there were mergers before and after this period. For instance, the United Fellowship for Christian Service, formerly the Woman's Union Missionary Society, merged into BMMF International in 1976. The Orinoco River Mission merged into The Evangelical Alliance Mission in 1980. See the Appendix for details of mergers of current member missions since their founding.

## ASIA COMMITTEE

After discussions on January 1, 1965 at Urbana, Illinois, executives of missions working in Asia recommended the appointment of a joint IFMA-EFMA Asia Committee. The approval for the committee was recorded in the January 18, 1965 IFMA Board minutes.

At its March 16, 1965 meeting, the IFMA Board approved the following:

> That Mr. Morris Rockness [OMF] be appointed chairman of the IFMA Asia Committee. It was further ordered that Mr. Marshall Davis [IM], and Mr. Philip Armstrong [FEGC] be the other members serving with Mr. Rockness, in addition to the executive secretary. This committee would also serve as the IFMA representatives on the proposed joint IFMA-EFMA Asia Committee.

The first meeting of the IFMA Asia Committee was held at Winona Lake, Indiana, on October 7, 1965. Asia and the Near East were thought to be its geographical area of interest. Suggested objectives of the committee were:

1. Encourage cooperation among IFMA missions in joint ventures, such as surveying and reaching new areas, special evangelistic endeavors, literature ventures, etc.
2. Collect and correlate information helpful to IFMA missions, a sort of communication center
3. During times of economic crises or disasters in a given area, provide some sort of machinery for IFMA missions to use in temporary relief work
4. When an indigenous need and subsequent request arises for a national Evangelical Fellowship, to encourage and help in the formation of such
   a. Avoidance of *de facto* representation by a group associated with the World Council of Churches
   b. Political representation before a government in the matter of visas
   c. Ventures by the national church which can only be accomplished through such a fellowship

Two weeks later, the committee met at Western Springs, Illinois, during the 1965 IFMA Annual Meeting. Representatives from member missions with an interest in Asia met with the committee. Committee functions were reviewed and clarification was requested of the board as to the geographic boundaries of the committee. With the appointment of an Islamics Committee in 1966, the Near East came under its area. The Asia Committee then represented only Asia.

The committee met during the 1966 Annual Meeting in Toronto. It was reported that the committee had interacted through correspondence on issues relating to the Congress on the Church's Worldwide Mission in Wheaton, Evangelism in Depth, and World Evangelical Fellowship. It was the consensus of the delegates meeting with the committee that the main function of the committee was to serve as a communication center for member missions working in Asia.

Into the 1980s, the committee functioned as a part of the joint Asia Committee, and reported on items of interest in the committee's report to the annual meeting. Communication of Asia information was shared through *IFMA News* and the publications of EMIS.

The committee arranged the programs for the Asia strategy meetings during IFMA Annual Meetings. Reports were given by representatives of member missions. Papers or special presentations were made on visa concerns in various Asian countries, contextualization of the gospel, theological education, urbanization, and unreached peoples.

From 1986 to 1991, the committee invited national evangelical leaders and missionary field leaders to give reports to the committee. IFMA Asia Committee funds were used to make grants to the Evangelical Fellowship of Asia, Asia Graduate School of Theology, Asia Theological Association, and to the 1990 Asia Missions Conference in Seoul, Korea.

The committee, in September 1986, followed up on the strategy session consideration of theological education and leadership training in Asia by recommending that we as Western sending missions recognize the need to be supportive of evangelical higher theological education that is available in Asia today. Therefore, we should in most cases:

1. Encourage Asian nationals to attend Bible schools and seminaries in preference to Western institutions
2. Encourage Western institutions of higher learning to share their professors with the Asian schools during sabbaticals and other appropriate times
3. Recognizing that some Asian students will need to study in Western schools, we would encourage that such study be only a small part of the total Asian graduate study program
4. Encourage our Asian theological leaders to develop lay leadership training programs for the local churches in

Asia. Our concern is to see such lay leadership training included in the post graduate degree programs so that the local church will be strengthened and encouraged in the task of developing lay leadership.

The committee received periodic reports from Dr. Dal Congdon, IFMA committee coordinator, who on behalf of the committee interviewed Asian graduate students at Wheaton College. The project was envisioned to help to ascertain "felt needs for the '90s in Asia." It was recognized that each of these students spoke from the experience of his/her own involvement in ministry and within the context of the country of that ministry.

Another project was gathering information on Theological Education by Extension (TEE) materials as a resource for member missions. A listing of publishers and distributors of TEE materials in different parts of the world was distributed to them, as well.

The IFMA Asia Committee continued to invite speakers to address subjects of concern on all of Asia, including China and Muslim countries, as well as the place of "tentmakers," or bivocational missionaries, and nonresidential missionaries.

In 1991, Dr. Frank W. Allen (SEND), IFMA Committee chairman, recommended that a standing committee on Asia not be reappointed, but that a reporter be named for each of five regions of Asia to supply pertinent information to be shared with member missions working in those regions.

At the 1991 Annual Meeting, the IFMA Board appointed Dr. David Michell (OMF Canada) as coordinator for Asia. He may ask others from any IFMA mission working in the area for assistance on a task-force basis, as needed.

## ISLAMICS COMMITTEE

The Islamics Committee was first appointed in 1966 with Dr. Francis Steele of North Africa Mission (Arab World Ministries) as chairman. The committee met each year during the annual meeting. Its purpose was to facilitate the activities of IFMA missions working among Muslims. It was to assist and supplement, rather than duplicate or complicate, the work of the Committee of Evangelical Missionaries to Islam (EMI) and the Fellowship of Faith for Muslims (FFM). These organizations had been in operation for a number of years. IFMA missions were represented in both of them.

The IFMA Islamics Committee saw its role as fostering cooperation and coordination of member missions in areas of literature, radio, correspondence courses, and student work. To this end, they have acted as liaison with the EMI, FFM, and International Fellowship of Evangelical Students (IFES).

The committee encouraged member missions to cooperate in the conference of the Committee of Evangelical Missionaries to Islam (EMI) in its conference held at America's Keswick, January 15-18, 1968.

Member missions were also informed that the FFM office in Toronto had a helpful bibliography on Islam. Evangelical Literature Overseas (Media Associates International) office in Wheaton also published a Muslim literature survey in 1967. ELO was a member of IFMA, and Media Associates International continues its IFMA membership.

Through 1972, the committee continued to alert member missions to seminars, workshops, and available literature to assist workers among Muslims. In its desire to spread information about opportunities for Muslim work and the need of more missionaries, a proposal was made to the IFMA-EFMA related Evangelical Missions Information Service (EMIS) to produce a *Muslim World Pulse*. That publication began with two issues in 1972.

Missions of IFMA and EFMA participated in a North American Conference on Muslim Evangelization that was convened at Colorado Springs, October 16-24, 1978. Rev. Gerald Swank of SIM was appointed chairman of an

Islamics Task Force in 1978 to represent IFMA and EFMA interests in the Islamic world.

The task force worked with Don McCurry of Samuel Zwemer Institute (SZI) in holding Muslim awareness seminars in 1980-1981, utilizing a special seminar notebook prepared by SZI. By the end of 1981, at least thirty seminars had been held.

A seminar on evangelism and church planting was held June 21-25, 1982 at the Billy Graham Center, Wheaton College, co-sponsored by IFMA, EFMA, and the Graham Center.

Missions were able to visit the Samuel Zwemer Institute during the 1984 IFMA-EFMA Study Conference in Pasadena at the U. S. Center for World Mission. The IFMA Islamics Committee was committed to support the seminars and research work of the Institute, which has now changed its name to Zwemer Institute of Muslim Studies (ZIMS).

From 1985 through 1991, the IFMA Islamics Committee remained active, sharing information, strategies, and concerns with member missions. For a little over a year, a part-time committee coordinator was made available by Frontiers. During his tenure, copies of *IFMA Minaret*, a confidential newsletter, was shared only with executives of member missions involved in Muslim work. An executive newsletter was continued on behalf of the committee by Arab World Ministries.

The committee met regularly during IFMA Annual Meetings and also conferred once or twice during the year by telephone conference calls. Papers were presented during annual meeting strategy sessions on subjects relating to Muslim evangelism, such as contextualization and bivocational missionary work.

SIM made copies available to member missions of a twenty-one-page document, *Guidelines for Muslim Ministry*, which came out of a consultation for SIM Muslim workers held in Monrovia, Liberia, in 1987.

At the joint strategy sessions in 1990 at the 11th IFMA-EFMA Study Conference in Northglenn, Colorado, the discussion was on human rights for Christians living under Muslim governments. It was profitable to review the various issues associated with identifying, categorizing, and publicizing violations. This proved to be of immediate value in publicizing the unjust imprisonment of three Egyptian Christians in Cairo. They were subsequently released.

Some IFMA committee members have had serious concerns about involvement of mission agencies in publicizing violations and the committee has not always agreed on an approach. Further work needs to be done in clarifying the role of the Zwemer Institute in monitoring and publicizing human rights violations.

At the 1991 IFMA Annual Meeting, Dr. Patrick Cate of International Missions spoke at a plenary session on "Islamic Ministries Post Desert Storm." The subject was continued in the strategy sessions, along with other ministry concerns of member missions.

The hostility of religious and government leaders in Muslim lands continues to make missions to Muslims one of the most difficult, but needed, mission endeavors.

At the 1991 Annual Meeting, Rev. William Saal (AWM) was named coordinator for Islamics, and may enlist others from IFMA missions to assist on a task-force basis, as needed.

## RELIEF COMMITTEE

The IFMA Relief Committee held its first meeting on December 19, 1967. Members were Rev. Ian Hay (SIM), Rev. Alfred Larson (UFM), Rev. Joseph McCullough (Andes Evangelical Mission), and the author.

The committee felt that IFMA could assist member missions in better understanding ways and means of helping people through social action, while at the same time maintaining the needed biblical perspective.

At its meeting in March 1968, Joe McCullough presented a paper on relief and social action. From that report the committee worked out guidelines for evangelical action on the mission field. The guidelines were included in the committee's report to the 1968 Annual Meeting for consideration. In response to a request from the IFMA Board, the committee met in January 1969 to amplify the section of the guidelines dealing with biblical principles. "Guidelines for Evangelical Social Concerns on the Mission Field" was distributed to member missions in March 1969.

## Guidelines for Evangelical Social Concerns on the Mission Field

I. Gain a clear understanding of the evangelical position regarding Christian social concern and relief
   A. The Biblical basis of social concern
      1. The nature of God (Mic. 6:8), of which the believer has become a partaker (II Pet. 1:4, Matt. 5:48)
      2. The commands of Scripture (Matt. 5:16; I Tim. 6:18, Tit. 3:8)
      3. The example of Christ's actions and teaching (Acts 10:38, Luke 9:13a, Luke 6:32-36
      4. The means by which faith is authenticated (James 2:14-18)
      5. It is a ministry to Christ Himself (Matt. 25: 34 45)
      6. It is of the essence of the Christian faith (James 1:27); the practical manifestation of love (Matt. 22:37-38)
   B. Goals of evangelical social concern
      1. To fulfill our obligation as individual members of humanity and as citizens of a "this world" society to promote *social justice* which is a "need of the individual, whose dignity as a person is at stake, and a society and culture, which would soon collapse without it." (*Christianity Today*, 8 October 1965, p. 6.).

2. Among the goals of social concern would be:
   a) The elimination of poverty
   b) The opportunity for employment
   c) Racial equality
3. Obedience to our scriptural mandate in this matter (as above)
4. To provide a "climate of acceptance" for the preaching of the gospel by demonstrating our concern for *all* the needs of man
5. As the church is in a sense the extension of the incarnation, so by identifying with and meeting human need (physical, moral, and spiritual), believers fulfill their "incarnational ministry"

II. Build a solid base of operation in each country
   A. There must be open communication. Fellow workers must be informed and must stand behind the plans so that the mission organization as a whole moves together.
   B. The national church organization must be involved. If the initiative comes from them, this is naturally the best; but they may be in need of mission guidance at this point. From the beginning the national church should be involved with personnel and planning.
   C. Wide cooperation among the Protestant groups in the country is essential for securing international aid. Local conditions will differ, but theological and ecclesiastical distinctions should not deter social concern programs as in other ministries of the church. Nevertheless, the base should be structured so as to assure evangelical leadership, and contingency plans developed in case the structure falls into undesirable directions under undesirable leadership.

III. Place qualified personnel in key positions
   A. Theologically and ecclesiastically sensitive persons should be able to oversee the general direction of the movement and provide it with a philosophy.

   B. Technically skilled and experienced personnel must be in charge of the day-by-day operation of the projects. Specialized knowledge of economics, sociology, political science, and certain technical skills are essential.

IV. Secure resources from as broad a spectrum of international agencies as possible

   A. The social service organization in a given country should be free to request and accept aid from any source that seems satisfactory. This should not imply theological compromise.

   B. The missions and national churches involved should be encouraged to channel their social service resources and program through the cooperative project when possible, rather than running a separate program.

V. Organize the program on sound business policies

   A. Qualified personnel should run the office, keep careful accounts and records, etc. Counterchecks must be provided so as to build public confidence in the organization.

   B. Definite plans, long and short-term, should be set forth. Provisions should be made for emergencies and disasters.

VI. Learn what services are available, how these are used in other countries, and the strong and weak points in every program.[22]

The Relief Committee recommended to the board that the World Relief Commission be considered the primary agency through which the IFMA would work. That was approved at the May 1969 IFMA Board meeting.

The Relief Committee requested Evangelical Missions Information Service (EMIS) to survey member mission's activities, including social concern and relief, and to catalog existing services, their affiliations and outreach.

In its report to the 1969 Annual Meeting, the committee shared the results of the EMIS survey, which found that fourteen IFMA missions were interested in or involved with major relief programs. Eighteen had limited interest or involvement. Only nine of the forty-one responding missions did not perceive a need for relief programs in their ministry situations. It was also reported:

> The IFMA Official Board favors cooperation with the World Relief Commission of the National Association of Evangelicals in our overall relief program. WRC, with its personnel, administrative facilities, contacts and know-how, has assured us of its willingness for IFMA Boards to work through it. In fact, WRC has already been of great assistance this year to a number of our Boards, especially in the areas of "emergency" and " disaster" relief. Plans are under way to explore ways and means of cooperation with WRC, which will, in turn, present a stronger program and image for evangelical missions. This will have much value with governments, national believers, and home constituencies.

At the committee's November 1969 meeting, Dr. Everett Graffam was invited to give an up-to-date report on the work of WRC. Working relationships between WRC and IFMA were discussed. It was reported that Mrs. Graffam, in accordance with an IFMA request, had prepared an article on relief work for the *Evangelical Missions Quarterly*, which was published in the Fall 1971 issue.

The IFMA Relief Committee remained active through 1971, making information available to member missions and coordinating activities with WRC. After the 1971 annual meeting, it was felt that the committee's work was completed and that the IFMA Executive Director could take care of the coordination between IFMA missions and WRC.

As executive director, the author was appointed to the WRC Special Advisory Committee and met regularly with the WRC Board during the 1970s. He met occasionally with the WRC Executive Director through the 1980s, and participated in the annual meeting of the larger advisory committee. During the past decade, the WRC has become much more directly involved with relief and development programs overseas, with its own staff working with leaders of national churches and organizations.

## EVANGELISM AND CHURCH DEVELOPMENT

Dr. George Peters, professor and head of the missions department at Dallas Theological Seminary, presented papers on saturation evangelism at the 1968 IFMA-EFMA Study Conference at Winona Lake, Indiana. He proposed "that we join with our sister churches in the different lands and together launch a program of several years of saturation evangelism, mobilizing all forces and means to bring the gospel to every creature."

It was the consensus of many IFMA delegates to the study conference that the Lord was speaking to IFMA to move forward unitedly in a concentrated and concerted effort, carefully and prayerfully planned, under the direction of the Holy Spirit. The IFMA Board stated at its November 1968 meeting:

> It is our conviction that national organizations on the various continents should be encouraged in every possible way to take the initiative in developing a program of saturation evangelism. We further recommend to our member missions that they strongly support these national organizations in such planning and implementation. It is agreed that a Committee on Evangelism be appointed to undertake a continuing study of such developments with periodic progress reports to the Official Board.

The committee worked for three years to see that IFMA missions were aware of information sources, workshops, and conferences on evangelism and church growth. When EMIS began including information on saturation evangelism and church growth/development in its publications, the Evangelism and Church Development Committee concluded that its informational responsibilities were being adequately covered by EMIS and other publications and workshops. The committee was discontinued, following its report to the 1971 Annual Meeting.

## NORTH AMERICA COMMITTEE

One of the realities of the last decades of the twentieth century is the increasing influx of ethnic peoples from all areas of the globe into Canada and the United States. This prompted the formation of a North America Committee to help to raise the awareness of all member missions of the opportunities available in North America to minister to representatives of most of the ethnic and national groups being served by member missions overseas.

At the IFMA Board meeting of April 8-9, 1981, the author pointed out the need for a committee for those who work with ethnic groups in North America. The appointment of a committee was approved. Six men were appointed on October 1, 1981 to serve on the initial committee. They were William Lottis (NAIM Ministries), chairman; Don Bjork (Worldteam); Joe Daniels (Africa Inland Mission); John Gillespie (Arctic Missions/InterAct Ministries); Ernest Heimbach (Overseas Missionary Fellowship); and George Johnson (Association of North American Missions—ANAM), consultant.

The committee arranged for the preparation of study papers for the annual meeting strategy sessions. In its first years, the committee stressed two areas of mission in North America. First, work among North America ethnic populations for prefield training for overseas ministry. Second, the redeployment of returning missionaries from overseas into North American ethnic ministry when they are home for permanent or long-term periods. It also encouraged ethnic ministry for missionaries in retirement.

Committee members participated in the Newcomers Forum that was co-sponsored by IFMA, EFMA, ANAM, and the Evangelism and Home Mission Association of NAE.

The committee has been involved in helping to document the significant ethnic changes and growth patterns in North America, and in passing the information on to IFMA missions. As a result of committee encouragement, a research project on this was completed under the auspices of the Billy Graham Center at Wheaton College. The findings of this project and the discussions at IFMA Annual Meetings helped to direct Art McCleary of the U. S. Center for World Mission (USCWM) to establish the USCWM affiliate, Doorstep Opportunities, an organization to serve as a vehicle for linking potential workers with ethnic ministry opportunities. It recently became Senior Ambassadors for Christ, affiliated with the USCWM, it will (1) link volunteers with opportunities in mission in North America and abroad, (2) assist mission agencies in recruiting and retraining long-term, part-time volunteers who live within commuting distance, and (3) link experienced returning missionaries with ethnic ministry opportunities in North America.

The emphasis of the IFMA North America Committee and the strategy sessions in 1990 and 1991, under the chairmanship of Dr. Earl Parvin (Berean Mission), was on the Hispanic and the Islamic presence in North America. The committee report to the 74th IFMA Annual Meeting in 1991 stated:

> Many people are still unaware that there are hundreds of Muslim student centers on the American university campuses and over 600 Mosques or centers to be found in 46 states. Islam is the third largest religion in the U. S. after Christianity and Judaism. Jews make up 2 percent of the population and Muslims .05 percent.
>
> Americans need to become aware that Muslim presses are turning out Korans and other

> literature specifically targeting the English-speaking American citizenry. They have determined to make the United States a Muslim country. The book, *Islamic Values in the United States* by Yvonne Yazbeck Haddad and Adair T. Lumis, Oxford Press, 1987, is worth noting.

At the 1991 Annual Meeting, the board named Dr. Parvin as coordinator for North America. He may enlist others from any IFMA mission working in North America for assistance on a task-force basis, as needed.

## THEOLOGICAL COMMISSION

An IFMA Theological Commission was named in 1981, not as a standing committee, but as a commission of theological consultants to assist the IFMA on theological issues and questions. Dr. Arthur Johnston of Trinity Evangelical Divinity School was named chairman. Dr. John H. Orme (William Tyndale College), Dr. George W. Peters (Dallas Theological Seminary), and Dr. Al Platt (CAM International) were named to the first commission. Others added in later years were Dr. Harold Lindsell, Dr. Robertson McQuilkin, Dr. Charles Ryrie, Rev. Charles Tipp, and Dr. John Gration.

At the 65th IFMA Annual Meeting at America's Keswick in September 1982, Dr. Johnston spoke on evangelism and social issues. His paper that was circulated to the delegates was "A Summary and Evaluation of CRESR, Consultation on the Relationship between Evangelism to Social Responsibility."

Dr. Arthur Johnston, along with Dr. Peter Beyerhaus of Germany and Dr. Myung Yuk Kim of Korea, prepared an evangelical evaluation of the World Council of Churches' sixth assembly in Vancouver, British Columbia, in 1983. This was shared with IFMA missions.

A copy of "Baptism, Eucharist, and Ministry," a study document of the WCC, was distributed to the commission members for their study.

Dr. Johnston met with the IFMA Board in 1984. He presented two papers. One was on theological trends relating to the growing relationship between the WCC and Roman Catholicism. The second was an evaluation of the WCC document, "Baptism, Eucharist, and Ministry." These were also shared with member missions.

In 1986, the board asked the commission for information on contextualization, hermeneutics, and liberation theology. In response in 1987, the commission chairman, Rev. Charles A. Tipp (BMMF/InterServe Canada) reported the following information sources:

1. Material on hermeneutics published by the International Council on Biblical Inerrancy
2. *Liberation Theology* by Dr. Emilio Antonio Nunez of Central American Theological Seminary in Guatemala, published by Moody Press
3. "A contemporary Evangelical View of Roman Catholicism" adopted by the World Evangelical Fellowship in 1986
4. *Issues in the Ecumenical Movement Today*, by Dr. Arthur P. Johnston, published as an NAE Occasional Paper in October 1985
5. "Baptism, Eucharist, and Ministry," book review by Dr. Mariano DiGangi, BMMF International Canada, in *Evangelical Missions Quarterly*, July 1985, pages 326-30

The report of the Theological Commission in succeeding annual meetings alerted member missions of WCC activities and other theological issues.

Dr. John H. Orme was named chairman of the commission in 1990 and 1991.

## FRONTIER PEOPLES COMMITTEE

The first meeting of the Frontier Peoples Committee was held in Chicago on February 23, 1982. The purpose for the committee was given as:

> To encourage IFMA member missions in addition to current ministries to give serious attention to the claims of unreached people groups presently without a viable church. In our role as the Frontier Peoples Committee, we see the need to help keep before our constituency the unfinished task and to stimulate member missions to take new steps where possible. At the same time, it is recognized that we are not appealing to missions for radical redeployment or criticizing existent work, but simply stressing the need for fresh personnel and resources to reach out to the frontiers or unreached people groups. While it is recognized that some redeployment may occur, yet the focus is on the mobilizing of new task forces and strategies to reach beyond into the thousands of unreached people groups.

At the 65th IFMA Annual Meeting at America's Keswick, Whiting, New Jersey, in September 1982 the "IFMA Frontier Declaration" was adopted.

**IFMA Frontier Declaration**

> We, the delegates to the 65th Annual Meeting of the IFMA, recognize the historical objective of our member missions has been that of pioneering church-planting evangelism. We declare our renewed determination to penetrate the remaining frontiers of those people who represent the final barriers to the completion of the Great Commission.
>
> We acknowledge with deep gratitude the blessing of God on our whole worldwide ministries, and we praise Him for the growing dynamic church, at home and abroad, that is our partner in this task.

YET, WE CONFESS:

That though we have been challenged repeatedly to mobilize people in specific prayer for specific fields, and though we agreed to the urgency of that challenge, little has been achieved;

That in many instances we have stayed too long in established ministries when our resources should have been redirected to new frontiers;

That we have not adequately challenged and trained others to share in evangelistic outreach;

That we have failed to prepare sufficient missionaries for the frontier task and to challenge them to a life commitment; and

That we have fallen short as missionary agencies in ministering to home churches in that we often have been more concerned about what we receive without adequate concern about what we can give.

WE THEREFORE DECLARE that we will be more attentive to the plaintive cry of a lost world and the compelling mandate for the Glory of God to fill the earth.

Whereas we rejoice in the momentous impact of evangelical missions in most countries of the world, yet we acknowledge that all of the world's peoples have not been reached. We reaffirm, therefore, that our chief and irreplaceable duty is to share the blessing of God with all those peoples, and that we are called anew to prayer, devotion, and sacrifice so that we can join with others to complete the remaining task.

To that end we reaffirm our highest strategic priority to be the planting of churches among the remaining peoples by the penetration of those frontiers. We will do this both by sending new

> forces to new fields and by conveying new vision in old fields.
>
> We further declare our belief in the primacy of evangelism, yet we humbly desire to follow our Lord by expressing deeds of love and mercy, especially among the poor and oppressed peoples of our world.
>
> We humbly accept renewed responsibility to churches to labor with them toward their full involvement in the penetration of frontiers. We are willing that our methodologies and structures be submitted to the urgent need of new outreach. In this effort our commitment is to nothing less than the accomplishment of our Savior's command to make disciples of all peoples.

The work of the committee during the following decade reminded member missions of one of the central purposes of the IFMA's founding missions—to reach the unreached. The committee reports, strategy sessions, brochures, and slide series provided tools to missions to help to keep their focus on this important priority of ministry.

The committee, under the leadership of chairman Larry Allmon of Gospel Recordings, maintained an office for several years at the U. S. Center for World Mission in Pasadena. The office was closed in 1991 due to lack of available staff and funding.

At the 1991 Annual Meeting, Dr. Howard Dowdell (Canadian Center for World Mission/SIM) was named coordinator for Frontier Peoples. Others from any IFMA mission may be enlisted for assistance on a task-force basis, as needed.

## JEWISH MINISTRIES COMMITTEE

Three Jewish missions joined IFMA during the 1980s: Jews for Jesus, American Board of Missions to Jews (Chosen

People Ministries), and American Messianic Fellowship. Sensing the need for fellowship and cooperation, delegates from those missions to the 1989 IFMA Annual Meeting in Lincoln, Nebraska, met together during the strategy session time. Rev. William Currie of American Messianic Fellowship had suggested the meeting.

As a result of that meeting, the Jewish Ministries Committee was appointed with Mr. Currie as chairman. Other members were Roy Adams of Chosen People Ministries and Baruch Goldstein of Jews for Jesus. In addition to working toward more cooperation among these three member missions, the committee urged other evangelical Jewish missions to consider membership in IFMA.

One of the goals of the committee was to help other IFMA missions to become aware of the opportunities for reaching Jewish people with the gospel in most countries of the world. They also wanted Third World churches that are related to IFMA missions to be aware of the biblical mandate for Jewish evangelism. Another concern was a perceived growing menace of anti-Semitism and insensitivity even among Christians, which must be exposed. The committee considered the vast changes in Eastern Europe and the opportunities for evangelism among emigres.

Jewish evangelism resource packets were made available to all participants at the 1991 IFMA Annual Meeting in Lancaster, Pennsylvania. At this annual meeting, Rev. Wesley Taber, American Messianic Fellowship, was named coordinator for Jewish Ministries. Others from IFMA missions having Jewish ministries may be enlisted for assistance on a task-force basis, as needed.

## NOTES

[1] *IFMA Prayer Bulletin*, February 1950, p. 1.

[2] Interdenominational Foreign Mission Association, Minutes of the Mission Executive's Retreat, 15-16 September 1960, p. 2.

[3] Ibid., p. 4.

[4] J. Herbert Kane, *Faith Mighty Faith*, (New York: Interdenominational Foreign Mission Association, 1956).

[5] Robert Hall Glover, *The Progress of World-Wide Missions*, rev. 4th ed. (New York: Harper & Brothers Publishers, 1939; rev. and enl.: J. Herbert Kane, 1960).

[6] Interdenominational Foreign Mission Association, Minutes of the Publicity Committee Meeting, 9 August 1955, p. 1.

[7] Interdenominational Foreign Mission Association, *Witnessing* (New York: Interdenominational Foreign Mission Association, 1959).

[8] J. O. Percy, comp., Mary Bennett, ed. *Facing the Unfinished Task* (Grand Rapids: Zondervan Publishing House, 1961).

[9] Richard Wolff, *The Final Destiny of the Heathen* (Ridgefield Park, N.J.: Interdenominational Foreign Mission Association, 1961).

[10] Harold R. Cook, *Next Steps* ( Chicago: Moody Bible Institute, 1949; rev., Ridgefield Park, N.J.: Interdenominational Foreign Mission Association, 1966).

[11] Letter from IFMA Committee on Latin America to Member Missions, 16 January 1950.

[12] Interdenominational Foreign Mission Association, Minutes of the IFMA Committee on Latin America, 20 March 1950, p. 1.

[13] Ibid.

[14] Interdenominational Foreign Mission Association, Minutes of Meetings of the Africa Committee, Meeting of 24 January 1950.

[15] Interdenominational Foreign Mission Association, Minutes of the Special Meeting of Representatives of IFMA Missions Working in Africa, 9 December 1959, p. 1.

[16] Interdenominational Foreign Mission Association, Minutes of Meetings of the Official Board, Meeting of 26 November 1957, p. 2

[17] Fay O. Richardson, "Office Administration," in *Reports and Findings of the 7th Annual Mission Executives Retreat* (Washington: Evangelical Foreign Missions Association, 1958), p. 19.

[18] Edwin L. Frizen, Jr., Introduction to *Mission Administration Manual*, rev. ed. (Ridgefield Park, N.J.; Interdenominational Foreign Mission Association, 1972), p. iii.

[19] Interdenominational Foreign Mission Association, Europe Committee, *Survey of Missions Working in Europe* (Ridgefield Park, N.J.: Interdenominational Foreign Mission Association, 1964).

[20] Interdenominational Foreign Mission Association, Minutes of Meetings of the Personnel and Student Affairs Committee, Meeting of 2 October 1968, p. 1.

[21] Interdenominational Foreign Mission Association, Report of the Cooperation and Comity Committee, 50th IFMA Annual Meeting, 25-28 September 1967, pp. 1-2.

[22] Interdenominational Foreign Mission Association Relief Committee, "Guidelines for Evangelical Social Concerns on the Mission Field" (Ridgefield Park, N.J.: Interdenominational Foreign Mission Association, 1969), pp. 1-2.

# 10

# RELATIONSHIPS

One of the first items on the agenda of the preliminary, exploratory meeting in March 1917 was the question raised by Charles Hurlburt of the Africa Inland Mission, How far can mission boards represented, and others upon similar basis, work together?

The three-fold purpose of the association stressed the cooperation and interdependence that was sought. The purpose was: (1) to secure spiritual fellowship and intercessory prayer, (2) to open the way to mutual conferences concerning missionary principles and methods, and (3) to make possible the bearing of a united testimony to the need of a complete and speedy evangelization of the world.[1]

The IFMA was irenic in its stance from its beginning. Opposition to denominational boards and others was avoided. Through its history, this positive stand has been maintained consistently.

Through the years, several missions that did not consider themselves denominational, such as the Christian and Missionary Alliance and the Association of Baptists for World Evangelism (ABWE), were refused membership in IFMA. The question arises, If IFMA had been open to this type of mission, would the other evangelical and fundamental mission associations have been formed? While the question is interesting, it cannot be answered definitely.

At the 1946 Annual Meeting, about a year after the

EFMA was organized, a question of IFMA membership standards was raised. It was asked, Why did not IFMA consider missions that were denominational, but yet were faith missions in their principles and practice? No answer was recorded.

In an address to the annual meeting in 1946, Ralph T. Davis said that IFMA must consider its relationship with the EFMA. After discussing the issues at length, the delegation of each mission met together to determine the position of its mission. Attorney Jacob Stam and Kenneth Strachan of the Latin America Mission and Paul F. Bobb of the Central American Mission were appointed to prepare a resolution. It stated:

> Whereas the IFMA appreciates the purpose of the Evangelical Foreign Missions Association in its desire to bring about a closer relationship of the two organizations; nevertheless, it is the sincere and deep conviction of this Annual Meeting that neither the best interests of the missionary enterprise nor of the IFMA and its respective member societies would be served by such a relationship. And, therefore, the IFMA regretfully declines the invitation extended to it by the EFMA.

The vote was unanimous to accept the resolution. The IFMA sought to maintain its independent position, in fellowship, but without official connection with any denominationally related organization. It did not want to enter into a relationship with the EFMA, which might hinder fellowship with the other fundamental missions, such as members of The Associated Missions of the International Council of Christian Churches (ICCC).

## INTERNATIONAL COUNCIL OF CHRISTIAN CHURCHES (ICCC)

The year 1950 was a decisive year in regard to evangelical missions relationships. At the first IFMA Board meeting of the year, Secretary August. B. Holm (SAIM) read a letter from Arthur G. Fetzer, general secretary of Baptist Mid-Missions, expressing his concern about "world conditions in these days of apostasy." Mr. Fetzer wrote:

> Believing that this situation should be faced and that fundamental missionary organizations, both denominational and interdenominational, should be united in a comprehensive program to offset and defeat these efforts of the World Council of Churches (WCC) and its affiliates, our Council has adopted the following resolution:
>
> "Resolved: That, due to the critical conditions existing in most mission fields of the world concerning the entrance of missionaries and the expansion of the work of evangelical agencies, conditions which are aggravated by the operations of the World Council of Churches and its affiliates, a service agency is needed to represent all sound evangelical missionary societies and to approach governments on behalf of member societies on such matters as missionary credentials, government approval, and property transfers.
>
> "Therefore, we invite the Interdenominational Foreign Mission Association of North America and The Association of Baptists for World Evangelism to join us in extending a call for the formation of such an agency, the date of the call, the initial procedure and the selection of the missionary agencies who will be invited to participate to be determined by mutual agreement. . . ."

> We are convinced that the issues at stake are far reaching and may, if the Lord tarries, affect the entire course of foreign missions within the next few years.[2]

The IFMA Board appointed a committee to follow up the invitation to meet with representatives of Baptist Mid-Missions and the Association of Baptists for World Evangelism. The board passed the following resolution to be used as a preliminary basis for the proposed meeting:

> Whereas The I.F.M.A. has consistently stood for the fundamentals of the evangelical faith; and
> Whereas The I.F.M.A. desires to maintain that testimony in these days of increasing apostasy; and
> Whereas Missions in the Foreign Fields as required by many Governments, are faced with obligation to work through Service Agencies (i.e., associations to represent missions before foreign governments in matters legal, economic and social);
> BE IT THEREFORE RESOLVED: That the I.F.M.A. strongly urge its member societies to safeguard the Evangelical testimony, individually and collectively, by: (1) continuing only in such associations as will meet the requirements of our testimony and work; or by (2) joining or forming as soon as possible, such service agencies as may be practical.[3]

At the same meeting, the board also expressed an interest in fellowship with the Independent Fundamental Churches of America (IFCA). Another resolution was adopted:

> Whereas the I.F.M.A. is a fellowship of Evangelical Faith Missions with a world-wide message; and
> Whereas the I.F.C.A. is a fellowship of Independent Fundamental Churches with a world-wide missionary vision;

> BE IT THEREFORE RESOLVED: that we express to the I.F.C.A. our desire to have a close fellowship with this association of churches in the interest of Foreign Missions.[4]

Less than a week later, the IFMA Committee on Relationships met on March 21, 1950 in the offices of the Association of Baptists for World Evangelism (ABWE) with J. Gordon Holdcroft of the Independent Board for Presbyterian Foreign Missions; Joseph M. Stowell, representing Baptist Mid-Missions; and Harold T. Commons of the Association of Baptists for World Evangelism.

After a full day of frank and prayerful discussion, agreement was reached to make every effort to strengthen and unify the evangelical testimony overseas against heathenism, anti-Christian ideologies, modern liberalism, and the ecumenical movement. Letters were sent to Vincent Brushwyler, Conservative Baptist Foreign Mission Society, and A. C. Snead, Christian and Missionary Alliance, to invite them to join the next meeting of this group.

Another meeting was held in April 1950 and good progress seemed to be made toward a Conference of Fundamental Missions. A meeting was set, but had to be cancelled when it was found that the men could not meet on Monday, June 5.

The next meeting was held October 2, 1950 in New York at the invitation of layman John Bolten of Park Street Church, Boston. This meeting included a mixture of NAE and EFMA men with IFMA leaders Ralph Davis (AIM), Kenneth Strachan (LAM), Vernon Mortenson (TEAM), and J. O. Percy (SIM). It was agreed that Joseph M. Stowell, Harold T. Commons, and J. Gordon Holdcroft be invited to the next meeting, which was held a few days later on October 19, under the leadership of Mr. Bolten.

The discussions at that meeting related primarily to areas of difficulty, differences of opinion on separation, and representation before governments. There was a good deal of discussion on these various points, particularly in the matter of separation, which was considered to be the crux of the whole matter. The following was passed unanimously:

1. That the IFMA and EFMA and the Missions Commission of the ICCC each appoint working committees to prepare proposals for the formation of an Association of Fundamental Missions, which proposals are to be circulated among the other committees for their study prior to the meeting of the Official Committee to be formed
2. That the Official Committee shall consist of three delegates of the IFMA, EFMA, and the Missions Commission of the ICCC together with Dr. A. C. Snead of the Christian and Missionary Alliance and our Chairman, Mr. John Bolten
3. That the Official Committee be prepared to meet at 10 A.M. on Tuesday, November 28th, at the Dorset Hotel, 30 West 54th Street, New York, New York, under the chairmanship of Mr. John Bolten[5]

At the 1950 IFMA Annual Meeting, Ralph T. Davis presented a paper, "Relationships," in which he outlined the possibilities before the IFMA relative to a wider cooperation. He concluded by asking the delegates to produce a clear statement of the IFMA position. A committee was appointed to draft a statement, and the following was adopted:

> The Interdenominational Foreign Mission Association of North America gathered in annual conference at Lansing, Michigan, October 21st to 30th, 1950, reaffirmed its stand on the fundamentals of the faith and its desire to continue as a distinctive association and fellowship of interdenominational faith missions dedicated to the primary task of world evangelization.

> The I.F.M.A. recognizes with concern the serious situation which faces the missionary enterprise today involving problems of testimony and relationship in the face of increasing restrictions from governments, and religious persecution. In view of the difficulties and perplexities in many missionary areas of the world, where conditions differ from the situation in the homeland, we plead for a united effort on the part of all fundamental groups to seek a solution which shall insure a clear testimony, a united front and a vigorous prosecution of the missionary undertaking, and to this end we express our willingness and desire to do all in our power to bring these purposes to pass.
>
> Constrained by the great evangelical responsibility which still faces the Christian church, and by the urgency of the hour, the I.F.M.A. would reaffirm the primacy of the great commission and appeal to all who love the Lord to give precedence in prayer and effort to this all-important task.[6]

There was full attendance at the next meeting of the three associations on November 18 at the Dorset Hotel. Agreement was reached on a number of positive steps. A smaller representative group was asked to meet on December 4, 1950 to finalize the organizational structure and basis of the proposed association. Unfortunately, due to illness, Dr. Commons, the representative of the ICCC missions, was not able to attend this meeting and was not able to give advance notice so that the meeting could be rescheduled. The proposed constitution was sent to the three associations for consideration. The ICCC missions representatives were not pleased with the wording of the documents.

Meeting together became increasingly difficult for the men representing missions associated with the ICCC because of the extremely hard line of separation taken by some ICCC leaders.

Another meeting was called by John Bolten for March 20, 1951. On March 14, Dr. Holdcroft, Dr. Commons, and Rev. Newton Conant sent a letter saying that they could not participate in the meeting, stating: "The primary reason for this is that we no longer have authority to represent the Foreign Missions Commission of the I.C.C.C." Dr. Stowell, representing Baptist Mid-Missions, was the only representative of that group who attended the meeting. An impasse was reached in the negotiations, and the bright hope for a possible federation of conservative evangelical missions did not materialize.

In 1968, the author arranged a meeting between IFMA and The Associated Missions of the ICCC. Two off-the-record meetings were held at IFMA with representatives of The Associated Missions and the IFMA. The sessions were friendly, but frank. Some misinformation was corrected, and it was helpful for the participants to get to know each other personally. However, basic disagreement on interpretation of the scriptural position on separation and unity could not be resolved. The meetings did bring a greater measure of understanding of the differing positions. Subsequent contact with a few of their leaders on an individual basis was encouraging, particularly in the demonstration of an appreciation and understanding of each other's ministries.

## EVANGELICAL FOREIGN MISSIONS ASSOCIATION (EFMA)

(Evangelical Fellowship of Mission Agencies)

In 1951, Iran Interior Mission and Far Eastern Gospel Crusade were the first missions to belong to both the EFMA and IFMA. Up to twelve missions have held joint membership in the two associations during the past forty years. Early in 1992, eight agencies were members of both: Every Home for Christ, Media Associates International,

Missionary Internship, Mission Aviation Fellowship, Partners International, Trans World Radio, U. S. Center for World Mission, and Zwemer Institute of Muslim Studies.

IFMA President Ralph T. Davis presented a paper, "The IFMA: Past, Present, and Future," to the September 1959 Annual Meeting. He called for the new officers to nominate a planning committee to give careful study of ways to strengthen member missions participation in IFMA, and to offer specific proposals. This struck a responsive chord, and there was approval to appoint a planning committee immediately to make a report during a later session of the conference.

One of the new Planning Committee's suggestions raised the question of holding the IFMA Annual Meeting at the same time and place as the EFMA Executives' Retreat in order for delegates of the two conferences to meet for prayer and discussion. As a rationale for this suggestion, the committee stated:

> *Interdenominational* is not *anti-denominational.* Therefore, let us avoid the danger of allowing ourselves to be isolated from others in the Lord's work who are not members of the IFMA, but who are truly serving the Lord. This need not diminish the importance of IFMA as a fellowship and as an instrument of help to new groups worthy of recognition. . . . Our IFMA groups need wisdom in all of these relationships, and the IFMA Annual Meeting should serve as a help to us in this. We need to study biblical principles involved, the trends in missionary and church work on the fields, the ways in which the work and workers can be used most effectively to contribute to the completion of the Lord's commission.[7]

At the March 1960 IFMA Board meeting, a letter from Clyde W. Taylor, EFMA's executive secretary, was read. He suggested the possibility of the executive committees of the IFMA and the EFMA meeting to discuss possible areas of cooperation in an effort to counteract the ecumenical movement. An approval motion stated "that the IFMA Executive Committee meet with the EFMA Executive Committee, should they so desire, bearing in mind that it must be made clear what the IFMA position is on cooperation with certain segments of EFMA." This was a particular reference to Pentecostal and charismatic missions. There is no record of such a meeting being held.

A major item for discussion at the special meeting of IFMA missions executives September 15-16, 1960 was areas of cooperation in relation to doctrinal, ethical, and comity standards.

After discussion on the IFMA purpose and its fellowship, Kenneth Strachan (LAM) and Francis Steele (NAM) made a motion that was adopted:

> Recognizing the tremendous pressures and demands of the crucial days through which the missionary enterprise is passing, we reaffirm the objectives outlined in our Constitution including specifically the following functions for both home base and fields: fellowship, promotion, accreditation, leadership coordination and service, and that we express our support for and encouragement to the leadership of the I.F.M.A. in the vigorous prosecution of each of these objectives in practical application to the peculiar requirements of our contemporary situation.[8]

Concerning a wider cooperation beyond the IFMA, the following statement was recorded:

> Without compromising our position, but, on the contrary, spelling out our theological position and stand against the ecumenical movement and recognizing the honest differences of opinion

> among fundamentalists, there should be an earnest seeking to work together with those of like precious faith.[9]

A committee to study relations while at the IFMA Executives Retreat presented its following report. The report was accepted, but it was not presented to an annual meeting for adoption as official policy until 1963.

The IFMA Executives Retreat in September 1960 recommended that the board canvas member missions regarding their position on further future cooperation with EFMA and The Associated Missions (TAM) of the ICCC. Mission amalgamations were discussed favorably, as was a projected conference with leaders of Christian colleges and Bible schools. These matters were committed to the board for further consideration and implementation.

The 1961 Annual Meeting program included a panel discussion on the question, Should interdenominational faith missions enter into a cooperative relationship in ecumenical evangelism? Consideration of that issue resulted in the following action:

> Resolved: That recognizing the imperative need for all-out evangelism on every field, especially in these crisis times, we would encourage our members to seek new means of cooperation with other IFMA missions and similar evangelical groups on their field in aggressive programs of mass evangelism. We believe evangelicals are sufficiently strong in many areas and should do this before liberal elements move in and create problems of association and cooperation.

At the same meeting, one revision to the IFMA Constitution made more explicit the authority of the association in relation to the areas of work and cooperation of its member missions. It stated:

> The Association, recognizing the autonomy of its constituent members, does not impose administrative restrictions as to their distinctive works or their areas of cooperation which do not violate our basic Christian ethics or doctrine as outlined in the Confession of Faith.

A paper was presented by Robert N. Thompson of Gospel Recordings, "The Problem of the Ecumenical Movement of the World Council and Its Avowed Aims of Engulfing National Churches." The IFMA Africa Committee, also, stressed the need for evangelical cooperation in light of ecumenical pressures, stating:

> Opposition to the gospel message and indigenous church growth is mounting and coming from many and various sources. One of these is the present ecumenical movement whereby faith missions would be bypassed as the W.C.C. establishes relationships with the national pastors and churches on the foreign field. Therefore, it is our recommendation that our member missions circulate information about this matter to our missionaries and leaders on the fields. That we seek to form evangelical fellowships among the African converts that would give them a united voice. The Africa Inland Mission reports great blessing from their first Conference where African leaders from all of their fields were brought together. The Sudan Interior Mission is encouraged by the progress made in the Nigerian Evangelical Fellowship. The South Africa General Mission reports that blessing has resulted from the evangelical fellowship on the Gold Coast. The North Africa Mission reports a fellowship of evangelicals in Morocco. We are grateful for this trend and it must be encouraged.

> Our faith mission personnel should further seek ways in which we can coordinate and work more closely together on the field.

At the November 1961 meeting of the IFMA Board, President Hubert Cook read a letter received from Milton Baker, president of the EFMA. Dr. Baker quoted a motion passed by the EFMA Board, which stated: "That the dates of the 1962 Retreat be set for September 10-14, and that we extend an invitation to the IFMA to meet with us in joint session." Dr. Baker then expanded on the invitation, saying in part:

> Though I believe communications have passed back and forth in the past regarding closer fellowship between our two groups, it would seem that the growing intensity of world events in both the religious and political realms force us to prayerfully search our hearts to see what we as evangelical mission leaders can do to encourage our co-workers and aid them in the work which the Lord has called them to do. . . .
>
> A joint Program Committee would undoubtedly come up with topics for discussion which would represent the best thinking of both groups. This Committee could also plan separate business sessions for the two organizations during the time of the retreat. This would not only preserve the autonomy of the two groups, but make it possible to carry out routine business matters.

The IFMA Board responded that the dates and place for the 1962 Annual Meeting was already set, but they would be happy to have the member missions consider the invitation for another year. This was a positive step toward the first joint conference of the two associations.

A letter was read from Fred G. Ferris, International Secretary of the World Evangelical Fellowship (WEF), asking that the IFMA clarify its position in regard to the WEF. In referring to the United States Board of the WEF, Mr. Ferris wrote:

> Another obvious weakness of the WEF in years gone by has been its policy of operating entirely apart from consultation with Mission Executives. I am making every effort to overcome this, and am seeking to have Mission Executives appointed to our Board. . . . If we are truly going to be the voice for evangelicals around the world and to adequately represent them, we must also have IFMA men helping to steer our program.
>
> I would appreciate any suggestions you might make, as to how we can go about establishing a closer relationship with the IFMA men, looking forward to the time when the WEF Board will be largely comprised of men from both the IFMA and EFMA.

The IFMA Board expressed appreciation for Mr. Ferris' letter but indicated it was not its prerogative to endorse the WEF, which would have to be done by its individual members.

Practical cooperation between IFMA and EFMA at that time remained in the joint committees, which were related to work overseas in Africa and Latin America. The major discussion at the IFMA Executive Committee meeting of December 19, 1961 related to the Evangelical Committee for Latin America (ECLA) meeting of the month before. The ECLA meeting approved detailed arrangements for a conference on evangelism (CLASE) to be held in Huampani, Peru. The Conference Committee was composed of mission representatives of IFMA, EFMA, and the Evangelical Missionary Alliance of England, along with a similar number of Latin evangelical Christian leaders. The IFMA Executive Committee endorsed the actions recorded in the ECLA minutes, thereby giving strength to evangelical cooperation in Latin America.

Cooperation of IFMA and EFMA in Africa was progressing at this time. The joint IFMA-EFMA Africa Committee approved a trip to Africa by representatives from the leadership of the two associations in order to encourage evangelical cooperation.

The stand of the IFMA before the Christian public was discussed by the board in September 1962. Action was taken to circulate the following board statement to member missions for their consideration:

> The I.F.M.A. is a free association of missions having a common doctrinal position and adhering to other standards of membership prescribed by the Constitution. To member missions is granted by our Constitution a full measure of autonomy within the limits of the above named standards in the realm of individual relationships and actions. Recognizing in these days the crucial importance of doctrinal fidelity, the I.F.M.A. as an organization makes as the theological basis of its cooperation with other organizations the basic fundamentals of Christian belief as expressed in the five points of the Niagara Statement of 1895, delineated as follows:
>
> 1. The verbal, plenary inspiration of the Scriptures and their inerrancy in the original manuscripts
> 2. The deity of Christ
> 3. The virgin birth of Christ
> 4. The vicarious substitutionary atonement of Christ
> 5. His physical resurrection and future bodily return

On the first day of the 1962 Annual Meeting, the IFMA Board discussed thoroughly the 1960 Executive Retreat statement on the IFMA position in relation to others outside the association. The statement was referred to the incoming board for their study and subsequent presentation to member missions for vote.

The 1962 Annual Meeting ratified the action of the board to set up the Africa Evangelical Office in Nairobi, Kenya—a joint IFMA-EFMA project—under the leadership of Kenneth Downing of the Africa Inland Mission.

At the same meeting, a letter from Louis L. King, president of the EFMA, was read. Dr. King invited the IFMA to meet with the EFMA September 30 - October 4, 1963 at Winona Lake, Indiana. The program would include joint study and discussion periods on mutually beneficial subjects, and separate business sessions for each association. The EFMA invitation was accepted "with the understanding that the Program Committee will work out a location for business sessions and committee meetings."

The Annual Meeting approved holding the 1963 Annual Meeting in cooperation with the EFMA in a joint study conference. The following resolution was passed:

> Resolved: That we, in view of the religious climate of the day at home and abroad, give all diligence to "stand fast in one spirit, with one mind striving together for the faith of the gospel," with praise to God for evidences of increasing fellowship and cooperation among IFMA missions and with other evangelical groups.

The IFMA Board, in January 1963, appointed a committee of Philip Armstrong (FEGC), Elrow LaRowe (IM), and Ralph Odman (UFM) to review the 1960 recommended Policy on Relationships to circulate to member missions in preparation for vote.

The author became executive secretary of IFMA on

September 1, 1963. The first joint conference with EFMA was held at the end of that month.

The 1963 Annual Meeting marked a milestone in the position of the IFMA on evangelical relationships. The main indication of a changed attitude toward relationship with the EFMA was that the two associations could come together in a joint study conference. Toward the end of the meeting, a recommendation from the board was approved for an invitation to be extended to EFMA to meet jointly again in 1965. Other actions on cooperation taken during this meeting were:

1. EFMA missions were invited to use any IFMA missionary pamphlets with their own imprint, at the same cost as IFMA missions.
2. Agreement was reached on recommended qualifications for membership in the proposed Association of Evangelicals of Africa and Madagascar (AEAM) as proposed by the joint IFMA-EFMA Evangelical Committee for Africa. Since evangelicals in each country must establish their standards of fellowship, we desire that our Africa missionaries be advised of our thinking on the subject. With many theological and organizational issues still being considered and debated in several African countries, we suggest the following regarding membership in any evangelical fellowship, national or regional, which may be established. Any mission, church, or individual joining such a fellowship shall promote and work in harmony with the stated purposes of the fellowship. Caution should be exercised concerning churches or missions maintaining affiliation with other organizations not in accord with the said purposes. As missions and national churches are clearly informed on current theological and organizational issues, we are confident that evangelicals will realize the undesirability of being affiliated with or affiliating with the World Council of Churches or its agencies. After an initial transitional period, evangelical fellowships will avoid

retaining in membership church or mission bodies that are or become related to the World Council of Churches or its agencies. However, it may provide membership without vote for individuals.

3. The IFMA Literature and Publicity Committee recommended that the IFMA Official Board take all necessary steps to launch a missionary journal in cooperation with the EFMA. The Annual Meeting approved this recommendation, and the IFMA Board appointed representatives to a Missionary Journal Committee. It later became the board of the IFMA-EFMA-sponsored Evangelical Missions Information Service (EMIS), publisher of *Evangelical Missions Quarterly*.
4. Approval was given for IFMA to name a Higher Education Committee and to invite EFMA to do the same. This became the joint Committee to Assist Ministry Education Overseas (CAMEO).
5. The policy statement on relationships, first suggested at the 1960 IFMA Executives' Retreat, was finally adopted, with only minor changes. See Appendix C.
6. The Official Board, feeling that one of the most significant things to come out of this joint conference was a guarantee of good faith in one another's Association, recommended that a joint EFMA-IFMA Committee on Comity be set up, and that the Presidents and Executive Secretaries serve on this committee. Motion was made, seconded, and carried that the IFMA appoint such a committee and invite the EFMA to do so.
7. Projection of another Congress on World Missions. After favorable consideration of another Congress to follow up the IFMA's Congress in 1960, it was suggested that dates after 1965 be considered, with EFMA being invited to participate. It was recognized that an Urbana Conference was scheduled in 1964, and another IFMA-EFMA study conference was projected for 1965. This action by the 1963 IFMA Annual Meeting was the initial move

toward the 1966 Congress on the Church's Worldwide Mission held at Wheaton College.

8. Final resolution on cooperation with EFMA adopted:
   Whereas a forward step has been taken in the interest of worldwide missions through the holding of this joint meeting of IFMA-EFMA leaders, and
   Whereas blessing has resulted in cooperative efforts of the two associations in specific projects in Africa and Latin America,
   BE IT RESOLVED that such joint efforts be continued and that the possibility of new ventures in cooperation be explored.

Among papers given at the conference, three were on evangelical cooperation and ecumenical dangers in Africa by Sidney Langford (AIM), Asia by Vernon Mortenson (TEAM), and Latin America by Wade Coggins (EFMA).[10]

It was recorded that three of the outstanding leaders of IFMA missions had died during the year: T. J. Bach of TEAM, Guy Playfair of SIM, and Ralph Davis of AIM. These men, no doubt, would have given approval to the steps taken toward evangelical cooperation. Seventeen years before the first meeting with EFMA, in 1946, Ralph Davis had asked the association to take a stand on its position regarding cooperation with the EFMA.

The positive response to the 1963 joint study conference and the action taken by the IFMA opened the way for cooperation between the two associations during the past twenty-nine years.

The basis for the continuing relationship between IFMA and EFMA was clearly stated in a resolution adopted by the 1965 IFMA Annual Meeting:

> Whereas the IFMA at its Annual Meeting in 1963 set forth a Statement of Policy on Relationships and whereas there exists a common adherence with the EFMA to a soundly evangelical position and dedication to the advance of the Gospel

> BE IT RESOLVED that the IFMA continue to cooperate with the EFMA in various joint efforts consistent with our aims and position and to fellowship in our common faith and problems, but, because of differing historical backgrounds and constitutional frameworks, the two organizations retain their distinctive identities without thought or purpose of amalgamation.

Occasionally through the years since 1965 the question of merger of the two association has been raised by an EFMA mission leader on a personal basis. The answer from IFMA always referred back to the 1965 Annual Meeting action as the continuing position of IFMA.

The author's executive director's address to the 1989 IFMA Annual Meeting, "Looking Toward the 90s," considered in detail the issue of IFMA relationship with other organizations, including EFMA.

It was apparent that 1989 was a time of leadership change in member missions and in the associations, as well. Rev. Paul McKaughan had been named to succeed Dr. Wade Coggins as executive director of EFMA, and IFMA had appointed a search committee for an executive director to succeed the author.

After the IFMA Annual Meeting in 1989, meetings were set up between the executive directors of the two associations and the executive-director designate of EFMA, Paul McKaughan, to discuss continued cooperation between IFMA and EFMA. Another meeting was projected between the two executive committees of the associations. The IFMA Board's position was to continue in the same relationship.

Before the meeting of the two executive committees could be held, the EFMA executive committee delivered a letter to the IFMA, requesting that the uniting of the two organizations be explored. The issue was considered, but the position of the IFMA did not change. IFMA was strong in its position of no merger with EFMA.

The meeting of the two executive committees met June 8, 1990 at Chicago's O'Hare Airport. In the all-day sessions, the past, present, and future relationship of the two associations was discussed in great detail. The meeting was concluded with the adoption of the following statement:

> On June 8, 1990 in Chicago, Illinois, a meeting was held of the Executive Committees of the IFMA and EFMA in which it was agreed to maintain the good working relationships through study conferences and workshops, which EFMA and IFMA have enjoyed through the past thirty years.

The basis for IFMA's continuing relationship with EFMA remains cooperation "without thought or purpose of amalgamation."

Both associations hold firmly to the theological fundamentals of historic biblical Christianity. They differ primarily in membership qualifications, procedures, and relationships. A majority of the founding missions of the IFMA were international organizations with sending councils or boards in different countries, including Canada, the United States, and British Commonwealth countries. IFMA missions were called interdenominational because they drew missionary workers and support from a variety of evangelical denominational and independent churches. The IFMA itself is not organizationally related to denominational structures or associations. Denominational and Pentecostal/charismatic mission agencies do not qualify for membership in IFMA.

The membership of EFMA consists of both denominational and independent mission agencies, including Pentecostal and holiness agencies. The EFMA is organizationally affiliated with the National Association of Evangelicals, and, through the NAE, is officially related to the World Evangelical Fellowship.

While the EFMA and the IFMA have each maintained its own identity, they have developed through the years a relationship based upon the recognition of the unity existing in the body of Christ and expressed through coordination and cooperation without compromise of distinctives or organic unity.

## ASSOCIATION OF CHURCH MISSIONS COMMITTEES (ACMC)

From the 1920s, IFMA missions on the West Coast sponsored meetings in their areas. Dr. John E. Jaderquist was the initiator of the IFMA cooperative missions conferences held on the Pacific Coast each year. He was active in IFMA from 1919 until his death in 1946. Dr. Jaderquist was appointed IFMA Western Representative in 1932 and was also a vice president of IFMA from 1935 to 1946.

One such meeting was the forerunner of the Association of Church Missions Committees. On April 22, 1973, an IFMA Consultation of Partners in Mission was sponsored by IFMA missions on the West Coast and was held at the Lake Avenue Congregational Church in Pasadena. Personnel from two IFMA missions—Mission Aviation Fellowship and International Missions—were in charge of the promotion and other arrangements. As the IFMA Executive Director, the author presided at the day-long consultation. There was good attendance of pastors, church missions committee members, professors, and IFMA missions personnel. Both churches and missions expressed appreciation for the presentations and discussions.

The following year, several who had attended this meeting—Peter Wagner, Ralph Winter, and their colleagues—called a meeting of mission committee chairpersons from churches across the United States with large missions programs. The meeting was named National Institute for Missionary Committee Chairmen and was held in Pasadena, June 14-16, 1974. The IFMA and EFMA Executive Directors served as consultants for this meeting, from which the Association of Church Missions Committees (ACMC) was formed.

During its relatively short existence, ACMC has done much to stimulate the growth of missions within evangelical churches of North America. There is great potential for ACMC's continued influence in the days ahead.

Many evangelical pulpits in North America are weak on missions. The average person in the pew is not convinced that the countless millions of people who have not heard the gospel are lost and eternally damned. They do not believe that those people who are apart from Jesus Christ are going to hell. The church needs to again be convinced that man is lost apart from Jesus Christ.

The IFMA has little contact with churches, so it must work with and through member missions and with and through the ACMC. The IFMA and its member missions must continue to cooperate with and to strengthen the ACMC in its vital ministry.

The IFMA has maintained a good cooperative relationship with ACMC since it was organized in 1974. The author has been a member of the ACMC Advisory Board from the beginning, and has participated in ACMC workshops and special projects. ACMC leaders are invited to participate in the IFMA Annual Meeting and special workshops, as well.

## ASSOCIATION OF NORTH AMERICAN MISSIONS (ANAM)

The Association of North American Missions (ANAM) was known during most of its fifty-year history as National Home Missions Fellowship (NHMF). Dr. Harry Ironside, pastor of Moody Memorial Church in Chicago, in 1941 pointed out the need for a "home missions" organization that would be comparable to IFMA. NHMF was organized in 1942 at Moody Church by a group of pastors and leaders of missions that were concentrating on the unreached of the United States. For over thirty years, NHMF's annual conference was held in conjunction with the home missions conference at Moody Church.

Organizational changes, along with its name change in 1980, made ANAM more like the IFMA in its operations and standards. In theological position and in supporting constituency, there has always been a close affinity.

IFMA and ANAM have participated together in the ethnic newcomers to North America committee and workshops. Seven missions hold membership in both IFMA and ANAM: American Missionary Fellowship, BCM International, Berean Mission, Helps International Ministries, Missionary TECH Team, Open Air Campaigners, and The Pocket Testament League. ANAM leaders are invited to participate in IFMA meetings and workshops. It is the desire of the IFMA that the two associations continue a close relationship.

## LAUSANNE COMMITTEE FOR WORLD EVANGELISM (LCWE)

The Lausanne Committee for World Evangelization (LCWE) published a 40-page document, *The Lausanne Story*, in 1987. A statement on page 18 reads:

> It is important to understand that Lausanne is a movement. It is not an organization of churches, it is not an organization which one "joins." . . . The Lausanne movement allows Christians and churches to maintain their denominational distinctives, while bringing them together for the singular purpose of world evangelization.

The leadership is a self-appointed *ad hoc* committee of seventy-five people from around the world, serving two-year terms, and eligible to serve a limit of three consecutive terms. The committee meets every two years. Dr. Leighton Ford currently chairs the fifteen-member executive committee, which acts on behalf of LCWE between its biennial meetings. Rev. Tom Houston, previously international director of World Vision, as international director heads the ongoing staff.

The IFMA Board authorized the author's participation in

Lausanne I and II, and several other Lausanne-sponsored meetings, but he has not served on any Lausanne committee. Only two or three IFMA mission leaders have served on a Lausanne committee. Neither the author nor the IFMA Board believes that attending a meeting as a participant establishes a relationship with the sponsoring group.

Through his participation in Lausanne II in Manila in 1989, the author sensed an apparent change in the Lausanne movement in at least three areas, which were disturbing.

The first area of concern is the participation of Roman Catholic clergy—men and women—in Lausanne II. When the author was informed by a Lausanne staff member that some Roman Catholics were anticipated, both as participants and as observers, he informed the IFMA Board. The board requested that a letter be drafted protesting the inclusion of Roman Catholics among the invited participants. It went out over the signatures of IFMA President John Beerley (UFM), Secretary Frank Severn (SEND), and Executive Director Frizen to the Lausanne leadership.

The responses from several of the Lausanne leaders stated, in essence, that the invitations to participate were left to the local selection committees, all unnamed. The overall participant selection had eight anonymous members from eight countries. The director of participant selection was Brad Smith of MARC/World Vision, who worked under Ed Dayton, director of the program committee for Lausanne II. At least a dozen other MARC/WV staff held key positions in leadership of the program and participant selection process. There is no doubt in the author's mind but that World Vision contributed much in funding and personnel to Lausanne and exerted enormous influence on the direction and position of the Lausanne movement.

In addition to the IFMA protest regarding Roman Catholic participation, many delegates, especially those from strongly Roman Catholic countries, were deeply offended by their inclusion.

The Lausanne leadership appears determined to continue to include Roman Catholics in their programs in spite of all protests from conservative evangelicals. In the July-August 1989 issue of Lausanne's *World Evangelization*, executive committee member Dr. Saphir Athyal wrote about the future of the Lausanne Movement:

> Essentially, its present structure will continue though other working committees will be added along with the development of regional and national networks. Some of the extreme right and left wing evangelicals may be disenchanted with it and leave. But the movement will provide the widest and most representative global link among the evangelicals of all segments of the Christian Church—Protestant, Orthodox, and Roman Catholic—that focus on the task of world evangelization.

After Manila 1989, the August issue of *MARC Newsletter* commented on the inclusion of Catholics, saying, "This turned out to be less of a problem than anticipated. Evangelistic concern usually becomes a unifying factor." The author's opinion is that MARC/WV does not recognize the extent of those not in agreement.

The author is convinced that the die is cast, that the Lausanne Committee for World Evangelization will become increasingly inclusive in all of its programs. It appears to be repeating the direction of the leadership of the Edinburgh Conference of 1910, which led into the World Council of Churches through a widely cooperative world-evangelization vision.

The second area of concern was the heavy emphasis on social justice issues emphasized in many of the plenary sessions and workshop groups. A quote in Lyn Cryderman's report on Lausanne II in the August 18, 1989 issue of *Christianity Today* demonstrates that emphasis: "'In 1974

[Lausanne I], we almost had to sneak in the message of social ministry,' said urban expert Ray Bakke. 'Now, it's almost all we hear.'"

Throughout the congress, there was almost no mention of the evangelistic, church-planting and discipling ministries of evangelical missions. Luis Palau, in his closing-day address, was one who gave a balanced presentation of what the gospel really is and is not. He also recognized the contribution of missionaries in world evangelization.

Dr. Harold Lindsell, a member of the IFMA Theological Commission, cautioned:

> Social action has become a driving force among Evangelicals and could easily quench their zeal for evangelism both at home and abroad. . . . Not that there is no place for social action. But when the proper relationship and the correct balance are changed, then social action gains an ascendance that does not belong to it."[11]

The third area of concern is the much greater emphasis on and manifestation of the charismatic influence in the Lausanne proceedings. The *Christianity Today* article also pointed this out. "To say the Lausanne movement is more open to Charismatics than it was in 1974 is to understate the obvious." The author attributes this over emphasis of Charismatics to the program committee in assigning Pentecostal (Four Square) pastor Jack Hayford to conclude an evening service under the topic "Power and Work of the Holy Spirit," and to give a charismatic invitation. According to *Christianity Today*, even Leighton Ford said that the program committee made a mistake in asking Dr. Hayford to conclude as he did.

The author has deep respect for Jack Hayford. He is an evangelical Christian gentleman, and a gifted expositor of the Scriptures. His song, "Majesty, Worship His Majesty," is a favorite among believers worldwide. Dr. Hayford's theological conviction is in the Four Square tradition, but the author has never known or heard of his forcing his position on others or his requiring that others hold the same views as his in the area of a Pentecostal or charismatic experience. In Manila 1989, he followed the request of the program committee.

As an association, the IFMA is not *anticharismatic;* it is *noncharismatic.* IFMA respects the theological stance of Pentecostals and Charismatics, and does not try to force a noncharismatic position on them. Individual member missions within IFMA may accept as missionaries those who are Pentecostal or Charismatic if they desire. But no mission that is considered a Pentecostal or Charismatic mission is accepted into IFMA membership.

Regarding the Lausanne Committee for World Evangelization, if, as it appears, the concerns mentioned and others that are not mentioned continue in LCWE, the author has serious reservations about participation by IFMA leadership in the future.

## WORLD COUNCIL OF CHURCHES (WCC)

A wide gulf exists between the IFMA and the World Council of Churches in regard to the Bible, human history, the church, and missions. After the WCC conference in Bangkok in 1973, Dr. Peter Beyerhaus wrote:

> I am convinced that the WCC has made up its mind to use all the means at its disposal to close the "missionary age" for all of its affiliated churches and mission agencies, as well as for all other institutions which it influences, and to implement its new understanding of "world mission." . . . The goal of the boldest ecumenical thinkers and leaders has grown increasingly clear: to construct a world community embracing all races, classes, religions, and political systems, united as far as possible under a common world

> government whose business will be the establishment of world peace. It is hoped that a universal church will be able to pave the way successfully for a universal government. Such a universal church would, however, not only be trans-confessional, it would also be unconditionally open to partnership with other religions and ideologies.[12]

There is no common biblical basis for cooperation between the IFMA and the ecumenical movement.

## WORLD EVANGELICAL FELLOWSHIP (WEF)

World Evangelical Fellowship is an international alliance of autonomous national and continental evangelical bodies. It traces its roots to the Evangelical Alliance founded in Britain in 1846. After disruptions due to the two world wars, it was officially reformed as the World Evangelical Fellowship in the Netherlands in 1951.

WEF provides a structure with which evangelicals worldwide may voluntarily identify themselves. It represents the church that is faithful to Jesus Christ and His teaching. It is a worldwide body that is thoroughly evangelical.

The World Evangelical Fellowship is a membership organization. Its members are national evangelical fellowships. WEF's membership has grown to 62 associations, representing 120 million believers. Full membership is open to any national or regional body that represents an adequate cross section of evangelicals in its area, is organized with a constitution and is in accord with the purpose and program of WEF, contributing annually to its support.

In North America, WEF's members are the Evangelical Fellowship of Canada, National Association of Evangelicals, and the National Black Evangelical Association. In addition, the WEF accepts international missionary organizations as associate members. Several IFMA missions have identified with WEF as associate members.

The members of WEF meet at six-year intervals in General Assembly. The ten members of the executive council are elected to represent global geographic areas in a balanced manner. The council, in turn, appoints an international director to direct the fellowship's day-to-day operations, and executive secretaries for the commissions it authorizes.

The commissions are standing bodies created to assist the WEF members in specialized areas, which currently are church renewal, missions, theology, and women's concerns. Their members are persons with appropriate expertise drawn from, and approved by, the member bodies.

The IFMA has no formal relationship with WEF. However, the IFMA Board approved the author's membership on the Missions Commission of WEF from its beginning in the 1970s until he stepped down as IFMA Executive Director in September 1991. The author also served on the commission's executive committee as its member from North America. The author was a member of the WEF North American Council, as well.

In contrast with the Lausanne position, WEF at its 1986 general assembly approved a clear theological position paper on the Roman Catholic issue.

Through national evangelical fellowships, WEF relates directly with many of the churches and church leaders associated with IFMA member missions. For a number of years, the author has encouraged cooperation with and participation in the World Evangelical Fellowship on every level possible.

## NOTES

[1] Interdenominational Foreign Mission Association, Minutes of Organizational Meeting, 29 September 1917.

[2] Interdenominational Foreign Mission Association, Minutes of the Official Board, 16 March 1950, pp. 1-2.

[3] Ibid., p. 2.

[4] Ibid., p. 3.

[5] Interdenominational Foreign Mission Association, Notes on meeting held in the Dorset Hotel, New York, 19 October 1950, p. 2.

[6] Interdenominational Foreign Mission Association, Minutes of Annual Meeting, 24-27 October 1950, p. 6.

[7] Interdenominational Foreign Mission Association, Minutes of the Annual Meeting, 27 September - 4 October 1959, pp. 36-37.

[8] Interdenominational Foreign Mission Association, Minutes of the Meeting of Mission Executives, 15-16 September 1960, p. 2.

[9] Ibid.

[10] Interdenominational Foreign Mission Association - Evangelical Foreign Missions Association, *Reports and Findings of the 1963 Annual Mission Executives Retreat* (Washington: Evangelical Foreign Missions Association, 1963).

[11] William J. Danker and Wi Jo Kang, eds., *The Future of the Christian World Mission* (Grand Rapids: William B. Eerdmans Publishing Company, 1971), p. 92.

[12] Peter Beyerhaus, *Bangkok '73* (Grand Rapids: Zondervan Publishing House, 1973), p. 107.

# 11

# COOPERATIVE COMMITTEES

For seventy-five years, the Interdenominational Foreign Mission Association has zealously guarded its independent status as a conservative evangelical association of nondenominational mission agencies. It has never been a member of any national or international church or organization. While holding firmly to the fundamentals of biblical Christianity, IFMA has maintained an irenic position toward other organizations.

For a number of years after the failure to bring together the IFMA, the EFMA, and The Associated Missions (TAM) into a cooperative fellowship, the IFMA remained aloof from official involvement with either group because of its desire to maintain an equal relationship with both groups. It was recognized that a simultaneous working relationship with both groups could not be achieved. The IFMA cautiously began to participate in cooperative committee activities with the EFMA, while maintaining its historic independence.

## SUMMER INSTITUTE OF MISSIONS COMMITTEE

The education and training of missionaries was one of the major subjects discussed at the EFMA-sponsored Missions Executives Retreat in 1955. Papers were given by Dr. Merrill C. Tenney, dean of Wheaton Graduate School; Dr. Paul G. Culley, dean of Columbia Graduate School of Bible and Missions; Dr. H. Wilbert Norton, dean of Education at Trinity Seminary and Bible College; and Dr. Charles Seidenspinner, president of Southeastern Bible College.

The Findings Committee recommended consideration of a Summer School of Missions, consisting of two four-week terms to be held on the campus of a Christian college or seminary. Faculty would be recruited from all evangelical sources to teach courses that would be available to students, missionaries, and missions executives. It was recognized that the summer school should be affiliated with an accredited institution. It was envisioned that this could pave the way for a permanent evangelical graduate school of missions. The Committee on Missionary Education was composed of Merrill C. Tenney, Paul G. Culley, Charles Seidenspinner, Wilbert Norton, Vincent Brushwyler, and J. B. Toews.

At the EFMA Missions Executives Retreat in October 1956, Dr. James Buswell III and Dr. Enoch Dyrness of Wheaton College were invited to meet with the committee. Plans were finalized for a proposed Summer Institute of Missions. The motion to the EFMA retreat recommended that "implementation of the report be placed in the hands of a committee to be composed of four members appointed by the EFMA, four members appointed by the Educational Commission of the NAE, the executive secretary of EFMA *ex officio*, and four members, which the IFMA shall be invited to appoint."[1] The motion passed without opposition.

IFMA missions represented at the retreat included Central American Mission, Far Eastern Gospel Crusade, International Missions, Latin America Mission, Regions Beyond Missionary Union, South Africa General Mission, The Evangelical Alliance Mission, and World Radio Missionary Fellowship.

A few weeks later, Rev. Ezra Shank reported the EFMA action to the 1956 IFMA Annual Meeting. The invitation for committee participation was referred to the board for action. The board met in November and after full discussion, appointed four members and two alternates.

Members were Vernon Mortenson (TEAM), Elrow LaRowe (IM), Frank Longman (AIM), and J. O. Percy (IFMA), with Ralph Davis (AIM) and Ezra Shank (SAGM) as alternates. It was agreed that IFMA should write to Dr. Seidenspinner, recommending that the American Association of Bible Institutes and Bible Colleges be represented on the Summer Institute of Missions Committee, also.[2]

At the 1957 Annual Meeting, Dr. Vernon Mortenson reported on the first Summer Institute of Missions held June 21 to July 19 at Wheaton College. In order to prepare himself better as a committee member, Dr. Mortenson had enrolled in the course, "Modern Missionary Methods and Trends," taught by Hubert Reynhout. The committee felt that the 1957 experience was basically positive, except for the small total enrollment of twenty-one in the two courses.

It was recommended that in addition to other courses, a graduate-level course be offered during the Wheaton Summer Inter-Session period, June 10-20, 1958. This course was open to mission field and home staff leaders only and was taken by the author, while he was on furlough from the Philippines. Entitled "Mission Leadership Seminar," it was taught by Dr. V. Raymond Edman, president of Wheaton College.

The Summer Institute of Missions continued for thirty years at Wheaton College. After summer and short-term missions courses were begun at other evangelical colleges and seminaries, the Summer Institute of Missions was absorbed into Wheaton's regular summer program.

## EVANGELICAL COMMITTEE ON LATIN AMERICA (ECLA)

At its meeting on December 20, 1957, the IFMA Executive Committee received a recommendation from the IFMA Latin America Committee that a joint committee with EFMA be formed. The creation of the Evangelical Committee for Latin America (ECLA) was approved. Hubert Cook (EUSA), Eldon Durant (GMSA), and Kenneth Hood (LAM) were designated as the original IFMA members. A letter from a member mission to the board resulted in sending a questionnaire to missions that had work in Latin America, inquiring about their position on committee work with the EFMA.[3]

A draft of the questionnaire was approved at the board meeting on March 12, 1958. The responses from the missions were mixed and inconclusive. However, the "joint committee" did meet in New York City on April 3, 1958, and approved cooperation to complete the detailed survey of Latin America begun by IFMA. This cooperation resulted in the publication of a statistical survey of 314 pages, plus a set of 30 large illustrative maps.[4]

The Latin America Committee report to the 1959 IFMA Annual Meeting generated discussion on the question of committee cooperation with the EFMA. The following motion was passed:

> That the IFMA authorize participation in a joint IFMA-EFMA Evangelical Committee on Latin America for consultation on missionary work in Latin America. . . . It is understood that the IFMA representatives of this joint committee shall constitute a Standing Committee on Latin America of the IFMA.

At the 1960 EFMA Executives' Retreat, R. Kenneth Strachan (LAM) delivered a paper presenting an outlined overview of evangelical missionary work in Latin America and its future. His conclusion stressed the need and importance of evangelical unity and cooperation.[5]

The joint Evangelical Committee on Latin America met at Moody Church in Chicago in December 1960 and discussed the Second Latin American Conference to be held in Peru in August 1961. It was thought that this WCC-related conference, sponsored by the large denominational groups, was attempting to attract conservative groups and to form Christian councils in every country. The committee pushed for a strong evangelical representation to give conservatives a voice without actual involvement in the World Council of Churches' activities.[6]

At the 1961 meeting, ECLA made plans for a consultation on evangelism to be held in conjunction with the evangelical Communications Conference already scheduled for September 1962. The evangelism consultation, *Consulta Latinoamericana Sobre Evangelismo* (CLASE), resulted in the formation of an evangelism committee in Latin America, *Comite Latinoamericano al Servicio de la Evangelizacion* (CLASE). This organization looked to ECLA for organizational and financial support.

ECLA continued to represent IFMA and EFMA missions and worked to promote various programs to strengthen the evangelical cause throughout Latin America. It became increasingly difficult for the committee and the officers of the IFMA and EFMA to keep up with the coordination of activities and information. In 1966 ECLA voted to request the loan of Vergil Gerber from the Conservative Baptist Home Mission Society to serve as executive secretary of ECLA.[7]

The ECLA office, under the leadership of Mr. Gerber, was set up in Wheaton, using space in a Conservative Baptist building. The office produced current information for member missions on all phases of evangelical ministry throughout Latin America. It became a service agency for mission leaders in North America and their representatives and counterparts in Latin America.

*Latin America Pulse*, published by ECLA, became a useful informational periodical. ECLA's special reports also kept mission leaders informed of developments throughout Latin America.

ECLA sponsored the Latin American Church Growth Seminar in September 1970 at Elburn, Illinois. The meeting drew up recommendations to strengthen evangelical church growth and ministries in Latin America. It was reported to be one of the most helpful projects sponsored by ECLA. It helped to strengthen evangelical cooperation throughout Latin America.

By 1975 relationships between missions and Latin evangelicals had become somewhat sensitive. For ten years the ECLA office had improved communications and provided many helps for IFMA and EFMA missions. However, the ECLA office was seen in a different light by Latin Americans. The committee became convinced that ECLA was perceived by some as a symbol of domination by North American missions. Instead of improving communication and cooperation between missions and church leaders, it was becoming a stumbling block. After prayerful consideration, "it was moved that ECLA be disbanded immediately as a separate organization with an appointed executive secretary and office. Carried."[8]

It was recognized that IFMA and EFMA would still need a low-key Latin America Committee. Telephone conference calls and correspondence largely replaced assembled committee meetings. The joint IFMA-EFMA corporation, Evangelical Missions Information Service (EMIS), assumed responsibility in December 1970 for publishing the *Latin America Pulse* and other special reports, so the information channel was still in place.

The committee sponsored several Latin American leaders to speak at IFMA-EFMA joint study conferences. It supported the two Quito, Ecuador, consultations on church-mission relations and subsequent regional conferences. It was represented on the *ad hoc* Puente (bridge) Committee with evangelical Latin leaders.

J. Allen Thompson, IFMA leader of the Latin America Committee, reported to the 1980 IFMA Annual Meeting that "the Latin America Committee posture is one of complete acceptance of Latin America leadership as equals and the mutual sharing of responsibilities in our quest for improved, more effective church-mission relationships."

The Latin America Committee in 1981 defined its role as a communication and service function for member missions. R. Allen Hatch was invited to serve as executive secretary of LAC with an office in Quito, Ecuador. He was loaned to IFMA-EFMA Latin America Committee by Mission to the World, Presbyterian Church in America. Mr. Hatch also served as coordinator of Puente. Until his sudden death in December 1989, Allen Hatch was an unusually effective representative of Latin evangelicals and North American evangelical missions. He had a unique combination of gifts and ministry. Allen Hatch was not replaced by IFMA and EFMA because they did not know of anyone capable of taking his place. He personified the bridge between evangelicals in North America and evangelicals in Latin America. Allen served Latin American evangelicals by:

1. Creating opportunities for interchange, dialogue, and reconciliation between evangelicals of differing backgrounds
2. Encouraging reflection on the mission and role of the Latin American church in fulfillment of the great commission
3. Promoting the renewal of the Latin American church by means of its involvement in missions

The Latin America Committee as a joint standing committee of IFMA and EFMA was terminated at the close of the Latin America Today conference that it sponsored in Glen Ellyn, Illinois, May 7-9, 1990. Joint IFMA-EFMA cooperative activities on Latin America will be handled in the future on a task-force basis.

## EVANGELICAL COMMITTEE FOR AFRICA (ECFA)

Concern over ecumenical activities in Africa affecting churches related to IFMA and EFMA Africa missions prompted an *ad hoc* meeting of twenty-three agencies at the Palmer House in Chicago, April 29-30, 1960. After reports covering seven major areas of the African continent, agreement was reached on the need for evangelical fellowships throughout Africa.

C. Reuben Lindquist of Berean Mission and Erik S. Barnett of Africa Inland Mission from IFMA and Milton Baker of Conservative Baptist Foreign Mission Society and Henry Hostetter of Brethren in Christ from EFMA were appointed to prepare a recommendation. The following resolution was adopted:

> Whereas there are definite trends in different parts of Africa to completely integrate missions and national churches, and
> Whereas the ecumenical movement is influencing many national African churches with the purpose of organizing one great African church under WCC leadership, and
> Whereas we believe that the truths of the Bible can best be perpetuated within the framework of evangelical fellowships established on a doctrinal statement containing the basic doctrines of biblical evangelical Christianity, therefore,
> BE IT RESOLVED: That we look with favor upon the collaboration of the secretaries of the Interdenominational Foreign Mission Association and the Evangelical Foreign Missions Association together with representatives of member groups having mission work in Africa, toward the establishing of evangelical fellowships with a view to preserving and advancing the evangelical cause . . . in Africa.[9]

There was consideration of strategy, literature, and a team to go to Africa, representing both IFMA and EFMA. Appointed to the joint committee were: C. Reuben Lindquist (BM), Raymond J. Davis (SIM), Sidney Langford (AIM), and David Johnson (TEAM) from IFMA; and George R. Warner (World Gospel Mission), Henry N. Hostetter (BIC), and Milton Baker (CBFMS) from EFMA.

The committee met in Wheaton in July 1960 to discuss "conditions in the various sections of Africa at the present time highlighting both the developments of nationalism and independence in the various countries, as well as new developments in the area of mission work and the national churches."[10]

IFMA and EFMA jointly sponsored a conference on Africa at Winona Lake, Indiana, on October 7, 1960. It was attended by sixty representatives from twenty-nine missions. Reports from all areas of Africa were given. Extensive discussion reaffirmed the resolution of the April meeting. It was agreed that missionaries and national leaders should prepare an adequate foundation for evangelical fellowship by giving instruction to the national churches concerning:

1. The fact that evangelicals are basically united by the great, fundamental truths of the Word of God
2. The unsatisfactory nature of the World Council of Churches, both as to its theological inadequacy and organizational goal of promoting the "One Church" concept throughout Christendom
3. The value of having closer cooperation among evangelical missions in the great task of proclaiming the Gospel and establishing indigenous churches which will be wholly reliant on the Lord Jesus Christ[11]

The joint committee met again at Moody Church in December 1960. The agenda consisted of three main items: (1) evangelical fellowships, (2) disposition of mission property, and (3) relief programs and subsidies for secondary schools.

During the discussion on establishing evangelical fellowships, Ralph Davis reported that Kenneth Downing, an AIM missionary, along with a national colleague, could make a survey in East Africa and may be available to travel to other areas, as well.

Unanimous approval was given to a motion by Vincent Brushwyler (CBFMS):

> That we constitute ourselves a Continuing Committee, representing both the EFMA and the IFMA, to survey the whole problem of the disposition of mission properties in Africa and to recommend some uniform procedure for all missions to follow in the light of present circumstances and developments.[12]

In 1961 the committee approved a trip by Clyde W. Taylor and an IFMA representative to Kenya, Rhodesia, South Africa, Congo, Ivory Coast, Liberia, Sierra Leone, and possibly to Senegal to hold two-day conferences in each place with a few key leaders. The purpose of the conferences would be spiritual fellowship, instruction in current ecumenical trends, and encouragement in evangelical cooperation, but not immediate organization at the time of the visit.

The meetings stimulated interest in cooperative efforts. It was the opinion of many who attended the conferences that an office was needed in Africa to assist in establishing fellowships in each country or region. The reaction of the joint committee was that establishing an evangelical office in Africa would be a new experiment for evangelicals. After lengthy discussion, the following action was taken:

1. As an initial step we recommend to the IFMA and EFMA Boards working in Africa the setting up of an office in Nairobi to stimulate the establishment of evangelical fellowships on a regional or national basis throughout Africa south of the Sahara
2. We ask the co-chairman of the committee, Rev. Sidney Langford, to explore the possibility of securing the loan of Rev. Ken Downing to operate this office for an initial period of two years
3. We ask IFMA and EFMA to approach their Africa boards to determine their willingness to participate in the proposed program and the necessary budget[13]

The IFMA Annual Meeting in December 1962 ratified the board's approval of establishing the Africa Evangelical Office and the first year's budget of $7,600.

Ken Downing (AIM), who was named general secretary of the Africa Evangelical office, was an observer at the All-Africa Christian Youth Assembly, December 28, 1962 - January 7, 1963. His report clearly demonstrated the ecumenical movement trends in Africa.[14]

Downing was able to schedule visits to several African countries to encourage evangelical cooperation and to assist in organizing evangelical fellowships. The ministry of the Africa Evangelical Office (AEO) was instrumental in fostering better relationships and cooperation throughout sub-Sahara Africa.

In preparation for an AEO conference projected for early 1966, Mr. and Mrs. Eric Maillefer were placed on loan by the Evangelical Free Church to assist Mr. Downing. A Swiss-born, French-speaking, naturalized American citizen, Mr. Maillefer was able to handle both French and English translation work for the office.

The urgent need for an African director was recognized. The Evangelical Committee for Africa in 1965 set as one of the goals of the 1966 Pan-African Conference of Evangelicals the naming of an African leader for the AEO.

The conference was held with 130 delegates from over 20 countries. Ten of the 12 existing Evangelical Fellowships in Africa were represented. The meetings were co-chaired by Assani Benedict of the Congo (Zaire) and David Olatayo of Nigeria. On motion by Aaron Gamede of Swaziland, the delegates voted unanimously to form a continent-wide evangelical fellowship. David Olatayo was named the first president of the new Association of Evangelicals of Africa and Madagascar (AEAM).

The Evangelical Committee for Africa continued its support of the AEO and through the AE0, the AEAM. Downing and Maillefer remained in the staff leadership of

AEO, working under ECFA, and in the AEAM working under the AEAM Executive Committee.

The first AEAM General Assembly was held at Limuru, Kenya, January 30 to February 6, 1969. ECFA minutes record that it was agreed that the long-range goal of AEO should be to merge into the AEAM with a gradual phasing out of the AEO, since the AEAM has the ability to function by itself. It was recognized that expatriates may continue to be needed to assist the AEAM in its outreach.[15]

At the November 1970 ECFA meeting, detailed consideration was given to the current working arrangements between the AEO and the AEAM, and plans for the 1972 General Assembly. It became apparent from correspondence that some of the issues could not be settled at a distance. Therefore, the committee requested Dr. Raymond Davis, general director of SIM, president of IFMA, and chairman of ECFA; and the author to go to Nairobi to represent ECFA in consultations with the Africa Evangelical Office staff, and to make themselves available to the AEAM Executive Committee as needed.

The trip took place in early December 1970, with many evidences that the Lord had prepared the way. Important matters were settled amicably during a special meeting of the AEAM Executive Committee. ECFA was asked to accomplish the merging of AEO into the AEAM as soon as possible, with AEO Executive Secretary Maillefer becoming the administrative secretary of AEAM. The AEAM General Assembly was postponed for one year, to 1973. Samuel Odunaike was appointed acting general secretary of the AEAM, replacing Ken Downing, until a full-time African leader could be elected. A number of other important matters of ECFA concern were accomplished during the trip.[16]

Administrative guidelines for the future conduct of ECFA were finalized in 1972. A number of committee meetings were held seeking ways to strengthen the program of AEAM and the national evangelical fellowships. Reports from

Africa indicated that an AEAM General Assembly in 1973 would be essential for the continuation of the association.

The general assembly meeting was successful in increasing the cooperation of evangelicals throughout Africa. One of the most important actions was the election of Rev. Byang Kato as AEAM General Secretary. Kato had previously served as general secretary of the Evangelical Churches of West Africa in Nigeria, and was completing work on a Doctor of Theology program at Dallas Theological Seminary.

ECFA was pleased to assist in strengthening the various programs of the AEAM, working closely with Dr. Kato. It was with a profound sense of loss that the committee received the news of the tragic death of Dr. Byang Kato by drowning, while on a family outing in Mombasa, Kenya, in December 1975.

Some of the Africa projects with which ECFA was involved included the development of the Bangui Evangelical School of Theology (BEST) in Central African Republic, various programs of theological education by extension including the production of programmed texts, literature coordination, and Christian education programs. Missionary personnel serving AEAM at this time included James Halbert on loan from Conservative Baptist Foreign Mission Society until the 1977 General Assembly, Eric Maillefer on loan from the Evangelical Free Church assigned as administrative secretary, and Roger Coon from the Africa Inland Mission serving as Christian education coordinator.

At the 1977 AEAM General Assembly held at Bouake, Ivory Coast, Dr. Tokunboh Adeyemo from Nigeria was elected general secretary. A few weeks after the meeting, the Bangui Evangelical School of Theology (BEST) for French-speaking areas was opened in Bangui, Central African Republic, with three missionary professors under the leadership of Dr. Paul White (AEF).

Another AEAM-related project that was formally organized was the Accrediting Council of Theological Education in Africa (ACTEA). Dr. Paul Bowers of SIM was the prime mover behind ACTEA.

By 1980 most of the ECFA meetings were conducted by telephone conference calls. Committee activities centered on financial or personnel concerns relating to AEAM and projects, such as BEST and ACTEA. Other projects for which funds were being secured and programs developed included the Nairobi Evangelical Graduate School of Theology (NEGST), the counterpart of BEST for English-speaking Africa, and the Christian Learning Materials Center, sponsored by the Christian Education Commission of AEAM.

The Fourth AEAM General Assembly was held in September 1981 in Malawi. Tokunboh Adeyemo is recognized as giving effective leadership to the AEAM. In his Africa-wide ministry on behalf of evangelical fellowships and churches, Dr. Adeyemo is responsible to the AEAM President and to the AEAM Executive Committee. AEAM is governed by its own African corporate documents and members. However, AEAM recognizes that it grew out of the Africa Evangelical Office, a ministry of the IFMA and EFMA Evangelical Committee for Africa. Thus, in the spirit of oneness, the AEAM and ECFA maintained an interdependent relationship of cooperation and fellowship.

Dr. Adeyemo was one of the speakers in 1984 at Inter-Varsity's Urbana (Illinois) student missionary conference. During that time, he and ECFA members met together. Dr. Adeyemo expressed his appreciation to IFMA, EFMA, and ECFA for the "founding" and continued support of the AEAM. He reported on the steady growth of the Nairobi Evangelical Graduate School of Theology, Bangui Evangelical School of Theology, and other AEAM programs. He also expressed special appreciation for the eighteen years of efficient service in the AEAM office by Eric Maillefer, on loan from the Evangelical Free Church in America.

Throughout the 1980s, the committee continued to share Africa information and concerns with member missions. In

1986 and 1988, ECFA sponsored Africa Update workshops in Glen Ellyn, Illinois, for evangelical missions executives, missionaries on furlough, African church leaders, and students. Among the speakers were Dr. Tite Tienou of Burkino Faso, Rev. Simon Ibrahim of Nigeria, Rev. Caesar Molebatsi of South Africa, and American black evangelist Dr. Howard Jones.

ECFA Chairman Harold Fuller (SIM) and Vice Chairman Richard Jacobs (CBFMS) participated in the Fifth General Assembly of the AEAM in September 1987 in Lusaka, Zambia. The 450 delegates from 37 African nations gave witness to the growth and influence of the AEAM, and to the national evangelical associations it represents throughout sub-Sahara Africa.

ECFA arranged for the speakers and program for the Africa strategy sessions during the tenth IFMA-EFMA study conference in 1987 in Orlando, Florida.

ECFA, the IFMA-EFMA Evangelical Committee for Africa, was terminated as a standing committee in 1988. The executive directors of the two associations and a person from each association, named as its Africa coordinator, were given the responsibility for the Africa interests of the associations. In the future, an IFMA-EFMA task force will be appointed for any cooperative project or program, as needed.

The two IFMA and EFMA coordinators for Africa prepared the program for the Africa strategy group sessions at the eleventh IFMA-EFMA study conference in 1990 at Northglenn, Colorado.

AEAM was assisted by IFMA and EFMA through quarterly financial grants from its inception until 1991. For many years, AEAM has also been assisted through the services of loaned missionary personnel. While there is constant need for consultation to maintain effective coordination of ministries, relations between the AEAM, IFMA, and EFMA remain at a high level of mutual confidence.

## COMMITTEE TO ASSIST MINISTRY EDUCATION OVERSEAS (CAMEO)

Dr. Harold Cook, director of the missions department of Moody Bible Institute, reported to the 1962 IFMA Annual Meeting the formation of an *ad hoc* Committee on Christian Higher Education Overseas. The inspiration for this group came from Dr. Howard Ferrin, president of Barrington College, after a trip to Africa. Dr. Ferrin met early in 1962 in New York with representatives of seven Christian schools. Later that year another group of school and mission representatives met in Wheaton. Discussion at these meetings centered on the need to assist Christian higher educational institutions abroad to realize their educational goals. Vernon Mortenson (TEAM) represented IFMA at the Wheaton meeting and was elected to the *Ad Hoc* Committee to Promote the Cause of Christ in Higher Education Overseas.

Contact was made with approximately one hundred evangelical schools in North America in an effort to mobilize faculty members to assist their overseas counterparts. Students were informed of the areas of educational opportunities and needs overseas. Dr. Harold Cook was particularly interested in this work because of a recently completed survey of twenty-two Bible institutes that he had made on a six-week trip through Latin America.

The program committee for the first joint study conference of the IFMA and EFMA in 1963 included a presentation and discussion on "Training National Leadership."[17] The Findings Committee recommended the formation of a cooperative committee of the IFMA and EFMA, with evangelical educators, to assist in the development of projects for higher education overseas. Dr. H. Wilbert Norton (Trinity College and Divinity School), chairman of the *ad hoc* committee, outlined the committee activities and the recommendation of the NAE Commission on Higher Education that a cooperative committee be formed.[18]

The IFMA appointed a Higher Education Committee and invited the EFMA to do the same.[19] Milton Baker (CBFMS) and Delbert Kuehl (TEAM) were appointed co-chairmen, and for twelve years they alternated as chairman and secretary of the meetings. Within the next few months, the joint Committee to Assist Missionary Education Overseas (CAMEO) was organized and five sub-committees appointed. They were: (1) Recruitment of Personnel, (2) Workshop and Area Studies in America, (3) Accreditation and Affiliation, (4) Interchange of Personnel, and (5) Curriculum and Textbooks. Each committee made surveys and gathered information to assist evangelical educators overseas. They outlined areas where CAMEO should give further assistance.

CAMEO representatives conducted workshops in Latin America and Africa in 1966. By the next year, authorization was given to request Dr. Raymond Buker, Sr. (CBFMS) to become part-time coordinator for CAMEO.[20] Dr. Buker served until 1975 when he was named consulting coordinator. John Gilmore (Free Methodist) was coordinator in 1975 and 1976.

During the years of Ray Buker, Sr.'s leadership, CAMEO was involved in popularizing the concept of theological education by extension (TEE) and programmed instruction (PI). The first mention of this program, which started in the Presbyterian Seminary in Guatemala, is recorded in the October 1967 CAMEO minutes. The following April, a seminar on TEE was held for mission leaders in Philadelphia. In December a TEE workshop was held at Wheaton College for field missionaries and executives.

The project to develop a directory of theological schools around the world was initiated in 1968 and published four years later.[21] CAMEO secured a grant for partial funding of this detailed project of 813 pages. Dr. Ralph Winter (Fuller School of World Missions), a Presbyterian missionary in Guatemala and one of the originators of the TEE concept, published a compendium of TEE materials in 1969, in which he included as Book II over 100 pages of material presented at the first CAMEO Extension Workshop.[22] One hundred twenty-one persons from 30 missions participated in that workshop.

In the "Foreword" of *An Extension Seminar Primer*, Dr. Buker traces the involvement of CAMEO in spreading the extension seminary concept:

> CAMEO carried the baton by introducing the concept through workshops among missionary leaders, first in the United States and then by workshops in South America, Africa, and Asia. The actual application of the principles of theological education by extension is the responsibility of the educational leaders on the mission fields of the world, both nationals and missionaries.[23]

Dr. Lois McKinney was loaned to CAMEO in 1972 by Conservative Baptist Foreign Missions Society. Headquartered in Brazil, she was a programmed-text writer and consultant in education for Latin America.

Workshops were conducted for several years by CAMEO in programmed instruction text production. Texts were produced by Fred and Grace Holland for Africa. The Hollands were loaned by the Brethren in Christ mission to work on this editorial project for all English-speaking Africa, under the auspices of the Association of Evangelicals for Africa and Madagascar (AEAM). Programmed texts were being produced in Asia and Latin America, as well.

In the early 1970s, CAMEO helped to support summer graduate courses in Latin America and Asia for teachers in schools for missionaries' children. Grants were secured to assist other professors, particularly theological, to finance short-term teaching overseas. This program was beneficial to theological schools overseas, and in North America it increased professors' awareness of theological education abroad.

CAMEO continued to review its mandates and priorities for programs. Dr. Fred Holland was named TEE coordinator to hold workshops overseas and in North America, including a series of workshops at Moody Bible Institute, Wheaton College, and Trinity Evangelical Divinity School. The Brazil project, directed by Lois McKinney, was extended to February 1978. By that time, it was expected that her internship program of theological education would be sufficiently established in Brazil to continue under local direction.

After the retirement of Raymond Buker, Sr. and the resignation of John Gilmore due to a new assignment overseas, the committee began to negotiate with Lois McKinney to see if she would be available to serve as CAMEO coordinator after completion of the Brazil project. Satisfactory arrangements were worked out between CAMEO, Dr. McKinney, and Conservative Baptist Foreign Mission Society (CBFMS).

With Dr. McKinney's coming to CAMEO in 1978, the title was changed from coordinator to executive director. The CAMEO name was also changed, from the Committee to Assist *Missionary* Education Overseas to the Committee to Assist *Ministry* Education Overseas. The office was set up in the IFMA building located in the village of Carol Stream on the north side of Wheaton. CAMEO's historical files were donated to the Billy Graham Center Archives at Wheaton College.

With a full-time executive director and part-time secretarial assistant, CAMEO was able to move forward under a revised set of short-range and long-range goals. The major contribution of CAMEO was in the overseas workshops and meetings held by the executive director in Africa, Asia, Europe, and Latin America. Dr. McKinney was, also, in demand as a visiting professor at a number of graduate theological schools throughout North America.

The overseas ministries of CAMEO were coordinated with evangelical theological groups, such as Asia Theological Association and the theological commissions of the

Association of Evangelicals of Africa and Madagascar and the World Evangelical Fellowship. The outreach and services of CAMEO were designed to enhance local, regional, and continent-wide educational ministries.

Dr. McKinney joined the faculty of the Wheaton College Graduate School in 1982, but continued as a member of the CAMEO Executive Committee.

Dr. H. Wilbert Norton, one of the founding members of CAMEO, accepted the invitation to become CAMEO's Executive Director. At the time when he helped to organize CAMEO, Dr. Norton was president of Trinity College and Divinity School. He later came to Wheaton Graduate School as professor of missions, and upon the retirement of Dr. Merrill Tenney, he became dean of Wheaton's Graduate School. Upon his retirement from Wheaton, Dr. Norton joined SIM and served three years in Jos, Nigeria. He assisted in the founding of SIM/ECWA's Jos Evangelical Theological Seminary and was its first principal.

Dr. Norton directed the ministries of CAMEO from 1982 until the fall of 1989 when he accepted a call from the Reformed Theological Seminary (Presbyterian Church in America) in Jackson, Mississippi, to join the faculty of missions and to help establish a doctoral program.

Under Dr. Norton's leadership, CAMEO continued to expand the influence of IFMA and EFMA in the strategic area of overseas ministry education. CAMEO was a strong catalyst in workshops on TEE and other forms of theological education. Networking with schools and professors in the Third World with counterparts in North America was a hallmark of CAMEO in the 1980s. Involvement with evangelical accrediting associations overseas was strengthened.

For several years, Dr. Norton worked hard to arrange consultation between seminary presidents and deans of North American schools and Third World schools. They were finally brought together in Manila in 1989.

Almost every CAMEO Board meeting during the Norton years included reports by visiting educators from overseas, as well as reports from CAMEO Board members on their current experiences overseas.

Cooperating with the Billy Graham Center Library staff and the Christian Librarians' Association, CAMEO assisted in the preliminary development of a library manual for overseas institutions. It is scheduled for publication in 1992.

CAMEO developed a consultative relationship with the Overseas Council for Theological Education and Missions. It approved the participation of Dr. Lois McKinney in the International Missionary Training Project of the World Evangelical Fellowship's Missions Commission.

After Dr. Norton's move to Mississippi, the IFMA and EFMA Boards considered phasing out the CAMEO office since other organizations, such as the Overseas Council for Theological Education and Missions, were now functioning in the areas of CAMEO's interest. With a sense of a job well done for almost thirty years, CAMEO office was closed in 1990 and CAMEO was discontinued as a joint project between IFMA and EFMA.

With the termination of CAMEO, IFMA set up its own Committee for Developing National Leadership. IFMA Executive Director Dr. John Orme, successor to the author, was named to represent IFMA in areas of education in which CAMEO had been involved. Dr. Orme holds a doctorate in theology from Dallas Theological Seminary and taught at CAM's Central American Theological Seminary in Guatemala for fourteen years.

## EVANGELICAL MISSIONS INFORMATION SERVICE (EMIS)

The decision to form a joint committee for the publication of a missionary journal was made at the first joint study conference of IFMA and EFMA in 1963. The man most responsible for proposing this ministry was Arthur F. Glasser. At that time, he was serving as director for North America of the Overseas Missionary Fellowship.

At the special 1960 IFMA Executives Retreat, Glasser was appointed, along with Ralph Davis (AIM) and Kenneth Strachan (LAM), to a special committee to make recommendations for strengthening IFMA. One of the suggestions was that the board consider existing IFMA publications "with special reference to developing a high-level quarterly magazine not unlike the *International Review of Missions.*"[24]

The IFMA Board, on September 29, 1960, appointed Dr. Glasser chairman of the Committee on Commissions to study the implementation of the former special committee's recommendations.

The IFMA Literature and Publicity Committee considered the question of a new mission magazine. They indicated that this had been discussed many times, and they had some doubt that the Christian public would subscribe to another magazine.

At the 1961 Annual Meeting, Arthur Glasser told of the study that eventuated in the book, *Missions in Crisis*, and commented, "This confirmed the need for an organ, a magazine of the format of *Practical Anthropology*, for our IFMA constituency that might function as a sounding board for a full and frank exchange of opinion, and which would encourage the participation of our IFMA membership through a reader's column, etc."[25]

There was the suggestion at the 1962 Annual Meeting that the IFMA publish a missionary digest magazine that would have articles of interest, as well as news items. Action was approved "that the matter of a missionary digest magazine be studied with a view to action by the Literature and Publicity Committee, with the help of Dr. Glasser."[26] A few months later, the Literature and Publicity Committee moved that Arthur Glasser investigate the possibility of an IFMA digest and bring a recommendation to the committee.[27]

This placed the issue back into the hands of Dr. Glasser. He was not able to make a recommendation to the committee before the 1963 joint study conference at

Winona Lake. When he was asked during the IFMA business session for a report of the Committee on Commissions, he mentioned that the committee report had been tabled at the last annual meeting. He then substituted a special report of the Literature and Publicity Committee, which was quite detailed and forceful. He presented the committee's concern about publications, the specific proposal for the quarterly, suggested contents, overall thrust, and practical aspects. He concluded by asking if "this should be a joint IFMA-EFMA project, with a mutual sharing of costs."[28]

The report was referred back to the full committee for their recommendation. After further investigation, the committee felt it would be possible to obtain personnel and funding for the journal. The annual meeting directed the board to take the steps necessary to start a new publication in cooperation with the EFMA. Vernon Mortenson (TEAM), Ralph Odman (UFM), James Reapsome (Belgian Gospel Mission/*The Sunday School Times*), and the author were appointed to the Committee for the Missionary Journal.

The following purpose statement was adopted at the first joint committee meeting on December 4, 1963:

**Purpose**

> The purpose of the journal will be to glorify God through the encouragement and inspiration of evangelical Christians who are dedicated in obedience to the command of Jesus Christ to the proclamation of the Gospel of the Son of God to the whole world. It pledges loyalty to the Bible, the inspired Word of God, and to the truth it proclaims.
>
> Reporting: The journal should inform of events and trends vital to the cause of missions, interpreting them in the light of the evangelical position.

> Stimulating: The journal should stimulate evangelical leaders of missions and national churches to write expressing their views on problems vital to the ongoing of the evangelical witness. It should stimulate and encourage the total missionary force in the application of effective strategy and methodology to their work.
>
> Linking: The journal should be a channel of communication linking the missionary force and the church constituency in a better understanding of basic problems and victories.
>
> Edifying: The journal should not overlook the possibility of having a devotional ministry to its readers.
>
> Helping: There should be practical helps giving clear instructions on how to undertake certain projects—a "workshop" or "how-to-do-it" page.
>
> Reviewing: The journal will have an important ministry in reviewing current books of importance in the field of missions. Giving excerpts or reviews of articles of importance will, also, be an important function of this section.[29]

The name, *Evangelical Missions Quarterly*, was approved. It was agreed that the target of the magazine would be the total missionary force, at home and abroad. A clear policy was adopted to ensure the distinctively evangelical character of the publication.

James Reapsome, board member of Belgian Gospel Mission and editor of *The Sunday School Times*, was named managing editor, which would be on a part-time basis. Members of the first EMQ Editorial Committee were Philip Armstrong (FEGC/SEND), Horace Fenton, Jr. (LAM), Ralph Odman (UFM), Jack Shepherd (C&MA), and executive secretaries of the IFMA and EFMA.[30] It would be published by a new corporation set up jointly by IFMA and EFMA, the Evangelical Missions Information Service (EMIS), which is responsible to IFMA and EFMA Boards.

The subscription rate was set at $3.00 per year with special rates for bulk subscriptions.

The Articles of Incorporation for the Evangelical Missions Information Service (EMS) was recorded in Washington, DC, on March 27, 1964. The Constitution and Bylaws, prepared by Wade Coggins of EFMA and the author, were adopted April 24, 1964. Member missions had sent in 2,062 subscriptions by July and $767 in initial grants. The first issue was published in the fall of 1964, just one year after the concept was approved. The first issue presented the rationale for the new journal and a statement of definition, purpose, and belief in its conservative evangelical stand.[31]

After the first year of publication, Arthur Glasser replaced Ralph Odman on the Editorial Committee. A staggered term had been established for the board to ensure continuity. The same system was applied to the Editorial Committee. A search was begun for an executive director for EMIS who would develop the information service ministries.

To focus on the need and potential for an EMIS research center and to build on the conclusions of the Congress on the Church's Worldwide Mission, a small group of IFMA and EFMA missions leaders and consultants met May 29 - June 3, 1967 at Glen Eyrie, Colorado Springs, Colorado. The findings of this meeting—on the subjects of Church Development, Mass Media, Institutions, and Unity—are still relevant.[32]

The National Liberty Foundation in 1967 offered the services of Dr. Osborne Buchanan, Jr., on a part-time basis, to assist in the development of the EMIS program. The executive committee accepted and appointed Dr. Buchanan as acting executive director.

Action was taken by the EMIS Board to take over the functions of the Congress on the Church's Worldwide Mission Continuing Committee. Vergil Gerber, congress coordinator, was appointed a special consultant to EMIS on matters related to the congress follow-up.

After considering the development of a research program, a recommendation was made to IFMA and EFMA in

1967 to cooperate with other evangelical groups and educational institutions in terms of research projects and a research library facility. Evangelical Missionary Research Library was proposed as the name, and the Chicago area was suggested as the eventual permanent location of the envisioned library.

Negotiations were made with the Conservative Baptist Home Mission Society for the services of Vergil Gerber on a loan basis for EMIS. At the 1969 EMIS annual board meeting, Dr. Gerber was named executive director; and Dr. Buchanan was appointed assistant to the executive director. Wheaton, Illinois, was chosen as the site of the new EMIS headquarters. *Pulse* editions for Africa and Asia, similar to the *Latin America Pulse*, were authorized.

During 1970 the executive directors of IFMA, EFMA, and EMIS "met with representatives of Wheaton College regarding plans for a dynamic resource center for the study of world missions and evangelism. The plan would provide library and depository facilities for receiving the documents of evangelical missions and for future study and research in these areas."[33]

Approval was given by IFMA, EFMA and the EMIS Board to develop the Evangelical Missions Research Library in conjunction with Wheaton College. In 1971 the name of the proposed library was changed to Center for the Study of World Missions. Agreement was reached in principle that a separate nonprofit corporation be established to finance and control the center.[34]

After various studies and meetings over several years, the project was tabled for lack of funding. The vision for the library and archives became a reality in 1980 after the Billy Graham Evangelistic Association and Wheaton College completed the Wheaton College Billy Graham Center, which includes an extensive library and archives on evangelism and nondenominational mission agencies. The most up-to-date technical knowledge was used in designing, furnishing, and maintaining this facility.

EMIS served IFMA and EFMA in organizing and directing GL '71. This study conference, held in 1971 at Green Lake, Wisconsin, gave serious consideration to the important issue of church/mission tensions under the theme, Missions in Creative Tension. This will be considered in more detail in Chapter 12, Conferences.

The EMIS travel coordination department was of practical assistance to IFMA and EFMA missions. To help reduce the cost of furlough travel, group flights were arranged to various cities in Asia and Africa. The service was most successful to Africa. J. Morris Rockness was loaned to EMIS for two years by Overseas Missionary Fellowship to help in the initial operation of this service. After some experience, the program was carried on by selected mission agencies for EMIS, making charter flights available to IFMA and EFMA missions.

Approval was given in 1973 for EMIS to develop overseas seminars and workshops, working with appropriate IFMA-EFMA committees or appropriate overseas bodies. The EMIS Executive Director was authorized to participate in church growth/evangelism workshops, as funds were provided apart from the EMIS operational budget. Vergil Gerber participated in 1972 in a pilot workshop in Venezuela in his dual role of executive director of both EMIS and the Evangelical Committee for Latin America. The workshop ministry developed into one of the most effective contributions to evangelical pastors and other church leaders worldwide. By 1979 over seventy workshops were conducted in some fifty countries.[35]

In addition to the renewed vision and impetus to grassroots evangelism and church growth, the workshops have served to strengthen evangelical cooperation. The workshops were held only at the invitation and under the auspices of a local or regional evangelical fellowship. Some fifty people from many different countries served with Dr. Gerber as resource personnel in the workshops. The travel expenses for the resource people were met through designated contributions and grants. Local expenses and arrangements were cared for by the sponsoring committee.

Gerber stepped out of his EMIS administrative role of executive director in 1981. As director of ministries, he continued to conduct the workshops and was free to work on writing and editing projects. His book, *God's Way to Keep a Church Going and Growing*, which grew out of the original Venezuela workshop, was published in over fifty languages. The English edition had eleven printings, including two in India and one in the Philippines.

The ministries and services of EMIS are used by many evangelicals beyond the personnel of IFMA and EFMA, which form its basic constituency. The full cooperation of member missions has contributed greatly to the effectiveness of EMIS. Of special note has been the complete participation of the Conservative Baptist Association, Conservative Baptist Foreign Mission Society, and Conservative Baptist Home Mission Society. Since 1969, the EMIS office has had office space made available by each of these organizations. The cooperation of the various departments throughout these years has been invaluable.

EMIS, because of its publications, is a well-known expression of IFMA and EFMA cooperation. Missionaries of the two associations still make up the major block of subscribers to *Evangelical Missions Quarterly*.

Jim Reapsome who had served since 1964 as part-time employee as editor of *Evangelical Missions Quarterly* (EMQ), *Pulse*, and *Missionary News Service* was named full-time executive director of EMIS in 1982. Vergil Gerber was named ministries consultant. Additional editorial and marketing assistance was secured in 1983.

Throughout the 1980s and into the 1990s, the EMIS publications and services continued to increase in effectiveness. In an effort to assist the struggling Association of Evangelical Professors of Missions (now Evangelical Missiological Society), a section was included in each issue of EMQ from 1984 to 1987, focusing on the issues relating to the AEPM.

The publication of *Missionary News Service* was discontinued with the last issue of 1987 in favor of a redesigned *World Pulse*. The new format has a growing response from readers. Most respondents indicate much appreciation for Jim Reapsome's back-page editorial, "Final Analysis," in each issue.

EMIS is now in its twenty-ninth year.

## COMMITTEE ON BIBLE SOCIETY CONCERNS

The United Bible Societies issued a brochure in June 1968, *Guiding Principles for Interconfessional Cooperation in Translating the Bible*. The interpretation of *Guiding Principles* in some overseas locations brought the issue to the IFMA and EFMA. Evangelical mission leaders had questions regarding the possibility of the American and United Bible Societies producing a common edition of the Bible.

Dr. Robert Taylor, general secretary of the American Bible Society (ABS), was invited to speak at the 1968 IFMA-EFMA joint study conference to clarify Bible Society issues. He spoke of the historical development of the Bible societies under the title, "Good News for Modern Man."[36]

A joint IFMA-EFMA statement on Bible translation was presented. After discussion, the associations were asked to follow up with the Bible Society.

A joint Committee for Bible Society Concerns was appointed and met frequently with American Bible Society leaders for several years to express in more detail some of the evangelical concerns. In further response to committee questions, the ABS prepared a pamphlet, *Evangelicals and the Bible Cause*. A clear understanding was reached between the committee and the Bible Society. However, an explanatory statement on the inside back cover had not been seen by the committee prior to the pamphlet's printing. The wording of this statement was misinterpreted by those who had not participated in the committee interaction. The committee requested that the paragraph be corrected in future editions.

After two years of meetings, considering questions or information submitted by missionaries of IFMA and EFMA, the committee finished its assignment. Since no further questions were received, the joint Committee for Bible Society Concerns was not reappointed.

The associations do not perpetuate or proliferate joint committees unless there is a call from member missions, demonstrating a felt need.

## EVANGELICAL ASIA COMMITTEE

The first cooperative Asia Committee was appointed in 1965 under the co-chairmanship of J. Morris Rockness of OMF and Sam Wolgemuth of Youth for Christ. At its first meeting, a report was given on Asia and developments affecting evangelicals. Consideration was given to the purpose of the committee and relationships. Regarding the World Evangelical Fellowship, it was noted that while the EFMA has a direct relationship through the NAE, the IFMA does not have such a relationship with WEF.

After the 1966 Congress on the Church's Worldwide Mission, the committee recommended that IFMA and EFMA encourage their missionary and national church bodies to work together to form national evangelical fellowships.

With the beginning of *Asia Pulse* under EMIS, the Asia Committee became less active. One of the difficulties facing coordination of work in Asia is the diversity of cultures, religions, languages, and the vast geographical spread of the area.

In 1975 the committee held an Asia Briefing in Washington, DC. The day before the briefing, the committee met to consider its current function and organization. Leonard Tuggy, Asia secretary of the Conservative Baptist Foreign Mission Society, was named Asia Information Coordinator for the committee. For the Asia Briefing, the committee and other mission executives interested in Asia met first at the State Department for sessions with three Asia specialists. In the afternoon, the group went to the Brookings Institution for presentations by two of their research scholars on China and Japan. Feedback indicated that the sessions at the Brookings Institution were particularly helpful.

Two resource people provided background information at the 1977 Asia Briefing. David Adeney of the Overseas Missionary Fellowship and the Evangelical Fellowship of International Students handled the morning session on Christianity in China. In the afternoon, a State Department Asia Desk man spoke. There was a positive response to the briefing for the good balance between an experienced churchman and a State Department representative.

Resource people for the 1980 Asia Briefing included a State Department official and specialist on Asia from the University of Alabama. Dr. Bong Rin Ro (Asia Theological Association) and Dr. Saphir Athyal (Union Biblical Seminary, Pune, India) spoke, as well, and reports on Indonesia were given.

The committee agreed that the Asia Briefing sessions should continue to be informational meetings, rather than planning or strategy sessions. Sponsorship of Asia Briefings has been the committee's primary function.

From 1981 to 1990, the committee arranged programs for the strategy sessions during IFMA-EFMA study conferences. Grants from committee funds were given to assist the Asia Theological Association, Asia Graduate School of Theology, and Evangelical Fellowship of Asia. The committee chairmen and executive directors of the two associations met with U. S. State Department officials in Washington, DC, to seek ways to improve the missionary visa situation in Asia.

One Asia Briefing was held during these years. It was convened April 1-2, 1986 in Des Plaines, Illinois. Presentations were made on theological education, evangelical fellowship, and mission agencies in Asia. Update Reports were given on Hong Kong, Indonesia, Philippines, and Taiwan.

The joint IFMA-EFMA Asia Committee was not

reappointed in 1991. Joint Asia activity will be on a task-force basis upon the recommendation of the associations' executive directors.

## EVANGELICAL CHINA COMMITTEE

During the China Cultural Revolution in the 1960s William Kerr of the Christian and Missionary Alliance invited evangelical mission personnel and Chinese Christian leaders to meet occasionally to share information on the emerging China situation. They took the name Evangelical China Study Group. One of their major concerns was to generate prayer for China, particularly for the Christians in their time of great need.

Mr. Kerr gave an informative China awareness presentation at the 1972 EFMA Mission Executives' Retreat. Even though it appeared that missions would not be able to enter China for many years, he urged preparation for that eventuality. The first step was to stimulate prayer interest. Then to urge young people to seriously study China, encourage laymen to plan to go there, urge overseas Chinese Christians to prepare to go back at any cost, and to begin the long process of preparing potential missionaries.[37]

An Evangelical China Consultation sponsored by the Study Group was held at America's Keswick, Whiting, New Jersey, October 16-18, 1973 to encourage interaction between Chinese Christian leaders in North America and interested evangelical mission personnel, regarding responsibility toward China. Jonathan T'ien-en Chao presented a paper, "Prospects for Future Mission Work in China." Mr. Chao concluded with a challenge to Chinese churches and mission agencies in North America to form an Evangelical China Committee to work out a comprehensive China strategy for the next two decades. He said that the Chinese church in diaspora and foreign missions must find ways to cooperate for the evangelization of China. He further said that this is a task that "is so great that it requires no less than a concentrated effort of the entire Chinese Church assisted by a united effort of the churches in other lands."[38]

The IFMA and EFMA leaders of the Evangelical China Study Group met during the first conference of the North American Congress of Chinese Evangelicals (NACOCE). The sessions of NACOCE '74 were held at Wheaton College, August 26-31, 1974. The committee, representing the Evangelical China Study Group, met with the NACOCE leadership to express appreciation for the opportunity to cooperate with NACOCE in prayer and study on behalf of the evangelization of the Chinese people worldwide.

A follow-up China Consultation was held May 1975 in Chicago's Chinatown. All groups connected with IFMA, EFMA, and NACOCE were urged to send representatives to take part in the presentation and to discuss the possibility of forming a new cooperative organization of the Evangelical China Committee. The presentations of the consultation were helpful, and the interaction was stimulating, but NACOCE representatives were not authorized to officially join a cooperative organization. The *ad hoc* committee was reorganized, but one by one the Chinese members withdrew, feeling that they were not the right ones to represent the Chinese Christian community. One Chinese brother ventured that this would not be realized until after NACOCE '77 or perhaps into the 1980s.[39] It was recommended that IFMA and EFMA officially establish the Evangelical China Committee to replace the *ad hoc* committee and continue to work toward NACOCE participation.

The first official meeting under IFMA and EFMA sponsorship was held September 27, 1976. Edvard Torjesen was elected chairman; William Kerr, vice chairman and secretary; and the author was elected treasurer. Action was passed requesting The Evangelical Alliance Mission to release Mr. Torjesen to serve part-time as coordinator for the committee. Objectives were outlined and support was requested from the associations to enable the committee to implement its program.

Mr. Torjesen had been reared in China by CIM missionary parents, and later served as a missionary with TEAM in Taiwan. He spent the first months as coordinator visiting Chinese churches and Bible study groups to get their recommendations for committee goals and activities. His visits were received with appreciation. The publication of *Chinese World Pulse* was started in cooperation with EMIS.

Negotiations with David Adeney (OMF) produced plans for China Consultations in 1979. Nearly one hundred people participated in the California meeting and seventy-five in New Jersey. Among the recommendations coming from these meetings was a mandate to involve NACOCE as a full partner in the Evangelical China Committee.[40]

Contact with Dr. Eddie Lo, pastor of First Evangelical Church of Glendale, California, and the chairman of NACOCE '80, resulted in the appointment of four members to the committee by NACOCE. The enlarged committee met October 1, 1979 to reorganize and to determine steps toward implementing goals.

When Dr. Ed Torjesen was assigned to Europe by TEAM, Dr. Donald Douglas of Far Eastern Gospel Crusade/SEND was named administrative coordinator. However, more than part-time help was needed to accomplish the work that had been approved. When arrangements could not be made for Dr. Douglas to give full-time, Dr. Eddie Lo was asked to be director. Dr. Alan Gates, formerly of Taiwan with the Conservative Baptist Foreign Missions Society, was loaned to serve as associate director. With the opening of an office July 1, 1980, the name was changed to Evangelical China Office. A foundation grant was received to provide for setting up the office and the first year's budget.

The Evangelical China Office and the China Program of the Graham Center at Wheaton College jointly sponsored a China Consultation. Limited to fifty invited leaders of missions and Christian organizations, it was held at Wheaton College, April 29 - May 1, 1981. Major emphasis was on developing a coordinated effort toward China among evangelicals. The cooperation of IFMA, EFMA, and NACOCE was a major breakthrough in cooperation between evangelical Chinese leaders in North America and evangelical mission executives.

The China Office began a resource center on developments in China and the preparation of Chinese-language editions of *Chinese World Pulse*. A slide/tape presentation on China was produced for use by the Christian public.

Dr. Lo consulted with Chinese Christians in the People's Republic of China and participated in the 1981 Chinese Congress on World Evangelization in Singapore.

Another China consultation was co-sponsored with the Wheaton Billy Graham Center China Program in 1982.

Because of personnel and financial needs, the Pasadena office was closed July 31, 1982. The IFMA and EFMA each then appointed a China coordinator to work with the executive directors and Wheaton College China Studies director. China consultations were held in Wheaton in 1985 and 1987. With the Wheaton College China Studies director's leaving that position, and with the leadership of the IFMA and EFMA in transition, the China consultations have been on "hold."

## PERSONNEL COMMITTEE

The IFMA Board met in an extended session at Williams Bay, Wisconsin, September 24-26, 1964. The retreat was planned to give time for an in-depth study of various issues affecting the ministry of member missions. Two of the agenda items were redeployment of missionaries and student recruitment. As a result of considering these personnel matters, a Committee on Student Affairs was envisioned. It was established the following week during the IFMA Annual Meeting, with Virgil Newbrander (FEGC/SEND) and Delbert Kuehl (TEAM) as members.

That same week they met at the invitation of the Moody Bible Institute Missionary Union to discuss "Present Problems/Situations of the Student Missions

Group." Student group leaders from various campuses met with representatives of IFMA, EFMA, Inter-Varsity Christian Fellowship, and Moody Bible Institute staff.

At the Urbana Missionary Conference a few months later, the student missions leaders met again with members of IFMA and EFMA committees. From this meeting, the students organized themselves into a national Student Coordination Committee with the core leaders appointed from schools in the Midwest. The IFMA and EFMA committees met to discuss ways to assist the student groups when requested.

Inter-Varsity appointed Evan Adams as assistant missionary director in April 1965. His responsibility was to promote missionary interest on Christian campuses. He worked closely with the Student Coordination Committee and the Committee on Student Affairs in planning regional workshops for Student Foreign Missions Fellowship groups. Student initiative was encouraged and taken. Included among these student leaders were Paul Bowers, Mark Senter, David Langford, Jim Plueddemann, Philip Schwab, and Tom Chandler, who have continued service as missionaries, ministers, and professors.

Detailed discussion on relationships between student groups, Inter-Varsity staff, and the IFMA and EFMA committees was recorded at the June 9, 1966 meeting in Wheaton. Later at the 1966 IFMA Annual Meeting, the scope of the committee was expanded to include other personnel matters. The committee was asked to have charge of a session at the 1967 IFMA Annual Meeting. A workshop was held in Detroit, December 15, 1967.

During the 1968 joint study conference, the IFMA and EFMA Personnel and Student Affairs Committees met together. David Howard, who had just been appointed to the missions staff of Inter-Varsity, mentioned that each association would have two representatives on the new Inter-Varsity Advisory Committee. Plans were made for a joint literature program for recruitment purposes and a cooperative campus team to visit three campuses in the Northeast. There was agreement to work closely with evangelical professors of missions.

The workshops on personnel matters became an annual event. The committee members on the Inter-Varsity Advisory Committee reported regularly on their activities. The literature project to produce recruitment brochures was coordinated with EMIS, which published them.

The annual personnel workshop stimulated an intermission orientation course in California, starting in 1971. Mission Aviation Fellowship was a prime mover in this program, working with Evan Adams (IVCF).

Representing the IFMA and EFMA committees, Warren Webster (CBFMS) and the author (IFMA) presented papers at a Wheaton College meeting of the Association of Evangelical Professors of Missions in August 1971. Later that year, the IFMA and EFMA committees merged into a joint IFMA-EFMA Personnel and Student Affairs Committee. Guidelines were adopted and committee activities became primarily devoted to preparation of the annual workshop.

In 1977 the Personnel and Student Affairs Committee shortened its name to IFMA-EFMA Personnel Committee. After twenty years of conducting helpful annual workshops, the IFMA-EFMA Personnel Committee and the Evangelical Missions Information Service remain the only two surviving standing joint committees of the IFMA and EFMA.

## EFMA/IFMA/ACMC TASK FORCE ON EVALUATION

The evaluation of missionaries, mission agencies, and church missions programs was brought up at the 1976 IFMA-EFMA study conference. These issues had been raised earlier that year in *Forum*, a publication of the Association of Church Missions Committees (ACMC). The three associations agreed to forming a joint task force, with the executive director of each naming the members from his organization. Three members from IFMA, three from EFMA, and four from ACMC were chosen. The executive directors served *ex officio*. Rev. William Crouch (SIM) was named chairman.

Over a two-year period, questionnaires were sent to member missions and churches. Responses were circulated to task-force members for their input. All of this information was reduced to a draft report prepared by the task force chairman. The twenty-five page booklet, *A Preliminary Report of the EFMA/IFMA/ACMC Task Force on Evaluation*, was published September 16, 1977. It was distributed to task force members and to members of the associations.

A reworking of the material received in response to the circulation of the preliminary report produced the 50-page booklet, *Evaluation: A Research Report Based on The Preliminary Report of the EFMA/IFMA/ACMC Task Force on Evaluation*, published by ACMC in 1978.

It is divided into three parts: the evaluation of the mission agency, the evaluation of mission personnel and their work, and the church's self-evaluation on its level of involvement. A copy of the questionnaire for evaluating the mission agency was sent to IFMA and EFMA member missions to alert them to the types of information that may be requested from them by their supporting churches.

Although some members of the task force were able to meet together when attending other conferences or meetings, it was regrettable that distance, costs, and time did not permit a face-to-face meeting of *all* members at any time.

## CONCLUSION

The joint committees have provided the framework for the IFMA and EFMA to cooperate in the projects mentioned in this chapter and in the conferences and congresses to be discussed. Out of these joint programs have come study papers, articles, books, guidelines, and helps for missionaries, and home and field administrators.

Theological confusion and ecumenical pressures were primary factors that led IFMA to relax its independent stance and consider closer ties with other evangelicals during the past forty years. It was evident that missions with similar purposes and biblical convictions should stand together in the cause of world evangelization. In order to secure evangelical unity against apostasy, the IFMA sought to broaden its relationships with other evangelical mission associations, including The Associated Missions of the International Council of Christian Churches and the Evangelical Foreign Missions Association (Evangelical Fellowship of Mission Agencies).

It was not possible to facilitate a working agreement with The Associated Missions (TAM) of the International Council of Christian Churches (ICCC) or The Fellowship of Missions (FOM), which separated from TAM.

During the 1980s, a series of meetings and seminars were held with the leadership and some members of the Association of North American Missions (ANAM). A good relationship exists between the two associations.

Cooperative programs continue with EFMA.

## NOTES

[1] "Committee on Missionary Education Minutes," *Reports and Findings of the 5th Annual Mission Executives Retreat* (Washington: Evangelical Foreign Missions Association, 1956), p. 10B.

[2] Interdenominational Foreign Mission Association, Minutes of the Official Board Meeting of 19 November 1956, p. 1.

[3] Interdenominational Foreign Mission Association, Minutes of Meetings of the Official Board Meeting of 10 February 1958, p. 2.

[4] Clyde W. Taylor and Wade T. Coggins, eds., *Protestant Missions in Latin America: A Statistical Survey* (Washington: Evangelical Foreign Missions Association, 1961).

[5] R. Kenneth Strachan, "An Appraisal of the Evangelical Conservative Missionary Enterprise in Latin America, and its Future," *Reports and Findings of the 9th Annual Mission Executives Retreat* (Washington: Evangelical Foreign Missions Association, 1960), pp. 24-27.

[6] Interdenominational Foreign Mission Association - Evangelical Foreign Missions Association, Minutes of the Evangelical Committee on Latin America, Meeting of 3 December 1960, p. 1.

[7] Interdenominational Foreign Mission Association - Evangelical foreign Missions Association, Minutes of the Meetings of the Evangelical Committee on Latin America, Meeting of 13 April 1966, p. 1.

[8] Interdenominational Foreign Mission Association - Evangelical Foreign Missions Association, Minutes of the Meeting of the Evangelical Committee on Latin America, Meeting of 2 October 1975, p. 1.

[9] Interdenominational Foreign Mission Association - Evangelical Foreign Missions Association, Minutes of the Joint Africa Meeting, 29-30 April 1960, p. 2.

[10] Interdenominational Foreign Mission Association - Evangelical Foreign Missions Association, Minutes of Program Committee, Joint Conference on Africa, 26 July 1960, p. 1.

[11] Interdenominational Foreign Mission Association - Evangelical Foreign Missions Association, "Letter to Missions Working in Africa," 15 November 1960.

[12] Interdenominational Foreign Mission Association - Evangelical Foreign Missions Association, Minutes of Joint Africa Committee, 3 December 1960, p. 2.

[13] Interdenominational Foreign Mission Association - Evangelical Foreign Missions Association, Minutes of Joint Africa Committee, 15 November 1961, p. 1.

[14] Interdenominational Foreign Mission Association - Evangelical Foreign Missions Association Evangelical Committee for Africa, "Reports from Africa Evangelical Office," 11 February 1963.

[15] Interdenominational Foreign Mission Association - Evangelical Foreign Missions Association, Minutes of Meetings of the Evangelical Committee for Africa, Meeting of 26 September 1969, p. 2.

[16] Edwin L. Frizen, Jr., "Report of Special Africa Trip," Evangelical Committee for Africa, 22 December 1970, pp. 1-5.

[17] Interdenominational Foreign Mission Association - Evangelical Foreign Missions Association, *Reports and Findings of the 1963 Missions Executives' Retreat* (Washington: Evangelical Foreign Missions Association and Interdenominational Foreign Missions Association, 1963), pp. 64-74.

[18] H. Wilbert Norton, "Report to the IFMA-EFMA Joint Meeting," 1 October 1963, pp. 1-3.

[19] Interdenominational Foreign Mission Association, Minutes of Annual Meeting, 30 September - 4 October, 1963, p. 27.

[20] Committee to Assist Missionary Education Overseas, Board of Directors' Meeting, 4 April 1967, p. 1.

[21] Raymond B. Buker, Sr., and Ted Ward, Comp., *The World Directory of Mission-Related Educational Institutions* (South Pasadena: William Carey Library, 1972).

[22] Ralph D. Winter, ed., *TheologicaI Education by Extension* (South Pasadena: William Carey Library, 1972)

[23] Ralph R. Covell and C. Peter Wagner, *An Extension Seminary Primer*, with a Foreword by Raymond B. Buker, Sr. (South Pasadena: William Carey Library, 1971), p. ix.

[24] Interdenominational Foreign Mission Association, Minutes of the Mission Executives Retreat, 15-16 September 1960, p. 4.

[25] Interdenominational Foreign Mission Association, Minutes of Annual Meeting, 13-15 September 1961, p. 17.

[26] Interdenominational Foreign Mission Association, Minutes of Annual Meeting, 11-13 December 1962, p. 23.

[27] Interdenominational Foreign Mission Association, Minutes of Literature and Publicity Committee, 19 March 1963, p. 2.

[28] Interdenominational Foreign Mission Association, Minutes of Annual Meeting, 30 September - 4 October 1963, p. 19.

[29] Interdenominational Foreign Mission Association - Evangelical Foreign Missions Association, Minutes of IFMA-EFMA Joint Committee on Missions Quarterly, 4 December 1963, p. 2.

[30] Minutes of the Board of Directors, *Evangelical Missions Quarterly*, 25 February 1964, p. 4.

[31] Editorial Committee, "Missionary Faith.," *Evangelical Missions Quarterly*, Fall 1965, pp. 4-8.

[32] Evangelical Missions Information Service, *Report of the Findings: Missions Study Conference* (Springfield, Pennsylvania: Evangelical Missions Information Service, 1967).

[33] Evangelical Missions Information Service, Minutes of Board of Directors' Meeting, 16 November 1970, p. 1.

[34] Evangelical Missions Information Service, Minutes of Board of Directors' Meeting, 5 May 1971, pp. 2-3.

[35] Vergil Gerber, Evangelical Missions Information Service, Annual Report, 1979, p. 20.

[36] Robert T. Taylor, "Good News for Modern Man," *Reports of the 1968 Mission Executives Retreat* (Washington: Evangelical Foreign Missions Association and Interdenominational Foreign Mission Association, 1968), pp. 44-49.

[37] William Kerr, "China," in *Reports of the Annual Mission Executives' Retreat* (Washington: Evangelical Foreign Missions Association, 1972), p. 18.

[38] Jonathan T'ien-en Chao, "Prospects for Future Missions Work in China," *Evangelical Perspectives on China*, ed. Donald E. Douglas (Farmington, MI: Evangelical China Committee, 1976), p. 109.

[39] Edvard Torjesen, "China Committee Report," Interdenominational Foreign Mission Association, Annual Meeting, 1-3 December 1975.

[40] Interdenominational Foreign Mission Association - Evangelical Foreign Missions Association, Minutes of the Evangelical China Committee, 5 May 1979, p. 2.

# 12

# CONFERENCES

One of the three purposes of the IFMA given in the original Articles of Agreement drawn up at the Organizational Meeting on September 29, 1917, was "to open the way to mutual conferences concerning missionary principles and methods."

## BIBLE AND MISSIONS CONFERENCES

The first IFMA-sponsored conferences, apart from the annual meeting, were Bible and missionary conferences. The first one was held in July 1924 at Montrose, Pennsylvania. The purpose was "for prayer, teaching, testimony, the discussion of mission matters and for fellowship."[1] These conferences continued through the twenties, thirties, and forties, with noted pastors and missions personnel speaking.

The early IFMA conferences attracted many missions-minded people. As the Bible and missionary conferences moved from the East across the country, the emphasis remained on Bible teaching and missions. They were slanted, however, toward the laity—to challenge them to become more deeply interested in missions by prayer, service, and support.

In the fifties, there were fewer IFMA-sponsored Bible and missionary conferences. The emphasis focused more on the missions. Conferences began to be designed to carry out Article I of the IFMA Constitution, which had been changed, "to promote mutual helpfulness and conferences concerning missionary principles and practice."

## MISSION ADMINISTRATION SEMINARS

For several years in the early 1950s, various mission executives on whom responsibility for administration rested expressed the hope that it would be possible to get together to talk about some of the down-to-earth questions that confront administrators and office managers. To come to grips with these questions, administrators from the Far Eastern Gospel Crusade (SEND), The Evangelical Alliance Mission, Baptist Mid-Missions, and Conservative Baptist Foreign Mission Society met, with IFMA General Secretary J. O. Percy as chairman. Three days in May and two days in September 1957 were spent discussing problems and trying to put answers into simple words. The result was a series of papers on essential home office activities, which were made available to all evangelical groups. The *Manual on Mission Administration* was published by the IFMA early in 1958, and revised and reprinted later that year.

At the 1961 Annual Meeting, an IFMA Business Administration Committee was appointed—Philip Armstrong (FEGC/SEND), Vernon Mortenson (TEAM), and J. O. Percy (IFMA). They were commissioned to arrange a seminar for IFMA mission administrators before the end of the year. Twenty people gathered to discuss Social Security coverage and Internal Revenue Service regulations. This meeting resulted in the publication of a *Supplement to the Manual on Business Administration.*

The January 1963 conference was attended by fifty administrators from thirty missions, mostly IFMA. The discussions centered primarily on Social Security, IRS regulations, and the 1961 supplement to the manual. It was from this meeting that the recommendation came to schedule such conferences on a regular basis, rather than calling meetings only as problems arose.

The subject area broadened for the February 1965 IFMA Conference on Mission Administration to include management, salaries, legislation, Canadian tax matters, financial systems, mailings, investments, and capital giving. The number attending increased to ninety-four.

The 1967 Mission Management Seminar had 110 participants. Sessions focused on several aspects of management, office systems, Social Security, and tax matters.

A completely revised *Mission Administration Manual* was distributed at the 1969 conference. Called the 6th IFMA Mission Administration Seminar, 157 people attended from 104 Christian organizations. Sessions on use of computers and discussions of the various sections of the manual were the major focus.

The emphasis of the 1972 seminar at Wheaton was on computerization, work simplification, tax matters, and a presentation of the Overseas Resources Counselors' Balance Sheet Approach to salary management. A revised edition of *Mission Administration Manual* was issued at the 1972 seminar.

At the Mission Administration Seminar held at Wheaton College in 1975, financial planning, information management, office systems, and salary management were the areas covered. Kenneth Hansen of ServiceMaster brought the keynote address, "Dynamic Christian Management." The keynote address and the morning devotionals are consistently rated very high on the evaluation sheets.

Seminar participants in 1975 requested that a task force be appointed to prepare an accounting and financial reporting guide for missionary organizations. It was determined that a standard guide for missionary organizations was needed as a matter of Christian stewardship to assist churches and individual donors to better understand and compare financial statements of the missionary organizations they support. The IFMA invited two men from EFMA missions to serve on the Accounting Task Force set up to prepare the guide.

The 1977 *Discussion Draft of Standards of Accounting and Financial Reporting for Missionary Organizations* was circulated at the October 1977 seminar, in which 144 participated. Major consideration was given to the discussion draft, which was on accounting for not-for-profit missionary organizations. There were sessions on retirement, overseas office systems, taxes, and planned giving. The IFMA Mission Administration Seminar was immediately followed by an Overseas Resources Counselors' Seminar, which all participants of the IFMA seminar were encouraged to attend.

During the next two years, the IFMA Business Administration Committee and the IFMA Accounting Task Force worked on a new edition of the *Mission Administration Manual* and the *Accounting and Financial Reporting Guide for Missionary Organizations.* Both were ready for distribution at the 1979 Missions Administration Seminar. Discussion of sections of these books was the main emphasis of the conference.

In 1982, the IFMA Board approved the expansion of IFMA's accounting committee to include representatives from Christian Ministries Management Association (CMMA), now Christian Management Association (CMA); the Evangelical Council for Financial Accountability (ECFA); and members of the accounting profession, to expand the guide in order for it to be more applicable to Christian ministries other than missions agencies. The IFMA already had included two representatives from the EFMA on the IFMA's Accounting Task Force that produced the *Accounting and Financial Reporting Guide for Missionary Organizations* published in 1979 with reprints in 1981 and 1984.

The enlarged committee, known as the Evangelical Joint Accounting Committee (EJAC) chaired by Eldon Howard (SIM), worked hard to produce the *Accounting and Financial Reporting Guide for Christian Ministries*, published jointly by IFMA, EFMA, CMMA, and ECFA in December 1987.

The 1981 IFMA Mission Administration Seminar theme was "The Mission Administration Process: How to Do It." The 1984 seminar focused on "Relating to Our Home Constituency."

The 1986 seminar sessions were organized into five tracks of nine sessions in each: (1) Publications and Media, (2) Business and Accounting, (3) Church Relations, (4) Computer Applications, and (5) Resource Development. Five tracks with six sessions in each were planned for the 1988 seminar: (1) Business and Accounting, (2) Church Relations, (3) Communications, (4) Computer Applications, and (5) Resource Development. A three-track seminar with eight sessions in each was arranged for the 1991 Mission Administration Seminar: (1) Business and Accounting, (2) Church Relations, and (3) Resource Development.

Participation in the IFMA Mission Administration Seminars through the years has come from a wide range of evangelicals, including EFMA missions, missions not affiliated with IFMA or EFMA, and other Christian organizations.

In the early years of the IFMA Business Administration Committee, it was carried on largely by Philip Armstrong (FEGC), Vernon Mortenson (TEAM), and J. O. Percy (IFMA).

During the author's twenty-eight years as executive director, the IFMA Business Administration Committee was chaired by only a few men, all exceptionally qualified and capable. They were, in the order in which they served: Rolf Egeland (TEAM), Richard Oestreicher (SEND), Eldon Howard (SIM), Don Brugmann (GEM), and Ewart Hodgins (Trans World Radio-TWR). Other members were equally as capable. Jack Phillips from SIM Canada headed up the committee in Canada, as well as serving on the U. S. committee. He spent much time and energy in his efforts to help IFMA Canadian missions, as well as a host of other agencies. His contribution to mission business administration in Canada is invaluable.

Eldon Howard and his successor, Don Mortenson (TEAM), chaired the IFMA Accounting Task Force that produced the accounting guide. This group put in countless hours over several years, producing four discussion drafts that were widely circulated for feedback, before putting the guide into its final form as the *Accounting and Financial Reporting Guide for Missionary Organizations.*

Scott Holbrook, chief financial officer for Gospel Missionary Union, was appointed chairman of the Business Administration Committee by the board at the 1991 IFMA Annual Meeting. He had been a member of the committee since 1986.

## COOPERATION AND AMALGAMATION COMMITTEE WORKSHOPS

The IFMA Board at its March 1965 meeting discussed at length the possibilities and benefits of mission mergers. The conclusion was that a committee on amalgamations should be appointed to survey the past and recommend possibilities for future mergers.

A survey was taken of member missions in order to compile information on missionary personnel on loan to other agencies, redeployment, association by contract agreement, and mergers. The survey revealed that only six of forty-one IFMA missions were considering merger possibilities. Twelve had already had merger experience. Only sixteen others saw advantages in a merger.

Dr. Paul Culley, dean of Columbia Graduate School of Missions, was invited to speak on amalgamation of missions at the 1966 Annual Meeting. The following year the committee prepared sample basic organizational documents for the formation of a new combined mission into which several existing missions could merge. IFMA missions were divided into three groups, according to type of missions: (1) service agencies, (2) church planting, and (3) international organizations. A fourth group was made up of those that did not attend the other workshops. A separate workshop was planned for each of the four groups. The author was commissioned by the committee to meet with eight to ten people from each group for informal talks on intermission cooperation and merger. Committee members participated when possible.

The first workshop was held at Missionary Internship in December 1968. Background information was given on various aspects of cooperation and merger, after which the executives talked among themselves about possibilities.[2]

At the second workshop in June 1969, George Thomas of Christian Service Fellowship spoke on merger procedures. Case studies of intermission cooperation at home and on the field were presented.

A few months later, a third workshop was held. This one was for international missions, agencies having sending boards in more than one country, which make up a significant segment of IFMA membership. Internal relationships of international missions often present difficulties in cooperation and merger.

The fourth and final workshop in the series was held in May 1970 for the missions that had not attended any of the three others. Dr. Edmund Clowney of Westminster Seminary gave a series of Bible studies on the unity that Christ requires of His church.

The workshops provided a relaxed setting for executives to share organizational philosophies, visions, and concerns. They provided the catalyst for several missions to continue discussions that led to mergers and were helpful in facilitating better cooperation. Evaluation of the workshops by the participants was positive.

A thick notebook of photocopied material from these sessions is still available from the IFMA office. Several missions request copies each year. There have been over twenty mergers within IFMA during the author's years as executive director, and greater cooperation among member missions in projects, such as candidate orientation schools, etc.

The Cooperation and Amalgamation Committee (formerly the Amalgamation Committee, then the Cooperation and Comity Committee) challenged missions to seriously consider closer cooperation and merger. It attempted to create an atmosphere that would make it increasingly difficult for IFMA missions to enter areas occupied by evangelical missions without consultation and cooperation with them.

A paragraph in *IFMA Standards* under the section on "Operational Standards" states:

> Each mission conducts a thorough survey before entering a new geographic area or people group. Before starting the ministry, consultation is held with other evangelical missions and/or churches working in the area or among the people group.

See the Appendix A for the *IFMA Standards*, which gives requirements for membership in IFMA.

## COLLEGIATE MISSIONS SEMINARS

For many years, IFMA missions have been involved in programs for college-age young people. Most have supported the Urbana conferences of Inter-Varsity Christian Fellowship. Speaking to student groups in secular and Christian schools is a top priority for most missions. Some IFMA mission leaders in the Northeast wanted to stimulate more mission interest among Christian students in their area and wondered if a conference similar to the Southeastern Regional Student Missionary Conference was feasible.

Dick Bailey, candidate secretary of International Missions, called a meeting in January 1973 to discuss possibilities of beginning student missionary conferences in the Northeast. A Steering Committee was formed under the auspices of IFMA. The first conference was planned for October 1973 at Camp Streamside, Stroudsburg, Pennsylvania. It dealt with: (1) Mission Anthropology and Non-Christian Culture; (2) How to Start a Church from Zero; (3) Discipling and Leadership Training; (4) Working with the National Church; and (5) Who Is Responsible for Evangelism? Dr. Gordon MacDonald gave the opening address, "The Biblical Basis for the Local Indigenous Church." Other speakers included national church leaders and missionaries. The first seminar was well received by students and missionaries.

Ten overseas national students and church workers contributed positively to the program. Some students wanted to participate in planning future seminars. Several were appointed to the Steering Committee and sub-committees. However, since the schools they represented covered a large geographical area and student schedules were tight, it was difficult to arrange meetings with more than one or two student representatives at a time.

To further strengthen coordination, Lee Howard, a staff member of Inter-Varsity Christian Fellowship and working with its Student Foreign Missions Fellowship (SFMF), was added to the Steering Committee. The 1974 seminar was held at Pinebrook Conference Center. The theme, "Missions in Times Like These," considered opportunity, discipline, and crisis. Sixty-nine students attended from eleven schools, along with forty missionaries representing twenty-one missions.

"Missions Alive in '75" was the theme of the next seminar. Both student and missionary participation dropped from previous years. The students appreciated the quality of the program and the personal attention they received from the missionaries. It was recommended that future seminars be sponsored by the Student Foreign Missions Fellowship. It was desired that more student involvement be generated.

Since no group of students came forward to take up this responsibility, the Steering Committee decided to hold one more seminar under IFMA sponsorship. In spite of extensive promotion on campuses, student participation was disappointing. When a number of the Steering Committee members were transferred overseas or to other parts of the country, the committee was not reappointed.

It was agreed that the initiative for such seminars must come from student leaders themselves. Mission leaders were quite willing to assist in any arrangements requested by the students, but did not believe they should continue the leadership of such an effort. The seminars were held annually from 1973 through 1976. IFMA missions subsidized them.

# COOPERATIVE CONFERENCES

The IFMA Annual Meetings are designed so that member missions can interact on issues of mutual concern. EFMA meetings are the same. After IFMA and EFMA began cooperating in joint committee activities, it was logical for the two associations to join in a combined study conference.

## IFMA-EFMA STUDY CONFERENCES

The first combined meeting was held September 30 - October 4, 1963 at Winona Lake, Indiana. It was a study conference that dealt with: (1) The Candidate Problem, (2) The International Student, (3) An Analysis of Islam, (4) Training National Leadership, and (5) A National Missionary Movement. The last paper was given by Raymond J. Davis, general director of Sudan Interior Mission (SIM), who described the missionary outreach of the SIM-related churches in Ethiopia and Nigeria. Reports were given of surveys of developments in Africa, Asia, and Latin America.

The Congress on the Church's Worldwide Mission, held at Wheaton College, April 9-16, 1966, was IFMA-EFMA sponsored. See Chapter 10, Congresses.

In 1968, the two associations were together again in a study conference at Winona Lake. Major emphasis was given to studying two issues: (1) Evangelism in Biblical Perspective and Contemporary Experience, and (2) Winning Roman Catholics in the Post Vatican II Era. Other sessions featured Bible translations and missionary candidates. Special speakers were Professors Merrill C. Tenney (Wheaton Graduate School), George W. Peters (Dallas Theological Seminary), C. Peter Wagner (Fuller School of World Mission), and J. Herbert Kane (Lancaster Bible College, later at Trinity Evangelical Divinity School).

Sponsored by the joint IFMA-EFMA Evangelical Missions

Information Service, the two associations held the Green Lake '71 Conference, known as GL '71, at Green Lake, Wisconsin. Next to the 1966 Wheaton Congress, it was the most significant conference sponsored by the IFMA and EFMA. *Missions in Creative Tension*, the conference compendium remains a valuable resource book on evangelical mission and church relations. All five parts of this book contain helpful material vital to an understanding of mission and church relations. While the conference emphasized relations to the church overseas, there are significant items included on relations to the sending churches, as well.[3]

Part 1 of the compendium, "Studies from a Preliminary Retreat," includes all papers and finding of the IFMA Board Retreat, June 1971. The "Feedback Summary" is an overview of church and mission questions. Part 2, "Advance Study Papers for Delegates," gives the two preliminary study papers and various orientation materials. Part 3, "The Conference Handbook," provides a full set of materials given to the delegates, including all major papers and a select bibliography on church/mission relations. Part 4, "A Sampling of Early Response," gives evaluation feedback responses from delegates—overseas nationals, pastors, educators, students, and mission personnel. The Appendix is a reprint of the Summer 1971 *Evangelical Missions Quarterly*, which was devoted to special articles for GL '71 preparation.

The 378 delegates interacted on the papers of 4 major speakers. Jack F. Shepherd (C&MA) spoke on church-mission relations at home. Louis L. King (C&MA) and George W. Peters (DTS) each gave two papers on mission-church relations overseas. Edmund P. Clowney (Westminster Seminary) gave four Bible studies on the church.

More than twenty years after GL '71, mission and church relations remains one of the main concerns of missions. Today there are many new pastors of mission-minded churches, many new overseas national church leaders, and many new missions executives and administrators who would profit from a study of this material.

Members of the Association of Evangelical Professors of Missions (AEPM) were invited to join the IFMA and EFMA for the next three study conferences, all held at TWA Breech Training Academy, Overland Park, Kansas, in 1973, 1976, and 1978. In 1973, the church and mission theme was continued. Five overseas national church leaders gave major presentations, followed by panel responses and interaction. This dialogue was a forward step in the direction of mutual understanding and trust, a necessary foundation for building a spirit of interdependence.

In 1976, World Evangelism and the Future was considered from many viewpoints. Projections for missions in the 1980s were made by thirteen church, missions, and school leaders. The book that came out of the 1976 IFMA-EFMA study conference, *Evangelical Missions Tomorrow*, has been used as a textbook in preparing missionary candidates and in continuing education for field missionaries.

The 1978 conference emphasized crucial issues facing evangelical missions in relation to diverse political systems. It was designed to help missionaries understand the influence of their own political systems on their theology and practice, and to prepare them to cope with systems different from their own. It was to provide help for missionaries under totalitarian regimes, and to assist them in preparing the church for life in a hostile society. Historian Earle E. Cairns in four addresses gave the historical perspective and biblical basis for church/mission relations to civil authority. The addresses, papers, and findings of the study conference were published in *Christ and Caesar in Christian Missions*. The material in this book, published by William Carey Library, is still relevant today.

The next joint conference was held September 28 to October 2, 1981 at TWA Breech Training Academy, having the theme, "Serving Our Generation: A Way of Life."

The theme for the 9th IFMA-EFMA Study Conference held in 1984 was "Biblical Balance in Modern Missions." Holding the meetings at the U. S. Center for World Mission in Pasadena gave many delegates their first opportunity to visit that campus and to see missions, research organizations, and educational programs centered there.

The Association of Evangelical Professors of Missions was invited to hold its annual meeting concurrently with the study conference. Most of the speakers and panel members were members of AEPM. Dr. Pablo Perez of Mexico and Dr. Chris Marintika of Indonesia represented overseas churches and training institutions. Other major speakers included professors Dr. David Hesselgrave of Trinity, Dr. Ron Blue of Dallas, Dr. Terry Hulbert of Columbia, and pastor Paul Cedar of Lake Avenue Congregational Church in Pasadena.

The 10th IFMA-EFMA Study Conference was held in Orlando, Florida, in 1987 with the theme, "Focusing the Vision." The Bible teacher was Rev. Ajith Fernando, national director of Youth for Christ in Sri Lanka. Other speakers included professors Dr. Kenneth Gangel and Dr. Michael Pocock of Dallas Seminary; Rev. Stanley Davies, general secretary of Evangelical Missionary Alliance, Great Britain; Pastor Leith Anderson, Wooddale Church, Edina, MN; Rev. Luis Bush, coordinator of COMIBAM '87, Sao Paulo, Brazil; and Dr. William Taylor, executive secretary of the WEF Missions Commission.

"Confronting Change" was the theme of the 11th IFMA-EFMA Study Conference in Northglenn, Colorado, in September 1990. Dr. David Howard, World Evangelical Fellowship International Director, Singapore, was the daily Bible teacher. Other major speakers were Dr. Eugene Williams, American Missionary Fellowship on "The Concept of Change;" Dr. Leith Anderson of Wooddale Church on "Change in the Church;" Rev. Paul McKaughan, the new executive director of EFMA on "Change in Missions;" and Dr. William Taylor, WEF Missions Commission on "Two-Thirds World Missionary Training." The AEPM also met during the meetings.

The value of the joint meetings lies largely in the provocative plenary meetings, the small-group sessions, and the one-on-one discussions between meetings when people get to know and understand one another and each other's organization and ministry.

## MEDICAL CONSULTATION

Overseas missionary medical personnel began raising questions about the future of medical missions in the fast-changing world situation. A few IFMA and EFMA executives asked that a consultation be arranged for mission administrators and medical personnel. A two-day Consultation on the Future of Medical Missions was held at Missionary Internship, Farmington, Michigan, March 8-9, 1977. Medical missions was considered in relation to governments, the national church, interagency cooperation, and the future role of medical missions. Participants had come with lists of subjects and questions that required consideration. The program was set up with a process format that encouraged full participation and interaction of each one in the group. The workshop enabled doctors, nurses, and administrators, working within their groups, to gain insights and find answers applicable to their own particular situations.

## PERSONNEL WORKSHOPS

The IFMA Personnel and Student Affairs Committee began holding workshops for personnel staff in 1967. The committee presented a panel discussion on recruitment of candidates at the annual meeting and determined from the response to hold a Recruitment Seminar at Missionary Internship in Farmington, Michigan, December 15-16, 1967.

For the next three years, the separate committees of the IFMA and EFMA met together occasionally and participated together in the IFMA's December workshops. In 1968, the emphasis was on a review of forms and recruitment procedures; in 1969 on candidate orientation; and in 1970 on coping strategies.

The IFMA and EFMA Personnel Committees began working as a joint committee in 1971. They jointly sponsored the December 1971 workshop, which considered adult and youth communication problems.

The seminars of 1972 to 1974 were devoted to the general subject of personnel evaluation. During these sessions, the participants studied how to develop instruments for evaluation of candidates and missionaries. Dr. Ted Ward of Michigan State University and now at Trinity was the chief resource person.

Continuing Education was the subject of the 1975 sessions. This topic was continued in 1976, with particular emphasis on the effect a continuing education program has on the missionary family. A missionary's first term on the field is one of the most difficult periods of his missionary career. Even though that period is usually supervised by field staff, rather than home leadership, the committee decided that the 1977 seminar should focus on the frustrations, development, and integration of the first-term missionary. Fifty-five participated.

A change of pace was planned for the 1978 seminar, held at the Assemblies of God Conference Center, Springfield, Missouri. Missionary Personnel Recordkeeping was the subject. Candidate processing records, appointed missionary records, and legal and security matters were discussed. The sessions were geared to both large and small organizations, with presentations and demonstrations of both manual and electronic approaches.

The 1979 workshop was held at Missionary Internship, with a continuation of the 1977 theme of the first-term missionary. Under the title, "Field Structures and the New Missionary," the role of veteran missionaries in promoting a positive initial term for new missionaries was pursued.

The committee decided to go back to the basic issue of recruitment for 1980. Resource people were from Christian organizations specializing in work among college students. Dr. Christy Wilson (Gordon-Conwell Seminary) spoke on the need of mission involvement in recruiting "tentmakers."

The personnel workshop continued to be held from 1981 through 1990, using the services of Missionary Internship in Farmington, Michigan. However, since the number of participants grew to as many as 109, the sessions were held in local churches. The 1991 workshop was held at the Clarion Hotel, Farmington Hills, Michigan.

Workshop themes for the decade were:

1981 - Process of Missionary Candidates
1982 - Preparing the Candidate for the Field
1983 - Interviewing Skills
1984 - Prefield Orientation and Training Program
1985 - Functions of the Personnel Department
1986 - Developing Missionary Leadership
1987 - Candidates from Bruised Backgrounds
1988 - The Personnel Worker's Professional and Private Life
1989 - Spiritual Factors in Missionary Effectiveness
1990 - Rethinking Missionary Recruitment
1991 - Choosing the Right People for Missionary Service

The joint Personnel Committee and the smaller Program Committee take their responsibilities very seriously in order to produce an annual workshop that is well accepted and that accomplishes its purposes. The committee regularly invites others to meet with them, including evangelical professionals from industry, such as Pepsico and 3M, representatives from Inter-Varsity, Navigators, Campus Crusade, professors of missions, professional counselors, and student leaders.

The staff at Missionary Internship have provided much of the logistical support.

The *Personnel Committee Handbook* was produced in 1987, and a compilation of workshop materials was begun.

A survey taken during the introductions from year to year show that up to a half of the participants were new to their personnel department responsibilities. This reflects a large turnover in personnel departments. Special sessions for the new personnel workers were tried occasionally. In 1990 a special session for new workers was held following the regular workshop. Feedback indicated that it was helpful and appreciated.

A special three-day workshop was held in May 1991 for new personnel workers, in addition to the regular December 1991 personnel conference, which marked the 25th annual personnel workshop since the IFMA began them in 1967.

Whatever the name—conference, consultation, seminar, or workshop—sponsorship of such meetings is one of the IFMA's productive services to its missions. From technical mission administration and personnel recruitment to subjects of mission philosophy, theology, and strategy, missions leaders are looking for the help that they receive in IFMA-sponsored meetings.

During the past twenty-five years, there has been a significant change in executive leadership among IFMA missions. New administrators are appointed to home-staff positions each year, making it necessary to repeat workshop emphases from time to time. One great benefit is that the meetings also provide the new executive with the opportunity to get to know and to interact with experienced administrators from other missions who have similar responsibilities.

## NOTES

[1] Interdenominational Foreign Mission Association, Special Meeting, 9 July 1924, p. 1.

[2] Interdenominational Foreign Mission Association, Minutes of Cooperation and Comity Committee, 2 April 1968, p. 1.

[3] Vergil Gerber, ed., *Missions In Creative Tension* (South Pasadena: William Carey Library, 1971).

# 13

# CONGRESSES ON WORLD MISSIONS

There were several historic conferences on missions prior to 1960: New York, 1854; London, 1888; New York, 1900; and Edinburgh, 1910. Participants included those from main line denominations, as well as representatives from faith missions and other organizations that remain theologically fundamental. Fifty years had passed since Edinburgh, possibly the most revolutionary missions conference in history. There had been two major wars, the Bolshevik Revolution, and smaller wars and revolutions. Technological advances in travel and communication had brought the most remote people to our door. Nations were instantly aware of each other's problems and conditions. There had been a revolution in morals and thought. Ghana had received her independence in 1957, and nationalism was on the rise. The world was in upheaval in 1960.

In half a century, the world's population had increased by 75 percent, and a large percentage of the total was under twenty-five years of age. It seemed that North Americans had just about reached the zenith of affluence. There were more unevangelized people than ever before! In a world of upheaval and change, two things remained constant: (1) the sinfulness of man and his need of redemption, and (2) the truth of God's saving grace through Jesus Christ.

The leadership of IFMA sensed an urgency about arousing

Christians in North America to the lateness of the hour and the need for speedy evangelization of the world. Mission agencies needed to develop strategies to complete the mandate of Jesus Christ. The Congress on World Missions was envisioned to help to meet these needs.

## CONGRESS ON WORLD MISSIONS

In 1958, while cooperative efforts with the EFMA were in the embrionic stage, the IFMA was concerned about the lack of widespread commitment in Christian schools and churches to the fulfillment of the great commission.

The focus of the 1958 IFMA Annual Meeting was a reevaluation of the nondenominational missions movement. The following was adopted that year:

> With an overwhelming sense of the immensity—but also of the extreme urgency, of the great unfinished task of world evangelization, and having regard to the lateness of the hour,
>
> WE RESOLVE most humbly to yield ourselves afresh to the Lord of the harvest. It is our prayer that we may thus be used of Him to hasten the consummation, by reaching speedily those who are still waiting the coming of the messengers of Christ. Thus shall the Church be completed and He shall see the travail of His soul and be satisfied.
>
> BE IT FURTHER RESOLVED: that we call upon Christian young people, everywhere to rise in force for the speedy occupation of the remaining unevangelized portions of the world field and for the Church of Jesus Christ to encourage and support a mighty missionary advance.

C. Gordon Beacham (NAM), elected to the IFMA Board in 1958, was appointed immediately to chair a committee to plan a congress on world missions for 1960. In his report to the 1959 Annual Meeting the next year, Beacham announced:

> Fifty years after the great Edinburgh Missionary Conference of 1910, half the world still remains unevangelized. To help meet this urgent spiritual challenge, the IFMA proposes to convene a Congress on World Missions December 4-11, 1960 in Chicago, Illinois.

J. O. Percy and C. Gordon Beacham were named congress coordinators to work out all arrangements. Five committees were appointed to handle the program, publicity, prayer, finance, and research. Publicity began fifteen months before the conference.

The Congress on World Missions was held at Moody Memorial Church in Chicago December 4-11, 1960. Possibly never before in the history of missions in North America did so many evangelical missionaries gather in one place—about 500 altogether, including 400 serving with IFMA member missions.[1] Possibly never before in conservative evangelical circles had so many noted Bible teachers, evangelists, prominent educators, missionary statesmen, and widely-recognized national church leaders made up the speakers' roster of a conference on world evangelization. And possibly never before had so many fundamental pastors, professors from Christian schools, and laymen gathered with such a group for the single purpose of looking at the world in its desperate spiritual need and considering what to do about it.

Of the 27 major speakers only 5 were mission executives. Other speakers were pastors, professors and school administrators, leaders of other conservative evangelical organizations, and 7 national church leaders representing the non-North American world helped to give a global perspective to the Congress. They also participated with missionary leaders in nightly forum sessions. Others attending included 800 pastors and several thousand lay Christians. The congress resolutions reminded the Christian world that the unfinished task of world evangelization was greater by far than it was 50 years before at the Edinburgh Conference of 1910, which led to the formation of the World Council of Churches and a subsequent loss in missionary vision on the part of many mainline denominations.

A major objective of the congress was to influence pastors and leaders of Christian educational institutions. They, in turn, were to arouse young people to the urgency of fulfilling the great commission. Believers in North America were to be stirred to support a forward thrust in foreign missions by prayer and financial support.

The host pastor, Dr. Alan Redpath of Moody Memorial Church, delivered the opening address, and Dr. Theodore Epp of Back to the Bible Broadcast had the closing session. During the eight days, thirty-six messages were given and were published in the congress compendium, *Facing the Unfinished Task*, which includes summaries of research and panel discussions. Compiled by J. O. Percy and edited by Mary Bennett, it was published by Zondervan in 1961.

Speakers repeatedly spoke of increasing population, false religions, economic unrest, and governmental controls. The spiritual condition of the world's multitudes was made unmistakably clear. Speaker after speaker presented the response to these challenges as obedience to the mandate in the Word of God to disciple the nations, to preach the gospel to every creature, and to seek to mobilize every member of the body of Christ.

Many assembled for the Congress felt that a document, simple and decisive, should be prepared by a representative committee and presented to the congregation gathered on Friday evening, December 9. The committee was comprised of three mission leaders, one pastor, one Christian educator, and one layman. The following document was presented and eventually distributed to all present who desired a copy:

## Congress on World Missions

### Resolutions

At the Congress on World Missions held in Moody Memorial Church, Chicago (December 4-11, 1960) with approximately 500 missionaries, 800 pastors, and several thousand lay Christians in attendance, the work of Christ throughout the world was brought under review. It was concluded that:

We face a new period of drastic upheaval and unparalleled change in the world.

We face the unfinished task of evangelization in a time of a population explosion that makes this task greater by far than that declared at the Edinburgh Conference of fifty years ago.

We face the fact that we, as a group of born again believers, live in a day when the world's need is overwhelming.

In this knowledge we confess that "we know not what to do," but we would also say with God's servant of old, "our eyes are upon Thee, O Lord."

THEREFORE BE IT RESOLVED:

I. That we reaffirm the urgent necessity of an intimate and continuing closer relationship with God. It must be understood by each individual believer that we are "laborers together with God" and that fellowship and power can only be attained through the abiding fulness of the Holy Spirit working in and through us.

II. That we urge a closer working partnership and spiritual fellowship between missions, between the missionary and the national

Christian, and between the missionary and the home church. This mind of unity, which was also in Christ Jesus, does not require union of organization or uniformity of action, but finds practical expression in love and like-mindedness in this common effort.

III. That we express awareness of the fact that this technical age of scientific achievement makes it possible, as never before, to reach every tribe and nation on the face of the earth with the message of redemption through Jesus Christ. The increase of literacy in underdeveloped areas, the potential of the printed page, the recording of remote languages, the development of radio, and T.V., and the facilities of communication in general must be considered providential aids for the speedy evangelization of all the world.

IV. That we recognize that this new era of challenge and responsibility calls for a careful appraisal and an immediate adjustment of the missionary enterprise. There is no place for pessimism. The criticalness of the hour propels us forward to meet the opportunities of open doors and of reaching needy souls with the gospel.

V. That we declare the need for a total mobilization of all the resources of the church of Jesus Christ, both in terms of men and means, in order that the total evangelization of the world may be achieved during the immediate generation. This demands the total personal commitment of each individual believer. This is the challenge to, and responsibility of, each one of us and of the church as together we proceed to the task.[2]

It was recognized the following day by the IFMA Annual Meeting that the resolutions adopted had failed to include any direct statement on the Word of God. A motion was approved, "that the Congress Committee prepare a news release . . . , bearing in mind the need for a special emphasis on our trust in the inerrant Word of God."[3]

Testimonials from pastors and laymen indicated a positive influence on their lives. The IFMA Board must have been pleased with the results of the Congress. A month later they discussed a possible conference in Hamilton, Ontario, for 1964 to be patterned after the congress in Chicago. A Continuing Congress Committee was appointed and a fund established for future congresses. At the invitation of Dr. Redpath, the board approved another congress to be held at Moody Church in 1964 in connection with the Church's centennial. However, plans for future congresses were soon tabled. Mr. Percy resigned as IFMA executive secretary, and Dr. Redpath left the Moody Church pastorate.

Twenty years after the 1960 Congress on World Missions, Dr. George W. Peters commented on the congress messages, recorded in *Facing the Unfinished Task*, saying they "should be read by everyone of us for inspiration as well as for education. Some of the finest mission messages that ever have been preached were preached at the Congress by men of God from all over the United States and elsewhere."[4]

The next congress in which the IFMA was involved was the Congress on the Church's Worldwide Mission, which it co-sponsored with the Evangelical Foreign Missions Association in 1966.

## CONGRESS ON THE CHURCH'S WORLDWIDE MISSION

With theological confusion and ecumenical pressures increasing, it was necessary for evangelicals to define their position on existing issues and to focus on the biblical mandate.

When IFMA President Vernon Mortenson (TEAM) called for expressions from the 1963 Annual Meeting, regarding holding another congress on world missions, the delegates went on record favoring one to be held after 1965. They recommended that this be discussed with the EFMA. The IFMA Board at its meeting on March 10, 1964, after naming the committee to work on the congress on world missions, voted to recommend to the EFMA that they name a committee to meet with the IFMA committee to make recommendations in regard to a congress on world missions in 1966.

The EFMA agreed to co-sponsor the congress. The joint IFMA-EFMA committee adopted the name Full Congress Committee. It met first on July 13, 1964. The initial order of business was to make recommendations on the congress name, purpose, delegate representation, date, and place. The executive secretaries of the two associations—the author (IFMA) and Clyde W. Taylor (EFMA)—were named to be the Program Committee. IFMA President Vernon Mortenson (TEAM), and EFMA President Louis King (C&MA) were co-chairmen. The Conservative Baptist Foreign Missions Society loaned Vergil Gerber to be congress coordinator.

By April 1965, detailed plans for the Congress on the Church's Worldwide Mission had been approved, and Wheaton College had been reserved for April 9-16, 1966. The purpose statement was constructed in some detail to set the tone for the congress. Copies were sent to all potential speakers and delegates. The final wording was:

> Because of the injection of new definitions and unwarranted interpretations of Scripture into the overall mission of the church by some ecumenists, including new concepts of the theology of missions, the strategy of world evangelism, and Biblical authority, and
>
> Because these new definitions tend to foster religious syncretism, a wide acceptance of the

> doctrine of universalism, and the substitution of inter-church aid for world evangelism, and
>
> Because of the incompleteness of worldwide Gospel outreach, and
>
> Because of common problems in mission-church relationships, and
>
> Because of the need for evangelicals to demonstrate to the world that we stand agreed on basic doctrinal beliefs, fellowship, and the defense and proclamation on the Gospel,
>
> In adoration of the Triune God and in obedience to His infallible Word, we shall seek, through the Congress on the Church's Worldwide Mission:
>
> > To relate to the Word of God the entire task of missions, its mandate, message and method,
> >
> > To evaluate our present achievements in an effort to improve our strategy and methods,
> >
> > To motivate and to involve all evangelical Christians in the task of world evangelism and church development.[5]

Thus, the major congress issues were clearly identified and enumerated as being: (1) the drift of the ecumenical movement toward syncretism, (2) universalism and a "new evangelism," (3) the unfinished task of world evangelization, (4) mission-church relationships, and (5) the need for a demonstration of evangelical unity.

"God's Gift to the Church," the keynote address by Dr. Louis L. King, focused on Jesus Christ, the head of the Church. Other Bible expositions covered mission and the Church's authority, mission and the Church's message, mission and the Church's endowment, mission and the Church's nature, and mission and the Church's consummation. Ten study papers covered the relation of the mission of the Church to syncretism, neo-universalism, proselytism, neo-Romanism, church growth, foreign missions, evangelical unity, evaluating methods, social concern, and a hostile world.

A few months before the meetings, the congress committee commissioned Dr. Harold Lindsell to prepare a brief that would put the congress in historical and missiological context, which would be sent to all speakers and their consultants, and circulated as a news release. He mentioned the stewardship responsibility and obligation facing evangelicals in the light of the challenge. Lindsell concluded, "The clarion call has gone forth to those who share this heritage to join in a Congress which has for its compelling aim to bring into new focus the Biblical mandate to evangelize the world."[6]

The congress registered 938 official delegates from 71 countries, along with a number of observers. One hundred fifty mission boards sent delegates, 50 were non-IFMA-EFMA agencies. Thirty-nine special mission interest groups, 55 schools, and 14 non-North American mission agencies were represented.

The major document to come from the congress was the twenty-eight-page *Wheaton Declaration*, which summarized the concerns of the ten major papers. The recommendations of the twenty-five discussion groups were processed by group recorders and then distilled by five recorder-editors. The results were further processed with the author of the original paper and his consultants.

Speaker Gilbert W. Kirby, who at the time of the congress was principal of London Bible College in England and executive secretary of World Evangelical Fellowship, wrote, "How it was possible to produce the final draft of the 'Wheaton Declaration' from the many and varied contributions submitted by the different study groups remains a mystery."[7] The answer is that the Full Congress Committee, Review Committee, International Advisory Committee, and a few theological and editorial consultants met each evening after all sessions were over to put the document into its final form.

As one of the student delegates, Wheaton College senior David Morris, wrote:

> The integrity of the Congress shined through the clear, open structure leading into the final declaration. It became truly representative of evangelicalism's position on present problems. Prayer and the Scriptures characterized the Congress, not as ornaments, but as the basic fiber. The discussion groups, the actual focus of the Congress itself, were clear examples of Christian love, the spirit by which we are to be known in the world. There was straightforward equality: my voice carried as easily as the opinion of a missionary executive.[8]

The authority for the consensus was the inspired, authoritative, inerrant Word of God. The supreme task of the church was clearly identified as the mandate that the gospel of Jesus Christ must be preached to the people of every tribe, tongue, and nation.

Each major section of the *Wheaton Declaration* was divided into three parts: underlying issues, witness of the Scriptures, and the declaration. The assembled delegates unanimously adopted the declaration on the final morning, recognizing that it was a true consensus after eight days of interaction and corporate study. In presenting it, Co-chairman Louis King clearly indicated it was prepared by fallible, finite people, and that it was subject to correction and change as God gives new insights.

The section that raised most questions, demonstrating the need for further study and more precise definitions, was "Mission—and Foreign Missions." The search for clearer understanding of the relationship of the missions agency and the church at home and overseas was continued at the IFMA-EFMA study conference, Green Lake '71.

Following adoption of the declaration, the delegates stood and, in unison, solemnly read the Covenant:

IN SUPPORT OF THIS DECLARATION
WE
the delegates here assembled in adoration of the Triune God with full confidence in Holy Scripture, in submission to the Lord Jesus Christ, and looking for His coming again
DO COVENANT TOGETHER
for God's eternal glory, and in response to the Holy Spirit, with renewed dedication, and in our oneness in Christ as the people of God,
TO SEEK
under the leadership of our Head, with full assurance of His power and presence,
THE MOBILIZATION OF THE CHURCH
its people, its prayers, and resources,
FOR THE EVANGELIZATION OF THE WORLD
IN THIS GENERATION
so, help us God!
AMEN.[9]

Dr. Eugene L. Smith, then executive secretary of the World Council of Churches in New York, attended the congress as an observer from the National Council of Churches of Christ in the U. S. A. Dr. Smith called the congress "a notable gathering, superbly organized, representing a larger number of missionaries than any previous missionary assembly in North America, seriously and creatively considering the evangelistic task of the Church in today's world."[10] He further observed:

> One development of major importance in recent years has been the increasing cooperation between the EFMA and IFMA, of which this Congress is a major result. The Congress has historic significance for the participating agencies, both in the convergence of currents which made it possible, and in the initiative it

> represents for coming to grips with contemporary problems and opportunities in fulfilling the Great Commission.[11]

The Full Congress Committee met a few weeks after the congress to finish its business affairs. It approved the use of remaining funds for translating the declaration into some of the major languages of the world. It also recommended its dissolution as a committee, which had completed its assignment. It further recommended that a committee be appointed to seek ways of implementing the *Wheaton Declaration*, giving priority to the covenant made to seek to evangelize the world in this generation.

The 1966 IFMA Annual Meeting enthusiastically endorsed the *Wheaton Declaration* by adopting a series of implementing resolutions:

> That we as individuals and member missionary societies will be actively engaged in implementing the Declaration by:
>
> 1. Seeking to study and apply its principles in our own ministry and service
> 2. Diligence in distributing the Declaration in our own organizations and among our own personnel
> 3. Careful attention that our missionaries on the fields become involved in the implementation of these principles
> 4. Sharing the truths and implications of the Declaration with the national churches and church leaders among whom we labor
> 5. Emphasizing wherever possible in our contacts with supporting churches in the homeland the importance of these principles
> 6. Including a careful presentation of these principles in the orientation and training of our workers

7. Diligence in continuing the study of the broad areas covered in the Declaration
8. Seeking to observe the guidelines of the Declaration in our relationships with and witness to Roman Catholics and other religious groups not sharing our biblical orientation
9. Aggressively promoting church growth in harmony with the principles enunciated
10. Preserving and expanding with gratitude to God the vital spirit of evangelical unity in the Wheaton Congress and Declaration as distinguished from organizational union

That we appeal to the entire evangelical community at home and abroad to join us in establishing, applying, and continuing these principles by:

1. Encouraging the use of the *Wheaton Declaration* and the Congress studies in Seminary, Bible College, and other Christian educational curricula
   a. Seminars for missions professors and other instructors ought to be planned in which authors of Congress study papers and selected missions strategists review the structure and content of curricula and recommend such revisions or additions as may be indicated
   b. Specific questions ought to be gleaned from the Declaration and study papers for graduate research and for thesis preparation
   c. A broad range of material suitable for class discussion, term papers and other assignments ought to be discovered in these materials

2. Encouraging all who love and minister the Word of God to intensify their study of the Scriptures in areas relating to the eternal punishment of the lost and to the call of redemption and reconciliation which is the responsibility of the saved
3. Encouraging the planning of specialized conferences on various segments of the Declaration, and the use of this material wherever appropriate at every level of communication.[12]

The joint Congress Continuing Committee was responsible for allocating subsidies for publishing the *Wheaton Declaration* and *The Church's Worldwide Mission* in various languages. Within one year of the congress, the declaration had been published in 8 languages, totaling 57,000 copies. In addition to 10,000 copies of *The Church's Worldwide Mission* in English, it was published in Korean, Chinese, and French.

Members of the continuing committee produced a series of questions on the ten declaration topics for use by missions, national churches, pastors, and missionaries in their implementations of the declaration.[13] The committee worked with Evangelical Missions Information Service in arranging for the 1967 Missions Study Conference held at Glen Eyrie, Colorado Springs, May 29 - June 3, 1967. Four topics were studied in depth: (1) church development, (2) unity, (3) mass media, and (4) institutionalism. The Congress Continuing Committee's functions were later absorbed by EMIS.

The congresses on missions that the IFMA sponsored or co-sponsored had a positive impact on participants. The books and materials published after the meetings extended their impact.

The 1966 Congress on the Church's Worldwide Mission was widely recognized for its treatment of ten important missiological issues. The *Wheaton Declaration* through translation was made available to many people around the world who do not read English. Reflecting on the Wheaton Congress, George Peters stated in 1975 at the EFMA Missions Executives' Retreat:

> I have no hesitation to say that the year 1966 is going down in history and will be recorded by historians sometime in the future as the most significant year of evangelicalism in this century. It was in that year when evangelicals hoisted their sails and evangelicalism set its face and force to meet the future and the world in bold evangelism. In the spring of that year, the Wheaton Congress convened, a congress of tremendous significance.[14]

At that same meeting, Charles Tipp of Ontario Bible College presented a paper, "Reflection on the Wheaton Congress." Tipp stated:

> While the Wheaton Congress was largely North American in its composition, it did bring together the two large mission families of EFMA and IFMA, plus other independent evangelical missions. This has proved most fruitful and is a demonstration of the kind of unity that is most desirable. . . . I believe the Wheaton Congress provided the most comprehensive forum for evangelical interaction since Edinburgh in 1910.[15]

## THE IFMA AND OTHER INTERNATIONAL CONGRESSES AND MEETINGS

The IFMA is cautious about its participation in international congresses and meetings, being careful that cooperation is limited to those having sponsors that affirm the historic biblical Christian faith.

In 1958, when the IFMA Congress Committee and Board were working on plans for the 1960 Congress on World Missions, J. O. Percy (IFMA) was approached by Larry Love about a proposed conference on world evangelism, which was to be convened in 1960, also. Mr. Love was reported to be working full-time for the Billy Graham Evangelistic Association as director of the conference that was planned to be held either in Europe or the United States. Love had been authorized by the board of the Billy Graham Evangelistic Association to invite Mr. Percy to be a member of the planning committee for the evangelism conference, along with Dr. Harold Ockenga, Dr. V. Raymond Edman, and Dr. Clyde Taylor. J. O. Percy indicated that Love was assured by the Billy Graham Association that no liberal or modernist would have any part in the planning, program, or speaking.[16]

One further meeting was reported between Mr. Love and Mr. Percy. Afterwards, however, Mr. Percy expressed doubts as to the advisability of his serving on the committee, although he was willing to attend the next meeting of the planning committee.[17] There is no record of further IFMA involvement in this conference that was held at Montreux, Switzerland, August 16-18, 1960 in which thirty-three evangelical leaders from twelve countries participated.[18]

An invitation was extended to the author to attend the World Congress on Evangelism in Berlin in 1966, which was a tenth anniversary project of *Christianity Today.* The IFMA Board decided he should attend as an observer and should visit the work of as many member missions as possible while in Europe.

Three years later, the author and eight other IFMA-related men were among thirty who participated in the Saturation Evangelism Consultation held in Leysin, Switzerland, August 28 to September 4, 1969. Dr. George Peters was chairman of that international consultation. A full report is given in the book, *Mobilizing for Saturation Evangelism.*[19]

The author was designated to represent the IFMA at the 1969 Latin American Congress on Evangelism (CLADE) in Bogota, Colombia. The IFMA Board carefully considers every invitation extended to the executive director. An example is seen in the action taken relative to participation in the 1974 International Congress on World Evangelization held in Lausanne, Switzerland, July 16-25.

> Moved: In light of the assurance of the Planning Committee members that they desire the Congress to be 100 percent evangelical, we authorize Mr. Frizen to attend the Congress as a participant. Carried.
>
> The following factors were also taken into consideration by the Board in making this decision:
>
> 1. The general purposes of the IFMA as stated in the Constitution include the promotion of conferences concerning missionary principles and practice and concern for the speedy and complete evangelization of the world.
> 2. At the Congress it is planned to have special missions sessions.
> 3. Attendance at a congress or special conference like ICOWE by Mr. Frizen does not in any way commit the IFMA or any of its member missions to participate in or join any resulting program or organization.
> 4. Individual IFMA missions are free to allow their personnel to participate or not to participate in evangelical meetings like ICOWE.[20]

History will confirm that the 1974 Lausanne Congress marked the recognition of evangelical leadership from Third World areas of Africa, Asia, and Latin America. Up to this time, the stature of national leaders and the potential of the church overseas had not been fully realized, especially by evangelical Christians in North America.

Two major weaknesses of the Lausanne-sponsored Consultation on World Evangelization, held at Pattaya, Thailand, June 16-26, 1980, were disturbing. First, a number of nonevangelicals were granted observer status, which they interpreted by ecumenical rules to take advantage of the miniconsultation sessions for the propagation of their ideas. This made it more difficult to come to consensus agreement. Second, it appeared that there was an imbalance in the participation selection process. There were too few evangelism and church-planting missionaries and nationals invited, compared to the number of pastors and professors from the United States, and paramission delegations from the U. S. and elsewhere.

Maintaining a close relationship with leaders of the Association of Evangelicals of Africa and Madagascar (AEAM) has been a high priority within IFMA. Personal friendship and contact are important in establishing and maintaining understanding between Westerners and leaders from the Third World. Upon the recommendation of the joint Evangelical Committee for Africa, the IFMA Board approved the author's attending the first four AEAM General Assemblies. The first three, in 1966, 1969, and 1973, were held in Limuru, Kenya. The fourth, in 1977, was in Bouake, Ivory Coast.

IFMA President Philip Armstrong (FEGC/SEND) and the author participated in a consultation of missions association leaders from Asia, Europe, and North America, held in Atlanta in June 1973. In August that year, the executive director was an invited consultant to the first All-Asia Missions Consultation in Seoul, Korea. A Presbyterian pastor, Dr. David Cho, was coordinator for this meeting from which the Asia Missions Association developed.

The church in Latin America was beginning to develop a worldwide missionary vision. One of the limiting factors has been a dependency relationship with foreign missions.

The first Quito Consultation held December 4-9, 1976 was planned and directed by Latin Americans. The church/mission consultation resulted in a large step forward toward an interdependent partnership. The executive directors of the IFMA and of the EFMA were asked to lead a special session on North American missions structures and methods of finance.

The All-India Conference on Mission and Evangelism Committee invited the author to be a consultant at the January 1977 meeting in Devlali, India. He gave a report on IFMA and its member missions at a plenary session, led some of the small-group work sessions, and was a missions consultant in others.

Immediately after the Devlali Conference, the author joined leaders of missions associations from India, Korea, Hong Kong, Brazil, Germany, Great Britain, and North America for a consultation in Bombay. Discussions included: (1) Third World Missions—Reality, Prospects, and Problems, (2) Creating a World Missions' Forum, (3) Developing National Associations of Missions, and (4) The Status of Asian-Based Missionary Efforts. The organizing of the Missions Commission of the World Evangelical Fellowship (WEF) came out of that meeting.

The Asia Missions Association invited the author to represent Western missions at their General Assembly meeting in Singapore, November 1978. It was held in conjunction with the Asia Leadership Conference on Evangelism. He was one of the speakers at a combined session of the two conferences. He served as a consultant in the Asia missions seminars and as a resource person at the AMA meetings.

The author was a nonmember participant in the meetings of the Missions Commission of the World Evangelical Fellowship in Bad Liebenzell, West Germany, in January 1979. The worldwide evangelical missionary movement was reflected by the twenty-seven participants representing all continents. Theodore Williams, executive secretary of the

WEF Missions Commission and general secretary of the India Missions Association, wrote:

> One of the dominant concerns in tune with the theme was that of partnership in missions. The task is too great to be accomplished alone by any one section of the church. The church in the six continents must gather up her forces in a partnership that is not only challenging, but also effective in the cause of missions.[21]

Three other meetings were convened by the World Evangelical Fellowship Missions Commission in the 1980s. As members of the commission, the executive directors of IFMA and EFMA represented the two associations. The 1982 meeting was held in Bangalore, India. In 1986, the commission met in Singapore in conjunction with the WEF General Assembly. The 1989 sessions were held in Quezon City, Philippines, prior to the Lausanne II meetings in Manila.

The purpose of Missions Commission meetings is to provide a world missions forum and to build constructive relationships between the older Western mission structures and the emerging Third World missions. Overseas leaders, and most Westerners, want to experience interdependence and true partnership. African and Asian leaders particularly are quick to indicate that they do not want Western leaders to abdicate their responsibility for leadership in missions.

Other international congresses and conferences in which the author participated included Wheaton '83, COMIBAM '87, GCOWE 2000, and Lausanne II in Manila '89.

Having the theme, "I Will Build My Church," Wheaton '83 was sponsored jointly by WEF Theological Commission and Lausanne Committee for World Evangelism.

COMIBAM '87, the Ibero-American Missions Congress, was held in Sao Paulo, Brazil, in November 1987. Most of the 2,700 delegates were from Latin America, with others from Spain, Portugal, and North America. The congress initiated a national church missions movement throughout

Latin America with follow-up missions congresses held in a number of countries. The WEF Missions Commission is cooperating with COMIBAM to help produce missions literature in Spanish. Helps to train prospective Latin missionaries is one of the continuing needs in undergirding the missions interest.

GCOWE 2000, the Global Consultation on World Evangelization by AD 2000 and Beyond, was held in Singapore January 5-8, 1989. Consultation materials revealed that hundreds of programs for world evangelization have been launched. The participants represented many of the active plans in operation by denominational and nondenominational agencies in countries around the world.

A Great Commission Manifesto came from this consultation. It closed with the affirmation:

> We believe it is possible to bring the gospel to all people by the year 2000. This can be accomplished with sufficient dedication, unity, and mobilization of available resources, powered and directed by God.

One of the negative features of that meeting, from a conservative evangelical position, was that, without prior notice, the *ad hoc* committee had invited several Roman Catholics as participants. The author was among those who protested to the leaders of the consultation.

An AD 2000 and Beyond movement and organization grew out of the consultation, under the leadership of Dr. Thomas Wang and Rev. Luis Bush. The IFMA Board requested the IFMA Executive Committee to meet with these men, and to prepare a response to the AD 2000 movement. After the meeting, the following response was made:

> MSC [moved, seconded, carried] to affirm the stated direction of the AD 2000 Movement headed by Dr. Thomas Wang. We wish to encourage Dr. Wang and his associates as they endeavor to

> fan the flame of a growing vision among churches around the world toward completing the task of discipling the nations as we approach the year 2000.
>
> We appreciate and support Dr. Wang's statements that Roman Catholics will not be included as members or participants within the AD 2000 Movement, nor will they be invited to be participants at forthcoming consultations. We see the Roman Catholic World as part of our missionary task along with all peoples, regardless of their religious affiliation, who have not heard with understanding the message of salvation by grace through faith in Jesus Christ alone.
>
> We are committed to participate with evangelical churches around the world in the mobilization of a growing missionary movement aimed at the evangelization of the world by the year AD 2000. We must obey our Lord's command to disciple the nations until He comes![22]

Lausanne II was held in Manila, Philippines, July 11-20, 1989. This congress offered the participants a wide variety of workshops and programs in addition to the plenary sessions. The author reported many benefits from the congress, but also gave three concerns arising from the meetings:

1. The stated intention of Lausanne leadership to make Lausanne a movement that "brings together the widest and most representative global link among evangelicals of all segments of the Christian Church—Protestant, Orthodox, and Roman Catholic—that focus on the task of world evangelization"
2. The over emphasis on issues of justice and social concern for the poor almost to the exclusion of the great commission, with the result that the social issues tended to eclipse the need for world evangelization

3. The inclusion of a Pentecostal emphasis/invitation in a plenary session of the congress

Growing out of the IFMA Board discussion on the position and perceived future direction of the Lausanne movement, the IFMA Executive Committee was requested to prepare a statement on Roman Catholicism. The committee reviewed the World Evangelical Fellowship position paper, "A Contemporary Evangelical Perspective on Roman Catholicism." The concluding paragraph of the WEF study provided the basis for the preparation of an IFMA statement. The following was approved:

> Our submission to the Bible, God's Word, requires us to hold high the cardinal truths of the historic apostolic faith as proclaimed in the Reformation: *sola scriptura*, *sola gratia*, *sola fide*, *sola Christo*, all to the glory of God.
>
> Standing in that faith we encounter many obstacles in Roman Catholicism as it manifests itself today, which seriously impede fellowship and cooperation between IFMA missions and Roman Catholicism. These obstacles are insurmountable as long as there is no fundamental reformation according to the Word of God in the Church of Rome. We consider the members of the Roman Catholic Church to be part of our mission field and are constrained by the commission of our Lord, and by His love, to proclaim the gospel to all people, including those who are Roman Catholic.[23]

In an editorial in the *Evangelical Missions Quarterly*, Jim Reapsome wrote:

> Some skepticisms about international congresses is warranted. . . . It may be time to declare a moratorium on international

> congresses. . . . The question is, When are we going to back off and ask ourselves the hard questions about their value? And if we find they aren't worth the time, money and effort, who is going to stop the process?[24]

A call for a moratorium on international congresses is well placed in the North American and Western context. However, many national leaders from other areas of the world who represent small Christian minorities in their countries do not accept this concept. They believe Western leaders have experiences and information to share with them in such meetings, and that lessons learned by all will help in the completion of world evangelization.

While the IFMA Board agrees that hard questions should be asked before planning a worldwide congress, it does realize the importance of the opportunities afforded for consultation with IFMA-related leaders, both missionary and national, and non-IFMA-related leaders, as well. Thus, if such congresses of evangelicals are going to be held, the board considers it important for the executive director to represent the association at such meetings.

For any congress to be of lasting value, the reports and findings must be studied and implemented by Christians in North America: missions staff, pastors, lay leaders, professors, administrators; and overseas by missionaries and national leaders.

## NOTES

[1] "Report on Congress," *IFMA News*, January 1961, p. 3.

[2] Ibid., pp. 6-7.

[3] Interdenominational Foreign Mission Association, Minutes of Annual Meeting, 10 December 1960, p. 9.

[4] George W. Peters, "Missions in Review - Missions in the Future: Consider Your Ways" (Address given at the 63rd IFMA Annual Meeting, 22-25 September 1980, Photocopied), 1.

[5] Interdenominational Foreign Mission Association - Evangelical Foreign Missions Association, Minutes of the Full Congress Committee, 2-3 April 1965, p. 1.

[6] Harold Lindsell, ed., *The Church's Worldwide Mission* (Waco: Word Books, 1966), p. 3.

[7] "A Critical Look at the Wheaton Congress from Five Perspectives," *Evangelical Missions Quarterly*, Fall 1966, p. 7.

[8] Ibid., p. 9.

[9] Lindsell, *The Church's Worldwide Mission*, p. 237.

[10] Harold Lindsell, "Precedent-Setting in Missions Strategy," *Christianity Today*, April 29, 1966, p. 43.

[11] Eugene L. Smith, "Congress on the Church's Worldwide Mission," *International Review of Missions*, October 1966, p. 457.

[12] Interdenominational Foreign Mission Association, Minutes of Annual Meeting, 3-8 October 1966, p. 9.

[13] Interdenominational Foreign Mission Association - Evangelical Foreign Missions Association, Minutes of the Congress Continuing Committee, 28 December 1966, p. 3.

[14] Evangelical Foreign Missions Association, *Report of the Annual Mission Executives Retreat*, September 29 - October 2, 1975 (Washington: Evangelical Foreign Missions Association, 1976), p. 5.

[15] Ibid., p. 12.

[16] Interdenominational Foreign Mission Association, Minutes of the Official Board, 19 December 1958, pp. 5-6.

[17] Interdenominational Foreign Mission Association, Minutes of the Executive Committee, 11 March 1959, p. 2.

[18] Johnston, *The Battle for World Evangelism* (Wheaton: Tyndale House Publishers, 1978), p. 164.

[19] Clyde W. Taylor and Wade T. Coggins, eds., *Mobilizing for Saturation Evangelism* (Wheaton: Evangelical Missions Information Service, 1970).

[20] Interdenominational Foreign Mission Association, Minutes of the Official Board, 17-18 September 1973, p. 4.

[21] Theodore Williams, ed., *World Mission—Building Bridges or Barriers?* (Bangalore: World Evangelical Fellowship Missions Commission, 1979), p. iii.

[22] Interdenominational Foreign Mission Association, Minutes of the Executive Committee, 18-20 September 1989, p. 3

[23] Ibid., pp. 2-3.

[24] James W. Reapsome, "Time for a Moratorium on Congresses?" *Evangelical Missions Quarterly* 16 (April 1980): 86-87.

# PART FOUR

# LOOKING AHEAD

# 14

# MISSIONARIES IN CROSS-CULTURAL MINISTRY

It has been demonstrated in earlier chapters that the founders of IFMA missions emphasized pioneer evangelism to penetrate the frontiers of unreached people groups. That has remained a major focus. IFMA missions have been innovative in their efforts to evangelize unreached, hidden people of the world, pioneering in such ministries as education, medicine and health care, missionary radio and TV, gospel recording, Bible translation, and missionary aviation. Almost any occupational training, educational major, and working experience can be used in cross-cultural missions.

The 14th edition of *Mission Handbook USA/Canada Protestant Ministries Overseas* lists in alphabetical sequence forty-nine categories of ministry activity, from agricultural assistance through youth ministry. IFMA Canadian and U. S. missions are listed under forty-six of those activities. The author is aware of IFMA missions that have missionaries in the remaining categories of psychological counseling, purchasing service, and translation work other than Bible translation, as well.

The largest listings of IFMA missions are found under evangelism (personal and small group), church planting/establishing, and Christian literature production and distribution.

## PHYSICAL NEEDS AND SOCIAL CONCERNS

Evangelicals have sometimes been accused of neglecting the social implications of the gospel. Such charges have been made by those who have never seriously studied the role of nondenominational missions in the areas of physical needs and social concerns. Throughout their histories, IFMA missions as a whole have demonstrated that such neglect has not been true of nondenominational missions. A study of individual missions will reveal impressive records of involvement in these areas.

In their book, *Missions in Crisis*, Eric Fife and Arthur Glasser wrote of the exploited, underprivileged masses of mankind and their desire for justice. Before their student leadership and teaching roles, both had missionary experience with IFMA missions, Fife with North Africa Mission/Arab World Ministries and Glasser with China Inland Mission/Overseas Missionary Fellowship. They wrote:

> It is not fully appreciated at home that the Church has had no small part in precipitating this ferment by means of its missionary outreach. She has brought literacy and education to many parts of the world. She has taught the importance and dignity of the individual. She has planted the seeds not merely of personal and spiritual revolution through Christ, but also of social and economic revolution.[1]

Dr. J. Herbert Kane, another China Inland Mission missionary who became a distinguished professor of missions, wrote of involvement that evangelical missions have had in social ministry. He said:

> By all odds the early missionaries were a special breed . . . Single-handedly and with great courage they attacked the social evils of their time—child marriage, the immolation of widows,

> temple prostitution, and untouchability in India; the opium trade, gambling, foot-binding, and infanticide in China; the slave trade, the liquor trade, and the destruction of twins in Africa. In all parts of the world they opened schools, hospitals, medical colleges, clinics, orphanages, and leprosaria. They gave succor and sustenance to the dregs of society cast off by their own people. At great risk to themselves and their families, they fought famines, floods, pestilence, and plagues. They were the first to rescue unwanted babies, educate girls, and liberate women. They reduced languages to writing, translated the Scriptures, and taught the people to read, thereby opening to them a whole new world of ideas.[2]

The author has heard Dr. Earle Cairns, noted author and historian, say many times that evangelicals have been at the forefront of meeting human needs and social concerns.

The roles of four of the oldest IFMA missions were mentioned earlier. The Woman's Union Missionary Society and Bible and Medical Missionary Fellowship (InterServe) were founded because of unmet spiritual and social needs of neglected women of Asia. Ramabai Mukti Mission and Home of Onesiphorus (Kids Alive International) were organized to help meet the needs of neglected children of Asia.

Pioneering evangelistic and church-planting IFMA missions through the years have devoted a large portion of missionary staff and budget to educational, medical, and other social needs of those among whom they worked.

One of the ten major subjects studied in detail during the IFMA-EFMA-sponsored Congress on the Church's Worldwide Mission in 1966 was "Mission and Social Concern." After studying the issues and the witness of the Scriptures, the delegates declared:

> That, we reaffirm unreservedly the primacy of preaching the gospel to every creature, and we

> will demonstrate anew God's concern for social justice and human welfare.
>
> That, evangelical social action will include, wherever possible, a verbal witness to Jesus Christ.
>
> That, evangelical social action must avoid wasteful and unnecessary competition.
>
> That, when Christian institutions no longer fulfill their distinctively evangelical functions they should be relinquished.
>
> That, we urge all evangelicals to stand openly and firmly for racial equality, human freedom, and all forms of social justice throughout the world.[3]

The IFMA followed up that declaration by appointing a relief committee. Reported in Chapter 9.

## OVERSEAS DEVELOPMENT AND SELF SUPPORT

Some IFMA missions have been involved in various types of community development projects, particularly in Africa and Asia among low-subsistence level believers and refugees.

Counselors and teachers serve in inner city programs, helping street kids, drug and alcohol addicts, AIDS victims, prisoners, deaf, blind, and visually handicapped.

Newer member missions, such as Mission: Moving Mountains, Spiritual Overseers Service International, and World Reach, send out teams of missionary evangelists, disciplers, community development, and primary health care workers. North American workers are preferably placed in teams with national evangelists and church planters.

The IFMA founding missions, particularly the SIM, AIM, AEF, and WUMS/InterServe, are heavily involved in relief and development projects in cooperation with related national churches. Some of the specialties involved are public health instructors and project coordinators, agriculturalists, foresters, veterinarians, water specialists, vocational instructors, construction designers and supervisors, engineers, mechanics, and small business developers.

Among other missions providing training programs in church-related community development programs are United World Mission and World Outreach Fellowship.

The objective of some of these development projects is to enable the nationals to upgrade their standard of living and to increase their incomes. They, in turn, will then be able to support their national pastors and national missionaries in cross-cultural ministry, as the SIM-related Evangelical Churches of West Africa in Nigeria are doing.

## ROLE OF WOMEN

What would have been the progress of worldwide missions without women? The extent of their ministry and the results of their efforts are immeasurable. Not only have women made a significant contribution to world evangelization, but women have often been the ones to pioneer new methods and new fields, as well as remote, primitive, and often dangerous, geographic areas. The stamina, courage, and commitment of women missionaries have often exceeded that of men.

Women have been considered full missionaries in IFMA missions from the beginning. This includes wives, as well as single workers. It has already been mentioned that Woman's Union Missionary Society and Bible and Medical Missionary Fellowship (InterServe) both started as "woman's" missions. Women made up the WUMS board, women made up a significant portion of the supporting constituency, single professional women were the overseas missionary staff—doctors, nurses, educators. Ramabai Mukti Mission in India had North American single women who worked alongside Indian workers in medical, educational, social service, evangelistic, and Bible-teaching ministries.

The first party of missionaries from North America to sail for China with J. Hudson Taylor in the fall of 1888 consisted of six men and eight women. This pattern has continued for well over a century, with more women than men going to the mission fields of the world with many

IFMA and other nondenominational missions.

As with the 1888 CIM party, single workers were the norm. The women, even more than the men, must have realized the difficulties facing them in the radically different living conditions in China.

> For the mission offered anything but an easy billet. No promise of salary; Chinese dress and ways of living; pioneering journeys; loneliness in the far interior; no marriage for at least two years; yes, and the privilege of preaching and living Christ where He had never yet been named—this was the attraction.[4]

The love of Christ has constrained women, single and married, to enter missionary service in obedience to God's leading. A study in 1965, *The Role of Single Women in Missions* by David Cornell of Worldwide Evangelization Crusade (WEC International), found that single women in Protestant missions were serving as their primary work in a wide range of ministries, from pioneer and general evangelism to radio, recording and printing technicians, and engineers. In the order of their numbers, women served in general missionary work, educational, medical, literature, business, and radio/recording.[5]

Through the years, single women have not been limited to supporting roles. They have been effective pioneer evangelists and church planters. Administration is one of the areas where women are not well represented, except as office workers. While some IFMA missions include women on their field and home councils, there are only a few that have women in executive staff positions.

In the decade from December 1980 through December 1990, the number of married women missionaries serving with IFMA missions increased by a total of 1,019. During the same period, the number of single women missionaries serving with IFMA missions decreased by 411.

Reports from seminaries during the past decade indicate that the number of women enrolled has been increasing.

## NORTH AMERICAN STATISTICS

The 14th edition of *Mission Handbook USA/Canada Protestant Ministries Overseas*, published in 1989; did not give the total number of missionaries that are represented by the various associations of missions. However, the 13th edition that was published in 1986 does give a table that is helpful in indicating a general trend.[6]

OVERSEAS CAREER PERSONNEL TOTALS

| Affiliation | 1953 | 1968 | 1985 |
|---|---|---|---|
| NCC/DOM | 9,844 | 10,042 | 4,349 |
| CCC/CWC | 572 | 1,873 | 234 |
| EFMA | 2,650 | 7,369 | 9,101 |
| IFMA | 3,081 | 6,206 | 6,380 |
| Independent/unaffiliated | 3,565 | 11,601 | 19,905 |
| Less doubly affiliated | (1,113) | (2,941) | (660) |
| TOTAL | 18,599 | 34,150 | 39,309 |

NCC/DOM - National Council of Churches, Division of Overseas Ministries

CCC/CWC - Canadian Council of Churches, Commission on World Concerns

The missionaries of IFMA member missions are understated in this table since missionaries in cross-cultural ministry among ethnics in North America are not included. One of the big differences between the IFMA and EFMA figures is that EFMA has the three large non-church planting groups: Inter-Varsity Christian Fellowship, Campus Crusades, and Operation Mobilization.

The table does indicate that there has been a sharp decline in the missions of mainline denominations that are associated with the Division of Overseas Ministries and the Commission on World Concerns in Canada.

The numerical growth of North American overseas missionaries has been greatest among evangelical missions that are not associated with IFMA, EFMA, or the ecumenical mainline denominations. These include five Baptist groups: Southern Baptist, Baptist Bible Fellowship, Baptist Mid-Missions, Baptist International Missions, and Association of Baptists for World Evangelization. Nondenominational unaffiliated evangelical agencies with solid growth are Youth With A Mission, Wycliffe Bible Translators, and New Tribes Mission.[7]

Evangelicals make up the largest block of North American Protestant missionaries in cross-cultural ministries.

IFMA MEMBERSHIP STATISTICS

As of December 31, 1990, the 71 member missions representing 38 Canadian and 66 U. S. corporations, reported the following cross-cultural missionaries* and home staff:[8]

| | From North America | | From Other | |
|---|---|---|---|---|
| Staff | Canada | U.S.A. | Countries | Total |
| Career | 1,158 | 5,873 | 1,014 | 8,045 |
| S-T (1-3 yrs) | 92 | 455 | 59 | 606 |
| Summer-1 yr. | 327 | 1,307 | N/R | 1,634 |
| | 1,577 | 7,635 | 1,073 | 10,285 |
| Home Staff: | | | | |
| With Miss. Status | 287 | 1,176 | 117 | 1,580 |
| W/O Miss. Status | 151 | 753 | 28 | 932 |
| Total | 2,015 | 9,564 | 1,218** | 1 2,797 |

*Cross-cultural missionaries only. Does not include anyone working with his own ethnic or language group.

NR = Not Reported

**A number of missions did not report figures for some or all of the categories under "From Other Countries." IFMA estimates a conservative total of at least 3,000.

At December 31, 1991, there were 72 member missions, representing 105 distinct corporations—38 in Canada and 67 in the United States. The compilation of the full personnel report for December 31, 1991 has not been completed.

## NON-WESTERN MISSIONS

These sending countries are referred to by some people as the third world. This term is not appreciated by many nationals from the areas of Africa, Asia, and Latin America. Others refer to the countries of those continents as the developing nations, while others call them the two-thirds world.

It is the responsibility of the church in every land to respond to the missionary mandate—to evangelize its own people and those beyond. The primary outreach of world evangelization has been borne by mission agencies of the Western world. While some from developing nations have for years realized that missionary outreach is not only the responsibility of the West, the numbers sent and supported from non-Western countries have been relatively few.

However, during the last three decades, the churches in Africa, Asia, and Latin America have increasingly become involved in cross-cultural ministry, both within their countries and internationally. About 80 percent of these non-Western missionaries serve within their own countries in cross cultural ministry. The remaining approximately 20 percent serve outside their own countries, either in cross-cultural ministry or with their own language or cultural group in another country. Example: Chinese from the Philippines working among Chinese in Hong Kong.

Dr. Larry Pate has studied this missions movement extensively and concluded that in 1988 non-Western missionaries from Africa, Asia, and Latin America totaled

35,924. In 1980 only 13,238 such missionaries were reported. The net gain in eight years was 22,686. If that growth rate continues, the number of non-Western Protestant missionaries will equal the number of Western Protestant missionaries in six years, by 1998.[9]

The most recent statistic that the author has seen is in a 1992 article by Phil Bogosian from the U. S. Center for World Mission's Division of International Mobilization, which states, "The number of Two-Thirds World (TTW) missionaries has gone from 39,000 to 49,000 in just the last two years."[10]

## NOTES

[1] Eric S. Fife and Arthur F. Glasser, *Missions in Crisis* (Chicago: Inter-Varsity Press, 1961), p. 21.

[2] J. Herbert Kane, *Understanding Christian Missions* (Grand Rapids: Baker Book House, 1974), pp. 328-29.

[3] Harold Lindsell, ed., *The Church's Worldwide Mission* (Waco: Word Books, 1966), p. 235.

[4] Dr. and Mrs. Howard Taylor, *"By Faith:" Henry W. Frost and the China Inland Mission* (Philadelphia: China Inland Mission, 1938), p. 96.

[5] David Cornell, *The Role of Single Women in Missions* (Fort Washington, PA: Worldwide Evangelization Crusade, 1965), p. 2.

[6] Robert T. Coote, "Taking Aim on 2000 AD" in *Mission Handbook: North American Protestant Ministries Overseas*, 13th ed. (Monrovia, CA: Mission Advanced Research and Communication Center, 1986), p. 39.

[7] John A. Siewert, "Overview of the Survey" in *Mission Handbook: USA/Canada Protestant Ministries Overseas*, 14th ed. (Monrovia, CA: Mission Advanced Research and Communication Center, 1989), pp. 54-55.

[8] "Statistical Report," *IFMA News*, Third Issue 1991, pp. 10-13.

[9] Larry D. Pate, *From Every People* (Milpitas, CA: OC Ministries, 1989), pp. 17, 34, 51.

[10] Phil Bogosian, "Training the Two Thirds World Missionary," *Mission Frontiers*, March-April 1992, p. 36.

# 15

# CHALLENGES AND DETERRENTS

The IFMA has been known through its long history for its strong biblical position, its high standards relating to finance and integrity in operations, and for its position on relationships. The chief executive officer of each member mission, or a representative, is asked each year to sign an Adherence Affirmation saying that the mission continues to be in agreement with the IFMA Bylaws, Confession of Faith, Standards, and Policy on Relationships.

Through the years, particularly in his executive director's reports and addresses to IFMA Annual Meeting, the author strongly emphasized that IFMA must remain strong in a number of areas.

## IFMA FOUNDATION

The foundation of IFMA, as the author sees it, is in three strata: theology, prayer, and unity, with the base stratum being theology.

### THEOLOGY

The IFMA's biblical foundation is sound theology based on the authority of the inerrant, infallible, Word of God. The Confession of Faith clearly states IFMA's position. However, it is a danger to assume that IFMA and its member missions will always adhere to this statement.

Change can be subtle and gradual. The leadership of IFMA must constantly be alert to maintaining a strong biblical position. IFMA must be diligent and vigilant in following its Policy on Relationships.

There is a growing rejection of the authority of the Bible. Some evangelical theologians no longer clearly stand for inerrancy or infallibility of the Scriptures. If this drift continues, it will adversely affect evangelical missions as did the theological drift in the ecumenical community affect missions in the mainline denominations. IFMA must be unwavering on the inerrancy of the Scriptures.

The IFMA must stand firm in its conviction that man is eternally lost apart from Jesus Christ, and that its primary task is proclaiming the message of God's redemptive plan through faith in the finished work of Christ.

## PRAYER

The second stratum of IFMA's foundation is prayer. Missions is God's work. He will build His church. God uses man as an instrument, which must be empowered by the Holy Spirit for the task. We are commanded to pray. There are two requirements to answers to prayer: (1) we are to abide in Christ, stay in His will, and (2) His Word is to abide in us; it is to be a vital part of our lives. It is important that we who are involved in missions should pray. It is scriptural that we develop strong prayer backing from other believers.

## UNITY

The third stratum of IFMA's foundation is unity. The purpose of unity as expressed in John 17 is that the world will believe the gospel message. While the nature of unity is basically spiritual, there needs to be a visible expression of that unity. IFMA delegates, along with others at the 1966 Congress on the Church's Worldwide Mission, affirmed in the *Wheaton Declaration:*

WE THEREFORE DECLARE

That, we are one in Christ Jesus, members of His body, born again of His Holy Spirit, although we may be diverse in our structured relationships.

That, we will endeavor to keep the unity of the Spirit in the bond of peace so that the world may believe.[1]

However, the author strongly emphasizes that *IFMA must guard against unity at the expense of biblical truth.*

## MAINTAINING STANDARDS

The IFMA has insisted on strict compliance with its standards in every area. The association did not set itself up as an accrediting agency for nondenominational missions, but that function has been ascribed to it by churches and others through the years. The major purpose of IFMA standards is to assure the Christian public that IFMA members subscribe to a strong conservative evangelical theological position, and practice financial and operational integrity in North America and overseas. They are worthy of support by prayer and finances.

## POLICY ON RELATIONSHIPS

The policy on relationships, as well as the standards, were approved by the membership of the association. The IFMA insists on strict adherence to it. See Appendix C for its full text.

## THEOLOGICAL ISSUES

There are a number of theological issues that are strong forces against world evangelization. A few are mentioned that must be continually guarded against.

## NEO-UNIVERSALISM

There is an attempt to promote a concept of universalism on the basis of biblical proof texts. One argument is that as man's fall was universal, so divine deliverance is set forth as including all. Thus, all men will ultimately be saved. There are within evangelical churches and schools those who believe that a loving God will not send anyone to hell. Universalism pierces the heart of missionary obedience. There is no urgency in carrying out the great commission if it is believed that all men will ultimately be saved.

## SYNCRETISM

Syncretism is combining different beliefs into one system—belief in Christ with other religious belief. The most common statement is that there are many roads to heaven; through Christ is only one way. Syncretism in a variety of forms compromises the uniqueness and finality of the message of redemption through Jesus Christ. Among other Scripture, it totally ignores, denies, or discredits the words of Jesus in John 14:6 where He said that He is the way and that no one comes to God except through Him.

## CONTEXTUALIZATION

Contextualization can be good. However, there are dangers in attempting to make theology culturally relevant. Syncretism has been recognized as a major danger in contextualization. In trying to make the gospel message relevant, Christians are open to political interpretations of the gospel, which, they believe, will solve the grave social problems of the world. In some cases, biblical theology has been replaced by a theology of liberation. Dr. Harold Lindsell said this theology of liberation is "nothing more or less than Marxism with a thin veneer of Christianity thrown over it."[2]

## NEO-SOCIAL GOSPEL

There appears to be a growing tendency among some evangelicals toward a neo-social, or holistic, approach to the gospel. There is an increasing emphasis on hunger, health, living conditions, development, and justice. Some evangelicals are equating this to the gospel message of salvation, saying they are equal and inseparable. Some say that man's spiritual life is indivisibly rooted in all of his conditions—physical, mental, and social—and that the mission program must minister to the whole man in every aspect of his life and relationships.

Harry Boer wrote:

> Had it been stated that man's spiritual life is *affected* by his conditions, we would agree. But it is hardly true that his spiritual life is *rooted* in his conditions. It is *rooted* alone in his relationship to God. It is the glory of the life of the Spirit that it transcends and overcomes conditions. In the Bible and in the history of the Church many of the finest testimonies to the power of the Christian faith are found in a setting where conditions were at a minimum—persecution, loneliness, poverty, sickness. The heroes of faith recorded in Heb. 11 did not exercise their faith under favorable conditions.[3]

The author wholeheartedly concurs with Dr. Boer when he also said:

> The church has not been charged with the reformation of social and economic conditions. She has been charged with the task of declaring the power that is in Christ, the new life, which, when it lives in men, will issue in social and economic improvements. This task the church

> discharges through the proclamation of the gospel. For this reason every true missionary is a walking social revolution.[4]

The charge by some liberals and evangelicals that people who live in poverty, persecution, and oppression will not listen to the gospel message and respond is not valid. Historically, it simply is not true. The author, along with many missionaries, has witnessed strong churches under such conditions. Such charges limit the work and power of the Holy Spirit. They subordinate Christ to conditions.

We are concerned about human needs and justice, but that ministry should grow out of the ministry of the gospel. We must be sure that in today's world with the emphasis on physical needs, we do not permit programs and activity to obscure or minimize the priority of preaching the gospel message of individual salvation.

A study of the history of various IFMA missions will reveal an impressive record of ministering to physical needs. Some such ministries date back well over a hundred years.

## ECUMENICAL DIALOGUE

Pressures for ecumenical dialogue may increase. There is danger in evangelicals participating in theological dialogue with nonevangelicals. The author underscores two things: (1) the urgent need for all evangelical missionaries to have thorough conservative theological education, and (2) the persistent and consistent implementation of the IFMA Policy on Relationships.

## THE GROWING OCCULT, SPIRITISM, WITCHCRAFT, AND DEMON POSSESSION

These are issues that cannot be ignored. There should be serious, prayerful study of them.

# OTHER ISSUES

Some forces affecting Christianity are getting stronger and more aggressive. There are a number of socio-political forces, as well, that may be deterrents, or challenges, and/or opportunities relating to evangelical advances toward world evangelization. We live in a hostile world. It is hostile toward missions because it is hostile toward God and His Son, the Risen Christ. We can expect hostilities to intensify as we approach the end of the age. These issues are not new. The list is by no means exhaustive. The author has not attempted to put them in order of importance, which could vary from area to area and from mission to mission. Some will be mentioned without comment.

## THE POLITICAL CLIMATE

Missions can expect to work in areas of increasing opposition. The material in the book, *Christ and Caesar in Christian Missions*, edited by the author and Wade Coggins, and published by William Carey Library, is still relevant. It came out of the IFMA-EFMA Study Conference in 1978, which studied crucial issues facing Christian missions in relation to diverse political systems. The book is to provide help for missionaries under totalitarian regimes, and to assist them in preparing the church for life in a hostile society.

## THE RAPID SPREAD OF ISLAM

This is attributed to a high birth rate and the acceleration in evangelistic fervor of Muslims. Danger lies not only in the militant opposition to Christianity, but to the rise of Muslin influence in the West. Islam is the fastest growing major religious group in the world. One out of every five people is Muslim. If the current population rate continues, by 2000 almost one-fourth of the world's population will be Muslim.

The IFMA North America Committee reported to the 1991 Annual Meeting that Muslims have vowed to make the United States a Muslim country. There are hundreds of Muslim Student centers on university campuses and over 600 mosques or centers in 46 states. Islam is the third largest religion (.05 percent) in the U. S., after Christianity and Judaism (2 percent).

## GROWTH OF WORLD'S POPULATION

As of September 1991, the estimated population of the world was 5,400,000,000 (5.4 billion).[5] If the current net rate of gain continues, the world's population will double by the year 2022.

## INCREASING ETHNIC POPULATION IN NORTH AMERICA

The number of ethnic people in Canada and the United States pouring in from all continents continues to grow. Projections are hard to estimate because of the difficulty in determining the number of illegal aliens entering each year.

The second largest ethnic group in the U. S. is Hispanic. Its population is estimated to be twenty million, with 89 percent living in nine cities. It is projected that there will be twenty-nine million Hispanics in the U. S. by 2000.

All of these ethnic people—the native Americans included—represent an enormous opportunity for cross-cultural ministry. It is a vast mission field at the doorstep of IFMA missions. While several IFMA missions specialize in North American ministries, others should target some of these groups for evangelism and church planting, especially the groups whose culture is the same or similar to the areas where the missions now work.

## THE WORLD'S CITIES

Approximately 45 percent of the world's people live in cities. It is expected to be 60 percent by 2020. Urban evangelism and church planting must be a priority in the strategy of each mission.

### FOREIGN STUDENTS IN NORTH AMERICA

The hundreds of thousands of students from overseas that are studying in Canada and the United States demands that missions give more attention to reaching them with the gospel while they are in North America. They represent the future leaders of their countries. Some organizations are concentrating on reaching them, but their efforts are not enough. The evangelical church is failing to reach out to them. Many are lonely. They want friendship. They long to be invited into a North American home, but most of them will return to their homelands without ever crossing the threshold of one.

### DIVORCE AND ITS EFFECTS, THE DRUG PROBLEM, THE RISING COST OF MISSIONS, INSUFFICIENT PERSONNEL, INTERNATIONAL DEBT, AND INFLATION

All of these, along with many others, have been emphasized as having an impact on world evangelization, and must be dealt with by the mission in charting its course for the future.

## CONCLUSION

Almost every year during his tenure as executive director, without apology the author made a plea to the IFMA Annual Meeting to remain strong, committed to the authority of the inerrant Word of God. Again, the author charges each one to stand firm in the resolve to reach the unreached—wherever they are—with the good news of God's saving grace through Jesus Christ. Man *is* lost apart from Jesus Christ. The reason we are committed to reaching the unreached is so they *will* escape God's wrath and eternal damnation. That concept is not popular in today's world, but obedience to Jesus Christ demands it. He gave the mandate to take the message of God's redemptive plan to all people

In the days ahead, which will certainly bring increasing pressures to soften IFMA's position—to compromise, may God give grace to stand absolutely, unreservedly, unswervingly, and solely on His unchanging Word.

## NOTES

[1] Harold Lindsell, ed., *The Church's Worldwide Mission* (Waco: Word Books, 1966), p. 232.

[2] Harold Lindsell, "Evangelicals and the 1980s," in New Horizons in World Mission, ed. David J. Hesselgrave (Grand Rapids: Baker Book House, 1980), p. 44

[3] Harry R. Boer, *Pentecost and Missions* (London: Lutterworth Press, 1961), p. 240.

[4] Ibid., p. 241.

[5] "Population Update," *Population Today*, September 1991, p. 9.

# 16

# MISSION STRUCTURES

Alvin Toffler's book, *The Third Wave*, focuses on structures of the emergent society of tomorrow and uses the metaphor of colliding waves of change. His First Wave, the agricultural revolution, took several thousand years. The Second Wave is the industrial revolution and took only three hundred years. His Third Wave is the new civilization, which is facing the deepest social upheaval and creative restructuring of all time.

Two, and possibly three, of these waves of change are simultaneously impacting many of the countries and people groups that IFMA missions are attempting to reach with the gospel of Jesus Christ. Probably most of our mission structures are what Alvin Toffler calls Second Wave institutions. He points out that beginning about 1955 we entered into the discontinuity between the Second Wave industrial model and the Third Wave of synthesis of disparate factors and disciplines. If we follow his thinking, it appears that if we are to be realistic about the accomplishment of our objectives in world evangelization—evangelizing the emerging contradictory civilization—our agencies must be open to change. He said:

> It does little good to forecast the future . . . if the forecast springs from the premise that everything else will remain unchanged. For nothing *will* remain unchanged. The future is

> fluid, not frozen. It is constructed by our shifting and changing daily decisions, and each event influences all others.[1]

Toffler reasons that Second Wave civilization placed an extremely heavy emphasis on our ability to dismantle problems into their components. It rewarded us less often for the ability to put the pieces back together again. Most people are culturally more skilled as analysts than synthesists. This is one reason why our images of the future, and of ourselves in that future, are so fragmentary, haphazard, wrong. He says that we stand today on the edge of a new age of synthesis. We are likely to see a return to putting the pieces back together again.[2]

Alvin Toffler's observation that people are better analysts than synthesists applies to us in missions. We have been better at examining the parts than we have in combining separate elements to form a coherent whole.

In a survey of eighty-four IFMA member missions in 1982, the author asked for the five major issues before them. Response indicated that present structures, systems, principles, and practices were not thought to be adequate to cope with contemporary and future situations. Evaluation is essential. Whether we realize it or not, most of us are either *resisting* or *creating* change.

Paul Hopkins observed that the call in ecumenical circles for a moratorium of finances and personnel from the West was aimed at mission structures more than at the missionary.[3]

## ELEMENTS FUNDAMENTAL TO WORLD EVANGELIZATION

In considering the international factor of missions and relationships in relation to penetrating frontiers, there are several elements that are fundamental to any serious attempt to evangelize the three billion plus people who are still unreached.

## A PASSION FOR THOSE WITHOUT CHRIST

An absolute conviction of the lostness of man apart from Jesus Christ is basic. Nothing else will do. Scripture clearly teaches that there is no other means of salvation (John 14:6; Acts 4:29), and that there are only two destinies open to man (Matt. 13:49-50, 25:41; II Thess. 1: 8-9; Rev. 20:12-15). Scripture also teaches that someone must take the gospel of God's saving grace through Jesus Christ to them (Rom. 10:9-15; Matt. 28:19-20; Mark 16:15-16).

Will God send a person to hell who has never heard the gospel? Scripture says that the only way to be saved is by grace through faith in Jesus Christ. He declared Himself that He is the *only* way. Scripture teaches that faith comes by hearing the Word of God which comes by preaching—someone must be the messenger. Scripture also teaches that through creation and conscience all men have some knowledge. God is just.

At the 63rd IFMA Annual Meeting in 1980, Dr. George Peters told of a fellow student who asked their professor, "What is God going to do with those people who die in ignorance?" The professor sat for a moment, his eyes becoming glassy with tears, then he said, "Brother, that I have to leave to God. But, I have an even more serious question, What is God going to do with the church that leaves them in ignorance?"

## PRIMACY OF EVANGELISM

Evangelism must be an obsession. The basic element in mission outreach is the primary place of evangelism, not just in word but in deed. Evangelism, witness, was the direct command of Jesus to His disciples; it is the commission to the church. Other ministries should reinforce evangelism, not replace it. Over-specialization and institutionalism have tended to deflect from pioneer evangelism. Once the church is established with mature national leadership, the main body of the missionary force should move on to other unreached areas, leaving behind a *minimal* and *temporary* counseling staff, if needed by the church. *Mobility must characterize mission strategy.*

## COMMITMENT TO REPRODUCE STRUCTURES FOR EVANGELISM

A conviction of the lostness of man will motivate the missionary to immediately teach the new church its responsibility for the fulfillment of the great commission, and counsel it in establishing its own mission structure for ministry. It is the responsibility of the mission not only to penetrate people groups, but to teach the new church it has planted to also penetrate other people groups and to establish evangelizing, church-planting congregations. *Pioneering new frontiers should be a reproductive process.*

## EFFICACY OF PRAYER

A prominent characteristic of IFMA missions has been the faith principle which recognizes and utilizes the power of prayer. Pioneering evangelism with its physical, mental, and spiritual oppression demands a powerful concentration of prayer support. Over one billion Muslims, more than one billion Chinese, and seven hundred thousand Hindus who make up the majority of the unreached have historically been the most resistant to the gospel. Penetrating these groups with the gospel of God's saving grace through Jesus Christ will require a special moving of the Holy Spirit.

## DEVOTION AND COMMITMENT

Devotion to God and to His Word, and an unswerving commitment to His will is required. God's will is not an option. It is not negotiable. Eber J. Hazelton, a long-time missionary with OMF, said:

> The try-it-and-see attitude of the present day is simply doubting God and is in no way the surrender of the will to the Lord or a commitment to Him. It is denying the lordship and the wisdom of God . . . It is better that none of the Lord's money and time be spent on a person still deciding whether God's will suits him.[4]

The problem missions face in the area of leadership for lack of experienced workers is directly related to the need for commitment. Missions are pushed to make room for short-term workers when what is needed is *commitment without reservation.*

The "instant" mentality in North America will not work. It takes time to learn the language, acquire cross-cultural understanding, gain acceptance and credibility, and to disciple new believers to maturity.

Long-time OMF Overseas Director Denis Lane stated:

> The thought of being effective in three months is just laughable. Do we imagine that we can come into a situation for a few months or even a few years and in that time communicate something really relevant and worthwhile to people whose thought forms and cultural communications are so different? Is that not the worst kind of cultural imperialism?[5]

Commitment to the 12,000 people groups unreached with the gospel demands selfless, what-ever-the-cost, lifetime willingness. It means commitment to hard, demanding work. It demands Christ's attitude that He came into the world not to be ministered to, but to minister, to be a servant.

Commitment may mean renunciation of possessions, rights, recognition, homeland, North American life style, family, friends. For what? Possibly for reproach, rejection, persecution, loneliness, suffering, and even death. The missionary must not only be willing to take up his cross, but be willing to die on it

## CAREFUL SELECTION OF MISSIONARIES

Missionary candidates must be carefully and thoroughly screened. Rather than relying on questionnaires sent to names listed as references, letters should be written to those persons, explaining the type of information the mission needs before appointing and sending one overseas. Explain that the mission is concerned about stewardship of human resources and in helping the prospective candidate find the place where he/she can be the most effective in ministry, as well as being concerned about the outlay of enormous financial resources in sending one to the field who becomes a dropout. In that letter, let the prospective candidate's reference know that you will follow the letter up with a telephone call. Be sure to emphasize that all information, written and/or oral, will be considered confidential. *Then keep it confidential.*

The mission must be diligent in finding out about personality, character, and integrity. Is he/she disciplined, conscientious, thorough? How does he/she handle personal problems? Problem solving in ministry? What are attitudes toward money? His/hers? The mission's? Other possessions? Relationship to others?

Better screening and selection, along with broad and thorough preparation for cross-cultural ministry and pre-field orientation to the mission, and thoughtful and prayerful placement of personnel will significantly reduce attrition among the missionary force, from dropouts while on the field and resignations while on furlough.

It is *quality* of workers that is needed before *quantity.*

## PLACEMENT OF PERSONNEL

Along with careful *selection* of missionary personnel goes the careful *placement* of personnel. It is the responsibility of the board of directors and those who are delegated to make assignments of personnel to prayerfully and carefully seek to place each person in the place that he/she can be the most effective for God. One of the most wasted resources in the cause of world evangelization is human resources. There is vast waste in financial and physical resources, much of which is through the proliferation of missions agencies. But one of the most serious and significant wastes related to reaching the unreached results from the assignment of personnel.

God creates people to be different from each other. He gives abilities and degrees of abilities, different interests, desires for service. There is too much filling slots in order to maintain the status quo. There are far too many square pegs in round holes. There are ministries and projects that have long ago fulfilled the purposes for their existence. There must be regular evaluation of the mission's programs, projects, and overall strategy. There should be regular and systematic evaluation to determine when it is time to strategically withdraw from a ministry or to discontinue it. No ministry or project should be the property of or controlled by a missionary or a donor that necessitates its continuance when it is not in the best interest of the overall ministry of the mission.

Too often a gifted, well prepared missionary becomes a square peg in a round hole, or just fills a slot. The usual result is that the missionary becomes a dropout, or the missionary loses his/her enthusiasm and potential for effectiveness.

When a missionary has investigated an agency and has chosen to serve under its administration, it is expected that the missionary will be submissive to authority and willingly serve where assigned. It is also to be expected that the powers that be place personnel where they are best qualified to serve and can be the most effective in ministry.

One thing is certain: God will hold the boards of mission agencies accountable for the stewardship of personnel.

## THOROUGH PREPARATION FOR CROSS-CULTURAL MINISTRY

This cannot be emphasized too much. It is imperative that prospective missionaries have a thorough understanding of the preparation requirements for cross-cultural ministry and that they get broad and thorough preparation. A new age is here and it demands proficient missionaries who thoroughly understand the target people and their culture, and that they are thoroughly trained to work among them. It may be that they will work alongside missionaries from other nations. The missionary must be prepared for working with multinationals, for mutual acceptance, friendship, and joint action.

Dr. J. H. Oldham, the organizer of the 1910 Edinburgh Conference and the founding editor of the *International Review of Missions*, stated many years ago:

> I am more and more convinced that the question of the right selection and training of missionaries is beyond all comparison the major question in the whole missionary enterprise. The really critical period in a missionary's career is his first term of service. . . . A great deal of the instruction given before he sails is lost to him because he cannot relate it to anything in his life."[6]

Preparation for cross-cultural ministry should include a broad range of subjects. Broad and thorough preparation is necessary whether the place of ministry will be in North America, the modern cities of the world, or in the remote areas of the developing nations.

Saturation in the Word of God comes first, then a good knowledge of theology. A thorough knowledge of the people among whom the missionary will work is mandatory. That will require speaking the language or languages, a study of anthropology, sociology, ethnology, and linguistics.

Knowledge of the people should include a broad geographic study of the country/area. Where it is, what/who surrounds it, its relationship to neighboring countries, its political system, economic, social, and religious structures. Limiting and contributing factors in the political, economic, and social. It is important that the missionary understands these if he/she is to understand the target people and if he/she is to be an effective ambassador for Christ among them. There is much about other cultures that can be appreciated and enjoyed.

When one lives in a country other than one's own, that which is heard or read can be more accurately interpreted if one has a good knowledge of the political, economic, social, geographic, and religious context from which it comes.

Acquiring a thorough knowledge of the culture requires a positive attitude, discipline, and hard work. *Cultural sensitivity is often the key that unlocks the door of opportunity to witness.*

There have been too many hindrances to ministry caused by those who have not bothered to learn about the receptor people, to develop cultural sensitivity. When one evangelical Western missionary makes a gross error because of his cultural ignorance, it affects the ministry of all Christians, national and expatriate. It has an adverse effect on the cause of Jesus Christ. *Insensitivity to the culture of the people among whom one is ministering in the name of Christ is inexcusable.*

## THE INCARNATIONAL APPROACH

As the hymn says, Jesus Christ left his throne in heaven and His kingly crown to come to Galilee. He temporarily gave up His position, power, and riches to accomplish that which God the Father sent Him to do. God's incarnate Son was born humbly into a humble family and identified Himself with poor, humble people, spending most of his earthly life among them. At times, He dealt with the wealthy, the learned, and the religious leaders of that culture.

Whether God sends the missionary to work among the rich, the educated, the religious leaders, or the poor, the missionary must have an incarnational commitment and attitude.

Going into another cultural setting, one must submerge the nonessential aspects of his/her culture, whether one is from a Western or other non-Western culture. The nonessentials may be many things, a political system, a seemingly affluent or superior lifestyle, type of clothing, church architecture, order of worship services, music. One must submerge the tendencies to want to be in control, to be the leader, the urge to get things done in a hurry. Much of the world is slow; it does not hurry; time is not important. Patience is required in teaching and training, as well as in learning. It is necessary to maintain an attitude that one has much to learn from the host culture.

There are essentials of the missionary's culture that must be retained, such as that which pertains to solid biblical foundations and scriptural principles, hygiene and medicine, literacy and education, development projects and techniques that may lead to life in Christ, better health, improved income and standard of living for the receptor people.

The missionary must contextualize his lifestyle and his message as much as possible without compromising biblical teaching and a strong, clear Christian witness. The missionary must always keep focused on the reason for being there: to clearly present God's plan of redemption through Jesus Christ, and to disciple those whom the Holy Spirit draws to God. God chooses the missionary for that ministry; God ordains the missionary for that ministry. That is a promise, as well as a motivation.

## FLEXIBILITY

While mission structures must provide for orderliness and competence, they must not crush spontaneity or stifle responsiveness to new ideas. Some mission structures are totally inflexible, and provide no room for flexibility. It is extremely necessary that the missionary be willing to live and work within an ordered framework, but individual initiative, innovation, and creativity must not be quenched.

This does not mean that the missionary should do that which is right in his/her own eyes, but an atmosphere should be maintained that is conducive to strategic change. The author believes that flexibility characterized the founding missions of IFMA seventy-five years ago. It is even more imperative that it characterize missions today.

One should, to the best of ones ability, determine that one can work efficiently, effectively, and in agreement within the framework of an agency before joining it and committing oneself and one's ministry to its direction. The missionary volunteer must look very carefully at the structures, principles, and practices of each agency with which he/she is considering serving. It is recommended that one interview missionaries that serve with those organizations, if possible.

# ORGANIZATIONAL PATTERNS

The *international factor* in IFMA missions begins with the organizational structure of most members of the association. There are four types of mission organizations: (1) single home base, single field; (2) single home base, multiple fields; (3) multiple home bases, single field; and (4) multiple home bases, multiple fields.

The first two structures, having single home bases, are sometimes referred to as *homogeneous* missions. They have one sending office that sends missionaries primarily from one country. The last two, having two or more home bases, are called *international* mission organizations.

For purposes of administration, it is simpler to be a homogeneous mission with only one home base. However, with the addition of other home bases comes the possibility of more recruits, more financial backing, more prayer support, and increased possibility for wider penetration of frontier areas of the world.

For some years several IFMA missions have accepted missionaries from the national church in emerging or developing nations, and have sent them in cross-cultural ministry to existing areas of their involvement. The OMF has councils that are made up of nationals in several Asian countries. They screen candidates and assist in raising their support. SIM has such a council in Asia for processing its Asian missionaries. Africa Inland Mission has worked out an agreement with the CAM-related national missionary agency to send Latin Americans to work in Africa. OMF, SIM, AIM, SEND, and others have councils in European countries.

## MISSION/NATIONAL CHURCH RELATIONSHIPS

During the modern missions movement, a number of patterns of mission/national church relationships have emerged, from paternalism or mission dominance on one side to full integration or fusion of mission into the church on the other.

In denominational circles, particularly mainline denominations, full integration or fusion seems to be the pattern. The merging of the mission into the church as a necessity to achieve oneness of the church came alive at the International Missionary Council's Jerusalem Conference in 1928. It accelerated after the Whitby Conference in 1947. The number of missionaries has greatly decreased. Currently, most are serving the national church in specialized ministries, with a heavy emphasis on education, development, and social concerns—not evangelism. Regarding the Melbourne Conference in 1980, William Nottingham wrote, "Melbourne says to the whole world . . . that the exploitation of the poor is the first item on the international agenda! . . . In a way, Melbourne represents the full integration of the World Council of Churches and the International Missionary Council."[7] Dr. Daniel T. Niles, from Sri Lanka and former secretary of evangelism for the WCC, said, "When a missionary church is reduced to the bare function of a recruiting agent of personnel and finances to support another church, then the heart of missionary conviction has been betrayed."[8]

Among evangelical missions the most prominent patterns of mission/national church relationships would probably come under *modified dichotomy* and *modified fusion*. These vary from mission to mission, and the pattern of relationships often varies from country to country within the same mission.

What is the answer? The author proposes that neither mission nor national church must dominate the other, *but both should work in association, joining together in a relationship as equals, in order to accomplish jointly that which neither can accomplish alone.*

The author calls this relationship *association with identification*, which is a form of modified dichotomy. *Association* is to join in a relationship, a partnership. *Identification* is to consider as equal. Association must be an *equal partnership*. A partnership may be an arrangement where one partner puts up one thing and the other partner puts up another. The national church does not have an equal part of what the mission has, and the mission does not have an equal amount of that which the national church has. So they each pool their equally important, but different, resources.

Dr. Max Warren noted that three essential factors in partnership are: (1) involvement, (2) acceptance of responsibility, and (3) acceptance of liability. He said:

> Involvement and the acceptance of both responsibility and liability presuppose the continuity within the partnership of each partner.

> There can be no question of absorption whereby the identity of the partners is lost. The terms of our definition—involvement, responsibility, liability—are meaningless unless this conscious identity of each partner survives.[9]

Although related as equal partners in association, the mission and the church must retain their distinct identities. Under this association, missionaries as a field conference decide the matters that only concern themselves. But as equal partners and distinct entities, the mission and the church must together plan and implement the program.

The larger church bodies established by IFMA missions, such as the Evangelical Churches of West Africa (ECWA) related to SIM in Nigeria and the Africa Inland Church (AIC) related to Africa Inland Mission in Kenya, have desired integration of mission field personnel into the church. One factor that has preserved the missionary vision of these large churches is the strong indigenous church missionary societies, developed with the encouragement and help of the SIM and AIM, which are now penetrating cross-cultural frontiers both within and without their countries.

A negative aspect of fusion into the national church could be that mobility of missionary personnel is curtailed. Missionaries may be kept too long as counselors or in institutional work, rather than being able to move on into other areas of pioneer ministry.

The author concurs with Climenhaga and Jacques about church and mission membership. During the period of equal partnership, the missionary should identify with the mission and not the national church. The line of the missionary's responsibility traces back through the field conference and mission agency to the home sending churches. The national worker should identify organizationally with the national church and not with the foreign mission. He should not be invited to serve as a member of mission committees. Rather, he should be encouraged in the formation of a strong national church administration to which the mission should relate itself in joint conduct of the work and to which church body the work can be progressively turned over. The national then does not find his normal sphere of service carrying out policies and purposes of a foreign mission agency subject to its supervision. Rather, the national should serve on a committee in the context of his own church organization, and participating on a *joint* mission/national church committee.[10]

Thus, the national and the missionary should each continue in his own organizational context of church and mission: the permanent (church) and the temporary (mission); one responsible to local churches and the other to a foreign mission. When nationalization of the work will have been completed and the mission organization withdraws, any missionary remaining temporarily to serve in any capacity should serve with the national church and under the national church. At the time the mission withdraws, the mission and the national church should agree on a definite date for the withdrawal of the mission personnel that remains on temporary loan to the church.

The mission and the church must seek a clear understanding of what constitutes a mature church. If both are not certain on this, it could have disastrous effects on the church, the mission, and world evangelization. Evidence indicates little danger that evangelical agencies will withdraw too soon. Rather, the danger does exist that the main body of the missionary force will stay beyond the time when the church can function on its own with minimal temporary assistance, if any. The mission must keep its primary purpose of pioneer evangelism and church planting in focus and continually be seeking new frontiers to penetrate.

Integrity, trust, openness, friendship, genuine fellowship, and interdependence are qualities the association with identification must have to fulfill its role in evangelization.

These must be demonstrated by both the mission and the national church.

One of Max Warren's papers was written on Matthew 18:19, which says that if two people agree to ask for something from God, He will do it for them. Dr. Warren focused attention on the word *agree* and interpreted the Greek original as that of the symphony, as harmony. He said that agreement is much deeper than uniformity of outlook. The two who pray may see many things from quite different points of view. Far from making agreement difficult, prayer is the essential without which harmony is impossible. Harmony of relationships is possible only through friendship, and prevailing prayer can only be experienced when there is genuine fellowship. Dr. Warren also pointed out that the following verse, Matthew 18:20, says that when two or three are gathered in Jesus name, the fact that He is there with them is the key to everything else. Prayer must be *in His name.* To gather in His name implies *harmony of intentions* and a deep *fellowship of obedience.* Personal relationships are thus perfected by the Person of Christ and prayer prevails.[11]

In this partnership of *association with identification,* shared responsibilities may be limited in the early beginning of the new church. Ultimately, shared responsibilities must include all matters of mission field activity related to the church, including policy, finance, administration, and personnel. Several items need to be clearly set forth in the agreement and are discussed below.

## PERSONNEL

Assignment of personnel, missionary and national, is a joint decision during the period of equal partnership. The terms under which they are to work and to be released should be spelled out. It should be clearly understood that the missionary's service is primarily to the *unevangelized world.*

## FINANCES

Agreements regarding finances must be carefully made. The donor's intentions must be preserved and accountability must be required from both partners. The missionary's allowance will be paid by and through the mission and the national's is paid by and through the church. Larry Keyes of OC Ministries points out that perhaps the best general policy, in light of world nationalization and missionary indigenization, is to support special projects and allow the national churches to pay personal salaries of national workers.[12] There is aid to the church that is legitimate, this is in time of special emergency, such as earthquake, famine, flood, fire, that causes temporary need. The mission should be involved with the national church in developing self-help projects that will increase possibilities for personal sustenance, as well as support of the national church and its outreach.

A strong national church is one that is self-governing, self-propagating, self-supporting, and reproductive—sending its own members out in evangelism and cross-cultural ministry.

It is appropriate, under the consideration of finances, to emphasize again the life style of the missionary. Many take their style of life in North America with them at considerable cost to their supporters and to *identification*. Dr Petrus Octavianus said, "The foundation for integration as a living relationship is found in your willingness to (a) leave something behind, (b) become like your fellow worker in some aspects, and (c) suffer for others."[13] A more simple way of living than has often been exhibited in the past must characterize mission work if it is to be an equal partner with the national church in evangelism and church planting.

## OWNERSHIP OF PROPERTY

Generally, properties should be turned over to national church ownership as soon as possible. A clearly understood agreement should be reached in regard to details of the transfer of deeds and costs involved. Such agreements may vary in different countries. The agreement should cover the reserved use of certain properties for the mission as long as they are needed for agreed purposes. The future maintenance of properties must also be spelled out. In some cultures signed legal agreements can create more problems than they solve. In such cases, a letter of agreement can be prepared to refer to the issues agreed upon in the meetings. Such a letter will provide a record for future administrators in the mission and in the national church.

## INSTITUTIONS

Hospitals, schools, and other institutions are best controlled by independent corporations under the trusteeship of local Christians. Thus, institutional burdens will not sap resources the church needs in its responsibilities for evangelism and church development.

## KEYS TO GOOD RELATIONSHIPS

The *association by identification* agreement between mission and national church should be for a specified length of time. Upon termination, it may be reviewed by both mission and church. If circumstances warrant a continued association by identification, a new agreement can be negotiated.

*The main key in relationships is attitude.* A basic principle for achieving and maintaining a workable association is regular consultation and open discussions. An association can foster the principle of equality, which is vital to cooperation and unity.

It is evident that no one pattern of mission/church relationships is applicable to all situations of different cultures, missions, and churches. Missions must not look for an easy formula, nor to one that will necessarily apply to every field in which it is ministering. Serious study must continually be given to this vital issue. The mission must not allow itself to be taken by surprise by mission/national church tensions. Whatever pattern the relationship follows, the mission must remain free to move into new geographic areas of pioneer evangelism.

## MISSION/NATIONAL MISSION RELATIONSHIPS

If the Western mission joins with the national mission in efforts for penetrating frontiers, basically the same pattern of association with identification will apply. Each mission will be responsible for the salaries of its personnel. Again the author concurs with Larry Keyes:

> The basic purpose for suggesting this, of course, is to avoid the depressing problem of foreign dependence. It is demeaning for many missionaries to know that their basic existence is being influenced and determined by foreigners, not by one's own friends and Christian family. It stifles spiritual growth among national believers for there is little "stretch," little faith involved when basic mission salaries are assured from the outside and not dependent from within. The national church must be responsible to support those whom they send as missionaries and to send out no more than what they can adequately support.[14]

It is the responsibility of both the Western mission and the national mission as partners to trust God to supply all resources for joint efforts—finances and personnel. There are ways the Western mission can participate financially without subsidizing national missionary salaries, such as transportation, and office expense, and nationwide and regional joint projects.

# SENDING CHURCH/MISSION RELATIONSHIPS

For nondenominational missions the local sending church/mission relationship is a form of modified dichotomy. Theologically, the church and the mission are not equals; the mission is the servant of the church. Pragmatically, in the missionary task, the local church and the mission agency should recognize equality of partnership. The are mutually dependent. The relationship should be one of nonisolationism.

Most, if not all, IFMA missions recognize that the mission is the implementing arm of the church in cross-cultural ministry. The relationship should be more than financial. Interaction with each other will provide mutual benefit and assistance in building the body of Christ worldwide. If the sending church and the mission are to function effectively as partners in penetrating frontiers, there are several issues that need attention. Some are personnel, information, proliferation of organizations, in-depth relationships, and finances.

## PERSONNEL

A few years ago, the author received the following letter from a friend who had served overseas and was a well-known evangelical pastor. He wrote:

> I personally do not feel, as a pastor, that the mission boards are truly responsive to local churches and do not listen to what they have to say on a number of matters. For example, one outstanding matter is that of the missionaries they send to the field. They ask for references, but I have been appalled over the years as to how many missionaries have been sent out by missions who have subsequently proved to be totally unqualified and who could easily have

> been judged so, it seems to me, had there been further references sought and a more careful examination taken.

This is a two-way problem. One is that frank and honest references are needed from pastors and others. Second is that missions must be careful and thorough in their selection process.

On a number of occasions, when a mission has had problems with a missionary, the author has been told by a pastor or other referee that he had a feeling of hesitancy about recommending the missionary for service, but felt that if the Holy Spirit was leading one to the field, he did not want to stand in the way of the Holy Spirit's leading. If the mission is to be able to exercise its responsibility in screening and selection, as well as in the stewardship of human resources, an *honest, full evaluation* is absolutely necessary from those whose names have been given by the candidate as references. Even some mission board members have said the same, that if the Holy Spirit is leading the candidate into missionary service they do not want to hinder the Holy Spirit's leading. That may have some validity, but board members must be sure that the Holy Spirit is leading the candidate to that particular mission before accepting him/her. Board members, as well as pastors and other referees, must recognize their accountability before God.

## MISSION INFORMATION

This is an area that needs attention both in the area of *quality* of information and in *quantity* of information. The mission must see that information given out, whether orally or written, is accurate and a full and clear presentation is made so as not to distort the truth. As the implementing arm of the church in cross-cultural ministry, the mission should report its activities, including its successes and failures, to the church. The mission should keep the church fully informed about the over-all needs that relate to the evangelization of the world so the church can fulfill its responsibility. Missions must be honest with the sending church about the need for commitment to world evangelization—the need for the church to produce more career candidates and fewer short-term and summer workers. The church will be held accountable by God, as well, for its stewardship of its members and its finances.

## PROLIFERATION OF ORGANIZATIONS

It has often been said that perhaps nothing is more bewildering to the sending church than the proliferation of new missionary organizations and missions/church-related organizations. This situation could be prevented, or at least limited, if churches would be more careful in supporting Christian workers who are starting new organizations.

The proliferation problem is recognized by IFMA. Mission mergers are encouraged and for a number of years, the IFMA has had an Amalgamation and Cooperation Committee.

The author has said many times that he does not see how a sending organization with less than 200, and certainly not less than 100, can adequately service and direct its missionaries, and at the same time do realistic, thoughtful planning for ministry. Due to the high cost of missions, personnel needed for leadership, and governmental regulations, it will be increasingly difficult for small organizations to do effective work. The proliferation of organizations involves the serious question of proper stewardship of all resources.

Dr. Gordon MacDonald, at the time pastor of Grace Chapel in Lexington, Massachusetts, said:

> Perhaps, it can be said with some accuracy that the church is often divided on doctrinal lines while extra-church organizations tend to divide on personality lines. . . . We view with alarm the

> tendency for men to split and split again, starting new movements again, building buildings, purchasing computer time, mailing lists and expensive publicity material. . . . Every man who joins the rush to be a new "founder and director" will find some rationale to justify the existence of his movement.[15]

It must be recognized that small, new missions would not survive without the support of the church and its members. Therefore, to some degree, they must accept the responsibility for the proliferation. The majority of people support missions without first checking on the rationale for their existence, their financial credibility and accountability, their operational practices, the results of their stated ministry, and whether they belong to an association which requires that standards be met.

## IN-DEPTH RELATIONSHIPS

One of the problems of developing in-depth church/mission relationships is that both are somewhat paralyzed by the enormity of the task. Because of the multiplicity of churches, the mission cannot relate in depth to every supporting church, and likewise, because of the multiplicity of missions, the church cannot relate in depth to every mission agency.

It must be recognized that not every pastor or missions committee member has the time or interest in strengthening the relationship. Deeper involvement would be promoted if each church would support more fully a few missionaries, serving with only a few boards. A strong deterrent to church/mission relationships is the church missions committee's lack of understanding of the operations of a mission agency and of missions in general, and the lack of membership continuity on the committee.

## FINANCES

The relationship between the sending church and the mission agency should be more than financial. However, in the area of finances, the mission is obligated to full financial accountability to the sending church. This includes full disclosure when funds are being raised for special projects: the complete description of the project, its total cost, how it fits into the strategy of strengthening the national church and world evangelization, and how and by whom it will be administered. IFMA requires its members to submit a complete audited financial report upon request to anyone asking for it. For seventy-five years, the IFMA's high standards, including full financial disclosure, accountability, and fund-raising, have gained for it and its members a reputation of proven financial excellence and integrity.

# CONCLUSION

IFMA has been concerned for many years about church/mission relationships in North America. It has sponsored conferences, meeting with pastors to consider this subject. The concern does not arise out of the threat of "a drying up of home-base support." Missions need recruits, understanding of problems they face, and intercessory prayer.

The church at home is the sending *authority* and the mission is the sending *agency.* Missions must continually encourage the church to be more actively involved in the selection and sending process, according to the New Testament standard; assist the church in its efforts of mission education on all levels; impart to missionaries the necessity of maintaining a meaningful relationship with the local church; earnestly seek closer relationships with the church. The mission and church together must endeavor to mobilize the church for long-range commitment for missions.

Only superficial treatment has been given to some

serious issues. Many more pages would be required to give an adequate look at each, as well as at others. The reality of tensions has been acknowledged, but Satan, the master deceiver, must not be permitted to intimidate or to paralyze missions or churches with a sense of defeat.

It is true that missions leaders have been better analysts than synthesists. It is time to go beyond analyzing structures and relationships and to begin to synthesize the best elements into *action* for penetrating unevangelized areas and people groups still without a clear gospel witness.

## NOTES

[1]Alvin Toffler, *The Third Wave* (London: William Collins Sons & Co., Ltd., 1980), p. 145.

[2]Ibid.

[3]Paul A. Hopkins, *What's Next in Mission?* (Philadelphia: The Westminster Press, 1977), pp. 114-15.

[4] Eber J. Hazelton, *East Asia Millions*, December 1981 - January 1982, p. 141.

[5]Denis Lane, "Short-Term Commitment Is Just Not Enough," *East Asia Millions*, December 1981 - January 1982, p. 142.

[6]F. W. Dillistone, *Into All the World* (London: Hodder and Stoughton, 1980), p. 126.

[7]William Nottingham, "Cross-Cultural Mission at the Crossroads," *International Review of Missions*, October 1980, p. 438.

[8]Tracey K. Jones, Jr., "Mission, Unity, World Methodism and a Board of Missions," *International Review of Missions*, April 1966, p. 180.

[9]Max Warren, *Partnership: the Study of an Idea* (Chicago: Student Christian Movement Press, 1963), p. 13.

[10] Arthur M. Climenhaga and Edwin E. Jacques, "A Consideration of Principles in Missions-Church Relations," in *Facing Facts in Modern Missions* (Chicago: Moody Press, 1963), pp. 88-89.

[11] Dillistone, *Into All the World*, p. 96.

[12] Lawrence Keyes, "The New Age of Missions: Third World Missions," in *Perspectives on the World Christian Movement*, ed. Ralph D. Winter and Steven C. Hawthorne (Pasadena: William Carey Library, 1981), p. 758.

[13] Petrus Octavianus, "Frontier Mission Structures," in *Seeds of Promise*, ed. Allan Starling (Pasadena: William Carey Library, 1981), p. 102.

[14] Keyes, "The New Age of Missions: Third World Missions," pp. 758-59.

[15] Gordon MacDonald, "Closing Gaps between Missions and Home Churches," in *Church/Missions Tensions Today* (Chicago: Moody Press, 1972), pp. 68-69.

# 17

## A CRISIS OF BELIEF

Change has been a characteristic of society since creation. Change touches every person in one way or another. It is inevitable; it is unavoidable.

People deal with change in various ways. For those of us who are believers, we have God and His Word, The Bible. We believe God is sovereign and that He is changeless. He is the creator and the sustainer of all things. God is in complete control of all that touches our lives and of all that touches this world and all that is in it. Everything comes from God's hand, no matter who or what may have been the apparent agents. There are no "second causes."

Our sovereign God is changeless—immutable. He is the same yesterday, today, and forever. His *character* never changes. His *attributes* remain the same. God's *Word* is sure; it stands forever. His *standards* are absolute. God's standards in ethics and morality are absolute. They are changeless from generation to generation. They do not change from country to country, from social climate to social climate, from situation to situation. His standards are changeless.

Change on this earth is inevitable for all of us, but God is *sovereign*, *changeless*, and *eternal*.

Someone once said that *changes are challenges to the committed*. There are changes that have serious implications for world evangelization. There are changes that certainly are challenges to those of us who are committed to seeing that the good news of God's redemption through Jesus Christ goes to every part of the earth, to all people, and in a language that is clearly understood.

There is enormous change taking place in our world. It is change that has brought about some of the crises we see today—monumental problems of all kinds—poverty and starvation, environmental problems, economic, political, social, and technological.

John Lapp, executive secretary of the Mennonite Central Committee, asks the question, "So what time is it for Christian Mission in the 1990s?" He said that seven themes "leap out." One that he mentioned is:

> A profound yearning for meaning which often emphasizes traditional religious authority, fundamentalisms, or generates new religious entities. Harold Turner says, "The World has never seen more religious innovation and creativity than in the second half of the present century." The competitive nature of the major world religions is surely heightening. The overload of modernity has engendered widespread frustration, disorientation, and helplessness.[1]

James Davison Hunter said that "modern man suffers from a crisis of belief."

> Those particularly affected may then find attractive any meaning system which promises resolution—world views offering reliable moral and social coordinates by which to live.[2]

Many within missions have observed its gradual spread throughout evangelicalism. This crisis of belief is a direct result of change within our society. From the standpoint of evangelical missions in North America, it has the potential for seriously affecting the involvement in world evangelization by North Americans.

The crisis of belief did not happen overnight. It has developed over a long period of time, but accelerated during the last century, and especially since World War II, certainly among evangelicals. The growth of liberalism is traced in the first four chapters of this book, particularly in chapters one and four, up to the founding of IFMA in 1917. There was, however, in 1917 a clear distinction between liberal thought and conservative evangelical belief and practice. Now, a dangerous trend in North American evangelicalism is repeating the same erosion of orthodox faith and practice as liberalism did earlier.

## THE PERMISSIVE SOCIETY

"The permissive society, nurtured by the '60s, is probably here to stay," writes Richard Quebedeaux. "Sex is available premaritally, extramaritally, and nonmaritally to more and more Americans."[3]

The secular media has promoted the acceptability of sex apart from marriage. Abortions are available on demand, and divorce is easy to get.

There is a more tolerant attitude toward divorce and remarriage within the church. Homosexual lifestyles are increasingly acceptable, even within the church. These are direct results of a permissive society. It is a society characterized by personal freedom, no restrictions, and an anything-goes lifestyle.

There is no need to dwell on our spiritually-depraved society. We all live in it, we read about it, we see it every time we turn on a television set. We experience the erosion of God's standards in our own evangelical churches. Millions in North America are spiritually impoverished by their response to affluence and the unclear message from many evangelical pulpits.

Some evangelical pastors are changing their messages to conform to the people within the pews. The singles groups in many churches have more divorced than never-marrieds.

The influence of the sexually promiscuous, gays, and the divorced is seen in evangelicalism. There is also a blurring of belief about the lostness of man apart from God.

The 1970s was characterized by self-fulfillment. Young people lost faith in leadership and turned inward. They were the "me" generation. Self-fulfillment was a primary concern. Do whatever feels good; whatever gives pleasure. Everything was "I" centered. It is still prevalent in our society.

Today, those in the eighteen-to-thirty age group have been called the "I don't care" generation. Their age bracket has been labeled the "age of indifference," characterized as knowing less and caring less than any previous generation. Andrew Kohut, director of a study by the *Times Mirror*, concluded that young people are not so much disillusioned as indifferent. In commenting on this study, Jim Reapsome said that if this assessment is anywhere near reality, church and missions leaders need to be asking some hard questions about their futures. The first one should be, Why do the 18-to-30s care so little? He continued:

> Perhaps too many churches appear to be shelters from heavy world news. Perhaps people flee to the churches' comfort zones, rather than face the implications of a seemingly unending string of disasters: earthquakes, civil wars, famines, and so on. Perhaps the sermons tend to stress relief from personal ills, without showing concern for the people of the world outside the church.
>
> Do mission agencies significantly promote world concerns, or just parochial ones: their own work out of context (or perhaps out of step) with economic, political, social, and religious developments? How about the missionaries themselves? Do their letters and reports reflect mostly family and "ministry" concerns, rather than the larger concerns of the nations?[4]

## WHAT AMERICANS SAY ABOUT RELIGION/HOW THEY PRACTICE IT

Several studies indicate that there is a significant gap between what Americans say about religion and how they put it into practice in their daily lives. In its sixty-page report, *The Church Today: Insightful Statistics and Commentary* by the Barna Research Group, is an analysis of findings of nationwide Barna surveys over the previous two years. While research generally indicates that Americans "see the Bible as accurate, relevant, and helpful, they have problems making time to study it, concentrating enough to comprehend it, committing themselves sufficiently to adhere to it, or jeopardizing their social status by openly supporting it," the report asserts.[5]

Although 96 percent of Americans believe in God, the report cites as an example, up to one-fifth "acknowledge some type of universal spirit being called 'God' who is not the same God as referred to by orthodox Christians."[6] The report predicts:

> "While the '80s were a time of religious exploration, the '90s are likely to be a time of religious syncretism. . . . Americans will increasingly develop their own unique blends of pop religion, basing their theology and practice on a 'meet-my-needs' perspective. Religion will become highly personalized and less of a community experience for millions of adults. Rather than choose among Christianity, Judaism, Buddhism, and other religions, many individuals will create a hybrid faith, based upon the most appealing elements of a variety of religions."[7]

The Barna report further indicates that "Americans are beset by a tidal wave of spiritual ignorance and confusion." While "religion and spiritual beliefs" are accepted, it seems that they "exist as a mythical reality more than a substantive reality. . . . Clearly, something is amiss in people's understanding of Christianity and its application to American life."[8]

During 1982 to 1985, James Davison Hunter, associate professor of sociology at the University of Virginia and considered to be one of the most astute sociological observers of American evangelicalism, conducted an attitudinal survey of students and faculty at sixteen evangelical institutions of higher education: nine liberal arts colleges (Wheaton College, Gordon College, Westmont College, Taylor University, Messiah College, George Fox College, Bethel College, Seattle Pacific University, and Houghton College) and seven seminaries (Fuller, Gordon-Conwell, Westminster, Asbury, Talbot, Wheaton Graduate School, and Conservative Baptist Theological Seminary).[9]

Dr. Hunter stated that he made no attempt to predict the future of evangelicalism. Prediction was not the central concern of the survey, but it was, rather, to try to establish cultural trends in the evangelical movement.[10]

The sentiment among the coming generation is mixed, according to Hunter. It is clear that they know what they should believe but struggle with that. "Intellectually grasping the soteriological demands of orthodox Christianity is one matter; emotionally accepting them is quite another."[11]

While the conventional evangelical soteriology may be emotionally problematic, there appears to be wide recognition that it is socially problematic, as well. When asked what would most likely be *the first reason they would give* for trying to persuade someone to become a Christian, one out of ten (10 percent) said it would be to "escape the wrath of God and eternal damnation." When asked *the most important reason* for trying to persuade someone to become a Christian, Dr. Hunter found that one out of four (25 percent) said to "escape the wrath of God and eternal damnation." Yet most (67 percent) claimed *the first reason they would give a nonbeliever* would be either the "sense of meaning and purpose in life" coming from being a Christian or the fact that "God has made a difference in my life." Seminarians, likewise, expressed a recognition of the socially offensive nature of their views of the afterworld and of salvation in particular. Virtually one-half (46 percent) felt that under most circumstance or even all circumstances, to emphasize to nonbelievers that "they will be eternally damned in hell if they do not repent of their sins" was in "poor taste." One midwestern coed put it, "When you emphasize hell to a nonbeliever, you will tend to turn him off, and then you may never have another chance to talk to him. It comes off as being really arrogant."[12]

Overall, evangelicals have not, for all practical purposes, repudiated traditional Protestant theology on the matter of salvation, the research found. Dr. Hunter says that a dynamic is at work, nonetheless. As with their view of the Bible, it minimally represents a softening of earlier doctrinal certainties. He concludes, "Of their own salvation, they are confident. It is with regard to the salvation of others that there is ambiguity and doubt. The certainties characteristic of previous generations appear to be giving way to a measure of hesitancy and questioning."[13]

The author recommends a study of James Davison Hunter's 302-page *Evangelicalism: The Coming Generation* and the Barna Research Group's 60-page *The Church Today: Insightful Statistics and Commentary*, as well as its other reports. The Barna Research Group, Box 4152, Glendale, CA 91222, defines its purpose as "discovering solutions to the challenge of how to have significant impact for Christ in our complex, rapidly changing society."

There is a crisis of belief in North American evangelicalism. There is within our pews and evangelical institutions the belief that God is too loving, too good to commit anyone to eternal damnation. There is an increasing presence of universalism within evangelicalism—that everyone, in some way, will be saved in the end. This is totally contrary to God's Word.

A serious implication for missions is that many in evangelical churches and Christian schools do not believe that those who have not heard of God's saving grace through Jesus Christ are eternally lost. As a whole, the evangelical church lacks missionary enthusiasm.

Millions in North America are spiritually starved. For most, it is a result of how they have responded to change, to affluence, to the unclear message from the pulpit. When it comes to the eternal state of one who is outside of Jesus Christ, many evangelical churches are failing to make it unequivocally clear that the person is eternally lost. Hence, universalism is creeping in.

## GRACE, DISCIPLESHIP, AND OBEDIENCE

The condition of the church in Germany in 1937, as described by Dietrich Bonhoeffer in *The Cost of Discipleship*, is quite descriptive of the church, including many evangelical churches, in North America in the 1990s. He was concerned about "cheap grace," discipleship, and obedience.

"Cheap grace is the deadly enemy of our church," said Bonhoeffer, a young German theologian who was active in the German resistance, arrested by the Nazis in 1943 and executed by hanging in 1945. He observed that grace is represented as the church's inexhaustible treasury, from which she showers blessings with generous hand, without asking questions or fixing limits. The essence is that the account has been paid in advance. Because it has been, everything can be had for nothing. It is grace without price; grace without cost.[14]

In such a church, the world finds a cheap covering for its sins. No contrition is required, still less any real desire to be delivered from sin. Cheap grace means the justification of sin without justification of the sinner. Grace alone does everything and so everything can remain as it was before.

Cheap grace is the preaching of forgiveness without

requiring repentance, baptism without discipline, communion without confession. To Bonhoeffer, cheap grace was grace without discipleship, grace without the cross, grace without Jesus, living and incarnate.

True grace, or biblical grace, is what Bonhoeffer calls "costly grace." He wrote:

> Grace is costly because it calls us to follow, and it is grace because it calls us to follow Jesus Christ. It is costly because it costs a man his life, and it is grace because it gives a man the only true life. It is costly because it condemns sin, and grace because it justifies the sinner. Above all, it is costly because it cost God the life of His son: "Ye were bought at a price" and what has cost God much cannot be cheap for us. Above all, it is grace because God did not reckon his Son too dear a price to pay for our life, but delivered Him up for us. Costly grace is the Incarnation of God.[15]

Most evangelicals still believe Ephesians 2:8, that it is by grace through faith that one is saved. But to many, Jesus is Savior but not Lord. Grace and discipleship are inseparable. Costly grace has been turned into cheap grace without discipleship and obedience. Discipleship, or lordship, is an act of obedience to the call of Jesus Christ.

To the person who has experienced salvation by grace through faith in Jesus Christ, obedience is an obligation. One who has accepted God's forgiveness should demonstrate renunciation of a self-willed life, characterized by the self-fulfillment, "I" centered, and "I-don't-care" generations.

Bonhoeffer maintained:

> The only man who has the right to say that he is justified by grace alone is the man who has left all to follow Christ. Such a man knows that the call is inseparable from grace. But those who try

> to use this grace as a dispensation from following Christ are simply deceiving themselves.[16]

As in Germany and elsewhere, cheap grace has been disastrous to the church in North America, to the spiritual lives of many within it. The condition of some evangelical churches today is a consequence of making grace available to all at too low a cost. Cheap grace has contributed greatly to the crisis of belief, resulting in an erosion of conviction about the lostness of man apart from Jesus Christ and, thus, in participation in world evangelization.

## CONCLUSION

We acknowledge the reality, the severity, the implications of the change within society and within the evangelical church in particular. Meeting the challenge of change is not easy. It is not cheap. It is costly in time, effort, and commitment to stand firm on God's Word and its full proclamation. There must be no gap between what is believed and what is said.

God's standards do not change. This is not a popular position to take in these days of immorality and situational ethics. God will build His Church, but not without cost.

The evangelical church needs to get back to taking the fact of sin seriously. Sermons on sin, repentance, and God's judgment need to be returned to prominence from the pulpit. There seems to be little discernment of the signs of the times.

Evangelical pastors are a key to resolving the crisis of belief in North America. A revival among evangelicals could reverse the trend that seems to be creeping over evangelicalism. Unless there is an awakening among pastors in North America—and congregations—and within other evangelical institutions, the outlook for the twenty-first century seems rather dismal for the church in North America and for its role in world evangelization. A church that no longer teaches that man is eternally lost apart from Jesus Christ is not a sending or a missions-supporting church.

Mission agencies have an obligation to seek ways and opportunities to strengthen the church spiritually, and to endeavor to effect its return to the early church pattern.

## NOTES

[1] John A. Lapp, "Globan Mission in the 1990s," *Mission Focus*, December 1989, pp. 74-75.

[2] James Davison Hunter, *Evangelicalism: The Coming Generation* (Chicago: The University of Chicago Press, 1987), p. 8.

[3] Richard Quebedeaux, *The Worldly Evangelicals* (New York: Harper & Row, 1978), p. 15.

[4] Jim Reapsome, "Final Analysis: The 'I don't care' generation,'" *World Pulse*, 27 July 1990.

[5] *The Church Today: Insightful Statistics and Commentary* (Glendale, CA: Barna Research Group, 1990), p. 13.

[6] Ibid.

[7] Ibid., p. 54.

[8] Ibid., p. 14.

[9] Hunter, *Evangelicalism: The Coming Generation*, p. 9.

[10] Ibid., p. 14.

[11] Ibid., p. 39.

[12] Ibid., pp. 39-40.

[13] Ibid., p. 40.

[14] Dietrich Bonhoeffer, *The Cost of Discipleship* (1937; rev. and unabridged ed., New York: The Macmillan Company, 1963), p. 45.

[15] Ibid., p. 53.

[16] Ibid., p. 55.

# 18

# CONCLUSION

While we are concerned with the past, we must be profoundly oriented to the future. We can draw on the past to illuminate the present, and evaluate the past for making projections for the future. The three billion plus hidden and unreached people compel evangelicals to act. It would be incomprehensible at this hour not to make a concerted effort of thoughtful, prayerful commitment to a fresh thrust of evangelistic outreach. We must view challenges and deterrents from the perspective of past history, as well as from probable future developments. The eternal destiny of the billions who still are lost without Christ demands aggressive, purposeful, immediate action.

Within the fellowship of the IFMA there is diversity of thought and methodology. Far from being divisive, this diversity is a healthy factor that gives strength and vitality to the association and to its member missions. The common heritage of a strong conservative doctrinal position, and the mutual commitment to carry out the command to make disciples of all nations, is the foundation for the experienced unity.

Independence and individuality are a part of the North American way of life. One striking example of this in the area of missions is the number of mission boards. More are being organized each year.

The independence and fragmentation of evangelicals comes in part from the interpretation and application of biblical truths. While rightly stressing the priesthood of believers, evangelicals have largely ignored the biblical teaching on the unity of the body.

For the IFMA, unity is a key to world evangelization. There is strength in unity. A purpose of unity as expressed in John 17 is that the world might believe.

While holding to values of autonomy and self-reliance, IFMA independent faith missions must be pragmatic about the purposes as stated in IFMA Bylaws. The association provides an avenue for accomplishing goals that can best be achieved through a course of cooperation and accommodation.

New ways must be sought to take the good news of God's saving grace through Jesus Christ to the billions who are inaccessible by traditional means and to those who are within the possibility of personal witness. Bold, new steps must be taken for reaching the unreached billions. Evangelism must be the heart of all ministry.

Alvin Toffler said something in *Future Shock* that can be applied to the IFMA at this time:

> Every society faces not merely a succession of probable futures, but an array of possible futures, and a conflict over preferable futures. The management of change is the effort to convert certain possibles into probables, in pursuit of agreed on preferables.[1]

It is time now to deliberately and systematically address the question of what kind of action will be required in pursuit of the preferables. God did not call us to develop programs, but He did call us to action—to evangelize, to work with Him in building His Church.

There are challenges to world evangelization that are specifically related to performance. How each one is dealt with will determine the mission's effectiveness in evangelizing the world.

Every challenge, every deterrent must be faced squarely. What is the plan of action in view of the resurgence of ancestral and ethnic religions? What is the plan of action in view of world economics? What is our plan of action relating to the challenges of the cities; of the rapid spread of Islam; of the growth of the world's population; of universalism; syncretism; of insufficient personnel; of cultural sensitivity; of church/mission relations; of developing national leadership; of maintaining standards, and the numerous other challenges and deterrents to building the church of Jesus Christ?

*The greatest challenge facing missions today is the challenge of the unachieved.* The challenge of an unfinished task demands that past performance be honestly and thoroughly examined. Every facet of past mission activity must be examined. The lateness of the hour compels evangelicals to move forward with aggressive, purposeful, God-given direction. If evangelicals are serious about evangelizing the world in this generation, there must be absolute commitment of all resources to that end. Completion of the mandate does not depend on how many new workers can be recruited, nor how much money can be raised. It depends largely on how the human and financial resources that are available are used.

Several years before his death, Dr George Peters, who was chairman of the missions department at Dallas Theological Seminary, wrote to the author:

> The issues are principally theological, hermeneutical and structural. . . . I am deeply concerned for the future development of the evangelical cause, missions and the welfare of the churches. . . . May He . . . revive within the IFMA a more adventurous spirit and greater energy in evangelism. Let us keep in mind that movements and not institutions and establishments are attracting the people and money. IFMA

> must once more become the great evangelistic force which it was initially and experienced in an unusual way the blessings of God and the support of God's people. God is looking for dynamic evangelistic movements![2]

The immediate danger for the future of IFMA is that it will not utilize the potential for world evangelization that it unitedly possesses. The review of the history of IFMA reinforces the conclusion that cooperative programs can be effective. There is strength in unity. For IFMA missions, unity is a key to world evangelization. The IFMA *can* be a catalyst for finishing the unfinished task.

## NOTES

[1] Alvin Toffler, *Future Shock* (New York: Random House, 1970), p. 407.

[2] George W. Peters, letter to the author, 16 March 1981.

# APPENDIX A

## IFMA STANDARDS

Since its beginning in 1917, the Interdenominational Foreign Mission Association of North America has maintained definite requirements of its member missions. In the area of finances, from its beginning the Association has insisted that members demonstrate accountability of all funds received and practice full financial disclosure. Theologically, the IFMA has never wavered in its strong biblical position. The Association's high standards have gained for it and its members a reputation of proven excellence and integrity. Thus, the Christian public can support IFMA missions in full confidence.

### MEMBERSHIP STANDARDS

1. Each mission subscribes unreservedly to the IFMA Bylaws, Confession of Faith, Standards, and Policy on Relationships.
2. Each mission reaffirms annually in writing its adherence to IFMA Standards.
3. Each mission is approved by vote of the IFMA member missions and is reviewed regularly by the IFMA Board.
4. Each mission participates in activities of the IFMA, including the Annual Meeting, and contributes dues as determined by vote of member missions.
5. Membership is open to:
   a. Sending organizations involved in cross-cultural ministry which have as primary objectives evangelism and establishing and/or developing churches.
   b. Service organizations operating in support and furtherance of the objectives of evangelical cross-cultural missions and/or evangelical national churches.

## DOCTRINAL STANDARDS AND PURPOSE

1. Each mission has clearly stated articles of faith consistent with the IFMA Confession of Faith, and maintains a non-Charismatic orientation.
2. Each mission gives evidence satisfactory to the Association as to the purpose and rationale for its existence.
3. Each mission is involved only in programs and activities that are consistent with its stated purpose and those of the IFMA.

## ORGANIZATIONAL STANDARDS

1. Each mission is governed by an active board that demonstrates organizational control, including broad policy-making authority.
   a. The board is composed of at least seven members.
   b. A majority of the board members, and those in attendance at any meeting, are nonstaff and not immediate family members.
   c. The board meets at least semiannually.
2. Each mission has an active audit or finance committee, a majority of whom are nonstaff, which is responsible to:
   a. Maintain a direct line of communication between the board and the external auditors.
   b. Assist the board in fulfilling its fiduciary responsibilities relating to accounting and reporting practices.
   c. Insure that there is no conflict of interest in its financial operations.
3. Each mission has operated for at least five years as a tax exempt, religious or charitable not-for-profit organization registered or incorporated in Canada or the United States.
4. Each mission has sufficient personnel to make it a viable organization able to carry out its purposes and to meet IFMA standards.

## FINANCIAL STANDARDS

1. Each mission demonstrates financial responsibility by issuing an annual financial report prepared in conformity with

generally accepted accounting principles, audited by a chartered accountant or certified public accountant in accordance with generally accepted auditing standards.

2. Each mission prepares financial statements that are consistent with the IFMA-sponsored (Evangelical Joint Accounting Committee) *Accounting and Financial Reporting Guide for Christian Ministries*. Minimum financial statements include a balance sheet, a statement of activity, a statement of changes in financial position, and notes to the financial statements.
3. Each mission submits a copy of its audited annual financial report to the IFMA office, and will furnish a copy of its financial statements to the public upon request.
4. Each mission uses no more for its administration and fund-raising than is reasonable for its size and purpose.
5. Each mission exercises faith in God for the provision of needs without strong solicitation for funds.
6. Each mission uses all donated funds for the purposes for which they are accepted. No payment by percentage of receipts will be given to any consultant or persons involved in fund-raising activities.

## OPERATIONAL STANDARDS

1. Each mission maintains a reputation for integrity and stability in all its operations in North America and overseas, practices high ethical standards, and avoids all conflicts of interest.
2. Each mission conducts a thorough survey before entering a new geographic area or people group. Before starting the ministry, consultation is held with other evangelical missions and/or churches working in the area or among the people group.

## PERSONNEL STANDARDS

1. Each mission carefully assigns and supervises its personnel in order to practice good stewardship and achieve maximum effectiveness in the use of gifts, abilities, and training of missionaries and staff.

2. As an evidence of Christian integrity and mutual respect, any member mission considering recruitment of a person from another Christian organization is expected to consult with the leadership of that organization before entering into serious negotiations.
3. Any member mission considering acceptance into its fellowship a person under discipline or released for any reason by another Christian organization is expected to consult with the leadership of that organization before proceeding.

# APPENDIX B

## CONFESSION OF FAITH

The member missions do affirm and declare their belief in and defense of the historic Christian faith as set forth in the following:

1. We believe that the Bible, consisting of Old and New Testaments only, is verbally inspired by the Holy Spirit, is inerrant in the original manuscripts, and is the infallible and authoritative Word of God.
2. We believe that the one triune God exists eternally in three persons: Father, Son, and Holy Spirit.
3. We believe that Adam, created in the image of God, was tempted by Satan, the god of this world, and fell. Because of Adam's sin, all men have guilt imputed, are totally depraved, and need to be regenerated by the Holy Spirit for salvation.
4. We believe that Jesus Christ is God, was born of a virgin, died vicariously, shed His blood as man's substitutionary sacrifice, rose bodily, and ascended to heaven, where He is presently exalted at the Father's right hand.
5. We believe that salvation consists of the remission of sins, the imputation of Christ's righteousness, and the gift of eternal life received by faith alone, apart from works.
6. We believe that the return of Jesus Christ is imminent, and that it will be visible and personal.
7. We believe that the saved will be raised to everlasting life and blessedness in heaven, and that the unsaved will be raised to everlasting and conscious punishment in hell.
8. We believe that the Church, the body of Christ, consists only of those who are born again, who are baptized by the Holy Spirit into Christ at the time of regeneration, for whom He now makes intercession in heaven and for whom He will come again.

9. We believe that Christ commanded the Church to go into all the world and preach the gospel to every person, baptizing and teaching those who believe.

# APPENDIX C

## IFMA POLICY ON RELATIONSHIPS

In view of growing theological confusion and ecumenical pressures, the Interdenominational Foreign Mission Association has established standards to guide its relationships and those of its member missions.

> ASSOCIATION: IFMA is a voluntary association of interdenominational missions which have committed themselves to a testimony of fellowship and oneness in the body of Christ, working together without organic union but in mutual interdependence.
>
> COOPERATION: IFMA and its member missions encourage cooperation with all other evangelical groups which share basic doctrinal and operational agreement.
>
> FELLOWSHIP: Where evangelical groups hold distinctive doctrinal emphases that make cooperation difficult, IFMA acknowledges oneness in Christ through proper Christian respect and missions comity.
>
> COMMUNICATION: Where theological inclusivism and apostasy, as in the present Ecumenical Movement, make organizational association, cooperation, or fellowship with certain groups impossible, communication may be necessary on a nontheological level, especially in dealing with government authorities.

Member missions are urged to exercise discernment in the application of these standards in order that the essential unity and public testimony of IFMA may be maintained. In situations of uncertainty, the IFMA Board will assist any member mission in establishing such guidelines.

# APPENDIX D

## MEMBERSHIP 1917-1991: WHEN BEGAN; WHEN ENDED

During the 75 years of IFMA, 152 missions were accepted into membership. Of the 47 missions with a date in the Membership Ended column below, 19 merged with another IFMA mission; 2 merged with non-IFMA missions; IFMA terminated the membership of 7 missions; 6 withdrew because termination was imminent; 8 gave financial as the reason for withdrawal; 4 withdrew because of policy differences; and 1 left IFMA to join EFMA.

| Membership | | |
|---|---|---|
| Began | Ended | Mission |
| 1917 | | Africa Inland Mission/US |
| 1917 | | Africa Inland Mission/Canada |
| 1917 | | Central American Mission/US (CAM) |
| 1917 | | China Inland Mission/US (OMF) |
| 1917 | | China Inland Mission/Canada |
| 1917 | | Inland South America Missionary Union/ US (SAM) |
| 1917 | | South Africa General Mission/US (AEF) |
| 1917 | | South Africa General Mission/Canada |
| 1917 | | Sudan Interior Mission/US (SIM) |
| 1917 | | Sudan Interior Mission/Canada |
| 1917 | 1976 | Woman's Union Missionary Society/US (became United Fellowship for Christian Service and merged with Bible and Medical Missionary Fellowship, now InterServe) |
| 1918 | 1982 | Bolivian Indian Mission/US (became Andes Evangelical Mission merged into SIM) |
| 1918 | 1975 | Evangelical Union of South America/US (merged with Gospel Missionary Union) |
| 1918 | 1975 | Evangelical Union of South America/Canada (merged with Gospel Missionary Union) |

| | | |
|---|---|---|
| 1918 | 1953 | Bible House of Los Angeles |
| 1922 | 1946 | India Christian Mission/US |
| 1923 | 1989 | Ceylon & India General Mission/US (became International Christian Fellowship, merged into SIM) |
| 1923 | 1989 | Ceylon & India General Mission/Canada (became International Christian Fellowship, merged with SIM) |
| 1924 | 1927 | Heart of Africa Mission/US |
| 1924 | 1939 | Northeast India General Mission/US |
| 1929 | 1960 | American European Fellowship/US |
| 1929 | 1978 | Latin American Evangelistic Crusade/US (Latin America Mission/US) |
| 1932 | 1980 | Orinoco River Mission/US (merged into TEAM) |
| 1941 | 1974 | Soldiers and Sailors Gospel Mission/US (Gospel Mission of South America) |
| 1943 | 1969 | Sudan United Mission/US (merged into TEAM) |
| 1943 | 1969 | Sudan United Mission Canada (merged into TEAM) |
| 1943 | | Unevangelized Fields Mission/US (UFM) |
| 1943 | | Unevangelized Fields Mission/Canada |
| 1945 | | Scandinavian Alliance Mission/US (TEAM) |
| 1945 | | Scandinavian Alliance Mission/Canada (TEAM) |
| 1945 | | Russian Gospel Association/US (Slavic Gospel Association) |
| 1945 | | India Mission/US (International Missions) |
| 1945 | | West Indies Mission/US (Worldteam) |
| 1945 | | Gospel Missionary Union/US |
| 1948 | 1971 | Mexican Indian Mission (merged into UFM International) |
| 1949 | 1960 | Wycliffe Bible Translators |
| 1950 | | Slavic Gospel Association/Canada |
| 1951 | | Gospel Recordings/US |
| 1951 | 1971 | Belgian Gospel Mission/US (merged with Greater Europe Mission) |
| 1951 | 1955 | Iran Interior Mission/US (merged into International Missions) |
| 1951 | | Far Eastern Gospel Crusade/US (SEND) |
| 1952 | | Missionary Aviation Fellowship/US (Mission Aviation Fellowship) |

| | | |
|---|---|---|
| 1952 | | North Africa Mission /US (AWM) |
| 1952 | | North Africa Mission /Canada |
| 1952 | | Regions Beyond Missionary Union/US (RBMU) |
| 1952 | | Regions Beyond Missionary Union/Canada |
| 1952 | 1959 | European Evangelistic Crusade/US |
| 1952 | 1959 | European Evangelistic Crusade/Canada |
| 1952 | 1961 | Central Japan Pioneer Mission/Canada |
| 1953 | 1964 | Egypt General Mission/US (merged into UFM) |
| 1953 | | Berean Mission/US |
| 1953 | | International Missions/Canada |
| 1954 | | Greater Europe Mission/US |
| 1955 | 1966 | Japan Evangelistic Band/Canada |
| 1955 | | Ramabai Mukti Mission/US |
| 1955 | | Ramabai Mukti Mission/Canada |
| 1956 | 1983 | Japan Evangelical Mission/Canada (merged into TEAM) |
| 1956 | | The Pocket Testament League/US |
| 1957 | | Bible Christian Union/US |
| 1957 | | Bible Christian Union/Canada |
| 1957 | | World Radio Missionary Fellowship/US |
| 1957 | | World Radio Missionary Fellowship/Canada |
| 1958 | 1966 | Oriental Boat Mission/US (merged into International Missions) |
| 1958 | | Arctic Missions/US (InterAct) |
| 1958 | | West Indies Mission/Canada (Worldteam) |
| 1959 | | International Evangelism/US (Trans World Radio) |
| 1960 | 1974 | Worldwide European Fellowship/US |
| 1960 | 1962 | Mission to Orphans/US (merged into Worldteam) |
| 1960 | | Home of Onesiphorus/US (Kids Alive International) |
| 1960 | | Bible Club Movement/US (BCM) |
| 1960 | 1990 | Bible Club Movement/Canada |
| 1960 | | The Pocket Testament League/Canada |
| 1960 | | Greater Europe Mission/Canada |
| 1961 | 1990 | Far East Broadcasting Company/US |
| 1961 | 1974 | Global Gospel Broadcasts/US (Merged with Global Outreach) |
| 1961 | 1977 | Gospel Furthering Fellowship/US |

| | | |
|---|---|---|
| 1961 | 1989 | Latin America Mission/Canada |
| 1962 | 1971 | Central Alaskan Mission/US (merged into FEGC/SEND) |
| 1963 | 1987 | Evangelical Literature Overseas/US (merged into Media Associates International) |
| 1964 | 1968 | United Faith Mission/US (merged into Pioneer Bible Mission) |
| 1964 | 1990 | Far East Broadcasting Associates/Canada |
| 1966 | | Gospel Missionary Union/Canada |
| 1967 | | Gospel Recordings/Canada (Language Recordings International) |
| 1968 | 1978 | Missionary Services/US (merged into MAP International) |
| 1968 | 1990 | World Missions to Children /US (World Missions Fellowship) |
| 1968 | 1987 | World Missions to Children/Canada (World Missions Fellowship) |
| 1968 | | Bible and Medical Missionary Fellowship/US (InterServe) |
| 1968 | | Bible and Medical Missionary Fellowship/ Canada (InterServe) |
| 1969 | | Arctic Missions/Canada (InterAct) |
| 1970 | | Northern Canada Evangelical Mission/Canada |
| 1970 | | Overseas Christian Servicemen's Centers/US |
| 1971 | | Global Outreach/US |
| 1971 | | Global Outreach/Canada |
| 1971 | | Liebenzell Mission/US |
| 1971 | | Liebenzell Mission/Canada |
| 1972 | | Missionary Aviation Fellowship/Canada (Mission Aviation Fellowship) |
| 1973 | | North America Indian Mission/US (NAIM Ministries) |
| 1973 | | North America Indian Mission/Canada (NAIM Ministries) |
| 1973 | | Trans World Radio/Canada |
| 1974 | | Central American Mission/Canada (CAM) |
| 1974 | | Far Eastern Gospel Crusade/Canada (SEND) |
| 1976 | | South American Crusades/US (Impact International) |

| | | |
|---|---|---|
| 1977 | | Berean Mission/Canada |
| 1977 | | Christian Nationals' Evangelism Commission/US (Partners International) |
| 1977 | | Christian Nationals' Evangelism Commission/ Canada (Partners International) |
| 1977 | | International Christian Organization/US (Intercristo) |
| 1977 | 1990 | Language Institute for Evangelism/US (LIFE Ministries) |
| 1978 | | Portable Recording Ministries/US (PRM International) |
| 1978 | | United World Mission/US |
| 1980 | 1982 | Intercristo/Canada |
| 1981 | | Helps International Ministries/US |
| 1981 | | Janz Team/US (Janz Team Ministries) |
| 1981 | | Janz Team/Canada (Janz Team Ministries) |
| 1981 | | Missionary Internship/US |
| 1981 | 1986 | Prakash Association/US |
| 1982 | 1989 | Island Missionary Society/US |
| 1982 | | Canadian South America Mission |
| 1982 | | U. S. Center for World Mission |
| 1983 | | Missions Outreach/US |
| 1983 | 1990 | Missions Outreach/Canada |
| 1984 | | Jews for Jesus/US |
| 1984 | | Jews for Jesus/Canada |
| 1984 | | Romanian Missionary Society/US |
| 1984 | | Samuel Zwemer Institute/US (Zwemer Institute of Muslim Studies) |
| 1984 | | Venture Teams International/Canada |
| 1984 | | World Literature Crusade/US (Every Home for Christ) |
| 1985 | | Back to the Bible/US |
| 1985 | | Missionary TECH Team/US |
| 1985 | | Open Air Campaigners/US |
| 1986 | | American Board of Missions to the Jews/US (Chosen People Ministries) |
| 1986 | | BSSM/American Board of Missions to the Jews/ Canada (Chosen People Ministries) |
| 1986 | | Mexican Mission Ministries/US |
| 1986 | | Pioneers/US |

| | | |
|---|---|---|
| 1986 | | American Missionary Fellowship/US |
| 1986 | | Navajo Gospel Mission/US |
| 1987 | 1991 | Frontiers/US |
| 1987 | | Media Associates International/US |
| 1987 | | Navigators of Canada |
| 1987 | | World Reach/US |
| 1988 | | Mission: Moving Mountains/US |
| 1988 | | Spiritual Overseers Service International/US |
| 1988 | | Missionary Internship/Canada |
| 1989 | | Ambassadors for Christ/US |
| 1989 | | American Messianic Fellowship/US |
| 1989 | | European Christian Mission/Canada |
| 1989 | | International Development Organization (InterDev)/US |
| 1989 | | Rio Grande Bible Institute/US |
| 1989 | | World Outreach Fellowship/US |
| 1990 | | Christ for the Island World/US |
| 1990 | | Missionary Gospel Fellowship/US |
| 1991 | | Mahon Mission/US |
| 1991 | | White Fields/US |

# APPENDIX E

## MEMBER MISSIONS ON JANUARY 1, 1992; ABBREVIATIONS; DATES ORGANIZED; DATES ACCEPTED INTO IFMA

| | MISSION | MISSION ORGANIZED | ACCEPTED INTO IFMA U.S. | ACCEPTED INTO IFMA Can. |
|---|---|---|---|---|
| AEF | Africa Evangelical Fellowship | 1889 | 1917 | 1917 |
| AIM | Africa Inland Mission International | 1895 | 1917 | 1917 |
| AFC | Ambassadors for Christ | 1963 | 1989 | |
| AMesF | American Messianic Fellowship | 1887 | 1989 | |
| AMisF | American Missionary Fellowship | 1790 | 1986 | |
| AWM | Arab World Ministries | 1881 | 1952 | 1952 |
| BTB | Back to the Bible | 1939 | 1985 | |
| BCM | BCM International | 1936 | 1960 | |
| BMI | Berean Mission | 1937 | 1953 | 1977 |
| BCU | Bible Christian Union | 1904 | 1957 | 1957 |
| CAM | CAM International | 1890 | 1917 | 1974 |
| CPM | Chosen People Ministries | 1911 | 1986 | 1986 |
| CFIW | Christ for the Island World | 1983 | 1990 | |
| ECM | European Christian Mission | 1904 | | 1989 |
| EHC | Every Home for Christ | 1946 | 1984 | |
| GOM | Global Outreach Mission | 1943 | 1971 | 1971 |
| GMU | Gospel Missionary Union | 1892 | 1946 | 1966 |
| GR | Gospel Recordings USA | 1939 | 1951 | |
| GEM | Greater Europe Mission | 1949 | 1954 | 1960 |
| HIM | Helps International Ministries | 1976 | 1981 | |
| II | Impact International | 1959 | 1976 | |
| IAM | InterAct Ministries | 1951 | 1958 | 1969 |
| —— | Intercristo | 1967 | 1977 | |
| —— | InterDev | 1974 | 1989 | |
| IMI | International Missions | 1930 | 1945 | 1953 |

| | | | | |
|---|---|---|---|---|
| —— | InterServe | 1852 | 1968 | 1968 |
| JTM | Janz Team Ministries | 1956 | 1981 | 1981 |
| JFJ | Jews for Jesus | 1973 | 1984 | 1984 |
| KAI | Kids Alive International | 1916 | 1960 | |
| LRI | Language Recordings International | 1967 | | 1967 |
| LM | Liebenzell Mission | 1942 | 1971 | 1971 |
| MM | Mahon Mission | 1904 | 1991 | |
| MAI | Media Associates International | 1985 | 1987 | |
| MMM | Mexican Mission Ministries | 1954 | 1986 | |
| MAF | Mission Aviation Fellowship | 1945 | 1952 | 1972 |
| M:MM | Mission: Moving Mountains | 1978 | 1988 | |
| MGF | Missionary Gospel Fellowship | 1939 | 1990 | |
| MI | Missionary Internship | 1954 | 1981 | 1988 |
| MTT | Missionary TECH Team | 1969 | 1985 | |
| MOI | Missions Outreach | 1977 | 1983 | |
| NAIM | NAIM Ministries | 1949 | 1973 | 1973 |
| NGM | Navajo Gospel Mission | 1930 | 1986 | |
| NAV | Navigators of Canada | 1960 | | 1987 |
| NCEM | Northern Canada Evangelical Mission | 1946 | | 1970 |
| OAC | Open Air Campaigners | 1922 | 1985 | |
| OCSC | Overseas Christian Servicemen's Centers | 1954 | 1970 | |
| OMF | Overseas Missionary Fellowship | 1865 | 1917 | 1917 |
| PI | Partners International | 1943 | 1977 | 1977 |
| —— | Pioneers | 1979 | 1986 | |
| PRM | PRM International | 1967 | 1978 | |
| RMM | Ramabai Mukti Mission | 1889 | 1955 | 1955 |
| RBMU | RBMU International | 1878 | 1952 | 1952 |
| RMS | Romanian Missionary Society | 1968 | 1984 | |
| RGBI | Rio Grande Bible Institute | 1946 | 1989 | |
| SEND | SEND International | 1945 | 1951 | 1974 |
| SIM | SIM | 1893 | 1917 | 1917 |
| SGA | Slavic Gospel Association | 1934 | 1945 | 1950 |
| SAM | South America Mission | 1914 | 1917 | 1982 |
| SOS | Spiritual Overseers Service International | 1979 | 1988 | |
| TEAM | The Evangelical Alliance Mission | 1890 | 1945 | 1945 |
| TPTL | The Pocket Testament League | 1893 | 1956 | 1960 |
| TWR | Trans World Radio | 1952 | 1959 | 1973 |

| | | | | |
|---|---|---|---|---|
| UFM | UFM International | 1931 | 1943 | 1943 |
| UWM | United World Mission | 1946 | 1978 | |
| USCWM | U. S. Center for World Mission | 1976 | 1982 | |
| VTI | Venture Teams International | 1979 | | 1984 |
| WF | White Fields | 1955 | 1991 | |
| WOF | World Outreach Fellowship | 1981 | 1989 | |
| WRMF | World Radio Missionary Fellowship | 1931 | 1957 | 1957 |
| WR | World Reach | 1982 | 1987 | |
| WT | Worldteam | 1928 | 1945 | 1958 |
| ZIMS | Zwemer Institute of Muslim Studies | 1979 | 1984 | |

TOTAL: 72 agencies, representing 105 distinct corporations—67 in the United States and 38 in Canada.

# APPENDIX F

## NAMES UNDER WHICH CURRENT IFMA MEMBER MISSIONS HAVE OPERATED; MERGERS

| AFRICA EVANGELICAL FELLOWSHIP | Dates | |
|---|---|---|
| Names | From | To |
| Cape General Mission | 1889 | 1894 |
| South Africa General Mission | 1894 | 1963 |
| Africa Evangelical Fellowship | 1963 | |
| Mergers | Founded | Merged |
| Southeast Africa Evangelistic Mission | 1891 | 1894 |
| Lower Zambesi Mission | 1896 | 1900 |

| AFRICA INLAND MISSION INTERNATIONAL | Dates | |
|---|---|---|
| Names | From | To |
| Africa Inland Mission | 1895 | 1986 |
| Africa Inland Mission International | 1986 | |

| AMBASSADORS FOR CHRIST | Dates | |
|---|---|---|
| Names | From | To |
| Ambassadors for Christ | 1963 | |

| AMERICAN MESSIANIC FELLOWSHIP | Dates | |
|---|---|---|
| Names | From | To. |
| Chicago Committee for Hebrew Christian Work | 1887 | 1889 |
| Chicago Hebrew Mission | 1889 | 1953 |
| American Messianic Fellowship | 1953 | |
| Mergers | Founded | Merged |
| Hebrew Christian Fellowship | 1956 | 1963 |

| AMERICAN MISSIONARY FELLOWSHIP | Dates | |
|---|---|---|
| Names | From | To |
| First Day Society | 1790 | 1817 |

| | | |
|---|---|---|
| Sunday and Adult School Union | 1817 | 1824 |
| American Sunday School Union | 1824 | 1974 |
| American Missionary Fellowship | 1974 | |
| Mergers | Founded | Merged |
| New York Sunday School Union | 1816 | 1817 |
| Female Sunday School Union | 1816 | 1820 |
| Maranatha Settlement Association | | 1968 |

| ARAB WORLD MINISTRIES | Dates | |
|---|---|---|
| Names | From | To |
| North Africa Mission | 1881 | 1987 |
| Arab World Ministries | 1987 | |
| Mergers | Founded | Merged |
| Southern Morocco Mission | | 1961 |
| Algiers Mission Band | | 1965 |
| Dades Valley Fellowship | | 1982 |

| BACK TO THE BIBLE | Dates | |
|---|---|---|
| Names | From | To |
| Good News Broadcasting Association also known as Back to the Bible | 1939 | |

| BCM INTERNATIONAL | Dates | |
|---|---|---|
| Names | From | To |
| Bible Club Movement | 1936 | 1982 |
| BCM International | 1982 | |
| Mergers | Founded | Merged |
| Children's Temple | | 1967 |
| City Mission Association of Syracuse | | 1968 |
| Protestant Religious Education Services | | 1969 |
| Jack and Jill Bible Camp | | 1976 |
| Grace Settlement House | | 1979 |
| Children's Gospel Hour | | 1984 |
| Berean Band | | 1987 |
| Youth Ministries of Bible Christian Union | | 1988 |

| BEREAN MISSION | Dates | |
|---|---|---|
| Names | From | To |
| Berean African Missionary Society | 1937 | 1946 |
| Berean Mission | 1946 | |
| Mergers | Founded | Merged |
| Pacific Area Mission | 1954 | 1988 |

| BIBLE CHRISTIAN UNION | Dates | |
|---|---|---|
| Names | From | To |
| Organized in Estonia | 1904 | 1917 |
| Russian and Slovonic Bible Union | 1917 | 1929 |
| European Christian Mission | 1929 | 1954 |
| Bible Christian Union | 1954 | |

| CAM INTERNATIONAL | Dates | |
|---|---|---|
| Names | From | To |
| Central American Mission | 1890 | 1976 |
| CAM International | 1976 | |
| Mergers | Founded | Merged |
| Practical Missionary Training | 1950 | 1968 |

| CHOSEN PEOPLE MINISTRIES | Dates | |
|---|---|---|
| Names | From | To |
| Williamsburg Mission to the Jews | 1911 | 1924 |
| American Board of Missions to the Jews | 1924 | 1988 |
| Chosen People Ministries | 1988 | |

| CHRIST FOR THE ISLAND WORLD | Dates | |
|---|---|---|
| Names | From | To |
| Christ for the Island World | 1983 | |

| EUROPEAN CHRISTIAN MISSION | Dates | |
|---|---|---|
| Names | From | To |
| Organized in Estonia | 1904 | |
| Mission to Europe's Millions | 1962 | 1987 |
| European Christian Mission | 1987 | |

| EVERY HOME FOR CHRIST | Dates | |
|---|---|---|
| Names | From | To |
| Radio Tract Club - Canada | 1946 | 1952 |
| World Literature Crusade | 1952 | 1986 |
| Every Home for Christ | 1986 | |
| Mergers | Founded | Merged |
| Change the World Ministries | 1981 | 1988 |

| GLOBAL OUTREACH MISSION | Dates | |
|---|---|---|
| Names | From | To |
| European Evangelistic Crusade | 1943 | 1971 |
| Global Outreach | 1971 | 1984 |
| Global Outreach Mission | 1984 | |
| Mergers | Founded | Merged |
| Global Gospel Broadcast | 1948 | 1974 |

| GOSPEL MISSIONARY UNION | Dates | |
|---|---|---|
| Names | From | To |
| World's Gospel Union | 1892 | 1901 |
| Gospel Missionary Union | 1901 | |
| Mergers | Founded | Merged |
| Evangelical Union of South America | 1911 | 1975 |

| GOSPEL RECORDINGS U.S.A. | Dates | |
|---|---|---|
| Names | From | To |
| Gospel Recordings | 1939 | 1985 |
| Gospel Recordings USA | 1985 | |

| GREATER EUROPE MISSION | Dates | |
|---|---|---|
| Names | From | To |
| European Bible Institute | 1949 | 1952 |
| Greater European Mission | 1952 | |
| Mergers | Founded | Merged |
| Greek Evangelical Mission | | 1969 |
| Belgian Gospel Mission | | 1971 |

| HELPS INTERNATIONAL MINISTRIES | Dates | |
|---|---|---|
| Names | From | To |
| Helps International Ministries | 1976 | |

IMPACT INTERNATIONAL

| Names | Dates From | To |
|---|---|---|
| South American Crusades | 1959 | 1988 |
| Impact International | 1988 | |

INTERACT MINISTRIES

| Names | Dates From | To |
|---|---|---|
| Alaska Missions | 1951 | 1956 |
| Arctic Missions | 1956 | 1988 |
| InterAct Ministries | 1988 | |

INTERCRISTO

| Names | Dates From | To |
|---|---|---|
| International Christian Organization also known as Intercristo | 1967 | |

INTERDEV

| Names | Dates From | To |
|---|---|---|
| International Development Organization also known as InterDev | 1974 | |

INTERNATIONAL MISSIONS

| Names | Dates From | To |
|---|---|---|
| India Mission | 1930 | 1953 |
| International Missions | 1953 | |
| Mergers | Founded | Merged |
| Iran Interior Mission | 1923 | 1955 |
| Oriental Boat Mission (original name was South China Boat Mission) | 1909 | 1966 |

INTERSERVE

| Names | Dates From | To |
|---|---|---|
| The Indian Female Normal School and Instruction Society | 1852 | |
| Zenana Bible Mission | 1880 | |
| Zenana Bible and Medical Mission | 1880 | 1957 |
| Bible and Medical Missionary Fellowship | 1957 | 1979 |
| BMMF International | 1979 | 1986 |
| International Service Fellowship also known as InterServe | 1986 | |

| Mergers | Founded | Merged |
| --- | --- | --- |
| United Fellowship for Christian Service | 1860 | 1976 |

Woman's Union Missionary Society of America to Heathen Lands was organized in 1860. The name was later changed to Woman's Union Missionary Society in America, and in 1970 to United Fellowship for Christian Service, which merged with Bible and Medical Missionary Fellowship in 1976. Woman's Union Missionary Society was one of the founding missions of IFMA.

JANZ TEAM MINISTRIES

| Names | Dates From | To |
| --- | --- | --- |
| Janz Brothers Gospel Association | 1956 | 1978 |
| Janz Team | 1978 | 1982 |
| Janz Team Ministries | 1982 | |

JEWS FOR JESUS

| Names | Dates From | To |
| --- | --- | --- |
| Jews for Jesus | 1973 | |
| **Mergers** | **Founded** | **Merged** |
| South Africa Jews Society | 1953 | |
| became Hope of Israel Gospel Ministry | 1982 | 1989 |

KIDS ALIVE INTERNATIONAL

| Names | Dates From | To |
| --- | --- | --- |
| Home of Onesiphorus | 1916 | 1983 |
| Kids Alive International | 1983 | |

LANGUAGE RECORDINGS INTERNATIONAL

| Names | Dates From | To |
| --- | --- | --- |
| Gospel Recordings of Canada | 1967 | 1988 |
| Language Recordings International (a division of GR Canada) | 1988 | |

LIEBENZELL MISSION

| Names | Dates From | To |
| --- | --- | --- |
| Liebenzell Mission | 1942 | |

| MAHON MISSION | Dates | |
|---|---|---|
| Names | From | To |
| Christian Catholic Church in Zion | 1904 | 1946 |
| Mahon Mission | 1946 | |

| MEDIA ASSOCIATES INTERNATIONAL | Dates | |
|---|---|---|
| Names | From | To |
| Media Associates International | 1985 | |
| Mergers | Founded | Merged |
| Evangelical Literature Overseas (a member of IFMA, 1963-1987) | 1953 | 1987 |

| MEXICAN MISSION MINISTRIES | Dates | |
|---|---|---|
| Names | From | To |
| Mexican Militant Mission | 1954 | 1972 |
| Mexican Mission Ministries | 1972 | |

| MISSION AVIATION FELLOWSHIP | Dates | |
|---|---|---|
| Names | From | To |
| Christian Airmen's Missionary Fellowship | 1945 | 1946 |
| Missionary Aviation Fellowship | 1946 | 1984 |
| Mission Aviation Fellowship | 1984 | |

| MISSION: MOVING MOUNTAINS | Dates | |
|---|---|---|
| Names | From | To |
| Mission: Moving Mountains | 1978 | |

| MISSIONARY GOSPEL FELLOWSHIP | Dates | |
|---|---|---|
| Names | From | To |
| Migrant Gospel Fellowship | 1939 | 1942 |
| Missionary Gospel Fellowship | 1942 | |

| MISSIONARY INTERNSHIP | Dates | |
|---|---|---|
| Names | From | To |
| Missionary Internship | 1954 | |

| MISSIONARY TECH TEAM | Dates | |
|---|---|---|
| Names | From | To |
| Missionary TECH Team | 1969 | |

| MISSIONS OUTREACH INTERNATIONAL | Dates | |
|---|---|---|
| Names | From | To |
| Missions Outreach | 1977 | 1990 |
| Missions Outreach International | 1990 | |

| NAIM MINISTRIES | Dates | |
|---|---|---|
| Names | From | To |
| Marine Medical Mission | 1949 | 1964 |
| North America Indian Mission | 1964 | 1986 |
| NAIM Ministries | 1986 | |

| NAVAJO GOSPEL MISSION | Dates | |
|---|---|---|
| Names | From | To |
| Navajo Indian Evangelization Movement | 1930 | 1944 |
| Navajo Gospel Mission | 1944 | |

| NAVIGATORS OF CANADA | Dates | |
|---|---|---|
| Names | From | To |
| The Navigators of Canada | 1960 | |

| NORTHERN CANADA EVANGELICAL MISSION | Dates | |
|---|---|---|
| Names | From | To |
| Northern Canada Evangelical Mission | 1946 | |

| OPEN AIR CAMPAIGNERS | Dates | |
|---|---|---|
| Names | From | To |
| Open Air Campaigners | 1922 | |

| OVERSEAS CHRISTIAN SERVICEMEN'S CENTERS | Dates | |
|---|---|---|
| Names | From | To |
| Overseas Christian Servicemen's Centers | 1954 | |

| OVERSEAS MISSIONARY FELLOWSHIP | Dates | |
|---|---|---|
| Names | From | To |
| China Inland Mission | 1865 | 1951 |
| China Inland Mission/Overseas Missionary Fellowship | 1952 | 1965 |
| Overseas Missionary Fellowship | 1966 | |

| PARTNERS INTERNATIONAL | Dates | |
|---|---|---|
| Names | From | To |
| Chinese Native Evangelistic Crusade | 1943 | 1961 |
| Christian Nationals Evangelism Commission | 1961 | 1988 |
| Partners International | 1988 | |

| PIONEERS | Dates | |
|---|---|---|
| Names | From | To |
| World Evangelical Outreach | 1979 | 1984 |
| Pioneers | 1984 | |

| PRM INTERNATIONAL | Dates | |
|---|---|---|
| Names | From | To |
| Portable Recording Ministries | 1967 | 1985 |
| PRM International | 1985 | |

| RAMABAI MUKTI MISSION | Dates | |
|---|---|---|
| Names | From | To |
| Ramabai Mukti Mission | 1889 | |

| RBMU INTERNATIONAL | Dates | |
|---|---|---|
| Names | From | To |
| Livingstone Inland Mission | 1878 | |
| Congo Balolo Mission | | 1900 |
| Regions Beyond Missionary Union | 1900 | 1980 |
| RBMU International | 1980 | |
| Mergers | Founded | Merged |
| Peru Inland Mission | 1922 | 1948 |

| ROMANIAN MISSIONARY SOCIETY | Dates | |
|---|---|---|
| Names | From | To |
| Romanian Missionary Society | 1968 | |

| RIO GRANDE BIBLE INSTITUTE | Dates | |
|---|---|---|
| Names | From | To |
| Rio Grande Bible Institute | 1946 | |

| SEND INTERNATIONAL | Dates | |
|---|---|---|
| Names | From | To |
| Far Eastern Bible Institute and Seminary | 1945 | 1947 |
| Far Eastern Gospel Crusade | 1947 | 1981 |
| SEND International | 1981 | |
| Mergers | Founded | Merged |
| G. I. Gospel Crusade | 1945 | 1947 |
| Central Alaska Mission | 1936 | 1971 |

| SIM | Dates | |
|---|---|---|
| Names | From | To |
| Soudan Interior Mission | 1893 | 1896 |
| Africa Industrial Mission | 1896 | 1905 |
| Africa Evangelistic Mission | 1905 | 1906 |
| Sudan Interior Mission | 1907 | 1982 |
| SIM International | 1982 | 1991 |
| SIM | 1991 | |
| Mergers | Founded | Merged |
| Abyssinian Frontiers Mission | 1927 | 1927 |
| Bolivian Indian Mission | 1907 | |
| became Andes Evangelical Mission | 1965 | 1982 |
| International Christian Fellowship | | 1989 |
| from the 1969 merger of: | | |
| Ceylon and India General Mission | 1893 | |
| Poona and Indian Village Mission | 1893 | |
| Life Challenge | 1976 | 1986 |
| West Africa Broadcasting Association | 1950 | 1952 |

| SLAVIC GOSPEL ASSOCIATION | Dates | |
|---|---|---|
| Names | From | To |
| Russian Gospel Association | 1934 | 1949 |
| Slavic Gospel Association | 1949 | |
| Mergers | Founded | Merged |
| Russian and Eastern European Mission | 1927 | |
| became Eastern European Mission | 1950 | |
| became Euro Vision | 1986 | 1990 |

SOUTH AMERICA MISSION

| Names | From | To |
|---|---|---|
| Paraguayan Mission | 1914 | 1919 |
| Inland South America Missionary Union | 1919 | 1932 |
| South America Indian Mission | 1932 | 1970 |
| South America Mission | 1970 | |
| **Mergers** | **Founded** | **Merged** |
| Inland South America Missionary Union | 1902 | 1919 |

SPIRITUAL OVERSEERS SERVICE INTERNATIONAL

| Names | From | To |
|---|---|---|
| Spiritual Overseers Service Internat'l | 1979 | |

THE EVANGELICAL ALLIANCE MISSION

| Names | From | To |
|---|---|---|
| The Scandinavian Alliance Mission | 1890 | 1949 |
| The Evangelical Alliance Mission | 1949 | |
| **Mergers** | **Founded** | **Merged** |
| Door of Hope Mission | 1901 | 1959 |
| Sudan United Mission, North America | 1926 | 1969 |
| Peruvian Fellowship | 1956 | 1975 |
| Orinoco River Mission | 1920 | 1980 |
| Japan Evangelical Mission | 1950 | 1983 |

THE POCKET TESTAMENT LEAGUE

| Names | From | To |
|---|---|---|
| The Pocket Testament League | 1893 | |
| **Mergers** | **Founded** | **Merged** |
| Russian Christian Radio | 1961 | 1972 |
| Operation Campus known as Free Bible Literature Society | 1965 | 1986 |

TRANS WORLD RADIO

| Names | From | To |
|---|---|---|
| International Evangelism | 1952 | 1960 |
| Trans World Radio | 1960 | |

| UFM INTERNATIONAL | Dates | |
|---|---|---|
| Names | From | To |
| Unevangelized Fields Mission | 1931 | 1980 |
| UFM International | 1980 | |
| Mergers | Founded | Merged |
| World Christian Crusade | 1936 | 1949 |
| Alpine Mission to France | 1956 | 1962 |
| Egypt General Mission | 1897 | 1964 |
| Mexican Indian Mission | 1930 | 1971 |
| Safe Harbor Christian Servicemen's Center | | 1986 |
| International Asian Mission | 1979 | 1988 |

| UNITED WORLD MISSION | Dates | |
|---|---|---|
| Names | From | To |
| United World Mission | 1946 | |

| U. S. CENTER FOR WORLD MISSION | Dates | |
|---|---|---|
| Names | From | To |
| U. S. Center for World Mission | 1976 | |

| VENTURE TEAMS INTERNATIONAL | Dates | |
|---|---|---|
| Names | From | To |
| Team Ventures International | 1979 | 1983 |
| Venture Teams International | 1983 | |

| WHITE FIELDS | Dates | |
|---|---|---|
| Names | From | To |
| White Fields | 1955 | |

| WORLD OUTREACH FELLOWSHIP | Dates | |
|---|---|---|
| Names | From | To |
| World Outreach Fellowship | 1981 | |

| WORLD RADIO MISSIONARY FELLOWSHIP | Dates | |
|---|---|---|
| Names | From | To |
| World Radio Missionary Fellowship also known as HCJB | 1931 | |

WORLD REACH

| Names | Dates From | To |
| --- | --- | --- |
| World Reach | 1982 | |

WORLDTEAM

| Names | Dates From | To |
| --- | --- | --- |
| West Indies Mission | 1928 | 1978 |
| Worldteam | 1978 | |

Legal corporate names are:
Worldteam Canada, 1979
Worldteam International, 1987
Worldteam USA, 1987
Worldteam Associates, 1988

| Mergers | Founded | Merged |
| --- | --- | --- |
| Mission to the Orphans | 1944 | 1962 |
| Door to Life Mission | 1959 | 1963 |

ZWEMER INSTITUTE OF MUSLIM STUDIES

| Names | Dates From | To |
| --- | --- | --- |
| Samuel Zwemer Institute | 1979 | 1986 |
| Zwemer Institute of Muslim Studies | 1986 | |

# BIBLIOGRAPHY


Adolph, Paul E. *The Physical and Emotional Stress of Missionary Work.* Philadelphia: The Sunday School Times, 1959; rev. and enl.: Ridgefield Park, New Jersey: Interdenominational Foreign Mission Association, 1965.

Ahlstrom, Sydney E., ed. *Theology in America: The Major Protestant Voices from Puritanism to Neo-Orthodoxy.* New York: The Bobbs-Merrill Company, 1967.

Allen, Franklin W. *Breaking the Barriers: A History and Model of Church/Mission Relationships in the Philippines.* Singapore: Overseas Missionary Fellowship, 1990.

Ammerman, Nancy Tatom. *Bible Believers: Fundamentalists in the Modern World.* New Brunswick: Rutgers University Press, 1987.

Anderson, Gerald H., James M. Phillips, and Robert T. Coote, eds. *Mission in the Nineteen 90s.* New Haven: Overseas Ministries Study Center, 1991.

Austin, Alvyn J. *Saving China: Canadian Missionaries in the Middle Kingdom 1888-1959.* Toronto: University of Toronto Press, 1987.

Averill, Lloyd J. *Religious Right, Religious Wrong.* New York: The Pilgrim Press, 1989.

Bacon, Daniel W. *The Influence of Hudson Taylor on the Faith Missions Movement.* Singapore: Overseas Missionary Fellowship, 1984.

Barnett, Suzanne Wilson, and John King Fairbank, eds. *Christianity in China: Early Protestant Missionary Writings.* Cambridge, MA: Harvard University Press, 1985.

Barr, James. *Fundamentalism.* Philadelphia: The Westminster Press, 1977.

Bassham, Rodger C. *Mission Theology: 1948-1975 Years of Worldwide Creative Tension Ecumenical, Evangelical, and Roman Catholic.* Pasadena: William Carey Library, 1979.

Bateman, Charles T., ed. *Men and the World Enterprise: Addresses Delivered at the First National Conference, Laymen's Missionary Movement, Buxton, October 10-13, 1913.* London: Laymen's Missionary Movement, 1913.

Beach, Harlan P. *Geography.* Vol. 1 of *A Geography and Atlas of Protestant Missions.* New York: Student Volunteer Movement for Foreign Missions, 1901.

Beach, Harlan P., and Burton St. John, eds. *World Statistics of Christian Missions.* New York: The Committee of Reference and Counsel of the Foreign Missions Conference of North America, 1916.

Beard, Charles A., and Mary R. Beard. *The Making of American Civilization.* New York: The Macmillan Company, 1939.

Beaver, R. Pierce. "The Concert for Prayer for Missions." *Ecumenical Review*, July 1958, 420-27.

———. *Ecumenical Beginnings in Protestant World Missions: A History of Comity.* New York: Thomas Nelson & Sons, 1962.

———. "Missionary Motivation Through Three Centuries." In *Reinterpretation in American Church History*, edited by Jerald C. Brauer. Chicago: The University of Chicago Press, 1968.

———. *American Protestant Women in World Missions: History of the First Feminist Movement in North America.* Grand Rapids: William B. Eerdmans Publishing Company, 1980.

Bechtel, Paul M. *Wheaton College: A Heritage Remembered 1860-1984.* Wheaton, IL: Harold Shaw Publishers, 1984.

Beyerhaus, Peter. *Missions: Which Way?* Translated by Margaret Clarkson. Grand Rapids: Zondervan Publishing House, 1971.

Billy Graham Center. *An Evangelical Agenda: 1984 and Beyond.* Pasadena: William Carey Library, 1979.

Bingham, Rowland V. "Wiping the Slate." *Evangelical Christian*, January 1931, 1.

Bliss, Edwin Munsell. *The Missionary Enterprise: A Concise History of Its Objects, Methods and Extension.* New York: Fleming H. Revell Company, 1908.

———, ed. *The Encyclopedia of Missions.* 2 vols. New York: Funk & Wagnalls, 1891.

Bloesch, Donald G. *The Evangelical Renaissance.* Grand Rapids: William B. Eerdmans Publishing Company, 1973.

Boylan, Anne M. *Sunday School: The Formation of an American Institution 1790-1880.* New Haven: Yale University Press, 1988.

Brauer, Jerald C., ed. *Reinterpretation in American Church History.* Chicago: The University of Chicago Press, 1968.

Broomhall, A. J. *Barbarians at the Gates.* Book one of *Hudson Taylor & China's Open Century.* London: Overseas Missionary Fellowship, 1981.

———. *Over the Treaty Wall.* Book two of *Hudson Taylor & China's Open Century.* London: Overseas Missionary Fellowship, 1982.

———. *It Is Not Death to Die!* Book seven of *Hudson Taylor & China's Open Century.* London: Overseas Missionary Fellowship, 1989.

Broomhall, Marshall. *Our Seal.* London: The China Inland Mission, 1933.

Bush, Luis, and Lorry Lutz. *Partnering in Ministry: The Direction of World Evangelism.* Downers Grove, IL: Inter-Varsity Press, 1990.

Carpenter, Joel A., ed. *The Fundamentalist-Modernist Conflict: Opposing Views on Three Major Issues.* New York: Garland Publishing, Inc., 1988.

———, ed. *Modernism and Foreign Missions: Two Fundamentalist Protests.* New York: Garland Publishing, Inc., 1988.

———, ed. *The Premillennial Second Coming: Two Early Champions.* New York: Garland Publishing, Inc., 1988.

Carpenter, Joel A., and Wilbert R. Shenk, eds. *Earthen Vessels: American Evangelicals and Foreign Missions 1880-1980.* Grand Rapids: William B. Eerdmans Publishing Company, 1990.

CCCOWE Editorial Department, ed. *Chinese and Western Leadership Cooperation Seminar Compendium.* Hong Kong: Chinese Coordination Centre of World Evangelism (CCCOWE), 1980.

Chang, Lit-sen. *Strategy of Missions in the Orient: Christian Impact on the Pagan World.* Nutley, N.J.: Presbyterian and Reformed Publishing Company, 1970.

Chitwood, Oliver P., and Frank L. Owsley. *A Short History of the American People.* Vol. 1. New York: D. Van Nostrand Company, 1945.

Cho, David J., ed. *New Forces in Missions.* Seoul: East-West Center for Missions Research & Development, 1976.

Clark, J. Philip. *Biblical Missions vs. Ecumenical Missions.* Philadelphia: Biblical Missions, n.d.

Coggins, Wade T., and Edwin L. Frizen, Jr., eds. *Evangelical Missions Tomorrow.* South Pasadena: William Carey Library, 1977.

Coleman, Richard J. *Issues of Theological Warfare: Evangelicals and Liberals.* Grand Rapids: Wm. P. Eerdmans Publishing Company, 1972.

*Conference on Missions Held in 1860 at Liverpool.* London: James Nisbet & Co., 1860.

*The Continuation Committee Conferences in Asia 1912-1913.* New York: The Chairman of the Continuation Committee, 1913.

Cook, Harold R. *An Introduction to Christian Missions.* 15th ed., rev. Chicago: Moody Press, 1971.

———. *Strategy of Missions: An Evangelical View.* Chicago: Moody Press, 1963.

Costas, Orlando E. *The Church and Its Mission: A Shattering Critique from the Third World.* Wheaton, II.: Tyndale House Publishers, 1974.

Crow, Paul A., Jr. *The Ecumenical Movement in Bibliographical Outline.* New York: Department of Faith and Order, The National Council of Churches of Christ in the U.S.A., 1965.

Day, Richard E. *Bush Aglow; The Biography of D. L. Moody.* Philadelphia: The Judson Press, 1936.

Dayton, Edward R., and David A. Fraser. *Planning Strategies for World Evangelization.* Grand Rapids: William B. Eerdmans Publishing Company, 1980.

Dixon, A. C., Louis Meyer, and R. A. Torrey, eds. *The Fundamentals: A Testimony to the Truth.* 12 vols. Chicago: Testimony Publishing Company, 1910-1915. Reprint 4 vols. Los Angeles: Bible House of Los Angeles, 1917. Reprint. 4 vols. Grand Rapids: Baker Book House, 1972. Reprint. 4 vols. Edited by George M. Marsden. In *Fundamentalism in American Religion 1880-1950.* 45 vol. facsimile series. New York: Garland Publishing, Inc., 1988.

Dollar, George W. *A History of Fundamentalism in America.* Greenville, SC: Bob Jones University Press, 1973.

Douglas, Donald E., ed. *Evangelical Perspectives on China.* Farmington, Mich.: Evangelical China Committee, 1976.

Douglas, J. D., ed. *Evangelicals and Unity.* Abingdon, England: Marcham Manor Press, 1964.

———, ed. *The New International Dictionary of the Christian Church.* Grand Rapids: Zondervan Publishing House, 1974.

———, ed. *Let the Earth Hear His Voice: International Congress on World Evangelization, Lausanne, Switzerland.* Minneapolis: World Wide Publications, 1975.

Dowkontt, George D., *"Tell Them" or The Life Story of A Medical Missionary.* New York: Office of the *Medical Missionary Record,* 1898.

Dowkontt, George H. *The "Deadly Parallel:" A Comparison of Thomas Paine's "Age of Reason" with Harry E. Fosdick's "Modern Use of the Bible."* New York: George H. Dowkontt, M.D., 1926.

———. *Marvel Mantel.* New York: Loizeaux Brothers, 1940.

DuBose, Francis M., ed. *Classics of Christian Missions.* Nashville: Broadman Press, 1979.

Dwight, Henry Otis, H. Allen Tupper, and Edwin Munsell Bliss, eds. *The Encyclopedia of Missions.* 2d ed. New York: Funk & Wagnalls Company, 1904.

Eavey, Clarence B. *History of Christian Education.* Chicago: Moody Press, 1964.

Eller, D. B. "Frontier Religion." In *Dictionary of Christianity in America,* edited by Daniel G. Reid. Downers Grove, IL: Inter-Varsity Press, 1990.

Ellingsen, Mark. *The Evangelical Movement: Growth, Impact, Controversy, Dialog.* Minneapolis: Augsburg Publishing House, 1988.

Engel, James F., and Jerry D. Jones. *Baby Boomers and the Future of World Missions* Orange, CA: Management Development Associates, 1989.

Escobar, Samuel, and John Driver. *Christian Mission and Social Justice.* Institute of Mennonite Studies, Missionary Studies No. 5. Scottdale, Pa.: Herald Press, 1978.

Evangelical Foreign Missions Association. *Documents,* 1943-1990.

———. *Reports and Findings of the Annual Mission Executives' Retreats.* Washington: Evangelical Foreign Missions Association, 1952-1977.

Evangelical Missions Information Service. Minutes of the Board of Directors. Meetings of 1963-1991.

———. *Evangelical Missions Quarterly,* 1-28 (1964-1992).

———. *Report of the Findings: Missions Study Conference.* Springfield, Pa.: Evangelical Missions Information Service, 1967.

———. *Latin America Pulse,* 1-16 (1967-1981).

———. *Asia Pulse,* 1-13 (1970-1980).

Faulkner, Harold Underwood. *American Political and Social History.* New York: F. S. Crofts & Co., 1937.

Fey, Harold E., ed. *A History of the Ecumenical Movement Volume 2, 1948-1968.* Philadelpia: The Westminster Press, 1970.

Frizen, Edwin L., Jr. "Seoul '73 - All-Asia Mission Consultation." *Asia Pulse,* September 1973, 1-8.

Frizen, Edwin L., Jr., and Wade T. Coggins, eds. *Christ and Caesar in Christian Missions.* Pasadena: William Carey Library, 1979.

Frost, Henry W. *Miraculous Healing: A Personal Testimony and Biblical Study.* Grand Rapids: Zondervan Publishing House, 1979.

Gairdner, W. H. T. *"Edinburgh 1910:" An Account and Interpretation of the World Missionary Conference.* Edinburgh: Oliphant, Anderson & Ferrier, 1910.

Gasper, Louis. *The Fundamentalist Movement.* Paris: Mouton & Co., 1963.

Gerber, Vergil. "EMIS Annual Report, 1979," p. 20. Photocopy.

———, ed. *Discipling Through Theological Education by Extension.* Chicago: Moody Press, 1980.

Glasser, Arthur F. "Archival Alert—Rome 1980." *Missiology* 8 (1980): 389-93.

Goddard, Burton L., gen. ed. *The Encyclopedia of Modern Christian Missions.* Camden, N.J.: Thomas Nelson & Sons, 1967.

Gracey, Mrs. J. T. *Eminent Missionary Women.* Chicago: Missionary Campaign Library, 1898.

Hannah, John D. "The Social and Intellectual History of the Origins of the Evangelical Theological College." Ph.D. diss., The University of Texas at Dallas, 1988.

Hay, Ian M. "A Study of the Relationship between SIM International and the Evangelical Missionary Society." D.Miss. diss., Trinity Evangelical Divinity School, 1984.

Henry, Carl F. H. *Evangelicals at the Brink of Crisis.* Waco: Word Books, 1967.

Henry, Carl F. H., and W. Stanley Mooneyham, eds. *One Race, One Gospel, One Task, World Congress on Evangelism, Berlin, 1966, Official Reference Volumes: Papers and Reports.* 2 vols. Minneapolis: World Wide Publications, 1967.

Hesselgrave, David J., ed. *Theology and Mission: Papers Given at Trinity Consultation No. 1.* Grand Rapids: Baker Book House, 1978.

Hill, Patricia R. *The World Their Household: The American Woman's Foreign Mission Movement and Cultural Transformation, 1870-1920.* Ann Arbor: The University of Michigan Press, 1985.

Hoekstra, Harvey T. *The World Council of Churches and the Demise of Evangelicalism.* Wheaton,IL: Tyndale House Publishers, 1979.

Hoke, Donald E., ed. *Evangelicals Face the Future.* South Pasadena: William Carey Library, 1978.

Hopkins, C. Howard. *History of the YMCA in North America.* New York: Association Press, 1951.

———. *John R. Mott 1865-1955: A Biography.* Grand Rapids: William B. Eerdmans Publishing Company, 1979.

Howard, David M. *Student Power in World Evangelism.* Downers Grove, IL: Inter-Varsity Press, 1970.

———. *The Dream That Would Not Die: The Birth and Growth of the World Evangelical Fellowship 1846-1986.* Exeter: The Paternoster Press, 1986.

Howard, Philip E., Jr. "Forward by Faith." *The Sunday School Times*, November 18, 1950, 983-85.

Hudson, Winthrop S. *Religion in America.* New York: Charles Scribner's Sons, 1965.

Humphreys, Fisher, ed. *Nineteenth Century Evangelical Theology.* Nashville: Broadman, 1983.

Hutchison, William R. *Errand to the World: American Protestant Thought and Foreign Missions.* Chicago: The University of Chicago Press, 1987.

*Inland South America Missionary Union.* Edinburgh: The Inland South America Missionary Union, 1913.

Interdenominational Foreign Mission Association. Documents, 1917-1991.

———. Minutes of the Annual Meeting. Meetings of 1917-1991.

———. Minutes of the Committees. Meetings of 1917-1991.

———. Minutes of the Official Board. Meetings of 1917-1991.

———. Record of Dues Contributed by Member Missions, 1918-1922.

———. *IFMA News*, 1-42 (1950-1991).

———. *Missions Annual*, 1958-1962.

———. *Fiftieth IFMA Annual Meeting, September 25-28, 1967, Study Papers.* Ridgefield Park, N.J.: Interdenominational Foreign Mission Association, 1967.

———. *Accounting and Financial Reporting Guide for Missionary Organizations.* 1979 ed. Wheaton, II.: Interdenominational Foreign Mission Association, 1979.

———. *Mission Administration Manual.* Rev. ed. Wheaton, IL.: Interdenominational Foreign Mission Association, 1979.

Interdenominational Foreign Mission Association - Evangelical Foreign Missions Association. Minutes of the Joint Committees. Meetings of 1958-1991.

Johnson, James Turner, ed. *The Bible in American Law, Politics, and Political Rhetoric.* Philadelphia: Fortress Press, 1985.

Johnston, James, ed. *Report of the Centenary Conference on the Protestant Missions of the World Held in Exeter Hall (June 9th-19th), London, 1888.* 2 vols. New York: Fleming H. Revell, 1888.

Kane, J. Herbert. *Christian Missions in Biblical Perspective.* Grand Rapids: Baker Book House, 1976.

———. *A Concise History of the Christian World Mission: A Panoramic View of Missions from Pentecost to the Present.* Grand Rapids: Baker Book House, 1978.

———. *Life and Work on the Mission Field.* Grand Rapids: Baker Book House, 1980.

Kelley, Dean M. *Why Conservative Churches Are Growing: A Study in Sociology of Religion.* New York: Harper & Row, Publishers, 1972.

Kik, J. Marcellus. *Ecumenism and the Evangelical.* Philadelphia: Presbyterian and Reformed Publishing Company, 1958.

Lane, Denis. *Tuning God's New Instruments.* Singapore: World Evangelical Fellowship, 1990.

Latourette, Kenneth Scott. *Missions Tomorrow.* New York: Harper & Brothers Publishers, 1936.

———. *A History of Christianity.* New York: Harper & Brothers, 1953.

———. *The Christian World Mission in Our Day.* New York: Harper & Brothers, 1954.